Teacher's Edition

4 Workplace Plus

Living and Working in English

Joan Saslow

Edwina Hoffman
Dade County Public Schools
Series Advisor

Grace Tanaka
Santa Ana College
Pedagogical Advisor

Kristin Sherman
Teacher's Edition
Writer

LONGMAN ON THE **WEB**

Longman.com offers online resources for teachers and students. Access our Companion Websites, our online catalog, and our local offices around the world.

Visit us at **longman.com**.

Longman

Workplace Plus: Living and Working in English 4
Teacher's Edition

Pearson Education, 10 Bank Street, White Plains, NY 10606

Vice president, director of publishing: Allen Ascher
Senior acquisitions editor: Marian Wassner
Senior development editor: Marcia Schonzeit
Development editor: Trish Lattanzio
Vice president, director of design and production: Rhea Banker
Executive managing editor: Linda Moser
Associate managing editor: Christine Lauricella
Production manager: Liza Pleva
Director of manufacturing: Patrice Fraccio
Senior manufacturing buyer: Nancy Flaggman
Cover design: Ann France
Text design: Ann France
Text composition and art direction for Student Book: Word and Image Design Studio Inc.
Text composition for Teacher's Edition: Lehigh Press
Text font: 10/12 Palatino.

Illustrations: Craig Attebery: pp. 1, 8, 22, 23, 38, 50, 53, 134; Brian Hughes: pp. 17, 23, 30, 39, 42, 43, 44, 45, 51, 58, 99, 101, 107, 108, 123; NSV: pp. 11, 24, 29, 39, 50, 53, 57, 67, 70, 71, 80, 81, 85, 93, 94, 106, 109, 121, 136; Dusan Petricic: pp. 2, 16, 22, 31, 36, 72, 73, 78, 81, 100, 114; Meryl Treatner: pp. 6, 20, 34, 48, 62, 76, 90, 92, 96, 104, 113, 118; Anna Veltfort: pp. 5, 12, 17, 26, 40, 47, 54, 68, 82, 110, 124, 138; Word and Image Design: pp. 9, 15, 19, 37, 55, 75, 78, 79, 81, 93, 120, 128, 135, 137
Photography: Gilbert Duclos: pp. 2, 3, 7, 10, 16, 17, 19, 21, 25, 30, 31, 35, 36, 44, 45, 47, 49, 51, 58, 59, 63, 65, 72, 73, 74, 77, 86, 87, 91, 100, 101, 105, 114, 115, 119, 128, 129, 133

ISBN: 0-13-094353-3

1 2 3 4 5 6 7 8 9 10—WC— 08 07 06 05 04 03

Contents

Introduction to the *Workplace Plus* Teacher's Edition

What Is the *Workplace Plus* Course?

Workplace Plus: Living and Working in English is a complete course in English as a second language. This course prepares adults for self-sufficiency in the three principal areas of their lives: the workplace, the community, and the home. *Workplace Plus* integrates the CASAS Life Skill Competencies and SCANS Competencies and Foundation Skills with a complete language syllabus and relevant social language.

Communicative competence in English is of critical importance in achieving self-sufficiency. *Workplace Plus* applies the best of current second language acquisition research to ensure immediate survival, rapidly enabling learners to

➤ understand spoken and written general and employment-related language

➤ communicate in their own words

➤ understand the culture and civic expectations of their new environment and workplace.

To achieve these goals with efficiency and speed, *Workplace Plus* weaves together three integrated strands: workplace skills, language, and life skills.

Workplace Plus is designed to be used in a period of 60 to 90 classroom hours. This period can be shortened or lengthened, based on the needs of the group or the program.

Who Is the *Workplace Plus* Student?

The adult high-intermediate learner: *Workplace Plus 4* is designed for the adult learner who understands much spoken and written English but often communicates with difficulty and many errors. *Workplace Plus 4* is appropriate for multilevel intermediate classes, or for students who have completed *Workplace Plus 3*. A placement test is available for accurately placing students in the *Workplace Plus* series. The *Workplace Plus* student is an adult immigrant to the United States whose goal is to be able to communicate orally and in writing in all workplace and community activities.

What Is the *Workplace Plus* Approach?

Controlled introduction of language: To build confidence and ensure success, the *Workplace Plus* Student's Book controls the introduction and practice of language. All new words and grammatical structures are carefully and completely presented so that students acquire them with ease and speed. All language tasks and activities can be successfully accomplished by students of all ability levels, using the language learned in *Workplace Plus*.

Practical conversational models: Conversational models in *Workplace Plus* have been thoughtfully created to be practical in the work and life of all students in the class. Although all of the conversational models have workplace applicability, no model is so specific to one job or industry that it is not useful in others. A problem of many workplace textbooks is that they are too specific to the needs of one occupation, neglecting the communicative needs of other students in the class.

For example, a conversational model that presents language for describing problems of photocopiers would be of limited value to, say, short-order cooks. *Workplace Plus*, instead, has created conversational models that students of any occupation will find useful. This universality makes *Workplace Plus* broadly usable and effective for all students, and it speeds their arrival at self-sufficiency in any life or work path.

Authentic practice: In addition to the controlled productive tasks and activities in each Student's Book unit, a unique set of activities labeled *Authentic practice* exposes students to comprehensible language above their own productive levels and provides a rehearsal in dealing with it. This real-life rehearsal prepares students to meet their urgent need to function outside an English class and gives them practice responding to real spoken and written language they will encounter on their jobs, at home, and in their communities.

Activities for students of diverse levels within the same classroom: Every task and activity in *Workplace Plus* can be successfully completed by all students in the class. In addition, each two-page spread provides a closing activity labeled *Do it yourself!* in which students of diverse language abilities and levels can move ahead at their own pace.

A communicative ESL course with a dual workplace and life skill focus: *Workplace Plus* employs the most up-to-date language teaching methodology, emphasizing

➤ acquisition of vocabulary and social language

➤ presentation and practice of essential grammatical structures

➤ continual opportunities for controlled and free communicative practice in all four language skills of listening, speaking, reading, and writing

➤ frequent recycling and review.

Classroom Methodology

The following information has been provided to help you understand the underlying philosophy behind *Workplace Plus* and to offer some general suggestions for using the material. Specific suggestions for teaching every exercise in every unit are given in the interleaved *Teacher's Notes* pages of this Teacher's Edition. The extent to which you use these recommendations is up to you; all suggestions may not be appropriate for all groups, and you should tailor the lesson to reflect your own background, personal approach, and training, as well as the specific needs of your students.

Pair work and collaborative activities: On every page of *Workplace Plus*, opportunities for pair work, group work, and collaborative activities encourage students to take a more active and creative role in learning and allow the maximum number of students to participate. These activities encourage students to use their own language resources, making the lesson more personalized and meaningful. They also ensure that students have opportunities to initiate, as well as to respond to, conversation in English. Furthermore, in working together to solve problems, students get to know each other faster and become more independent, relying less on the teacher for guidance and ultimately taking more responsibility for their own learning. We recommend the following approaches for pair and group work activities:

➤ A student-centered approach: Some students, particularly those accustomed to teacher-centered lessons, may not immediately see the benefits of working in pairs or groups. The first time you use pair and group work, point out to students that working together allows them more time to practice English and allows you to listen to more students at once.

➤ Cooperative learning: Encourage students to help and learn from each other. Whenever possible, try to elicit answers from other students before answering a question yourself. If a student asks a question that was previously asked by another student, direct the question to the student who first asked the question. In restating information they have recently obtained in their own words, students internalize the language, increasing the likelihood that it will be retained.

➤ Seating arrangement: To ensure that students interact with a variety of partners, have students sit in a different location for each class. In multicultural classes, when dividing the class into pairs or groups, try to match students from different nationalities and backgrounds. One method of forming groups is to have students count off according to the number of groups needed. (The 1s work together, the 2s work together, and so on.)

➤ Teacher monitoring: Circulate during pair and group work activities, keeping students on task and offering help as needed. When dividing the class into pairs, avoid playing a partner role yourself, as this will limit your ability to monitor and offer assistance to the class. If faced with an odd number of students, create a group of three students, with a third role added as a helper to encourage eye contact and to correct mistakes.

➤ Building student confidence: Before asking students to speak in front of the class, build their confidence by having them rehearse language in pairs, in small groups, or as a class. Also, allowing students to collaborate on writing exercises, either by comparing their answers with a partner or by completing the activity in pairs, helps avoid the potential embarrassment of giving an incorrect answer when reviewing as a class.

➤ Time management: To keep students on task, set time limits for each activity. End activities before most of the class is finished to avoid dead time. Prepare additional activities for students who finish early. For example, have students who have finished practicing a *Pair work* conversation write the conversation that they created.

Correction: Most students of languages, particularly adult learners, like feedback and expect to be corrected when they make a mistake. However, studies have shown that it is repeated exposure to correct usage, rather than constant correction, that results in the internalization of new speech. In addition, excessive correction can embarrass and discourage students, making them reluctant to attempt the experimentation and practice that lead to language acquisition. We recommend the following approaches for providing effective positive feedback:

➤ Accuracy: For activities in which accuracy is the focus, such as in the *Practical conversations*, correct mistakes shortly after they occur. Immediate correction is important for controlled activities in which students need guidance in using the new language.

➤ Fluency: For activities in which fluency is the focus, such as the *Do it yourself!* activities, refrain from stopping the flow of student conversation with corrections. In these activities, accuracy is less important than the ability to improvise with known language. Developing improvisation skills is critical if students are to convert the English they have learned in the classroom into the English they need to function in their own lives. Interrupting students with corrections discourages this experimentation. Instead, take notes on common student mistakes and then review these errors as a class at the end of the activity.

➤ Self-correction: Students are often able to correct their own mistakes. First, allow the student to finish the thought; then show by sound or gesture that there has been a mistake. Try to indicate where the mistake was and give the student an opportunity to self-correct. Some techniques for eliciting self-correction include counting off each word of the phrase on fingers and pausing at the mistake, repeating the student sentence and pausing at the mistake, or prompting the student with a missing word. A less intrusive method is to correct the student's mistake by reformulating what the student said without stopping the flow of conversation. For example: *S: He have a car. T: Oh, he has a car? S: Yes, he has a car.* Note that this technique often prompts the student to self-correct.

➤ Selectivity: Don't discourage or overwhelm students by correcting every mistake. Focus corrections on the skills that are being taught or mistakes that prevent comprehension.

➤ Supportiveness: Above all, avoid making students feel pressured; give students enough time to think. Be careful not to stigmatize or embarrass students. Be aware that students from some cultural backgrounds may be sensitive to criticism in front of their peers and may prefer more private feedback.

Checking answers: For exercises or homework requiring a written response, have students check their answers with a partner. This encourages students to correct their own mistakes and also helps them avoid the possible embarrassment of giving incorrect answers in front of the entire class. When the class has finished comparing answers, review the correct answers as a class, either by eliciting the answers from individual students or by having volunteers write their answers on the board. In classes with time constraints, write answers on the board and have the class self-correct.

Repetition: Repetition of conversational models and new vocabulary within the *Practical conversations* sections helps students internalize correct word order, stress, and pronunciation. Note that the language that students repeat in these activities has been recorded twice on the cassette. After each recorded utterance, there is space for student repetition, followed by the recorded utterance again to confirm and reinforce pronunciation. Students listen to each utterance, repeat, and then listen again to the confirmation. Here are some tips for using repetition to facilitate learning:

➤ Open or closed books: For activities requiring students to listen and repeat, have students first listen while looking at the written form in their textbooks. This allows students to link the written form in the book to the sound they hear. In the next step, when students are asked to listen and repeat, have them listen and repeat with their books closed. This serves to reduce distractions and allows students to focus exclusively on listening and repeating rather than reading.

➤ Practice drills: Periodically, introduce short, fast-paced repetition drills to offer the class more pronunciation practice, reinforce word order or grammatical structures, and provide a change of pace. Start by modeling the new language and having the class repeat after you. Say the new language again and elicit further repetition from the class. Continue in this manner several times. Then say the language again, point to an individual student, and have that student repeat. Continue the drill by saying the language again and pointing to another student. Modeling the new language before and after each student's response helps students build auditory memory while providing students with a correct model for repetition.

➤ Pace: Keeping the pace of repetition drills lively gives the maximum number of students a chance to speak and maximizes their exposure to the language. If a student cannot respond or makes a mistake, move on quickly to another student and then return to the student who made a mistake. Maintaining the pace gives weaker students the time that they need to internalize and ultimately access new language.

Realia—bringing the outside in: Research has demonstrated that language is easier to comprehend and retain if presented in conjunction with sensory input such as pictures, sounds, props, and authentic documents. In addition, bringing real material into the classroom serves to motivate students and help them understand the relevance of their language study to their own lives.

The *Do it yourself!* and *Authentic practice* sections of *Workplace Plus* build students' understanding and competence with authentic documents by including near-authentic documents within the text itself. The *Teacher's Notes* include suggestions for enhancing this material with other realia, such as ads for work-at-home opportunities, terms of car-payment loans, and community college registration deadline information.

Elicitation: Asking questions keeps the class active and involved and helps you to identify what students understand and what they do not. An effective method for eliciting language from the class is first to provide a model that students understand and then to have them create language using the model. For example, before eliciting a list of weather adjectives from the class, provide examples by writing on the board several weather adjectives that students have learned. Some additional elicitation techniques to consider include the following:

➤ Warming up: Direct questions to the entire class before eliciting answers from individual students. This reduces the pressure on individual students to produce a response before they are ready and provides the class with a model of a correct response.

➤ Allowing one-word answers: It is not always necessary for students to answer in full sentences; often a one-word answer is sufficient to demonstrate understanding of the question and to respond appropriately. This encourages students to communicate using any relevant productive English they have previously acquired. Moreover, it allows students to speak "real" language from the start, as one-word responses are often more authentic in informal contexts than full-sentence responses.

➤ Pairing or grouping students: To maximize students' oral productivity, it is often helpful to provide opportunities for students to practice with a partner or in a small group before asking them to respond in open class.

Teaching multilevel classes: While it is rare for all the students in any adult education class to be at the same place in their language acquisition, those groups situated in a workplace setting are particularly diverse because students are often assigned to classes based on scheduling availability rather than language level. To accommodate diverse levels within the same classroom, we recommend the following approaches:

➤ Modeling: Use more advanced students to model activities. Advanced students, with their quicker comprehension time, are more likely to respond quickly and correctly. This will allow weaker students, who need longer exposure time to new language, to use the stronger students' responses as a model and respond successfully.

➤ Grouping: In pair and group work activities, varying your approach to grouping students keeps the activities fresh. Partnering more advanced students with weaker students encourages the class to help and learn from each other. Partnering students with similar ability levels also has advantages, as this allows pairs to speak at their own pace and level of production.

➤ Differentiating instruction: Optional and *Challenge* activities with varying levels of difficulty are suggested throughout the interleaved *Teacher's Notes* pages of this Teacher's Edition. Pairs or groups of students can be engaged in different activities at the same time, according to their levels of proficiency or learning styles.

The *Workplace Plus* Unit: General Teaching Suggestions

The following information has been provided to describe the features and offer general suggestions for getting the most out of each section of a *Workplace Plus* unit. More detailed procedures for teaching each exercise in each unit, as well as ideas for optional expansion activities and relevant notes on language and culture, are suggested in the interleaved *Teacher's Notes* pages of this Teacher's Edition.

Preview

The *Preview* page provides an introduction to each unit's content and is designed to activate students' prior knowledge and experience. Previous exposure to English enables the *Workplace Plus 4* student to discuss and make predictions about the content of a unit before it is fully presented. The *Preview* page consists of a *Warm up* activity and the *Unit objectives*.

Warm up: A picture, near-authentic document, or other illustration helps focus students on the content of the unit and provides them with an opportunity to relate what they already know. The interleaved *Teacher's Notes* pages of this Teacher's Edition contain numerous concrete suggestions for presenting the *Warm up* activity. Some general suggestions follow:

➤ Focus students' attention on the illustration in the *Warm up*. Ask questions that prompt students to look closely at the illustration and to speculate about the information represented.

➤ Ask questions that encourage students to relate the content represented in the illustration to their own lives and prior experiences.

➤ Summarize and check comprehension by eliciting answers to the question that precedes the illustration.

➤ Note that the illustration presented in the *Warm up* often reappears later in the unit. In-depth discussions of near-authentic documents with extensive text are more appropriate when the same or a similar document is presented the second time, as the purpose of the *Warm up* is more to generate interest than to master new material.

Unit objectives: Making students aware of unit objectives helps them to assess their needs, set learning goals, and evaluate their own progress. Being cognizant of what they should know and be able to do by the end of the unit may encourage students to take greater responsibility for their own learning and increase retention. Discussing the objectives also creates an opportunity to provide students with additional comprehensible input. The interleaved *Teacher's Notes* pages of this Teacher's Edition contain numerous concrete suggestions for presenting the *Unit objectives*. Some general suggestions follow:

➤ Read each objective out loud. Check comprehension by eliciting the meaning of words or phrases that might be difficult or unfamiliar to students.

If necessary, use simple definitions to explain new vocabulary.

➤ For each objective, elicit from the class examples of how to do what is described. If after prompts or hints the class is unable to provide any examples, move on to the next objective.

➤ Note that the objectives appear again at the end of the unit, where students are asked to check what they are then able to do.

 Practical conversations

This section provides natural, memorable conversation models that can be used in diverse, out-of-class situations. They show students the purposeful use of essential vocabulary and social language. Active vocabulary introduced on the *Practical conversations* page supports and reinforces the topics of the conversation and of the unit. In the controlled *Pair work* activities that follow each conversation, students use the words they know to manipulate the conversational model. In this way, students gain confidence and take ownership of the language, transferring the language to their own lives.

The interleaved *Teacher's Notes* pages of this Teacher's Edition contain numerous concrete suggestions for presenting the model conversations, *Vocabulary*, and *Pair work* activities on the *Practical conversations* pages. Some general suggestions follow:

Conversational model:

➤ Focus students' attention on the photo and any related illustration. Set the scene for the conversation by asking questions about the people, actions, setting, and content of the illustration. When asking questions, be mindful of what students are capable of answering; don't elicit information or language that students would not know prior to reading the conversation.

➤ For Exercise A, read the model conversation out loud or play the cassette. Have students listen and read with books open. If you read the conversation yourself, attempt to distinguish the two speakers by changing your voice or position for each role. Alternatively, have a student who reads clearly and comprehensibly play one of the roles. If possible, choose a student at the back of the room so that the class will be able to hear.

- Check that students understand the model conversation. One method is to ask the class comprehension questions about the conversation. For each model conversation, the *Teacher's Notes* offer concrete suggestions on how to check comprehension and convey the meaning of any new language that is introduced.

- For Exercise B, read the conversation again or play the cassette. With books open or closed—depending on students' needs or your preference, or alternating for variety—have students listen and repeat after each line. Encourage students to imitate the rhythm, stress, and intonation of the conversation as closely as possible. Correct where necessary, helping students to pronounce the language clearly.

Vocabulary:

- Focus students' attention on the illustrations in the *Vocabulary* box.

- Read each vocabulary word or phrase out loud or play the cassette. When pronouncing vocabulary, say each word clearly, but do not slow down to the point of sounding unnatural. You may wish to first say each word a little more slowly first and then at a natural speed.

- Note that singular count nouns are preceded by the indefinite article *a / an* in the *Vocabulary* box. Use the article when reading the words out loud to contrast singular count nouns from non-count nouns. For students of certain language backgrounds, the concept of count and non-count nouns provides a great challenge, even at this level; internalizing it is a lengthy process and the use of the indefinite article is an important first step.

- If necessary, clarify or reinforce the meaning of any words students have difficulty understanding. The *Teacher's Notes* offer suggestions on how to effectively convey ideas physically through the use of mime, gestures, tone of voice, pictures, flash cards, props, or other realia.

- You may wish to say some or all of the words in a sentence using known vocabulary to demonstrate usage, make them more memorable, and put them into the context of the unit. It may also be helpful to elicit from the class synonyms, antonyms, examples, and simple definitions of the words.

- Brainstorm and write on the board other similar words and phrases that students already know. List students' ideas in the same way that the *Vocabulary* is presented, for example, using the indefinite article or in gerund form. This provides students with more language to use in the *Pair work* activity and increases students' confidence by helping them realize how much English they have already acquired.

Pair work:

- For the *Pair work* activity (Exercise C), read the instructions out loud. Then model the conversation with a more advanced student to demonstrate that students should substitute their own words or the words provided.

- Note that for many *Practical conversations* models, a list of relevant language has been surprinted on the Student's Book page in the Teacher's Edition. This list has been provided as a summary of the productive-level language that students have learned in prior *Workplace Plus 4* activities and that could be substituted in the model. Actual student responses will vary, depending on each student's ability or ideas.

- Have students practice the *Pair work* conversation in pairs. The importance of this activity cannot be overstated, for it is in producing their own language in this controlled activity that students take their first steps toward truly free language.

- Circulate and offer help as needed. Be sure that students make eye contact during conversations to encourage natural pronunciation and tone. To review, have several volunteer pairs act out their conversations in front of the class.

Practical grammar

Each new grammar structure is clearly presented through examples followed by concise, controlled exercises to help students begin to use that structure. Grammar boxes generally offer examples rather than rules, except where necessary avoiding the use of terminology and concepts that might not be familiar to many students. Exercises provide written practice of the structures just taught while also offering further models of authentic language. For more thorough practice, many additional exercises appear in the accompanying workbook.

While grammar structures are formally presented in the *Practical grammar* section, exposure to the structures is integrated into the entire unit so that students have multiple opportunities to see and use them. For example, the *Practical conversations* section shows the grammar structure in action without requiring students to manipulate it. The grammar structures are also reinforced and practiced in the *Do it yourself!* and *Authentic practice* sections.

The interleaved *Teacher's Notes* pages of this Teacher's Edition contain numerous concrete suggestions for presenting the grammar structure and exercises. Some general suggestions follow:

➤ Inductive presentation: To present grammar with an inductive approach, start by providing numerous examples of the new structure in a natural context. Then encourage students to infer how to form or use the structure from the examples.

➤ Deductive presentation: Begin by presenting the concept and then follow it with examples from the grammar box. Involve students while you write these examples on the board.

➤ Exercises: Read the instructions out loud. If necessary, model how to do the first item in each task. Have students complete the exercises individually, in pairs, or in small groups. Circulate and offer help as needed. Before reviewing answers as a class, have students check answers with a partner.

➤ Authentic practice

Because adult immigrants must function in the world outside class immediately, even with the limited language they know, the *Authentic practice* sections provide opportunities for students to respond to language that they will encounter outside class.

This practice boosts students' confidence and decreases their potential panic when confronted with unknown language. In addition, these activities build the essential skill of improvisation: accessing known language in a spontaneous way to respond appropriately in the uncontrolled environment outside an English class.

Picture story: Students are presented with an illustrated conversation containing a mixture of known ("productive-level") language and not-yet-known ("receptive-level") language. The receptive-level language has been carefully chosen and extensively classroom tested for comprehensibility. Although students are encouraged to comprehend this new language through context—aided by carefully drawn illustrations—and through its similarity to language they know, it is not essential for students to know what every word means.

A variety of exercises follow the picture story. The purpose of the first exercise is to check students' comprehension of the conversation. In a subsequent exercise, students listen to statements or questions from the picture story and read an appropriate response from the text. A vocabulary exercise encourages students to use context in selecting their answer. In another exercise, students read receptive-level language models and select an appropriate response. The student's role (titled YOU) consists entirely of language students have already learned and is meant to serve as an example of what they can do with this language. These exercises further suggest to students how much language they already know and prepare them for success with the free-response *Do it yourself!* activities that conclude the section.

The interleaved *Teacher's Notes* pages of this Teacher's Edition contain numerous concrete suggestions for presenting the picture stories and accompanying exercises. Some general suggestions follow:

➤ Set the scene for the conversation. One method is to focus students' attention on the illustrations. For example, point to a picture and ask questions about the people, actions, and setting. When asking questions, however, be mindful of what students are capable of saying; don't elicit information or language that students would not know prior to reading the conversation.

➤ Read the conversation out loud or play the cassette. Have students listen and read with books open. If you read the conversation yourself, attempt to distinguish between or among the speakers by changing your voice or position for each role. Alternatively, have more advanced students read the other roles.

➤ Check that students understand the picture story. One method is to ask the class comprehension questions about the conversation. For each picture story, the *Teacher's Notes* offer concrete suggestions on how to check comprehension and encourage students to relate the content of the conversation to their own lives and prior experiences.

➤ For comprehension exercises, read the instructions out loud, and have students read the items individually. Then play the cassette or read the conversation a second time. Students complete the activity, referring to the picture story as necessary, and then compare answers with a partner. Review as a class.

➤ For exercises in which students choose a response, model the task by completing item 1 as a class. Copy the two answer choices from item 1 on the board. Read item 1 and elicit the correct response from the class. Demonstrate on the board that students should underline the correct response.

Working individually, students read the remaining items and underline the correct response.

➤ Have students compare answers with a partner and then take turns reading aloud the items and responses. If necessary, help students to pronounce their responses correctly by reading each answer and having students repeat.

Listening comprehension: By further exposing students to authentic models of both already learned ("productive-level") and comprehensible unknown ("receptive-level") language, these exercises reinforce students' confidence and skill in dealing with "real-world" encounters. Great care has been taken to ensure the comprehensibility of the receptive-level language. By encouraging students to use the pictures, context clues, intonation, and language they already know to understand new language, these activities demonstrate to students that it's not necessary to know every word in order to understand what is being said. As students increase their listening confidence, potential panic with unknown language outside of class will decrease.

The interleaved *Teacher's Notes* pages of this Teacher's Edition contain numerous concrete suggestions for presenting the *Listening comprehension* activities. Some general suggestions follow:

➤ Before class, read the tapescript to anticipate its content and language. Keep in mind—and point out to students—that a major cause of lack of comprehension is the natural panic that occurs when learners hear unknown words and that it is not necessary for students to understand every word to understand the selection. Again, if a student specifically asks for the meaning of a new word, give the meaning but avoid spending a lot of time on it.

➤ Before students listen to the selection, you may wish to tell them what they are about to hear by identifying the speakers, setting, or situation.

➤ To give students an idea of the "big picture," read the selection on the tapescript out loud or play the cassette while students listen with books closed.

➤ If you read the conversation yourself, attempt to distinguish the speakers by changing your voice or position for each role. Be sure to read in a clear, natural voice. Avoid slowing down your speech so much that it becomes unnatural. Instead, read the selection with a natural voice as many times as necessary for students to understand.

➤ Read the instructions out loud. Before having students listen again and complete the exercises, focus their attention on the specific listening task, such as listening for dieting facts and myths.

➤ Read the selection on the tapescript out loud or play the cassette as many times as necessary for students to complete the activities. Do not approach these exercises as "tests." Repeated exposure to each listening sample has substantial instructional value; increasing students' exposure to challenging language enhances their comprehension and confidence.

➤ Have students check their answers to the exercises with a partner before reviewing as a class.

➤ In *True story* activities, students have an opportunity to relate the content of the *Listening comprehension* selection to their own lives or prior experiences. Read the instructions for the *True story* activity out loud. Then model the activity by describing your own experience. Ask the class comprehension questions about your story to reinforce what information students should include when they talk about their own experiences in small groups. Circulate and listen as students discuss.

Ask Joan: In *Ask Joan*— an advice column that provides culture tips for newcomers—a humorous and personalized set of questions and answers prepares students to understand their rights and responsibilities and the civic and behavioral expectations of the North American community and workplace. Each column is followed by activities that build students' ability to function in the community and workplace with confidence. Again, the goal of this practice is to boost students' level of comfort and decrease their potential panic when confronted with unfamiliar situations.

The interleaved *Teacher's Notes* pages of this Teacher's Edition contain numerous concrete suggestions for presenting the *Ask Joan* feature. Some general suggestions follow:

➤ Play the cassette or read the letters. Pause after each letter and ask the class to identify the problem or suggested solution. To foster students' ability to capture the main idea, discourage the use of dictionaries. Point out that students do not need to understand every word to understand the question the newcomer has and the advice Joan offers in response.

➤ Encourage students to guess at the meaning of new words as much as possible. In this way, you will be preparing students to cope with readings outside class while also developing their ability to function independently without the aid of an instructor.

➤ You may wish to ask additional comprehension questions about what was read. Note that a single word or phrase is often sufficient to demonstrate understanding of the question and respond appropriately. Suggested comprehension questions are offered in the *Teacher's Notes*.

➤ Have students read the directions for each exercise, or read the directions out loud. If necessary, model the task on the board. Allow students a set period of time to refer to the reading as necessary and complete the exercises individually, in pairs, or in a small group.

➤ Have students check their work with a partner and then review answers as a class.

➤ You may wish to use the *Ask Joan* readings to point out in context the use of structures presented in the *Practical grammar* section or patterns of stress and intonation that can be heard on the cassette.

Authentic documents: Adult immigrants are called on daily to interact with written documents containing unknown language. For this reason, *Workplace Plus 4* provides practice with documents and other text types (including civics and consumer information from Web sites) similar to the ones they will encounter within the safe environment of the English class. These documents have been carefully constructed to be comprehensible yet challenging and authentic. The focus is on purposefulness; students practice dealing with such essential documents as magazine surveys and self-tests, written estimates for service, resumes, the Food Guide Pyramid, and a housing history form. In addition, the exercises that follow each document help students to develop critical thinking skills such as reasoning, problem solving, and decision making.

The interleaved *Teacher's Notes* pages of this Teacher's Edition contain numerous concrete suggestions for presenting activities based on near-authentic documents. Some general suggestions follow:

➤ Before formally presenting each document, allow students a set period of time to explore the document silently.

➤ Have students read without dictionaries to encourage them to read for general meaning rather than word for word. Again, encourage students to guess at the meaning of new words as much as possible.

➤ Read the document out loud or have students take turns reading it out loud.

➤ To check comprehension, you may wish to ask questions about the document. Suggested comprehension questions are offered in the *Teacher's Notes*.

➤ To prepare students for the task, read the directions to the exercise out loud. If necessary, model the task on the board.

➤ Allow students a set period of time to read the document again and then complete the exercise individually, in pairs, or in a small group.

➤ Have students check their work with a partner and then review answers on the board as a class.

 Review

Following each unit is a three-page, four-skill review that offers students an opportunity to check their progress. It also allows the teacher to identify any areas of particular difficulty that may require additional practice.

Exercise A (full-page illustration): A special feature of the *Workplace Plus* series is the full-page illustration located at the end of each unit. This open-ended activity is designed to elicit from students all the language they know—vocabulary, social language, and grammar. The picture provides a clear visual context for practice and helps students bridge the gap between language practice and authentic language use.

The picture can be used a number of ways for extensive oral practice. Working in pairs, in small groups, or as a class, students can find and name items in the picture, ask and answer questions about the picture, create conversations between the people in the picture, or take turns telling stories about people or situations in the picture. More specific suggestions for getting the most out of each illustration are given in the interleaved *Teacher's Notes* pages of this Teacher's Edition. Some general suggestions follow:

➤ Begin by allowing students time to look at the illustration. Note that, for some illustrations, students will have already practiced talking about a portion of the illustration in the *Do it yourself!* exercises earlier in the unit.

➤ In pairs, small groups, or as a class, students practice asking and answering questions, creating their own conversations for the people in the picture, and making up stories based on the illustration. For each illustration, several *Options* provide specific ideas for prompting students to tell stories and use essential content from the unit to say as much as they can about the picture.

➤ Circulate and offer help as needed. To encourage the risk taking and improvisation that are the major goals of these activities, avoid interrupting students with corrections. Instead, take notes on common student mistakes and review them as a class at the end of the activity. Encourage students to say as much as they can and to extend the suggested tasks as much as possible.

Other exercises: Completing the other *Review* exercises allows students to check their own ability to understand and use new language. The exercises review the essential content of the unit and include listening, speaking, reading, and writing tasks. Optional activities in the interleaved *Teachers' Notes* can be used to provide further practice as needed. Some general suggestions for presenting the *Review* exercises follow:

➤ Students work individually to complete the review exercises.

➤ Circulate to offer help as needed.

➤ Have students check answers with a partner. Review answers as a class.

➤ Identify any areas of difficulty that may require additional instruction and practice.

Composition: The last activity in each unit asks students to turn back to the full-page illustration at the beginning of the *Review* section. On a separate sheet of paper, students write about the picture. In their workplaces, students may need to write descriptions, short narratives, reports, and / or letters. This activity provides them with practice writing in a safe environment. Ideas specific to each picture and unit are included in the *Teacher's Notes* pages. Some general suggestions follow:

➤ Provide students with concrete approaches to writing about the picture. You may wish to use one of the options included in the *Teacher's Notes,* give students a choice of options, or assign options based on students' levels of proficiency. Model what is expected of students for each option.

➤ Advise students to look back through the unit for help and ideas as they write.

➤ Circulate to offer help as needed.

➤ You may want to keep student compositions that demonstrate effective writing or contain common errors to use as examples for future classes.

➤ If you ordinarily use process-writing techniques in your class, the *Composition* activity is an opportunity to practice peer correction. Students can then revise their drafts to incorporate classmates' suggestions.

Now I can: In the *Now I can* box at the very end of the unit, the objectives from the *Preview* page reappear in the form of a checklist. Having students check off what they are able to do after completing each unit helps them to take responsibility for their own learning and instills confidence and a sense of progress or achievement. General suggestions for using the *Now I can* box follow:

➤ Read the first item in the box out loud. Elicit from the class an example demonstrating that students can do what is described.

➤ In pairs, have students take turns reading each item in the box and giving an example of what they have learned. When students can provide an example, they should check that objective. For the items students weren't able to check, they should look back through the unit for ideas.

➤ When students are finished reviewing with their partners, read each item out loud and elicit an example from the class.

➤ Oral test: You may want to use the *Now I can* box as an informal evaluation. While students are working on the *Composition* activity, you can call them up individually and check their ability with two or three objectives.

Other unit features

Yellow notes: These "notes" are used throughout *Workplace Plus* as needed to provide students with additional vocabulary, variations of the vocabulary, or additional information. To help promote correct pronunciation, this element has been recorded on the audiocassette.

➤ To introduce the material, read the words on the yellow language note or play the cassette. Have students listen and repeat with books open.

➤ Note that the material has been recorded twice on the cassette. After each utterance, there is space for student repetition, followed by the recorded word again to confirm and reinforce pronunciation. Students listen to each utterance, repeat the words, and listen for confirmation.

Do it yourself!: Appearing at the end of each two-page spread and applying the language of that spread, *Do it yourself!* is designed to meet the needs of both single-level and multilevel classes. In these communicative and purposeful activities, students use the new vocabulary, social language, and grammar in a variety of creative or personalized ways. *Do it yourself!* helps students bridge the gap between the controlled practice of the textbook page and the natural use of language that will be necessary in the world outside of class.

Some examples of *Do it yourself!* activities are role-plays, discussions, personalized information charts, collaborative activities, and plan-ahead projects, all incorporating language students have just learned. Great care has been taken to ensure that students can perform the tasks successfully with the bare minimum of language presented for active use. However, students who have richer resources, experience, and ability will also be challenged by the open-ended nature of the tasks.

The interleaved *Teacher's Notes* pages of this Teacher's Edition contain numerous concrete suggestions for presenting the *Do it yourself!* activities. Some general suggestions follow:

➤ Spend as much time as necessary demonstrating the activity for your particular group of students. Keep in mind that the *Do it yourself!* activities are not intended to be a test and that the more support students receive, the more successful they will be in completing the task.

➤ Note that in many *Do it yourself!* activities an example has been provided on the Student's Book page that can be used to demonstrate the activity to the class. The *Teacher's Notes* for each *Do it yourself!* activity offer specific suggestions on how to effectively model each task.

➤ To encourage risk taking and experimentation, avoid correcting students until the end of the activity and praise them for creativity and expressiveness. Encourage students to take the activity in other directions and to extend the suggested tasks as much as possible. Have students say as much as they can.

Interleaved *Teacher's Notes* Pages

This Teacher's Edition contains page-by-page teaching suggestions specific to each new activity interleaved with the corresponding full-color Student's Book pages. The *Teacher's Notes* pages also contain boxed tapescripts of all material recorded on the audiocassettes and suggestions for optional expansion. In addition to the teaching suggestions, answers to the exercises are printed in color directly on the facing Student's Book pages for easy reference.

All teaching suggestions on the interleaved pages should be considered optional. Teachers are encouraged to use the techniques that have been successful for them in the past and to view the teaching suggestions on these pages as a practical menu of additional possibilities.

The interleaved *Teacher's Notes* pages include the following features:

Content: Serving as an at-a-glance summary of the exercise, this feature identifies all the teaching points presented in the exercise and any corresponding yellow language notes, including skills (e.g., *asking for an emergency repair*), the type of new vocabulary presented (e.g., *utilities*), and grammar (e.g., *non-action verbs*). Note that for lesson planning and compliance with curriculum guidelines, the *Scope and Sequence* chart on pages iv to vii in the Student's Book clearly spells out the following elements for each unit: Workplace Skills, Life Skills, Civics Concepts, Social Language, Grammar, and SCANS Competencies and Foundation Skills.

Procedure: The *Teacher's Notes* pages offer specific, concrete suggestions for presenting each exercise in the unit. Teachers are encouraged to experiment with their procedure to discover the techniques that work best for their classes.

Options: This element offers teachers many concrete ideas for supplemental activities, adding variety and fun to the lesson while allowing students more time to explore the teaching point. Note that some optional activities may not be appropriate for all settings or all classes. Teachers should use their judgment in selecting material that best meets the needs of their particular group. Optional material suggested in the *Teacher's Notes* includes the following:

➤ Realia: Props, pictures, and real information such as the student's name or job title are important aids in connecting the lesson to the student's real life outside the classroom.

➤ Games: Games in which students must utilize the teaching point in order to play help motivate students by making learning fun. Additionally, variations could also be offered that transform a textbook exercise into a game.

➤ Role-play: Acting out scenarios or conversations offers students the opportunity to rehearse using language in a natural context.

➤ Alternate presentations: Textbook material can often be presented and used in different ways to meet the specific needs of each class. Illustrations are particularly adaptable for different uses.

➤ Collaborative activities: Projects that students can complete together as a class or in groups, such as completing a chart on the board or brainstorming a list of information, encourage students to work together to solve problems and to take more responsibility for their learning.

➤ Graphic organizers: Having students organize content in a chart, diagram, or mind map helps them make sense of new information and makes difficult concepts more accessible. Graphic organizers can also promote interaction and help students efficiently gather and record information or ideas from their classmates. Presenting essential information clearly is a skill that may be helpful to your students in their workplaces.

Challenges: Intended to enrich the learning experience of more advanced groups or students, these optional ideas for supplemental activities increase the level of difficulty by introducing additional vocabulary or alternate methods of expression. As with *Options*, teachers should use their judgment in selecting material that best meets the needs of their particular group.

Tapescript: A boxed tapescript for each listening comprehension activity is included on the corresponding *Teacher's Notes* page for easy reference. Note that exercises marked with a 🎧 in the Student's Book include a listening component that has been recorded on the audiocassette.

If your students are ready . . . : Specifically targeted to the highly diverse and heterogeneous adult immigrant ESL classroom, these optional notes on language, culture, and civic expectations enrich the language experience of more advanced or academic students in multilevel groups. *Language notes* contain additional information on grammar and American language usage relevant to the lesson. In addition, because information about social customs may be as important as language for immigrant learners, *Culture / Civics notes* offer relevant background information on laws, customs, and traditions in North America. As always, use discretion in choosing which notes to include as some material might be above the level of your group.

Living and Working in English

Joan Saslow

Edwina Hoffman
Series Advisor

LONGMAN ON THE WEB

Longman.com offers online resources for teachers and students. Access our Companion Websites, our online catalog, and our local offices around the world.

Longman English Success offers online courses to give learners flexible study options. Courses cover General English, Business English, and Exam Preparation.

Visit us at longman.com and englishsuccess.com.

Longman

Contents

Scope and sequence

Unit	Workplace Skills	Life Skills	Civics Concepts	Social Language	Grammar
1 **Your life and work** page 1	• Prepares for job interview • Completes application • Requests letter of recommendation • Describes skills and abilities	• Engages in small talk • Gets to know someone • Asks for references	• Appropriate job interview dress and demeanor	How to • initiate conversations • give and accept compliments • get to know someone	• The present perfect continuous • Gerunds for describing likes, dislikes, and skills
2 **Your environ-ment** page 15	• Requests and gives directions inside a building • Offers and gives assistance • Gives directions to a place	• Demonstrates elevator etiquette • Gives directions for transportation • Uses maps and building directories	• Appropriate punctuality for social invitations	How to • extend and accept invitations • ask for directions • tell and ask others for directions • make plans to meet	• Imperatives for directions, warnings, requests, and suggestions • Indirect commands
3 **Your equip-ment and machines** page 29	• Tells employer about equipment breakdown • Troubleshoots a problem	• Discusses a product warranty • Completes a proof-of-purchase card • Uses telephone product service lines	• Rights afforded by product warranties • Employer expectations that workers report equipment breakdowns	How to • admit a possible error • reassure a worried person • empathize • express worry about consequences	• The passive voice • Review: Irregular past participles
4 **Your customers** page 43	• Explains a discontinued item • Discusses a safety recall • Offers to make good • Improves a quality-control problem • Offers service	• Requests a brand • Asks for service in a gas station • Acts on a product recall • Explains conditions • Writes consumer complaint letters	• Consumer Product Safety Commission and product safety recalls • Civic responsibility for the environment • EPA rules	How to • confirm another's opinion • express disappointment • express regret • offer an alternative	• *Used to* • Comparisons with *as* and *not as* • Review: Comparative forms
5 **Your time** page 57	• Understands consequences of lateness • Clarifies job expectations • Discusses payment, hours, and overtime pay	• Discusses payment • Computes pay • Understands importance of punctuality • Reschedules events	• Fair Labor Standards Act: minimum wage and entitlement to overtime pay • Company time vs. personal time	How to • reschedule events • provide reasons • interrupt politely • ask for repetition • ask for permission • clarify expectations	• Verbs followed by infinitives • Verbs followed by objects and infinitives

SCANS Competencies	SCANS Foundation Skills					
	Listening	**Speaking**	**Reading**	**Writing**	**Thinking**	**Personal Qualities**
• Interpersonal: Interprets and communicates • Information: Organizes data	Understands • small talk • interview questions	• Role-plays a job interview • Relates a personal experience	Reads • application forms • advice about interview etiquette	• Completes employment applications • Charts job skills • Writes a composition	• Classifies behavior as appropriate and inappropriate	• Demonstrates courtesy and sociability • Demonstrates self-management
• Information: Acquires and evaluates data related to locations • Interpersonal: Negotiates and plans with culturally diverse companions	Understands • requests for assistance • invitations • work-related directions	• Instructs co-workers • Relates a personal experience	Reads • maps, plans, and diagrams • advice about social behavior • handwritten directions	• Writes directions • Charts activities and locations • Writes an informal note • Writes a composition	• Interprets maps • Analyzes problems depicted in picture • Compares and contrasts map resources	• Demonstrates individual responsibility by assisting others • Demonstrates sociability
• Information: Acquires and evaluates data • Technology: Maintains equipment and troubleshoots problems	Understands • concerns over errors • equipment problems	• Describes equipment breakdowns • Uses telephone service lines • Relates a personal experience	Reads • warranties • advice about reporting breakdowns • a repair or replace order • service receipts	• Fills in a proof-of-purchase card • Charts machinery breakdowns • Writes a composition	• Interprets a product warranty • Compares and contrasts service receipts	• Demonstrates individual responsibility by reporting equipment breakdowns • Demonstrates integrity
• Interpersonal: Serves customers • Information: Acquires and evaluates data	Understands • product recall announcements • attributes of brands and products	• Role-plays a product recall • Offers to make good • Relates a personal experience	Reads • CPSC safety recalls • letters of complaint • advice about environmental hazards	• Writes a complaint letter and response • Charts defective products • Writes a composition	• Compares and contrasts consumer behavior in a native country with the U.S.A. • Compares and contrasts present and past life	• Demonstrates individual responsibility as it relates to the environment and product safety
• Resources: Knows how to allocate time • Information: Interprets and communicates information • Systems: Understands organizational systems	Understands • discussions of wages and hours • jobs and duties • employer's instructions	• Discusses payment and hours, hours, overtime pay • Advises co-workers • Relates a personal experience	Reads • employment policies and procedures • about minimum wage • job postings • advice about punctuality at work	• Charts occupations of classmates • Completes paragraphs • Writes a composition	• Compares and contrasts payment options • Understands consequences	• Demonstrates individual responsibility as it relates to punctuality • Demonstrates self-management • Demonstrates sociability

SCANS Competencies	SCANS Foundation Skills					
	Listening	**Speaking**	**Reading**	**Writing**	**Thinking**	**Personal Qualities**
• Interpersonal: Teaches others; Teams with partner • Information: Acquires and evaluates data; Uses computer to process information	Understands • conversations about bargains • information on unit pricing • conversations about ordering supplies	• Explains purchasing decisions • Orders over the phone • Relates a personal experience	Reads • unit pricing information and labels • about ordering online or by mail	• Charts information on units of measure • Completes a mail order • Writes a composition	• Compares and contrasts values • Draws conclusions • Classifies products by unit of measure	• Demonstrates self-management
• Interpersonal: Works on teams and teaches others • Information: Interprets and communicates information	Understands • conversations about disputes between neighbors	• Inquires about rules and laws • Advises others • Relates a personal experience	Reads • advice about community rules and laws • summons for violation of a rule	• Charts signs related to laws • Writes a composition	• Compares and contrasts customs and laws in a native country and U.S.A.	• Demonstrates sociability through consideration of others • Demonstrates individual responsibility for knowing the law
• Interpersonal: Negotiates and works in teams • Systems: Monitors and corrects performance • Information: Acquires and evaluates data	Understands • public service announcements about safe food-handling information	• Reports a food problem • Advises others on food safety • Relates a personal experience	Reads • medicine labels • about food safety • about over-the-counter medications	• Charts remedies for aliments • Writes a composition	• Analyzes medications • Compares food-handling customs • Applies warnings on medications	• Demonstrates sociability • Demonstrates integrity by representing employer honestly
• Interpersonal: Works in teams • Information: Acquires and evaluates data • Systems: Understands organizational systems	Understands • descriptions of banking services • conversations about credit	• Discusses debt • Inquires about credit counseling services • Relates a personal experience	Reads • credit card bills • about credit counseling services in the Yellow Pages • consumer information from the FTC Web site	• Charts bank services and accounts • Writes checks • Writes a composition	• Compares bank services • Solves debt-related problems • Decides how much to pay on a credit card bill	• Demonstrates individual responsibility to live within one's means • Demonstrates self-management of personal finances
Information: Interprets and communicates information Systems: Monitors and corrects performance	Understands • radio advice programs on interviewing "tips"	• Responds to an ad • Role-plays a job interview • Discusses career goals • Relates a personal experience	Reads • classified ads • advice about employee-boss communication	• Writes a cover letter to apply for a job • Completes a performance review form • Writes a composition	• Identifies reasons to change jobs	• Demonstrates sociability • Demonstrates individual responsibility by giving reasons for actions

Acknowledgments

The author wishes to acknowledge with gratitude the following consultants and reviewers—our partners in the development of *Workplace Plus*.

Regional Consultant Board

The following people have participated on an ongoing basis in shaping the content and approach of *Workplace Plus*:

Ann Belletire, Northern Illinois University–Business and Industry Services, Oak Brook, Illinois • **Sandra Bergman**, Instructional Facilitator, Alternative, Adult, and Continuing Education Program, New York City Board of Education • **Sherie Burnette**, Assistant Dean, Workforce Education, Brookhaven College of the Dallas County Community College District, Farmers Branch, Texas • **Michael Feher**, Boston Chinatown Neighborhood Center, Boston, Massachusetts • **Susan B. Kanter**, Instructional Supervisor, Continuing Education and Contract Training, Houston Community College-Southwest, Houston, Texas • **Brigitte Marshall**, Consultant, Albany, California • **Monica Oliva**, Educational Specialist, Miami-Dade County Public Schools, Miami, Florida • **Mary E. O'Neill**, Coordinator of Community Education, ESL, Northern Virginia Community College—Annandale Campus, Annandale, Virginia • **Grace Tanaka**, Professor of ESL, Santa Ana College School of Continuing Education; ESL Facilitator, Centennial Education Center, Santa Ana, California • **Marcia L. Taylor**, Workplace Instructor, Joblink, Ispat-Inland Inc., East Chicago, Indiana

Reviewers

The following people shared their perspectives and made suggestions either by reviewing manuscript or participating in editorial conferences with the author and editors:

Leslie Jo Adams, Santa Ana College–Centennial Education Center, Santa Ana, California • **Sandra Anderson**, El Monte-Rosemead Adult School, El Monte, California • **Marcy Berquist**, San Diego Community College District, San Diego, California • **Robert Breitbard**, District School Board of Collier County, Naples, Florida • **Ruth Brigham**, A.C.C.E.S.S., Boston, Massachusetts • **Donna Burns**, Mt. San Antonio College, Walnut, California • **Eric Burton**, Downington Area School District, Downington, Pennsylvania • **Michael James Climo**, West Los Angeles College, Culver City, California • **Teresa Costa**, The English Center, Miami, Florida • **Robert Cote**, Miami-Dade County Public Schools, Miami, Florida • **Georgette Davis**, North Orange County Community College District, Orange County, California • **Janet Ennis**, Santa Ana College–Centennial Education Center, Santa Ana, California • **Peggy Fergus**, Northern Illinois University–Business and Industry Services, Oak Brook, Illinois • **Oliva Fernandez**, Hillsborough County Public Schools–Adult & Community Education, Tampa, Florida • **Elizabeth Fitzgerald**, Hialeah Adult & Community Center, Hialeah, Florida • **Marty Furch**, Palomar College, San Diego, California • **Eric Glicker**, North Orange County Community College District, Orange County, California • **Steve Gwynne**, San Diego Community College District, San Diego, California • **Victoria Hathaway**, DePaul University, Chicago, Illinois • **Jeffrey L. Janulis**, Richard J. Daley College, City Colleges of Chicago, Chicago, Illinois • **Mary Karamourtopoulos**, Northern Essex Community College, Haverhill, Massachusetts • **Shirley Kelly**, Brookhaven College of the Dallas County Community College District, Farmers Branch, Texas • **Marilou Kessler**, Jewish Vocational Service–Vocational English Program, Chicago, Illinois • **Henry Kim**, North Orange County Community College District, Orange County, California • **Dr. Maria H. Koonce**, Broward County Public Schools, Ft. Lauderdale, Florida • **John Kostovich**, South Texas Community College–Intensive English Program, McAllen, Texas • **Jacques LaCour**, Mt. Diablo Adult Education, Concord, California • **Beatrice Liebman**, Miami Sunset Adult Center, Miami, Florida • **Doris Lorden**, Wright College–Workforce Training Center, Chicago, Illinois • **Mike Lowman**, Coral Gables Adult Education Center, Coral Gables, Florida • **Lois Maharg**, Delaware Technical and Community College • **Vicki Moore**, El Monte-Rosemead Adult School, El Monte, California • **Deborah Nash**, School Board of Palm Beach County Schools, West Palm Beach, Florida • **Cindy Neubrech**, Mt. San Antonio College, Walnut, California • **Patricia Peabody**, Broward County Public Schools, Ft. Lauderdale, Florida • **Joe A. Perez**, Hillsborough County Public Schools, Tampa, Florida • **Diane Pinkley**, Teacher's College, Columbia University, New York, New York • **Kay Powell**, Santa Ana College–Centennial Education Center, Santa Ana, California • **Wendy Rader**, San Diego Community College District, San Diego, California • **Don Robison**, Jewish Vocational Service–Workplace Literacy, Chicago, Illinois • **Richard Sasso**, Triton College, River Grove, Illinois • **Mary Segovia**, El Monte-Rosemead Adult School, El Monte, California • **Laurie Shapero**, Miami-Dade Community College, Miami, Florida • **Sara Shapiro**, El Monte-Rosemead Adult School, El Monte, California • **Samanthia Spence**, Richland College, Dallas, Texas • **JoAnn Stehy**, North Orange County Community College District, Orange County, California • **Margaret Teske**, Mt. San Antonio College, Walnut, California • **Dung Tran**, North Orange County Community College District, Orange County, California • **Claire Valier**, School District of Palm Beach County, West Palm Beach, Florida • **Catherine M. Waterman**, Rancho Santiago Community College, Santa Ana, California • **James Wilson**, Mt. San Antonio College, Walnut, California

To the teacher

Workplace Plus: Living and Working in English is a four-level course in English as a second language which starts at the absolute beginner language level.* The course prepares adults for self-sufficiency in the three principal areas of their lives: the workplace, the community, and the home. *Workplace Plus* integrates the CASAS life skill competencies and the SCANS Competencies and Foundation Skills with a complete civics and language syllabus and relevant social language.

Communicative competence in English is of critical importance in achieving self-sufficiency. *Workplace Plus* applies the best of current second language acquisition research to ensure immediate survival, rapidly enabling learners to:

- understand spoken and written general and employment-related language
- communicate in their <u>own</u> words
- understand the culture and civic expectations of their new environment and workplace
- cope with authentic documents they will encounter in their daily lives.

In order to achieve these goals with efficiency and speed, *Workplace Plus* weaves together four integrated strands: workplace skills, language, life skills, and civics.

Course length
Workplace Plus is designed to be used in a period of 60 to 90 classroom hours. This period can be shortened or lengthened, based on the needs of the group or the program. The Teacher's Edition gives detailed instructions for tailoring *Workplace Plus* to specific settings, circumstances, and student groups.

Components
Student's Book
The *Workplace Plus* Student's Book is a complete four-skill text, integrating listening, speaking, reading, and writing with workplace skills and life skills. The book contains 10 units, each one followed by a concise four-skill review section. For lesson planning and compliance with curriculum guidelines, the Scope and Sequence chart (on pages iv-vii) clearly spells out the following elements for each unit:

- workplace skills
- life skills
- civics concepts
- social language
- grammar
- SCANS Competencies and Foundation Skills

In order to facilitate student-centered instruction, *Workplace Plus* uses a variety of grouping strategies: pairs, groups, and whole class. In numerous activities, learners work with others to create a joint product. Those activities are labeled collaborative activities.

Two special features of the *Workplace Plus* Student's Book are <u>Do it yourself!</u> and <u>Authentic practice</u>.

Because learners have an immediate need to use their new language outside the class, <u>Do it yourself!</u> provides a daily opportunity for students of diverse abilities to put new language into their own words. This affords them a chance

---

* *Literacy Plus*, which precedes *Workplace Plus 1*, serves the combined ESL, literacy, and civics needs of the pre-literate beginner.

to "try their wings" in the safe and supportive environment of the classroom.

Authentic practice activities create a "living language laboratory" within the classroom. Learners practice responding to authentic models of spoken and written English with the limited language they know. In this way, students build their confidence and skill in coping with the language of the real world.

Audiocassettes

Because listening comprehension is a fundamental survival and success skill for new speakers of English, *Workplace Plus* includes a comprehensive listening strand in each unit of the Student's Book. In addition to listening comprehension activities, there are numerous other opportunities for learners to practice their listening skills. All exercises that appear on audiocassette are marked with a 🎧 symbol. A transcript of each listening comprehension activity is located on its corresponding Teacher's Edition page, for easy reference.

Teacher's Edition

An interleaved Teacher's Edition provides page-by-page teaching suggestions that add value to the Student's Book. In addition to general and day-by-day teaching suggestions, each teacher's page includes optional activities, challenge activities, and language and culture / civics notes that will help teachers demystify and explain new language and culture concepts to students. Answers to all exercises and the tapescript of each listening comprehension activity are also readily found on all pages.

Workbook

In addition to the ample opportunities for reading and writing practice contained in the Student's Book, the *Workplace Plus* Workbook contains further reading and writing exercises. The Workbook is valuable for homework or for in-class activities. An added feature is a test preparation activity for each unit, with CASAS-like and BEST Test-like items which ensure that learners can "bubble in" and cope with the formats of standardized language tests.

Teacher's Resource Binder

A three-ring binder contains a wealth of valuable items to enable busy teachers to customize their instruction and make the preparation of supplementary teaching aids unnecessary. The Classroom Booster Pack provided with the Binder features pair-work cards, vocabulary flash cards, grammar self-checks, photo chat cards, and extension activities for daily use. Correlations of *Workplace Plus* with state and federal standards are also included in the Binder.

The following additional teacher-support materials are also available: Student Progress Checklists, Pre- and Post-Tests and Achievement Tests, Skills for Test Taking, and industry-specific Job Packs that are correlated with Student's Books 1 and 2.

Placement Test

A simple-to-administer test places students accurately within the *Workplace Plus* series.

Workplace Plus Companion Website

The *Workplace Plus* companion website (www.longman.com/workplaceplus)

provides numerous additional resources for students and teachers. This no-cost, high-benefit feature includes opportunities for further practice of language and content from the *Workplace Plus* Student's Book. For the teacher, there are optional strategies and materials that amplify the *Workplace Plus* Teacher's Edition.

Student's Book unit contents
Each unit in the *Workplace Plus* Student's Book uses an integrated three-step approach.

1. <u>Practical conversations with integrated vocabulary</u>
Simple, memorable model conversations that are transferable to learners' own lives permit intensive practice of new vocabulary and key social language. These are followed by lively pair-work activities.

2. <u>Practical grammar</u>
Essential grammatical structure practice enables learners to manipulate the vocabulary and practical conversations to express ideas of their own.

3. <u>Authentic practice</u>
An entertaining picture story illustrates the authentic use of spoken target language and leads to a series of interactive comprehension tasks that help students cope with spoken language in the world outside the classroom.

A unique real-world reading enables students to understand culture and civics concepts of their new community and workplace. Then a series of authentic documents provides preparation for coping with the real documents students will encounter in the world outside the classroom.

<u>Review</u>
Following each unit is a three-page, four-skill review for learners to check their progress.

Author

Joan Saslow

Joan Saslow has taught English as a second language and English as a foreign language to adults and young adults in the United States and Chile. She taught workplace English at the General Motors auto assembly plant in Tarrytown, NY; and Adult ESL at Westchester Community College and at Marymount College in New York. In addition, Ms. Saslow taught English and French at the Binational Centers of Valparaíso and Viña del Mar, Chile, and the Catholic University of Valparaíso.

Ms. Saslow is the series director of Longman's popular five-level adult series *True Colors, an EFL Course for Real Communication* and of *True Voices*, a five-level video course. She is the author of *Literacy Plus*, a two-level series that teaches beginning literacy, survival English, and essential civics concepts to adult pre-literate immigrants. She is also author of *English in Context: Reading Comprehension for Science and Technology*, a three-level series for English for special purposes. In addition, Ms. Saslow has been an editor of language teaching materials, a teacher trainer, and a frequent speaker at gatherings of ESL and EFL teachers for over thirty years.

Series advisor

Edwina Hoffman

Edwina Hoffman has taught English for speakers of other languages in South Florida and at the Miccosukee Tribe of Indians, and English as a foreign language in Venezuela. She provided teacher training in a seven-state area for federally funded multi-functional resource centers serving the southeastern part of the United States. Dr. Hoffman taught English composition at Florida International University and graduate ESOL methods at the University of Miami.

Dr. Hoffman is an instructional supervisor with the adult and vocational programs of Miami-Dade County Public Schools in Miami, Florida. She has acted as a consultant, reviewer, and author of adult ESOL materials for over twenty years. A graduate of Middlebury College, Dr. Hoffman's doctoral degree is from Florida International University.

Living and Working in English

UNIT 1

Your life and work

 Preview

(For general suggestions, see *Introduction*, page Tviii.)

Warm up. Have you ever been interrupted at dinner by a telemarketer? What happened? What did you do?

Procedure:

➤ Before you open the book, provide students with an opportunity to get to know each other. Have them complete a "Find someone who" activity. You can create your own or use the one following. You can hand out photocopies with the sentences on them or write the sentences on the board and ask students to copy them on a piece of paper. Tell students to walk around the classroom and talk with their classmates. Next to each phrase, they should write the name of one student for whom the statement is true. They can use each name only once. If, for example, they write *Sandra* next to *is wearing jeans today*, they cannot write *Sandra* next to anything else. Share the completed sentences as a class.

Note: The structures used in this sample activity can be incorporated into the *Practical grammar* explanations on pages 4 and 5, so have students save their work.

Find someone who

1. is wearing jeans today _____

2. is working today _____

3. is studying at this school _____
   for the first time

4. drives to class every day _____

5. is planning a trip soon _____

6. never comes late to class _____

7. feels happy to be here _____

8. has a dog or a cat _____

9. thinks your city is exciting _____

10. likes pizza _____

➤ Have students open their books and look at the pictures. Ask questions about the pictures, such as *Who is in the picture on the left?* (a family) *What are they doing?* (eating dinner) *What interrupts them?* (a telephone call) *Who is in the picture on the right?* (The man is talking to a woman on the phone.) *Who is the woman?* (a telemarketer) *What is her job?* (maybe selling something) *Why do you think she is calling?* (She probably wants the man to buy something or give her something.)

➤ Read the *Warm up* questions. Have students look at the picture on the right and imagine the rest of the conversation. Elicit a variety of ideas from the class, such as *I'm sorry. We're having dinner right now; We're not interested; Can you send me something in the mail?*

If your students are ready . . .

Culture / Civics note: In the United States and Canada, people often tell a phone solicitor that they are not interested, and sometimes hang up. Students from other countries may have a different response to such a caller and find it difficult to do something that seems rude.

Unit 1 objectives

Procedure:

Note: Legislation passed in 2003 has changed the telemarketing business. Consumers can now place their names on a national "do not call" list. Telemarketers who call people on the list can be fined.

➤ Have students read the objectives. Ask them to put a check next to the objectives that they can do now and circle those they want to work on most.

➤ Ask students to underline any words they do not understand. Write any unfamiliar terms on the board. Some students may not be familiar with the concepts *good cause, telemarketer's sales solicitation, volunteerism,* and *fraud.* Give a quick explanation of these terms.

Your life and work

Preview

Warm up. Have you ever been interrupted at dinner by a telemarketer? What happened? What did you do?

Unit 1 objectives

- Agree to contribute to a good cause.
- Decline a telemarketer's sales solicitation.
- Understand the spirit of volunteerism.
- Avoid telemarketing fraud.

Model 1   Agree to contribute to a good cause.

🎧 **A.** **Listen and read.**

A: I'm collecting for the food pantry. Would you be willing to make a donation?

B: What did you say it was for?

A: The food pantry.

B: That's a good cause. I'd be happy to.

A: Thanks so much.

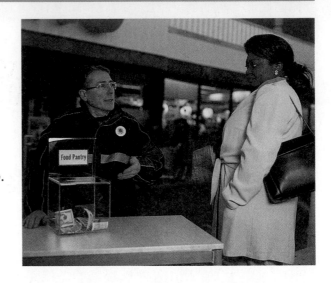

🎧 **B.** **Pronunciation and intonation practice.**

🎧 **Vocabulary**

Ways to volunteer

make a donation

volunteer some time

bake something for the bake sale

make a few phone calls

mail some letters

distribute some flyers

C. **Pair work.** **Ask for help with a good cause. Use these or your own cause.**

the homeless shelter	the food pantry
the scholarship fund	the hospital

A: I'm collecting for _____. Would you be willing to _____?

B: What did you say it was for?

A: _____.

B: That's a good cause. I'd be happy to.

A: ___1___.

[1]Thanks, That's great

2   Unit 1

Practical conversations

(For general suggestions, see *Introduction*, page Tviii.)

Model 1

Content: agreeing to contribute to a good cause, using the present continuous for an action in progress, identifying ways to volunteer, identifying good causes

Procedure:

A. Listen and read.

➤ Read the bar for *Model 1*. Ask students what *a good cause* is. If they don't know, give examples of causes and ask if each is a good cause. For example: *Is cancer research a good cause? Is freeing convicted murderers a good cause? What about giving money to a political party or enforcing a leash law for dogs?* Elicit from students that believing something is a good cause is subjective and that some people may think a cause is good, while others might find it silly or even wrong.

➤ To set the scene for the conversation, point to the photo and ask questions such as *Who do you see in the picture?* (a man at a table, a woman walking by) *What do you think the man is doing?* (collecting money) *What's on the table in front of him?* (a container for money donations) *Where are the people?* (in front of a store) *What do you think the woman is doing?* (shopping)

➤ Play the cassette or read the conversation. After students listen and read, ask comprehension questions such as *What is the man doing?* (collecting for the food pantry) *What does he want the woman to do?* (make a donation) *What is the woman's response?* (That's a good cause. She would be happy to make a donation.) *What is the cause that the man is collecting for?* (a food pantry, a place that gives food to people who need it)

B. Pronunciation and intonation practice.

➤ Tell students that they will listen to the conversation again and have the opportunity to repeat each speaker's lines. Play the cassette or read the conversation again. Encourage students to imitate the rhythm, stress, and intonation of the conversation as closely as possible. Correct where necessary.

Option: To help students improve their intonation, have them practice reading the conversation in pairs. Remind them that native speakers often link words when the first word ends in a vowel or when the second word begins with a vowel. For example,

native speakers might join *say* and *it,* creating *sayit.* Then have volunteers read the conversation aloud. Ask the other students to listen and note any linkages. Phrases that might naturally be linked because of vowel sounds include *yoube, tomakea, sayit, that'sa.*

Vocabulary

➤ Point to each picture and ask students what they see.

➤ Play the cassette or read the phrases and have students repeat the ways to volunteer.

Option: To elicit students' own experience, ask *Have you ever been asked to do one of these volunteer activities? Have you ever volunteered in one of these ways? Which ones? Which of these do you like doing?*

Option: Write on the board three headings: *Ways to volunteer, Advantages,* and *Disadvantages.* On the left, write each of the ways to volunteer listed in the *Vocabulary.* Ask students to brainstorm the advantages and disadvantages of each way. The chart might look something like the following:

Ways to volunteer	Advantages	Disadvantages
•Make a donation	Helps many causes	Costs you money
•Volunteer some time	Help people directly	Time consuming
•Bake something for the bake sale	Good if you like to cook	Have to be able to cook
•Make a few phone calls	Can do at home on your own time	Have to speak to people you don't know
•Mail some letters	Can fit into a busy schedule	You usually buy the postage
•Distribute some flyers	Meet people	May have to talk to people in English

C. Pair work . . .

➤ Brainstorm other causes that people might volunteer for, including *health clinics, social services, refugee programs, mentoring programs such as Big Brother / Big Sister, adult ESL programs, elementary schools, sports programs, holiday gift drives.*

➤ Model the conversation with a more advanced student. Play the role of Student A. Demonstrate that Student A mentions a good cause in the first slot and a way to volunteer in the second slot. Make sure students understand that they can use any of the ways to volunteer from the *Vocabulary* in the second slot. Student A then repeats the good cause in the third slot and expresses thanks in the last.

➤ Students practice the conversation with a partner, taking turns playing the roles of Student A and Student B. Circulate and offer help as needed.

T2

Model 2

Content: declining a telemarketer's sales solicitation, using the simple present tense with non-action verbs, identifying ways to decline an offer

Procedure:

🎧A. Listen and read.

➤ Read the bar for *Model 2*. Tell students to notice what the telemarketer's sales offer is.

➤ Direct students' attention to the photo. Ask questions such as *What is going on in the picture?* (A woman is on the phone.) *What is the man in the round photo looking at?* (a telephone book or other directory)

➤ After students listen to the conversation, check comprehension by asking *Who is the man?* (a telemarketer) *What is he selling?* (cell phone service) *What does the woman ask?* (Is this a sales call?) *How does she decline the telemarketer's offer?* (We don't take offers over the phone.)

🎧B. Pronunciation and intonation practice.

Option: Divide the class in half. Play the cassette or read the conversation and have half the class repeat Student A's lines and the other half repeat Student B's lines. Read the line with students if they have trouble.

🎧Vocabulary

➤ Have students look at the photo in the *Vocabulary* box. Have them describe the look on the woman's face or speculate about what she just heard.

➤ Play the cassette or read the expressions and have students repeat the ways to decline an offer, imitating the authentic intonation as closely as possible.

➤ Brainstorm other ways to decline an offer. Let students know that they can tell the telemarketer *Please take us off your list.* Then the company cannot call them again.

C. Pair work ...

➤ Model the activity with a more advanced student. Play the role of Student A to demonstrate using an expression from the *Vocabulary* to decline an offer.

➤ Have students practice the conversation in pairs, switching the roles of A and B. Circulate, answering questions if necessary.

If your students are ready ...

Language note: The telemarketer says *We have a special offer on cell phone service this evening.* Tell students that they may also hear *We're having a special offer*, which means we are running or conducting a special offer, not that we possess a special offer. In some regions, callers may say *We've got a special offer*, which is idiomatic and does not mean ownership.

If your students are ready ...

Culture / Civics note: In the United States, there are laws that restrict telemarketing. These restrictions include the following:

A telemarketer may only call between 8:00 a.m. and 9:00 p.m. A telemarketer may not call you if you have previously asked not to be called. According to legislation passed in 2003, consumers can place their names on a national "do not call" list. Telemarketers who call people on the list can be fined. Before starting a sales pitch, the telemarketer must tell you that the call is a sales call, the name of the seller, and what is being sold. If it is a prize promotion, the telemarketer must tell you that no purchase or payment is necessary to enter the contest or win the prize.

➤ Do it yourself!

(For general suggestions, see *Introduction*, page Txiii.)

Procedure:

A–B.

➤ Students should write down the name of one charity solicitation and one sales solicitation that they have actually received.

➤ Ask students for the names of the solicitors who have called them and list some of these names on the board or a transparency.

➤ Model a role play with a more advanced student. Ask the student to play the part of a telemarketer. Before you begin, make sure the student chooses a name for the company he or she represents and the product or cause. If the student is unsure, he or she can pick a name from the list. You will decline the offer. Role-play the conversation again and agree to the offer.

➤ Have students role-play the conversation, changing roles of telemarketer and recipient for more practice. Invite pairs to present their role play.

A. Listen and read.

A: Hello?

B: Good evening. This is the ABC Telephone Company. We have a special offer on cell phone service this evening.

A: Is this a sales call?

B: Yes, it is.

A: I'm sorry. We don't take offers over the phone.

B: Thank you very much.

B. Pronunciation and intonation practice.

Vocabulary

Ways to decline an offer

We don't take offers over the phone.

We're having dinner right now.

We're not interested.

We already have _____.

We don't need _____.

Your own way: _____.

C. Pair work. Decline a telemarketer's offer. Use the name of a business that has called you or a business you know.

A: Hello?

B: ___1___. This is _____. We have a special offer on ___2___.

A: Is this a sales call?

B: Yes, it is.

A: I'm sorry. _____.

B: ___3___.

[1]Hello, Good afternoon, etc.
[2]newspaper delivery, life insurance, etc.
[3]OK, thank you

► Do it yourself!

A. List one or more charitable and sales solicitations you have received.

Charities	Sales
Flood Emergency Relief Fund	Manny's Chimney Cleaning

B. Pair work. Role-play a conversation accepting or declining a solicitation from your list.

Practical grammar

The simple present tense and the present continuous

Use the simple present tense to talk about habitual actions and unchanging facts.

Lee **volunteers** at the community center every Sunday.

The American Cancer Society **provides** funds for cancer research.

Use the simple present tense with *never, sometimes, often,* and *always.*

I always **ask** telemarketers to send their offers in writing.

Use the present continuous for actions in progress.

He's **talking** to a telemarketer right now.

Don't use *never, sometimes, often,* or *always* with the present continuous.

~~I'm never going there. I'm often going there.~~

A. Complete each sentence with the simple present tense or the present continuous.

1. Water ___boils___ at 212°F.
   boils / is boiling

2. They always ___collect___ on Mondays.
   are collecting / collect

3. When she ___calls___, I never ___answer___ the call.
   calls / is calling   answer / am answering

4. I can't talk right now because we ___are eating___ lunch.
   eat / are eating

5. I ___don't accept___ sales offers over the phone.
   don't accept / am not accepting

6. ___Do you___ often ___volunteer___ at the hospital?
   Are you / Do you   volunteering / volunteer

B. Complete each sentence with the simple present tense or the present continuous. Use verbs from the box.

collect	donate	ask	talk	bake

1. I usually ___donate___ clothes to the American Red Cross when they ___ask___.

2. I can't distribute flyers this week, so I ___am baking___ something for the bake sale instead.

3. They never ___talk___ to telemarketers during dinner.

4. She can't come to the phone right now. She's out. She ___is collecting___ for the soup kitchen.

Practical grammar

(For general suggestions, see *Introduction*, page Tix.)

The simple present tense and the present continuous

Procedure:

➤ Ask students to take out the "Find someone who" activity that they completed on page T1. Put students in small groups to identify the verb form used in each clause in items 1 through 6. Ask them to answer these questions: *Which verb form—simple present tense or present continuous—is used? What cue words suggest the verb form to use?*

➤ Write student responses on the board. Ask for additional cue words used with the simple present tense and the present continuous. You may end up with a chart like this:

The simple present tense	The present continuous
Cue words: (item 4) *every day*, (item 6) *never*. Others: *often, sometimes, always, rarely, usually*	Cue words: (items 1, 2) *today*, (item 3) *for the first time*, (item 5) *soon*. Others: *now, right now, at this moment*

➤ Ask students to read the rules in the grammar box. Go over the example sentences and have students point out the cue words that suggest the verb form to use. Ask for additional example sentences that use the simple present tense to talk about habitual actions and unchanging facts and the present continuous to talk about actions in progress. Write students' examples on the board and underline the cue words.

A. Complete each sentence . . .

➤ To model item 1, write out the sentence with each possible answer inserted. Have students choose the correct sentence.

➤ Advise students to look for cue words as they are deciding whether to use the simple present tense or the present continuous.

➤ Have students complete the exercise individually and then check their answers with a partner. Review with the entire class.

Option: Have students add an adverb of frequency to each of the following statements to best describe their own behavior. For example, students may write *I <u>usually</u> contribute to charitable organizations* or *I <u>never</u> accept sales offers over the phone.* Have students read their sentences aloud. Elicit that the simple present tense is used in each of these sentences. Remind students that the simple present tense is used with *sometimes, always, never,* and *often.*

1. I contribute to charitable organizations.
2. I receive telephone solicitations during dinner.
3. I accept sales offers over the phone.
4. I tell telemarketers to take me off their lists.
5. I volunteer my time to help others.

Ask students to read their sentences aloud.

B. Complete each sentence . . .

➤ Write item 1 on the board and ask for volunteers to choose the appropriate verbs from the box to fill in the two slots *(donate, ask).* Once students have decided on the verbs, ask for the correct verb forms (the simple present tense: *donate, ask).* Have students underline the cue word *(usually)* that specifies the verb form.

➤ Remind students that the verbs in the box are often linked with prepositions. For example, we *collect for* a cause, *talk to* someone, and *donate to* an organization.

➤ Have students work individually to complete the sentences and then check answers with a partner.

Non-action verbs

Content: non-action verbs used with the simple present tense

Procedure:

➤ Write the heading *Non-action verbs* on the board. Explain that these verbs often express mental or emotional states or refer to the senses.

➤ Ask students to read the verbs in the box and describe any patterns they notice. Elicit that some verbs relate to the senses (for example, *What do the words "hear, see, smell, sound," and "taste" have in common?*), some to emotions (for example, *What do the verbs "like, love," and "hate" have in common?*), and some to mental states (for example, *What about "think, understand," and "know"?*).

➤ Under the heading, write *senses, emotional states,* and *mental states* and list the verbs from the box that fit under each category. With students, create example sentences such as *She feels tired, I hate calls during dinner, They know the food pantry is a good cause.* Point out that non-action verbs often express situations that exist not only in the immediate present but were probably true yesterday and will be true tomorrow. Give example sentences such as *Matt has two sisters, We're not interested in phone offers.*

Option: Continue using the "Find someone who" activity from page T1. Put students in small groups to identify the verb form used in each clause in items 7 through 10. Ask them to answer these questions: *Which verb form—simple present tense or present continuous—is used? Why?* Elicit that the simple present tense is used with non-action verbs. Share the completed sentences as a class.

Note: For a more complete list of non-action verbs, refer students to page 145.

C. Complete the conversation . . .

➤ Have students complete the exercise individually. Remind them to check whether the verb is in the boxed list of non-action verbs and also to think about the other restrictions related to using the simple present tense and the present continuous.

➤ Students can read the conversation in pairs to check their answers.

Option: Brainstorm ways to correct a speaker's mistake in pronouncing or reading a name. Such a list might include *That's Malino, not Balino* or *My last name begins with an M, Malino* or *That's M, as in Mary–Malino.* Have students work in pairs with Student A acting as a caller who mispronounces Student B's name. Student B can practice politely correcting the caller's pronunciation or spelling.

If your students are ready . . .

Language note: Although the general rule is not to use a continuous form with non-action, or stative, verbs, students may find evidence to the contrary. Some non-action verbs can be used in the present continuous because they have more than one meaning. For example, when *think* means *believe,* it is not used in the present continuous. However, when *think* refers to using your mind, it is used in the present continuous to emphasize that something is happening right now: *I am thinking about grammar.* Similarly, *have* is not used in the present continuous when it indicates possession, but it can be used in the present continuous in certain expressions: *She's having a baby, They're having a good time.* *Be* is used in the present continuous when it describes an action (*He's being difficult*) and not a state (*He's tired*).

Some non-action verbs can also be used in the present continuous to indicate a new development, something that is taking place now that wasn't happening before: *Now I'm remembering what happened that day.* Conversationally, some non-action verbs may be used in the present continuous to emphasize a temporary condition: *I'm loving this weather, They're looking good.*

➤ Do it yourself!

(For general suggestions, see *Introduction,* page Txiii.)

Procedure:

➤ Model the conversation with a more advanced student. Play the role of the caller in order to give the student an opportunity to respond appropriately to a telemarketer's offer.

➤ Remind students to choose the name of a company and of a product, service, or cause the telemarketer is selling or soliciting for.

➤ Working in pairs, students practice the telephone conversation, using as models *Model 2* on page 3 and Exercise C on page 5.

➤ Have volunteers present the conversation in front of the class.

Non-action verbs

Some verbs don't describe actions. Don't use the present continuous with non-action verbs:

appear, be, feel, hate, have, hear, know, like, look, love, need, remember, see, seem, smell, sound, taste, think, understand, want.

See page 145 for a more complete list of non-action verbs.

C. **Complete the conversation with the simple present tense or the present continuous.**

A: Hello?

B: Good evening. I _____am trying_____ to reach Mrs. Belinda Malino. Is this she?
  1. try / am trying

A: Well, I'm Mrs. Melinda Malino.

B: I'm sorry. How are you this evening, Mrs. Balino?

A: Fine, thanks. But we _____are eating_____ dinner right now. Is this a sales call?
  2. eat / are eating

B: No. I _____am not selling_____ anything now. I only _____need_____ a minute
  3. don't sell / am not selling   **4.** need / am needing

to tell you about a special offer for customers of Tri-State Telephone.

A: I'm sorry. We never _____take_____ offers over the phone.
  5. take / are taking

B: I _____understand_____. But I _____think_____ you'll like what I have
  6. understand / am understanding   **7.** think / am thinking

to tell you.

A: Please send your offer in writing. We'll be happy to look at it then.

B: Thank you very much.

➤ Do it yourself!

Pair work. Choose the name of a real company. Read Model 2 on page 3 again. Then continue the conversation for the two people in the picture.

A: Hello?
B: Good evening. How are you this evening?
A: Fine, thanks. . . .

Unit 1   5

A. Read the picture story again. Complete each sentence.

1. The proceeds of the bake sale are going to the ___homeless shelter___ .

2. The bake sale will be on ___Saturday___ at the ___railroad station___ .

3. Volunteers can donate something to sell, make a cash contribution, or work the
    ___booth___ .

B. Listen. Read each response out loud from the text.

Authentic practice

(For general suggestions, see *Introduction*, page Tx.)

Volunteerism and charity

Procedure:

🎧

➤ Ask questions about the pictures, such as *Who's in the pictures?* (two women) *Where are they?* (in a restaurant) *What do you think they're talking about?* (a bake sale). Remind students that baking something for a bake sale is one of the ways to volunteer that they read about on page 2.

➤ To help students practice discrete listening skills, direct them to keep their books closed while they listen to the story. To focus their listening, ask questions before they listen: *What has the first woman volunteered to do?* (run a bake sale) *How can the second woman help?* (She can contribute a pie, make a cash contribution, or help work the booth.) *How is she going to contribute?* (She's going to write a check.)

➤ Play the cassette or read the picture story. After students have listened, elicit the responses to the focused listening questions. If students missed anything, let them listen again.

➤ Have students open their books and read the picture story silently.

➤ Point out the use of the present continuous in the first picture (*We're setting up a booth at the railroad station*) and in the second picture (*I'm going to be out of town for two days*). Note that the present continuous is often used to talk about future plans as well as actions in progress right now.

➤ Make sure students understand words or phrases that may be unfamiliar to them. In the first picture, the woman uses the expression *run a bake sale.* Elicit synonyms such as *operate, have,* or *hold.* In the second picture, the woman says *A million people always show up for that!* Ask students if they think she really means a million people. Elicit the response that she is speaking figuratively, not literally, using exaggeration for emphasis. Jane responds with *Actually, on second thought.* If necessary, point out that this expression is used to indicate that the person has reconsidered something. In the last picture, the woman says *Better come early!* Remind students that *Better* is a reduction of *You had better* and is used for a strong suggestion or warning. Ask students to rephrase her

next statement *(We always run out of everything by two):* We have nothing left to sell by two.

A. Read the picture story again ...

➤ To model the activity, write the first item on the board and ask volunteers to fill in the blank. Have students read the picture story again to find the answers to the rest of the items.

➤ After students complete Exercise A individually, correct as a group.

🎧 B. Listen ...

➤ Tell students that they will listen to the tapescript or the cassette and then read aloud the responses from their text.

➤ Read each item in the tapescript out loud or play the cassette. Allow students to listen as many times as necessary to complete the exercise. If students have difficulty, prompt them by reading the response yourself.

Note: The speakers on the cassette for this exercise are different from those who recorded the text of the picture story. This has been done intentionally in order to give students the opportunity to hear a wide variety of voices.

Challenge: Use the prompts for Exercise B as a dictation. Have students listen to the questions and write what they hear. Allow students to listen as many times as necessary. Ask volunteers to write the questions on the board. Make corrections as a class. Students can then practice the prompts and responses with a partner.

Challenge: For an out-of-class assignment, ask students to find out the names of homeless shelters or food pantries in your community. Sources of information include religious organizations, social service agencies, and local newspapers or magazines. After the information has been collected, students can work in small groups to find out what services the organizations provide and what volunteer needs they have. The groups can generate questions, rehearse conversations, and actually call the organizations for information.

Tapescript

1. Would you be willing to contribute one of your wonderful pies?
2. Saturday's not great for me. But could I write you a check?

T6

C. Vocabulary...

➤ Write *show up, make it out, stop by, pick up,* and *run out of* on the board. To review the meaning of these phrases in context, have students reread the speeches in pictures 2 and 4 on page 6.

➤ Explain that the meanings of these verb and preposition combinations cannot be figured out simply by pairing the definition of the verb with the definition of the preposition. They form units that must be considered together. If necessary, go over the meanings of these phrases with the class.

➤ Model item 1 by writing the sentence on the board with the two choices listed below the underlined phrase. Ask students for the correct choice and circle *arrived* on the board.

➤ Have students complete the exercise individually and then correct as a class.

D–E.

➤ Have students answer individually and then compare responses with a partner before reading aloud the items and responses.

Option: After both students in each pair have practiced reading the items and responses in Exercise D, have Partner B close his or her book. Partner A then reads an item and Partner B responds from memory.

Challenge: Have students create sentences or questions for Exercise D that would give rise to the alternate response. For example, the alternate response for item 1 is *Is this a sales call?* A statement that might produce this response could be *This is Mark Hibler of Vacations, Unlimited. How are you this evening?* Write all the students' ideas on the board. Students can vote for the ones they like best.

If your students are ready...

Language note: Verb and preposition combinations, called phrasal verbs, are often difficult for non-native speakers because meanings are not always obvious. Also, phrasal verbs can be separable or non-separable. Separable phrasal verbs allow or require an object between the verb and the preposition. So, for example, students may see the phrase *make out the check* or *make the check out*. Similarly, students may see the phrase *pick up cookies* or *pick cookies up*. In other combinations, the verb cannot be separated from the preposition, so the object comes after: *run out of everything*. As a class, list the phrasal verbs from the picture story on page 6 and give example sentences that show whether each verb is separable or not.

➤ Do it yourself!

(For general suggestions, see *Introduction*, page Txiii.)

Procedure:

A. Write your own response...

➤ Working individually, students write responses to each question.

➤ Before students practice with a partner, have volunteers play the parts of the three speakers and read each speech balloon aloud. Answer each question yourself, giving students an opportunity to check the appropriateness of their own responses.

➤ Elicit examples of student responses and write them on the board. Answer any questions.

B. Discussion...

➤ Lead a class discussion about volunteering, using the questions in Exercise B as prompts. Additional prompts may include the following: *Did you volunteer here or in your home country? How do you feel about volunteering? What kinds of causes do you support? Do you support them with a check or cash, by volunteering at a booth, by baking something for a bake sale?*

C. Vocabulary. Circle the word or phrase closer in meaning to each underlined phrase.

1. They <u>showed up</u> too late to help set up the booth, so they worked it instead.
   left / (arrived)

2. <u>Make the check out to</u> the shelter.
   (Write the check to) / Throw the check away at

3. Not many homeless people <u>stopped by</u> the soup kitchen yesterday.
   (came to) / refused to come to

4. You can <u>pick up</u> cookies at the sale.
   (buy) / sell

5. When I got there, they had <u>run out of</u> everything. There was nothing left!
   (sold) / baked

D. Read each sentence or question. Underline your response.

1. "Would you be willing to work the booth?"

   YOU <u>With pleasure.</u>   **YOU** Is this a sales call?

2. "How many volunteers were at the soup kitchen?"

   YOU <u>A million!</u>   **YOU** Two. Tomato rice and chicken noodle.

3. "You could help run the booth."

   YOU <u>Actually, I won't be able to.</u>   **YOU** Better come early.

4. "Could you make a cash contribution?"

   YOU Sure. Who should I make   **YOU** <u>Absolutely. It's a good cause.</u>
   it out to?

E. Pair work. Take turns reading the items and responses in Exercise D.

➤ Do it yourself!

A. Write your own response. Then read each conversation out loud with a partner.

That's a good cause. Who should I make the check payable to?

YOU _____

Thanks for agreeing to volunteer at the booth. What time can you stop by to pick up the pies?

YOU _____

We've run out of baked goods. Could you please pick up some more at the supermarket?

YOU _____

B. Discussion. Has anyone ever asked you to volunteer? For what? What did you do?

Authentic practice

Avoiding telemarketing fraud

A. **Listening comprehension. Listen to the TV report. Then answer the question.**

Why do consumers complain about telemarketing? ___Answers will vary and may include___

___the following: calls are annoying, telemarketers call before 8 a.m. or after 9 p.m., they may be selling a fraud.___

B. **Pair work. Compare answers with a partner.**

C. **Listen again if necessary. Then check *True* or *False* for each statement, according to the report.**

		True	False
1.	Telemarketers sell products and services by phone.	☑	☐
2.	Con artists are honest salespeople.	☐	☑
3.	A free offer is always a fraud.	☐	☑
4.	You should always hang up on telemarketers.	☐	☑

D. **Answer the questions about a sales call you have received at home.**

1. Who called? _____

2. What time was it? _____

3. What questions did the caller ask? _____

4. What did the caller want to sell? _____

5. Did you buy anything? _____

6. If you bought something, how did you pay? _____

7. Are you happy with the product or service? _____

Authentic practice

(For general suggestions, see *Introduction,* page Tx.)

Avoiding telemarketing fraud

Procedure:

🎧 **A–B.**

➤ To help students anticipate the topic, ask them to read the heading in the bar. Ask *What is fraud?* Elicit the response that it is a deception or trick intended to take money from someone.

➤ Have students look at the pictures. Ask *What do you see in the pictures?* (a man and a woman from a television news program; the woman pointing to tips for preventing fraud).

➤ Read the instructions for Exercise A and the question out loud. Then read the selection on the tapescript out loud or play the cassette. Allow students to listen as many times as necessary to complete the exercises.

➤ Working individually, students answer the question in Exercise A and then compare answers with a partner.

🎧 **C. Listen again …**

➤ Have students read the statements in Exercise C and check whether they are true or false. If they are unsure of the answers, let them listen again.

➤ Review answers as a class and elicit students' help in changing false answers to make them true.

Challenge: After deciding if the statements are true or false, students can listen to the report again and write down the exact wording that led them to their decision. For example, on a separate sheet of paper, students might write *1. telephone solicitation as a new and effective way to sell products and services.*

D. Answer the questions …

➤ Remind students that not all sales calls are fraudulent. They may report on a legitimate call.

➤ Students work individually to answer the questions. Tell students to be as precise and complete as possible since they will be using their answers in Exercise E on page 9.

If your students are ready …

Culture / Civics note: The following tips are provided by the office of the Attorney General in Alaska. They may help your students avoid telemarketing fraud. For more information, refer students to this Web site:

www.law.state.ak.us/consumer_tips

A telemarketing sales pitch or charitable solicitation may be fraudulent if a telemarketer:

- says you've won a prize ….or that it is a "free" offer, but that you need to send money for fees, shipping, handling, insurance, etc.

- tells you that you have been pre-approved for anything that you have not requested yourself

- asks for your credit card number, bank account number, or social security number for any reason

- insists on an immediate decision to guarantee your participation in this wonderful opportunity or limited offer

- offers to have someone pick up your check at your home or office or requests that you use overnight mail. This can be a sign that the telemarketer wants to avoid inspection under the federal mail fraud law.

- confuses you with fast talk that he or she does not adequately explain

- keeps talking after you've said no

Tapescript

Man: And now we turn to Consumer Corner, a weekly feature of interest to consumers. Here's Julie Clark, our consumer reporter, with tonight's topic. Good evening, Julie. I know you have something very interesting for us tonight.

Woman: Good evening, Bill. Good evening, viewers. Can you name the number-one consumer complaint nationwide? If you said telemarketing, you're absolutely right. Just in case you don't know what telemarketing is, it's those annoying calls that arrive as soon as you've put dinner on the table or lowered yourself into a nice hot bath.

Man: What is telemarketing?

Woman: The term *telemarketing* was first used by telephone companies to promote telephone solicitation as a new and effective way to sell products and services. And although most telemarketers are honest, others are dishonest and take advantage of the situation, selling inferior products or—worse—collecting money and not delivering the merchandise ordered.

(Tapescript is continued on page T9.)

Tapescript (*continued from page T8*)

Remember: Telemarketers who do this are con artists. And the product they sell is a fraud.

Man: What can we do to protect ourselves from telemarketing fraud?

Woman: Well, there are some important steps any consumer can take. First of all: The law says that telemarketers cannot call you before 8 a.m. or after 9 p.m.

Next: Get the name and address of the company that is calling. Also, telemarketers have to tell you that they are selling something, that this is a sales call.

Con artists pretend that they are taking a survey or offering you something for free. Before you know it, they're selling you something, trying to get you to give them your credit card number. That's fraud.

Man: Why is it such a bad idea to give them your credit card number?

Woman: Well, if the call is a fraud, and the con artist who's calling you has your name and your credit card number, he or she can use that information to charge things with your card. Your card has been stolen, but you don't even know it's been stolen.

And finally: Before you pay for anything over the phone, ask the telemarketer to tell you the total cost of the goods you are buying.

Man: That's great advice. So you're saying (1) Get the name of the company. And (2) Get the total price before paying. That's great advice. It should go a long way toward preventing telemarketing fraud.

Woman: Oh, and one more thing. If you suspect fraud, or if the caller insists on continuing after you've said you're not interested, hang up the phone. *You're* not being rude. The caller is.

Man: As always, practical advice from Julie Clark. This is Bill Bell, with tonight's Consumer Corner report, thanking you for me and for Julie Clark. Good night.

E. True story . . .

➤ Model this activity by telling a true story about a sales call you received. Describe the call, covering all the questions given in Exercise D on page 8.

➤ After students practice telling their stories to a partner or a group, invite volunteers to share stories with the class.

➤ Elicit or point out any patterns in the calls, such as the types of businesses, the time of day, students' responses, their feelings about the calls.

FYI . . .

➤ Encourage students to investigate the FTC Web site. Depending on your students' previous experience using the Internet, you may need to help them with computer skills.

If your students are ready . . .

Culture / Civics note: In the United States and Canada, government and social service agencies often have a Web site, a place on the Internet where people can get information. People can access such Web sites by typing in the URL (Web site address) in the address box. A URL often begins with the letters http://www.

➤ Do it yourself!

(For general suggestions, see *Introduction*, page Txiii.)

Procedure:

A–B.

➤ Model the phone call with a student to show that the role play begins with the written conversation and then continues with the students' own words and ideas. Play the role of Partner B as a con artist or an honest salesperson. If necessary, repeat the conversation, making the other choice for the caller.

➤ Put students in pairs. Partner A answers the call. Partner B plays either a con artist or an honest salesperson. Have students continue the conversation and then switch roles.

➤ Lead a discussion about the role play. Read the questions from the book and extend the discussion by asking additional questions such as *Was it harder to play the role of a con artist or an honest salesperson? Why? Was it easier to respond to the con artist or the honest salesperson? What was the hardest thing to do on the phone? What consumer response was most effective against the con artist?*

E. True story. Look at the answers you wrote in Exercise D. Then tell your partner or your group about the sales call you received at home.

FYI. To file a complaint about a telemarketer with the Federal Trade Commission (FTC), download a complaint form from their Web site: www.ftc.gov

You can also write or call the FTC:

Federal Trade Commission
Consumer Response Center
600 Pennsylvania Ave. N.W.
Washington, DC 20580

Federal Trade Commission
Telephone: (877) FTC-HELP
Mon.–Fri., 9:00 a.m. to 8:00 p.m. EST

➤ Do it yourself!

A. Role play. Start with the conversation below, using your own words and ideas. Then continue until the end of the call.

Partner A: Answer the phone and respond to Partner B.
Partner B: Decide whether you are a con artist or an honest salesperson.

A: _____?
B: Hello. I'm calling from _____. Are you over eighteen years old?
A: _____.
B: We have a special offer for you tonight, if you'll just answer a few questions.
A: . . .

B. Discussion. Compare phone calls with your classmates. Was the telemarketer honest or a con artist? What did the consumer say?

Volunteerism in the local community

🎧 **A.** Read and listen to the letters.

Ask Joan

**Culture tips
for newcomers**

Dear Joan:

My son is a high school junior and he wants to volunteer in the fire department of our town. He says that a lot of his friends volunteer their time too. Joan, he's still a child, and he plans to go to college, not work in a fire department. This is a job for big men, not for teenagers! He could get hurt or killed. I don't understand. Joan, what should I do?

Nero in Nashville

Dear Nero:

Congratulations on having raised a wonderful, caring son! You must be very proud of him. Your son is participating in an important tradition of our culture: volunteerism. Many people consider volunteerism a responsibility of their membership in the local and larger community.

It's not unusual for teenagers to volunteer their time at the firehouse, the ambulance corps, or the local food pantry. At the firehouse, teens under the age of eighteen usually do not fight fires, although they receive training in firefighting techniques. But they participate in the maintenance of the fire trucks and other equipment, assist firefighters at the scene of fires, and help in chores at the firehouse. Whatever your son finally chooses as a career, the time he spends volunteering to help others in need is time well spent. So, don't worry, Dad. Just be proud.

Joan

Dear Joan:

I'm a homemaker and a part-time seamstress in my own home. My two children have graduated from high school (with honors!) and both are now studying in college. Joan, they both received scholarships. I am very grateful.

Now that my children are not at home, I have some extra time and I would like to volunteer. What do you recommend?

Grateful Grace

Dear Grace:

If you belong to a church, a synagogue, or a mosque, you will find opportunities there to volunteer in your local community in a variety of activities. Non-religious institutions such as the Boy and Girl Scouts, the League of Women Voters, the volunteer fire department and ambulance corps, soup kitchens, homeless shelters, and the local food pantry would also all be happy to have you as a volunteer. Many institutions accept donated goods and financial contributions in addition to your time. And remember, you may deduct charitable contributions from your income taxes.

The following quotation from a U.S. Government Web site on volunteerism expresses a core tradition of our culture: "The generous spirit of the American people has fostered a great and long-standing tradition of service." Your volunteerism expresses that spirit!

Joan

B. Check *True, False,* or *? (No information)* for each statement.

	True	False	?
1. Nero is a volunteer firefighter.	☐	☑	☐
2. Nero's son is in high school now.	☑	☐	☐
3. Nero thinks his son's volunteer work is dangerous.	☑	☐	☐
4. Now that her children are in college, Grace is not so busy.	☑	☐	☐
5. Grace belongs to a church, synagogue, or mosque.	☐	☐	☑

Authentic practice

(For general suggestions, see *Introduction*, page Tx.)

Volunteerism in the local community

Procedure:

⌒A. **Read and listen to the letters.**

➤ Ask students if they have seen advice columns before. If possible, bring in advice columns from a local newspaper. Explain that people write when they have a problem and ask for advice or an opinion about what they should do. The columnist writes back, and the letters are published in the newspaper. Ask students if the newspapers in their countries have advice columns.

➤ Explain that *Ask Joan* is an advice column for people who are new to this country and have questions about cultural expectations.

➤ Play the cassette or read the letters. Students listen and read silently. Pause after Nero's letter and ask *What is the problem? What will Joan's advice be?* Encourage students to make predictions and then have them listen to the response. Ask *What was Joan's response?* Repeat for Grace's letter and the response.

Option: Have students close their books and list the volunteer opportunities they can remember from the letters. Brainstorm other volunteer opportunities such as clothing drives, toy collections, and blood drives.

B. **Check . . .**

➤ Allow students to listen to the letters again, if helpful, and then have them complete the exercise. Remind them to check the column marked with **?** if the letters do not give any information.

➤ As students compare answers with a partner, circulate to answer any questions.

Challenge: To help students practice discrete listening skills, pass out slips of paper on which you have written the following words: *junior, college, wonderful, participating, tradition, ambulance, food pantry, chores, homemaker, church, synagogue, mosque, soup kitchens, homeless shelters, donated goods, charitable contributions.* Give everyone at least one slip. Depending on the number of students, you may have to write down some phrases more than once. Tell students that they are going to hear the letters again. When they hear the word on the slip of paper, they should stand up. If students miss their cues, play the cassette or read the letters again.

Challenge: Have students listen to the letters for the rising or falling intonation of items in a list. First have them locate the lists (teenager volunteer activities, volunteer activities at the firehouse, religious organizations, non-religious institutions). Then play the cassette or read the letters again. Have students mark the intonation above the listed items and then practice reading the lists aloud with a partner. Invite volunteers to read for the class. Discuss the general pattern of intonation in a list (rising intonation at the end of each item and falling intonation at the end of the list) and ask students to create their own lists (for example, what they need at the store, chores they have to do) to read aloud.

If your students are ready . . .

Language note: In these letters, Joan lists options for both Nero and Grace. In writing, items in a list are usually separated by commas, with *and* or *or* before the last item (*a church, a synagogue, or a mosque*). In speaking, the speaker indicates a list by using rising intonation at the end of each item and falling intonation on the last item.

C. Discussion...

➤ After students answer the questions individually, have them discuss their answers in small groups.

FYI...

➤ Explain the difference between federal programs (those run by the U. S. government) and national programs (nonprofit groups that are found throughout the country). Ask what students know about the programs listed. Tell them, or have them find out, which organizations have a local branch in your city or town. With the class, add other volunteer opportunities to the lists, or make a third list of local programs on the board.

➤ Have students check the HUD Web site for more information on volunteerism. Students may also want to compare volunteering in the United States and Canada after accessing the Canadian Web site.

Option: Put students in small groups. Have each group choose a national volunteer program to research. Each group should first brainstorm questions they want answered about the volunteer program. They can look the organization up in the phone book to see if there is a local office. Students can then call the office or go online to find out the answers to their questions. Questions might include *What kind of work do volunteers do? Do they need experience? How much time is usually involved? Do you need volunteers now?*

➤ Do it yourself!

(For general suggestions, see *Introduction*, page Txiii.)

Procedure:

A–B.

➤ Put students in small groups of mixed nationalities and have them fill in the chart with information from group members.

➤ Lead a discussion about volunteering in different cultures. Copy the chart on the board to list the different ways people help each other.

Option: To extend the discussion, read the following statements. Ask groups to agree or disagree with each statement and defend their opinions. Have volunteers from each group share their opinions with the class.

1. Charity should be left up to the individual.

2. The government is responsible for making sure everyone has food and shelter.

3. To be a good citizen, you must give time and/or money to help others.

4. The needs of the poor are adequately met by government agencies.

C. Discussion. Answer the questions. Then discuss with your classmates.

1. Why is Nero in Nashville worried? His son could get hurt or killed.

2. Is Joan worried too? no

3. What do teen volunteers usually do at the firehouse? Help in maintenance of fire trucks and other equipment, assist firefighters at the scene of a fire, help in chores

4. What is a volunteer? (Answers may vary.)

FYI. Read this information about volunteering from the Web site of the U.S. Department of Housing and Urban Development (HUD).

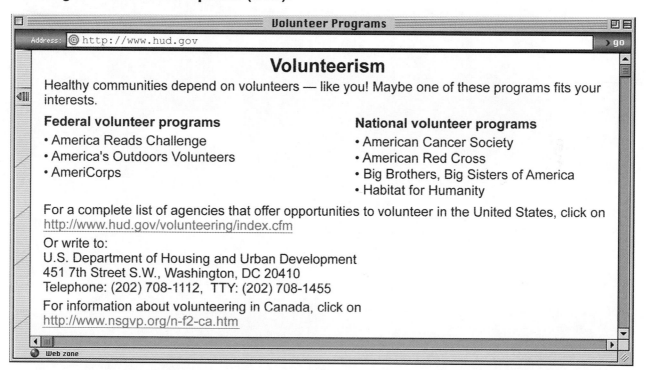

Volunteerism

Healthy communities depend on volunteers — like you! Maybe one of these programs fits your interests.

Federal volunteer programs
- America Reads Challenge
- America's Outdoors Volunteers
- AmeriCorps

National volunteer programs
- American Cancer Society
- American Red Cross
- Big Brothers, Big Sisters of America
- Habitat for Humanity

For a complete list of agencies that offer opportunities to volunteer in the United States, click on
http://www.hud.gov/volunteering/index.cfm

Or write to:
U.S. Department of Housing and Urban Development
451 7th Street S.W., Washington, DC 20410
Telephone: (202) 708-1112, TTY: (202) 708-1455

For information about volunteering in Canada, click on
http://www.nsgvp.org/n-f2-ca.htm

➤ Do it yourself!

A. In your home country, how do people help others? Fill in the chart.

Country	Donations or contributions	Volunteer opportunities
U.S.	United Way	soup kitchen at shelter

B. Culture talk. In the country you come from, is there a tradition of service to the community? How do people help each other? Do they collect money? Do they volunteer? Compare cultures with your classmates.

Review

A. Pair work or group work.

- Who are the people?
- What are they doing?

Ask and answer questions.

Create conversations.

Tell a story.

Say as much as you can.

Review

(For general suggestions, see *Introduction*, page Txii.)

Procedure:

A. Pair work or group work.

➤ Have students take turns pointing to and naming as many things as they can in the picture.

Ask and answer questions.

➤ Ask the class *Who are the people?* (a family preparing for a bake sale and a used clothing sale and a telemarketer) *What are they doing?* (The father is collecting used clothing for the sale, the mother is baking for the bake sale, the daughter is making a sign for the sale, the son and the telemarketer are having a telephone conversation.)

➤ Point to one person in the picture and ask questions such as *Where is this person? What is this person wearing? How does this person feel? Why do you think so?*

Option: Working in pairs, students can write their own questions about the picture. Elicit example questions before they begin, such as *Where are they? What does the sign say?* Create a game by separating the students into two teams. Teams take turns asking the questions team members have created. Give points for each correct answer.

Create conversations.

➤ Ask the class to choose one of the two pairs of people with speech balloons in the picture. Have students label the person on the left *A* and the person on the right *B*. Write *A:* on the board and elicit the help of the class in creating the first line of a conversation between the people. Then write *B:* and elicit a response. Continue adding lines to the conversation as a class, encouraging students to say as much as they can.

➤ With a partner, have students role-play the parts of the other pair in the picture. Circulate and listen to the conversations. Use prompts if necessary to help students extend the conversation, such as *What company does the woman represent? What is she selling? Do you think she's a con artist or an honest salesperson? Why do you think so? What can the son say to discourage the telemarketer?* Review the different ways people can decline a telemarketer's offer.

Option: After students have created the conversations suggested by the picture, give them a new task. Have them imagine conversations between different pairs, this time including the young woman at the table, and having a family member accept the telemarketer's solicitation.

Tell a story.

Option: Ways to volunteer. Have students point to the members of the family and explain the way in which each is volunteering. Brainstorm other possible ways to volunteer.

Option: Would you be willing ...? Imagine that a member of the family is making a telephone solicitation for donations for the sale. As a class, discuss possible questions the recipient might have, such as *Who did you say it was for? When is the sale? Where is it?*

Option: Right now! Have students summarize the activities in the picture. Encourage the use of the present continuous by asking such questions as *What is the young man doing right now? What is telemarketer saying right now?*

🎧B. Listening comprehension . . .

➤ To set the scene, tell students they will hear a conversation between a telemarketer and the man who answers the call.

➤ Play the cassette or read the conversation out loud while students listen with books closed.

➤ Have students open their books. Read the instructions out loud. Emphasize that students will be deciding whether the statements are true or false, based on the conversation they hear.

➤ Play the cassette or read the conversation as many times as necessary for students to complete the exercise.

Option: Have students rewrite the false statements to make them true.

C. Complete the conversation . . .

➤ If necessary, review the restrictions on using the present continuous and the simple present tense, including the categories of non-action verbs: the senses, mental states, emotional states, possession.

➤ Have students check answers with a partner. Review answers as a class.

Option: Have partners read the conversation out loud, changing roles for further practice.

If your students are ready . . .

Culture / Civics note: International law defines refugees as people who are forced to flee their country. They have run away because they are afraid that they will be hurt or killed because of their race, religion, nationality, membership in a social group, or political opinion. They are afraid to return to their own country because they believe their government cannot protect them. Both the United States and Canada accept a limited number of refugees each year. Refugees are given money, medical treatment, English-language classes, job training, and other services to help them start a new life.

Tapescript

Man: Hello?

Woman: Good evening. How are you this evening?

Man: Fine, thanks. But we're having dinner right now, and the baby's crying. Is this a sales call?

Woman: Actually, no. I'm calling on behalf of the Institute for Better Parenting. Do you have a moment to answer some questions?

Man: What was the name of the institute?

Woman: The Institute for Better Parenting.

Man: Are you selling something?

Woman: Not really. But we *do* have a special one-time free offer for new subscribers to our magazine, *Parent and Child.* Have you had an opportunity to see *Parent and Child* on the newsstand?

Man: No, I never have, . . . but as I said, we're having dinner right now, and . . .

Woman: That's because it isn't sold on newsstands. But if it were, it would cost $36.00 a year. But because you're a new parent, we'd like to offer you a subscription to *Parent and Child,* absolutely free, with no obligation for three months. Then, after three months, if you're not absolutely thrilled with *Parent and Child,* just send back the last month's issue and we won't bill you for any issues you have received.

Man: I'm sorry, but we never accept offers over the phone. If you'd be kind enough to send us the offer in writing, we'd be glad to consider the offer.

Woman: Well, the problem is that this offer is only good until Tuesday. It's a one-time offer, and as I said, it's absolutely free and there's no obligation, and [click]

B. Listening comprehension. Listen to the conversation. Then listen again and check *True* or *False* for each statement.

	True	False
1. The man says the family is eating.	☑	☐
2. The man wants to talk to the caller.	☐	☑
3. The caller is a telemarketer.	☑	☐
4. The caller isn't selling anything.	☐	☑
5. *Parent and Child* is the name of a magazine.	☑	☐
6. You can buy *Parent and Child* on the newsstand.	☐	☑
7. The caller is sending something in writing on Tuesday.	☐	☑
8. The man accepts the offer.	☐	☑

C. Complete the conversation with the simple present tense or the present continuous.

A: Hey, Mark. I _____ love _____ that car!
1. love / am loving

B: Thanks! What _____ are you doing _____ in this neighborhood?
2. do you do / are you doing

A: I _____ am picking up _____ used furniture for the refugee housing project.
3. pick up / am picking up

I _____ am trying _____ to set up a house for a new family this week.
4. try / am trying

B: That's a good cause. Refugees _____ have _____ absolutely nothing when
5. have / are having

they _____ get _____ here.
6. get / are getting

A: That's true. By the way, would you be willing to make a few phone calls for us?

We really _____ need _____ help.
7. need / are needing

B: How much time _____ do you need _____?
8. do you need / are you needing

A: About two million hours! No, seriously, if you _____ have _____ a few
9. have / are having

hours any evening this week, that would be great.

B: I _____ understand _____. Well, I _____ think _____ I can make it on Thursday.
10. understand / am understanding **11. think / am thinking**

D. Read each sentence or question. Underline your response.

1. "I'm collecting groceries for the women's shelter. Would you be willing to make a donation?"

   (YOU) Yes. Please drop it off at 4:00. **(YOU)** <u>Yes. What do you need?</u>

2. "What did you say you were collecting for?"

   (YOU) <u>The scholarship fund.</u> **(YOU)** I never take sales calls.

3. "Could you pick up some flyers to distribute this afternoon?"

   (YOU) <u>Sure. I'll stop by after work.</u> **(YOU)** There you go!

4. "I ran out of checks."

   (YOU) <u>You could make a cash contribution.</u> **(YOU)** We're not interested.

5. "We're running a clothing drive for the state hospital."

   (YOU) <u>That's great. I can volunteer some time.</u> **(YOU)** Did you run out yet?

E. Choose a word or phrase for each definition. Fill in the ovals.

1. selling goods and services over the phone

   (a) telemarketing **(b)** fraud

2. a dishonest person who lies to get a consumer's money

   (a) a con artist **(b)** a telemarketer

3. a dishonest offer, in which a person tries to steal money from a consumer

   (a) a telephone sales call **(b)** fraud

4. a person who helps others for no pay

   (a) a telemarketer **(b)** a volunteer

5. goods and services we give to people in need

   (a) donations and contributions **(b)** flyers and letters

F. Write a response. Use your own words.

"Telemarketers keep calling me during dinner. I need advice." ___(Answers will vary.)___

_____

G. Composition. On a separate sheet of paper, write about the picture on page 12. Say as much as you can.

> Now I can
> ❏ agree to contribute to a good cause.
> ❏ decline a telemarketer's sales solicitation.
> ❏ understand the spirit of volunteerism.
> ❏ avoid telemarketing fraud.

D–F.

➤ Students work individually to complete the review exercises.

➤ Circulate to offer help as needed.

➤ Have students check answers with a partner. Review answers as a class.

➤ Identify any areas of difficulty that may require additional instruction and practice.

Option: Have students practice Exercise D in pairs. One person reads the statement or question and the other reads the response.

Option: Have students write definitions for the words or phrases that are not defined in Exercise E.

Option: Have students share the advice they wrote in Exercise F.

G. Composition ...

➤ Provide students with concrete approaches to writing about the picture on page 12. Use one of the following options, give students a choice of options, or assign options based on students' level of proficiency. Model what is expected of students for each option.

➤ Advise students to look back through the unit for help and ideas as they write.

➤ Circulate to offer help as needed.

Option: Have students choose one of the pairs of people who are talking to each other in the picture, label the people *A* and *B*, and write an extended conversation for them. Have students use the same format as the model conversations on pages 2 and 3. Students can later role-play their conversations for the class.

Option: Have students number the people in the picture and then write two sentences about each one. To reinforce the grammar points in the unit, one sentence can describe what the person is doing right now, and the other can discuss the person's activities using a non-action verb.

Option: Have students write a paragraph about a sales call they received at home. They should include answers to the questions in Exercise D on page 8. If they answered previously about a fraudulent call, this paragraph should be about a legitimate call, and vice versa.

Challenge: Ask students to exchange compositions. Partners will peer-edit the compositions.

Now I can

➤ Read the first item in the box out loud: *Now I can agree to contribute to a good cause.* Elicit from the class an example of how to agree to contribute to a good cause, such as *The homeless shelter is a good cause. I'd be happy to make a donation.*

➤ In pairs, students take turns reading each item in the box and giving an example of what they have learned. When students can provide an example, they should check that box. For the items students weren't able to check, they should look back through the unit for ideas.

➤ When students have finished reviewing with their partners, read each item out loud and elicit an example from the class.

➤ Students can add examples of other skills they acquired while working on this unit.

Oral test (optional)

You may want to use the *Now I can* box as an informal evaluation. While students are working on the *Composition* activity, you can call them up individually and check their ability with two or three objectives.

UNIT 2

Your environment

 Preview

(For general suggestions, see *Introduction*, page Tviii.)

Warm up. Look at this section of a lease. What is a lease for? Have you ever signed a lease?

Procedure:

➤ Ask students to stand and sort themselves into groups according to the type of housing they live in. When students are grouped—perhaps into *apartment, house, condo*—form new small groups consisting of a student from each type of housing.

➤ To access students' own experience, ask the small groups to answer questions such as *Where do you live now? Do you rent or do you own? What are some differences between buying a residence and renting or leasing one?* (When you buy a residence, you usually take out a mortgage, you have monthly payments, you gain equity over time, you are responsible for upkeep and repairs; when you lease, the landlord is responsible for at least some maintenance and repairs, you pay rent each month, you have responsibilities toward the property.) *What are some advantages of renting? Of owning?* One student from each group should be the recorder and one the reporter of the group's ideas.

➤ Write *Advantages of renting* and *Advantages of owning* on the board. Elicit students' ideas from the reporters in each group. Your lists might look like the following:

Advantages of renting	Advantages of owning
Less money up front	Mortgage payments are
Landlord responsible	tax deductible
for major repairs	It's an investment that
May be cheaper	you can then sell or
	rent
More available	More stable

➤ Ask students to look at the sections of the lease. To encourage reading strategies, ask *What are the headings in this section of the lease?* (pests, utilities)

Remind students that headings help readers know what topics will be discussed.

➤ Check comprehension of terms. Ask *What are pests?* (bugs, rodents) *What are utilities?* (gas, electricity or power, cable, telephone) *Who is the lessee?* (the person renting) *Who is the lessor?* (the landlord or property owner).

➤ Have pairs of students read the sections of the lease and summarize the terms. Review the terms of the lease as a class, explaining difficult wording as necessary.

If your students are ready . . .

Language note: Tell students that they will see the *–or* (or *–er*) ending in *lessor* and the *–ee* ending in *lessee* attached to different base words. For example, elicit that an *employer* is the person who employs or hires (the boss) and that an *employee* is the person who gets employed or hired (the worker). Elicit that a *lessor* is the person who gives the lease, and the *lessee* is the person who receives the lease. Brainstorm other words with the same endings, such as *supervisor* and *supervisee,* and discuss the meanings of the words and the endings.

Unit 2 objectives

Procedure:

➤ Have students read the objectives. Ask them to put a check next to the objectives that they can do now and circle those they want to work on most.

➤ Ask students to underline any words they do not understand. Write any unfamiliar terms on the board. Some students may not be familiar with *tenant rights, the Fair Housing Act,* or *housing discrimination.* Give a quick explanation of these terms.

➤ Focus students' attention on the issues in the unit. Ask *What are housing emergencies?* (no heat, no hot water, a broken pipe) *What would you look for in a potential rental?* (safety features, evidence of good building maintenance, laundry facilities). Tell students they will learn more about these topics in the unit.

Your environment

 Preview

Warm up. Look at this section of a lease. What is a lease for? Have you ever signed a lease?

PESTS. Lessee is responsible for maintaining the premises free of pests and shall pay for any desired pest control services.

UTILITIES. Lessee shall pay all utilities, except when noted, upon the subject premises for the entire term of this Lease agreement. Lessee shall cause all utilities to be transferred to his/her name at the beginning of the Lease period. If Lessee shall fail to do so or should Lessee fail to pay any utility, Lessee shall be liable for any and all said charges and in addition shall also be liable to Lessor for a fee in the amount of $25 for each month or part thereof that this occurs as reimbursement for Lessor's time and expense incurred.

Unit 2 objectives

- Describe a housing emergency.
- Ask for housing repairs.
- Know what to look for in a potential rental.
- Understand tenant rights.
- Understand the Fair Housing Act.
- Act on housing discrimination.

Model 1   Ask for an emergency repair.

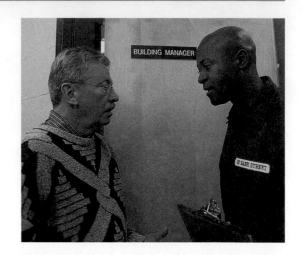

A. Listen and read.

A: I've got an emergency in my apartment.
B: What's the problem?
A: There's no heat.
B: I can look at that tomorrow.
A: I'm sorry. But this is urgent.
B: OK. I'll see what I can do.

B. Pronunciation and intonation practice.

Vocabulary

Household emergencies

A pipe burst.

The lock is broken.

The window is broken.

There's no heat.

There's no hot water.

There's no air conditioning.

C. Pair work. Ask for an emergency repair.

A: I've got an emergency in my apartment.
B: What's the problem?
A: _____.
B: I can look at that ____1____.
A: I'm sorry. But this is urgent.
B: ____2____.

¹this afternoon, next week, etc.
²OK. Just a moment, OK. I'll check it out now, etc.

Practical conversations

(For general suggestions, see *Introduction*, page Tviii.)

Model 1

Content: asking for an emergency repair, talking about household emergencies

Procedure:

A. Listen and read.

➤ Direct students' attention to the picture. Set the scene by asking questions such as *Who are the people?* (a tenant and a building manager) *Where are they?* (outside the building manager's office) *How do you know?* (There's a sign on the manager's door, and he's got a name tag on his shirt.)

➤ After students have listened to the conversation, check for comprehension. Ask questions such as *What is A's problem?* (There's no heat in his apartment.) *When does B say he can look at it?* (tomorrow) *What is A's response?* (It's urgent, meaning that tomorrow is too late.)

➤ Point out that, in *A's* first line, *I've got* is not the present perfect. It's an expression that means I have.

➤ Explain that *A's* response *I'm sorry* is not an apology for something the speaker has done but an expression of disagreement. *A* does not agree with *B's* plan to take care of the problem with the heat tomorrow.

B. Pronunciation and intonation practice.

➤ Tell students that they will listen to the conversation again and have the opportunity to repeat each speaker's lines. Play the cassette or read the conversation again. Encourage students to imitate the rhythm, stress, and intonation of the conversation as closely as possible. Correct where necessary, helping students to pronounce the language clearly.

Option: Have the class read the conversation chorally, with half the class reading *A's* part and half reading *B's* part. Then have students switch parts. Or have the entire class read one part while you read the other.

Vocabulary

➤ Compare the household emergencies to those the students volunteered when they discussed the objectives on page 15. Brainstorm other household emergencies. Your list might include these problems: *The ceiling is leaking, the basement is flooded, there's no electricity.*

➤ Point out to students that the expression *There's no . . .* is the same as *There isn't any . . .* Have students rephrase *There's no heat, hot water, air conditioning* using *There isn't any.*

➤ Play the cassette or read the phrases and have students repeat the household emergencies.

Option: Put students in small groups to discuss household problems that they are responsible for fixing vs. those problems that they have to get help for. Have students consider how their responsibilities change depending on whether they are renters or owners.

C. Pair work . . .

➤ Model the conversation with a more advanced student. Play the role of Student A. Make sure students understand that they can use any of the household emergencies from the *Vocabulary* in the first slot.

➤ Repeat the conversation playing the role of Student B. Make sure that students understand that they must use a future time in Student B's first slot. You can exaggerate the manager's unwillingness to cooperate by responding *Well, I can't look at that until Thursday* in the last slot.

➤ Students practice the conversation with a partner, taking turns playing the roles of Student A and Student B. Circulate and offer help as needed.

If your students are ready . . .

Language note: Point out that the first emergency states that *A pipe burst,* whereas the next two emergencies state *The lock is broken* and *The window is broken.* Direct students' attention to the use of the indefinite article in one emergency and the use of the definite article in the other situations. If necessary, explain that in the case of the lock and the window, we are looking at one specific lock and one specific window. In the case of a pipe bursting, it could be any one of the many pipes that provide water to the household.

Model 2

Content: extending a casual greeting, discussing an outage with another tenant, talking about utilities

Procedure:

⌒A–B.

➤ Read the bar for Model 2. Explain that *an outage* is a way of saying that something electrical doesn't work.

➤ To set the scene for the conversation, direct students' attention to the photo. Ask questions such as *Who do you think the people are?* (tenants, neighbors) *Where are they?* (in an apartment building lobby) Have students look at the corner picture of the TV. Ask *What's the matter with the TV?* Elicit or state the phrase *bad reception* and ask students to think about why the reception might be bad.

➤ Draw on students' experience by asking *How many of your neighbors do you know by name? Speak to on a regular basis? Feel you can call on for help?*

➤ Play the cassette or read the conversation and then check comprehension. Ask questions such as *What is the man's name?* (Peter) *What is the problem?* (Their cable is out.) *What is the woman going to do?* (check her cable and let Peter know)

⌒Vocabulary

➤ After students repeat the words, tell them that *power* is a synonym for *electricity*. We can say that *our power's out* or *our electricity's out*. We can also talk about *a power outage* although not *an electricity outage*.

➤ Relate to the students' experience by asking questions such as *Who has cable? Gas? Phones?* Explain that most people have electricity, but the other utilities may be less common. Ask whether students have satellite dishes rather than cable and cell phones rather than a land line.

C. Pair work . . .

➤ Model the conversation with a more advanced student. Play the part of Student B to demonstrate a negative response to Student A's question and describe a problem. Note that Student B says *Our* (or *My*) *cable, power, gas is out* but *Our* (or *My*) *phones are out*. Students can use *my* or *our*.

➤ Have students practice the conversation in pairs, stating a variety of problems with their utilities.

➤ Do it yourself!

(For general suggestions, see *Introduction*, page Txiii.)

Procedure:

A. Pair work . . .

➤ Direct students' attention to the picture on the right. Ask *What's the problem?* (There is a flood in the woman's kitchen.)

➤ Put students in pairs to create a conversation between the woman and the building manager. The woman reports the urgent problem and asks for help. Have pairs practice the conversation, switching roles for more practice.

B. Discussion . . .

➤ Ask volunteers to read the speech balloons at the bottom of the page and match each solution to a household emergency or outage.

➤ Students may see the term *super* rather than *building manager*. Explain that *super* is a shortened form of *superintendent* and is common in urban areas. *Superintendent* and *building manager* are often used interchangeably.

Option: Create a chart on the board. Write the headings *Problem, Called the manager, Called the utility company, Called a specialist, Fixed it myself*. Ask students what household emergencies they have had. As they describe the problems, write them in the left-hand column under the heading *Problem*. When you have a list of problems, ask *How many people called the building manager for this problem? How many people called the utility company? How many people called a specialist such as an electrician or a plumber? How many people fixed the problem themselves?* As students raise their hands, put a tally mark in each column. You might have a chart like the one following:

Problem	Called the manager	Called the utility company	Called a specialist	Fixed it myself
A power outage	///	ⱵⱵ ⱵⱵ //		
A broken pipe	////		//	/
A cable outage		////		
A broken lock	/		/	
A broken window	/			/

A. Listen and read.

A: Hi, Peter. How's it going?
B: Not great. Our cable's out. Is yours out too?
A: I hope not. I'll check and let you know.
B: Thanks.

B. Pronunciation and intonation practice.

Vocabulary

Utilities

cable   power   gas   phones

C. Pair work. **Tell another tenant in your building about an outage.**

A: Hi, _____. ____1____ ?
B: ____2____. _____ out. _____ yours out too?
A: I hope not. I'll check and let you know.
B: ____3____.

[1]How are you
[2]Not good, Terrible
[3]Thank you, I appreciate it, etc.

➤ Do it yourself!

A. Pair work. **Create a conversation for the tenant and the building manager.**

B. Discussion. **Have you ever had an emergency in your own house or apartment? What did you do about it?**

 I called the building manager.

 I called a plumber.

I called an electrician.

 I fixed it myself.

Practical grammar

The present perfect

Form the present perfect with *have* or *has* and a past participle.

She **hasn't paid** the rent yet.

Use the present perfect with *ever, never, already, still,* and *yet* for actions that have happened before now—if the exact time is not stated or not important, as in these examples.

Have you *ever* **signed** a lease?

She's *never* **had** an emergency in her house.

I've *already* **seen** that apartment.

We **haven't signed** the lease *yet*. They **haven't** either.

Do not use the present perfect when a time is stated. Use the simple past tense for actions that happened at a stated time in the past.

I **signed** it yesterday. (before now—exact time is stated) NOT: ~~I have signed it yesterday.~~

A. **Complete the paragraph with the present perfect.**

I _____'ve seen_____ thirty apartments in this city! I _____'ve looked at_____
　　　1. see   **2.** look at

every school and I _____'ve checked_____ the shops and services in every neighborhood
　　　　　　　　　　3. check

where I _____'ve thought about_____ renting an apartment. But I still _____haven't found_____
　　　　4. think about   **5.** not find

the right one! I _____haven't been in_____ a neighborhood that has a good elementary
　　　　　6. not be in

school that my children can walk to, a good selection of inexpensive restaurants, and

stores that stay open late. I _____'ve lived_____ in many cities, but now I have
　　　　　　　　　　　　　　7. live

to live here, and I _____haven't had_____ any luck yet.
　　　　　　　8. not have

B. **Complete each sentence with the present perfect or the simple past tense.**

1. I _____saw_____ that apartment on Monday.
   　　have seen / saw

2. My husband _____has already notified_____ the manager about the hot water.
   　　　already notified / has already notified

3. He _____hasn't called_____ me back yet.
   　didn't call / hasn't called

4. The maintenance staff _____came_____ this morning.
   　　　　came / has come

5. Our cable _____has never been_____ out. _____Has_____ yours?
   　was never / has never been　　Was / Has

Practical grammar

(For general suggestions, see *Introduction*, page Tix.)

The present perfect

Content: contrast between the use of the present perfect when an exact past time is not stated and the simple past tense when an exact past time is known

Procedure:

➤ Review the formation of the present perfect. Remind students that the past participle for regular verbs ends in *–ed*. They can refer to page 145 for the past participle of irregular verbs. If necessary, review the structure of negatives and questions in the present perfect.

➤ Have volunteers read the information in the box aloud. Make sure students understand the term *stated*. Ask students to circle the stated time in the last example sentence.

➤ Review the adverbs that indicate the use of the present perfect (*ever, never, still, yet, already*). Have students underline these adverbs in the first five example sentences.

➤ Remind students of the difference between the simple past tense (an action completed at a specific stated time in the past) and the present perfect (an action not completed, or one for which the past time is not known or not important).

A. Complete the paragraph . . .

➤ Tell students that they can contract the subject pronoun *I* with *have* in each sentence: for example, *I've seen*.

➤ After the students have completed the exercise, correct as a class.

➤ Point out the adverbs that cued the use of the present perfect: *still* in item 5 and *yet* in item 8.

Option: Ask students to write their own paragraphs about trying to find a place to live, a school, or a job. Tell them to use the present perfect at least five times. When they are finished, ask them to exchange paragraphs with a partner to read and correct.

B. Complete each sentence . . .

➤ To model item 1, write down the sentence with each possible answer inserted. Have students choose the correct sentence. Point out that the phrase *on Monday* states a specific time in the past and therefore requires the simple past tense.

➤ Have students complete the exercise individually and then check answers with a partner. Review as a class.

Option: To reinforce the use of the present perfect in questions with *ever*, play *Have you ever . . . ?* Ask students to write five questions that begin with *Have you ever*. The questions should be about things that most people have done, such as *Have you ever eaten fast food?* Have students sit in chairs arranged in a circle. One student stands in the middle of the circle and asks one of his or her questions. Students who can answer *yes* to the question must stand up and find a new place to sit. The student in the middle also tries to find a place to sit. The student left standing goes to the middle and asks a question. Play the game long enough so that most students have a chance to ask a question.

For and *since*

Procedure:

➤ Write example sentences on the board, underlining *for* and *since*. Use these sentences or create your own: *I've lived here for a long time, I've lived in my apartment for 10 years, I've had this VCR for three years, I've had my TV since 2000, I've worked at my current job since 1998.* Elicit the use of the present perfect with *for* and *since* to talk about actions that began in the past and that continue in the present.

➤ Review the use of *for* with numbers and intervals of time (for example, *for five years*) and *since* with a specific point in time (*since last Monday*). Write examples such as the following and ask students to add *for* or *since*: *(for) three weeks, (since) yesterday, (since) 2:30, (for) a month, (since) December.*

➤ Tell students that with *for* and *since* certain verbs (*work, live, study, teach*) have the same meaning in the present perfect continuous as in the present perfect. Read the pair of example sentences in the box and create other pairs with the class.

➤ Brainstorm with the class the non-action verbs that they remember from Unit 1. Tell students that non-action verbs take the present perfect rather than the present perfect continuous for actions that began in the past and continue to the present. Read aloud the example sentence in the box: *Ms. Drake has been our landlord for ten years.*

➤ Have students read the rules and the example sentences in the box silently.

C. Complete the paragraph . . .

➤ Have students complete the paragraph and compare answers with a partner. Review as a class.

Option: Have students interview a partner, using these questions as a guideline: *How long have you lived at your present address? How long have you lived in this city? How long have you worked at your present job? How long have you studied at this school?* Students can then write a paragraph or report to a group about their partners.

➤ Do it yourself!

(For general suggestions, see *Introduction*, page Txiii.)

Procedure:

A–B.

➤ Ask students to explain why the simple past tense is used for the last question on the form. ("Before that" is a "stated" time.)

➤ After students have completed the form, put them in small groups to brainstorm questions that a rental agent might ask.

➤ Write students' ideas on the board. Questions might include the following: *How long have you lived at your current address? Where did you live before that? What kind of work do you do? How long have you worked there? How many people are in your household? What size apartment are you looking for?*

➤ Have students work in pairs and role-play a conversation between a rental agent and a prospective tenant, using the information in their housing history forms and providing additional personal information as necessary. Have students switch roles for more practice.

Use the present perfect with *for* or *since* for actions that started in the past and continue in the present.
I**'ve lived** here *since 2002.* (I still live here.)
Ms. Drake **has been** our landlord *for ten years.* (She's still our landlord.)
With *for* or *since*, the present perfect continuous has the same meaning as the present perfect.
I**'ve been living** here *since 2002* = I**'ve lived** here *since 2002.*

C. **Complete the paragraph about actions that started in the past with *for* or *since*.**

Mr. Clark has been a tenant at 33 Riverside Drive _____since_____ April.
1.

But he has lived in New York _____for_____ over ten years. Mr. Clark has
2.

worked at the Starburst Room of the Claremont Hotel _____since_____ 1998.
3.

He has been an executive chef _____for_____ only the last year.
4.

➤ Do it yourself!

A. **Complete the housing history form about yourself.**

Green Tree Properties _____ Application and Housing History

Your name _____

What is your current address? _____

How long have you lived at that address? _____

Where did you live before that? _____

B. **Role play. Role-play a conversation between a rental agent and a tenant applying for an apartment. Use the information in your housing history.**

How long have you lived there?

I've lived on 11th Street since 1999.

Renting a house or apartment

A. Read the picture story again. Then check *True* or *False* for each statement.

	True	False
1. Landlords are always responsible for repairs.	☐	☑
2. If the tenant breaks a window, the tenant has to pay for the repair.	☑	☐
3. Tenants are always permitted to sublet their apartments.	☐	☑
4. Tenants can sublet for two years.	☐	☑
5. The man asks for more time.	☑	☐

B. Listen. Read each response out loud from the text.

Authentic practice

(For general suggestions, see *Introduction*, page Tx.)

Renting a house or apartment

Procedure:

➤ To set the scene for the picture story, ask questions about the pictures, such as *Who's in the pictures?* (a man and a woman) *Where are they?* (in a rental office) *What do you think they are talking about?* (the lease; renting an apartment)

➤ Play the cassette or read the picture story. With books open, students read along silently.

➤ Check for comprehension by asking questions such as *Who is having the conversation?* (a rental agent and a prospective tenant) *Does the tenant have to pay for repairs?* (only if the tenant is at fault, or has done something that caused the damage) *What does the tenant want to do with his apartment this summer?* (rent it to his uncle)

➤ Students may see some terms that are unfamiliar but whose meaning can be inferred from context: *at fault, fair enough, not off the top of my head, get back to you, take your time.* If necessary, explain.

Option: Have students read the speech balloons again. Ask *What questions does the man ask?* (Who's responsible for repairs? What do you mean, "at fault"? Is that a problem? Does that include cable? Do you mind if I take the lease home and get back to you tomorrow?) Have volunteers read the man's questions and the agent's answers.

A. **Read the picture story...**
➤ Have students read the statements and then reread the picture story.

➤ Have students individually check *True* or *False* and then compare answers with a partner. Students should be prepared to support their answers with direct quotations from the picture story.

Option: Students rewrite each false statement to make it true (for example, *Landlords are responsible for repairs unless the tenant is at fault*).

B. **Listen...**
➤ Tell students that they will listen to the tapescript or the cassette and read aloud the responses in their text.

➤ Read each item in the tapescript out loud or play the cassette. Allow students to listen as many times as necessary to complete the exercise. If students have difficulty, prompt them by reading the response yourself.

Challenge: Use the prompts for Exercise B as a dictation. Have students listen to the questions and write what they hear. Allow students to listen as many times as necessary. Ask volunteers to write the questions on the board. Make corrections as a class. Students can then practice the prompts and responses with a partner.

Tapescript

1. Have you had a chance to look over the lease?

2. Do you mind if I take the lease home and get back to you tomorrow?

C. Vocabulary...
➤ Have students complete the exercise. If necessary, let them refer to the picture story to use the context to infer meaning.

Challenge: Put students in pairs to write definitions for the words that were not used to complete the sentences. In item 1, for example, students write a definition for *leasing:* paying money to a landlord for the use of an apartment for a certain period of time. Encourage students to use dictionaries. As a variation, students can form two teams to write the definitions of the unused words. Each team can challenge the other to provide the word that matches their definition.

D–E.
➤ Have students answer the questions in Exercise D individually and then compare responses with a partner before reading aloud the items and responses.

Option: After both students have practiced reading the items and responses in Exercise D, have Partner B in each pair close his or her book. Partner A then reads the item, and Partner B responds from memory.

Challenge: Have pairs of students work together to write a statement or a question for each unused response in Exercise D. For example, in item 1, a statement that could elicit the response *Fair enough* might be *If you break it, you fix it*. Have students take turns reading the new items and responses.

➤ Do it yourself!

(For general suggestions, see *Introduction,* page Txiii.)

Procedure:
➤ Tell students to imagine that this rental agent is discussing their new lease with them. Have students write their own responses.

➤ Before students practice with a partner, have a volunteer play the part of the rental agent and read each speech balloon aloud. Respond to each statement or question for yourself, giving students an opportunity to check the appropriateness of their responses.

➤ Have students interview each other in pairs to check their responses.

C. Vocabulary. Choose one of the words or phrases to complete each sentence.

1. _____Subletting_____ is letting another person live in your apartment and pay
   Subletting / Leasing

   the rent when you are not there.

2. A _____lease_____ is a legal contract between a tenant and a landlord.
   utility / lease

3. "You are _____responsible_____ for payment" means you have to pay.
   responsible / included

4. _____Utilities_____ are basic services that tenants need.
   Sublets / Utilities

5. A flood or a fire can cause _____damage_____.
   damage / approval

6. When you cause a problem, you are _____at fault_____.
   at fault / fair

7. Tenants have to get their landlord's _____approval_____ before subletting.
   lease / approval

D. Read each question. Underline your response.

1. "What's the policy on repairs?"

   YOU If you break it, you fix it.   **YOU** Fair enough.

2. "Do you know the terms on sublets?"

   YOU Only if you're at fault.   **YOU** Not off the top of my head. I'll check.

3. "Do you mind if I ask you a few more questions?"

   YOU Absolutely not.   **YOU** Is that a problem?

E. Pair work. Take turns reading the items and responses in Exercise D.

➤ Do it yourself!

Write your own response. Then read the conversation out loud with a partner.

If you are at fault for any damage, you'll be responsible for the repair.   **YOU** _____

I don't know the answer off the top of my head. Can I get back to you on that?   **YOU** _____

Any other questions about the lease?   **YOU** _____

Tips for apartment hunters

a dead-bolt lock   a circuit breaker   a switch   a mouse trap

a bait trap   roaches

A. **Listening comprehension. Listen to the radio call-in show about renting an apartment or a house. Take notes on a separate sheet of paper as you listen.**

B. **Answer the questions in your own words.**

1. Who are Jack Mee and Irene from Moline?   a radio call-in host and a caller

2. What does Irene want to know about?   what to look for when renting an apartment

3. Jack Mee offers a lot of advice. In your opinion, which piece of advice is most important?   (Answers will vary.)

C. **Pair work. Compare answers with a partner.**

D. **Which subjects does Jack Mee give tips about? Listen again and then check the boxes.**

1. ☐ street lighting   5. ☑ electrical wiring
2. ☑ plumbing   6. ☑ pest infestation
3. ☑ appliances   7. ☑ maintenance
4. ☐ noise   8. ☑ laundry facilities

E. **Vocabulary. Match each term in column A with a related term in column B.**

	A		B
_f_	1. security	a.	smoke detectors
a	2. fire code	b.	trash
d	3. electrical wiring	c.	bait traps
c	4. pest infestation	d.	fuses and circuit breakers
b	5. common area neglect	e.	burners
e	6. appliances	f.	dead-bolt locks

Authentic practice

(For general suggestions, see *Introduction*, page Tx.)

Tips for apartment hunters

Procedure:

⌒A. Listening comprehension ...

➤ To help students attend to important information in the listening, ask them to read the bar above the pictures.

➤ To set the scene for the listening, ask students about the picture on the left: *Who do you think the man is?* (someone on the radio, a talk show host) Have students look at the pictures on the right and repeat the captions after you. Make sure students understand what each item is used for.

➤ Ask students to predict what the tips will be about. Elicit the topics *pests, security,* and *electrical concerns.* Brainstorm other issues that might be important to apartment hunters: *appliances, general maintenance, cleanliness, facilities on site.* Write students' ideas on the board.

➤ Tell students that the caller on the radio show is going to take notes about the tips and that they should too. To practice the important academic skill of note taking, ask students to write down the topics and then add details under these headings.

➤ Sequential connectors are important cues. To help students follow the listening and take good notes, brainstorm words and phrases that give the order of information (*first, second, third, next, then, finally*). Tell students to listen for these words.

➤ Read the instructions for Exercise A out loud. Then read the selection or play the cassette through once and have the students write down the main topics using the sequencing connectors. They should note nine points (*the neighborhood at night, security, emergency exits, plumbing, appliances, electrical problems, pest infestation, maintenance, laundry facilities*). Read the selection out loud or play the cassette again so students can write down supporting details. Have students compare notes with a partner.

Option: Have volunteers come up to the board and write down their notes for each of the nine points mentioned in the selection.

B–C.

➤ After students answer the questions individually, have them compare answers with a partner.

Option: In preparation for a class discussion, have students list reasons for their answer to item 3 and discuss the topic with their partners. Ask the class which piece of advice they thought was most important. Write students' reasons on the board. After the discussion, have students vote on the most important piece of advice.

⌒D. Which subjects ...

➤ Have students read the list of subjects.

➤ Let students listen to the selection again and then check the appropriate boxes.

➤ Have students check their answers with a partner, and then review as a class.

E. Vocabulary ...

➤ Tell students to go over the notes they took in Exercise A. Reading the main topics and the details will help them do the matching vocabulary exercise.

➤ Read the first item in column A and the related item in column B. Make sure students understand that they are to write the letter of the term in column B. Ask students if they noted any other terms under the topic *Security* (window locks).

➤ After students match the terms in column A with those in column B, have them compare answers with a partner. Review as a class. Ask if reviewing the notes helped them complete this exercise.

Tapescript

Jack: This is Jack Mee at "Rent Talk," W-A-L-K's call-in show with tips for tenants. Our number's 1-800-TENANTS, that's 1-800-836-2687. Let's go to our phones. Irene in Moline. Speak to me.

Irene: Jack?

Jack: Yes, Irene. You're on the air.

Irene: Thank you for taking my call. I was recently separated from my husband, and I'm looking for my own place. Tomorrow I'm going to see a bunch of apartments, and I don't know what to look for.

Jack: Do you live alone, Irene?

Irene: Well, I have a ten-year-old daughter.

Jack: OK. Let me make a few suggestions. Do you have a pencil and paper for a few tips? You might want to jot them down. They'll save you a lot of grief down the line.

Irene: OK, Jack. I'm ready.

Jack: First: Check the neighborhood at night. Does it feel safe? If you came home late with your daughter, would you feel frightened? If you took a

(Tapescript is continued on page T23.)

Tapescript (*continued from page T22*)

bus, could you walk from the bus stop without looking over your shoulder?

Irene: [writing] Hmm. Check the neighborhood at night. That *is* a good idea.

Jack: Second: Still thinking about security, check the doors and windows. Are there dead-bolt locks on the front and back doors? Do the windows lock?

Irene: [writing] Dead-bolt locks.

Jack: Third: And this might seem unnecessary, but check the emergency exits, fire stairs, and fire escapes, and see that there are smoke detectors. Fire code violations are common, especially if you're renting an apartment in a smaller building or a private home. Better safe than sorry.

Fourth: Check the plumbing. Look for leaks, drips, and evidence of past damage. You don't want to deal with burst pipes and ruined possessions.

Irene: You can say *that* again.

Jack: Fifth: Check the appliances. For example, turn on the stove. Raise and lower the oven temperature. Turn on the broiler. Turn on all the burners to make sure they all work.

Irene: That's a good idea.

Jack: Sixth: Look for electrical problems—frayed wires, blown fuses or tripped circuit breakers, missing switches, and the like.

Seventh: Look for evidence of pest infestation: roaches and other insects, mice, or worse, rats. Are there bait traps or sprays around, in cabinets and under sinks? You know where to check!

Eighth: Check the maintenance of the common areas: stairs, halls, basement, elevators. Is there trash or other evidence of neglect?

Ninth: Check laundry facilities. If there are no washers and dryers in the building, is there a laundromat in the neighborhood? And while you're at it, look for other facilities in the neighborhood: a supermarket, dry cleaner's, etc. Did you get all that?

Irene: I hope so! Those are good tips. Thanks, Jack. If I could ask you one more question.

Jack: I'm sorry. I've got another call waiting. Give us a call back and let us know how it goes. [click] This is Jack Mee at "Rent Talk," 1-800 T-E-N-A-N-T-S. Nathan, what's on *your* mind?

F–G.

➤ Have students work individually to complete the self-test.

➤ Model the activity in Exercise G by telling the class about your neighborhood and home. Give your answers from the self-test and add any other details.

Challenge: Tally the results for each question. Questions are worded so that a *no* answer indicates a potential problem. Put students in small groups to problem-solve the issues. Ask groups to fill in a chart like the one following. Planning action is important to getting students to be more proactive.

Problem	Possible solutions	Action steps
Don't feel safe in neighborhood.	Get to know neighbors, form a neighborhood watch.	Organize a meeting to discuss safety with neighbors.

Challenge: Ask students to write a composition based on one of the problems identified in the chart. Students can discuss a course of action for dealing with the problem using sequential or chronological connectors, just as Jack Mee did in the listening comprehension exercise on page 22. For example: *If you don't feel safe in your neighborhood, you should take action. First, call a meeting with your neighbors. Second . . .*

FYI . . .

➤ Read the list of other places to look for apartments. Ask students to raise their hands if they used any of these ways to find their apartment.

➤ Make sure students know what *word of mouth* is. Brainstorm people whose word-of-mouth recommendations students would trust.

➤ Have students investigate the Web site and report their findings. Ask questions such as *Would you use this Web site? Why? Why not?*

➤ Do it yourself!

(For general suggestions, see *Introduction*, page Txiii.)

Procedure:

A. Write a list . . .

➤ Remind students of the issues discussed in the listening comprehension selection and in the other exercises in this *Authentic practice* section.

➤ Have students in pairs or small groups brainstorm a list of questions to ask a rental agent.

B. Pair work . . .

➤ Model the role play with a more advanced student. Have the student use his or her own questions to play the role of the prospective tenant while you play the rental agent.

➤ Tell students they can use their own house or apartment as the model on which to base the answers to the questions the "tenant" asks.

➤ Ask volunteers to present their role play.

F. Complete the self-test about your house or apartment.

		yes	no
1	Do you feel safe in the neighborhood?	○	○
2	Do you feel safe in your apartment?	○	○
3	Does your door have dead-bolt locks?	○	○
4	Do your appliances work?	○	○
5	Do you have laundry facilities in the building?	○	○

G. True story. Tell your partner about your neighborhood and your apartment or house. Use your self-test for ideas.

FYI. A good place to look for apartments is this helpful Web site:

http://www.apartments.about.com/library/tools/bl_huntingchecklist.htm

Other places to look for an apartment:
- Ads posted on supermarket bulletin boards
- Real estate agencies
- Classified ads in the local newspaper
- Word of mouth

➤ Do it yourself!

A. Write a list of questions to ask a rental agent or building superintendent about an apartment or a house you are interested in.

Questions
1. *Is there a laundry room?*
2.
3.
4.

B. Pair work. Use the questions to create a role play between a tenant and a rental agent or building superintendent.

Fair housing and equal opportunity

A. Read about the Fair Housing Act.

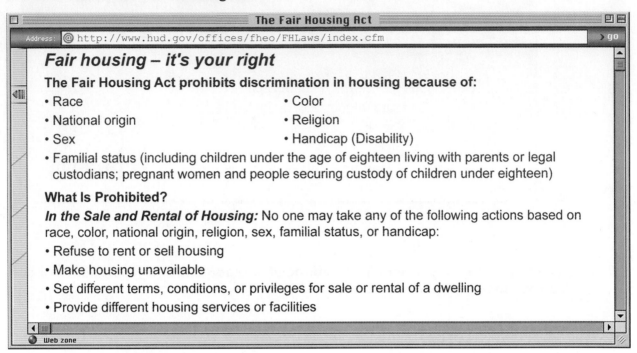

B. **Vocabulary. Read the definitions. Then complete each sentence with one of the words.**

a. **an act:** a law
b. **a right:** a legal permission
c. **prohibit:** not permit, prevent
d. **refuse:** not give permission
e. **disability:** a physical or mental condition that makes everyday actions difficult; for example, being hearing impaired

f. **discrimination:** illegally refusing to treat certain people equal to others because of a difference or disability
g. **a complaint:** a legal document that says a person has been unlawfully discriminated against
h. **a dwelling:** a place to live—a house or an apartment

1. We filed a _____**complaint**_____ when the landlord said we couldn't have the
   _{complaint / discrimination}

   apartment because we have two young children.

2. It's my _____**right**_____ to rent an apartment, no matter what my religion is.
   _{act / right}

3. Although I have a _____**disability**_____, the landlord can't refuse to rent me
   _{dwelling / disability}

   an apartment.

4. This apartment lease _____**prohibits**_____ pets. It has a no-pet policy.
   _{prohibits / permits}

Authentic practice

(For general suggestions, see *Introduction*, page Tx.)

Fair housing and equal opportunity

Procedure:

A. Read about ...

➤ Have students read the information on the Fair Housing Act. Ask them to focus on identifying the seven factors that cannot be used as a basis for discrimination and the four actions that are specifically prohibited.

➤ Make sure students understand the meaning of *race, national origin, sex, familial status, color, religion,* and *handicap.* Put each word or phrase on the board and ask the class for examples for each category.

➤ With students, discuss the meaning of the actions that are prohibited. Have students reword these actions to make sure they understand the meaning. Be sure students understand the difference between *renting* and *selling.*

➤ To demonstrate the relevance of the Fair Housing Act to the students, ask them to look at the seven factors again and identify those that apply to them.

Option: Coming up with strategies to remember key information is an important academic skill. Brainstorm with the class strategies that could help them remember the information in the reading. Write the strategies on the board. Ideas might include *remembering the first initials, creating a mental picture, linking the concepts to something already known.*

Challenge: Have students access the Web site whose address is given at the top of the monitor screen. Ask them to summarize the additional information they read about the Fair Housing Act.

B. Vocabulary ...

➤ Have volunteers read the eight definitions aloud. Discuss and reword as necessary to make sure students understand the terms and definitions. Ask students for examples of each term and together create example sentences.

➤ Brainstorm other disabilities. Write them on the board.

➤ Point out that some of the terms (*an act, refuse, a complaint*) have other definitions. Elicit these other meanings and remind students to use the context to determine the specific meaning.

➤ Have students complete the sentences. Then correct as a class.

Challenge: All of the words in the *Vocabulary* belong to word families, words that are different parts of speech but have the same base. Have students work in pairs to identify nouns and verbs with the same base. The list may include *act, action; prohibit, prohibition; refuse, refusal; disability, disable; discrimination, discriminate; complaint, complain; dwelling, dwell.*

C–D.

➤ Put students in pairs or small groups to read the case studies and then discuss whether the landlord has committed a violation of the Fair Housing Act in refusing to rent to the person.

➤ Have students give advice about how to handle the situation to each person.

Option: Assign one case study to each pair of students. Give students about 10 minutes to prepare a role play between the prospective tenant and the landlord that presents the issues. After students have presented their role play, ask the class to identify the issues and vote on whether the landlord committed a violation of the Fair Housing Act.

Option: Print out the complaint form from HUD and give a copy to each group. Ask students to fill out the form based on the situation in one of the case studies. Circulate and offer help as needed.

Option: Refer students to the picture story on page 20. Point out that the prospective tenant has a disability and is in a wheelchair. Ask *Is the rental agent discriminating against the man because of his handicap? How can you tell?* Have students suggest how landlords can encourage or discourage tenants with disabilities. If necessary, suggest that a building may or may not have wheelchair access, doors that are wide enough to accommodate wheelchairs, or bathrooms that can accommodate wheelchairs.

➤ Do it yourself!

(For general suggestions, see *Introduction*, page Txiii.)

Procedure:

A. Discussion . . .

➤ If your students come from different countries, put them in small groups according to home country.

➤ Ask them to discuss the three questions according to practices in their country. Tell students to be prepared to offer specific examples to support their discussion.

B. Culture talk . . .

➤ Explain that students will now be "ambassadors" to a new group to whom they will explain housing rights in their home country.

➤ Form new groups of students consisting of "ambassadors" from different home countries.

➤ Have groups discuss the differences and similarities between their countries in terms of housing rights and discrimination.

➤ Lead a class discussion about housing rights in various countries. Be sure to include whether discrimination occurs, what factors affect discrimination, and what tenants do about suspected discrimination.

C. Critical thinking. Read the case studies. Did the landlord commit a violation?

Chen

1. Warren Chen is blind. He has a specially trained dog that helps him in his daily activities outside of his home. He has an appointment to talk about renting an apartment. When he arrives for the appointment, the landlord says she's sorry, but the apartment has a no-pet policy.

Martin

2. Jolie Martin makes an appointment to see an apartment. When the rental agent learns that she is Haitian, he tells her that the unit is unavailable and that the building is full.

Hasan

3. Mohammad Hasan calls and leaves a message that he would like to see a house that is advertised in the local paper. The office doesn't call him back to make an appointment. Mr. Hasan suspects that the landlord doesn't want to rent to Muslims, so he calls again about the same apartment but leaves another name. The landlord calls back immediately and makes an appointment.

Johnson

4. Marjorie Johnson wants to rent an apartment. When she arrives to see it, the landlord tells her that the apartment is no longer available.

Schwartz

5. Milton Schwartz is a single father with six children. He wants an apartment with three bedrooms. The landlord says he doesn't have an apartment that big.

D. Discussion. Explain your answers in Exercise C to your group or partner. Use the Fair Housing Act on page 24 for support. (To download an official complaint form from the U.S. Department of Housing and Urban Development (HUD), click on www.hud.gov.)

➤ Do it yourself!

A. Discussion. Discuss the questions about housing rights in your home country.

1. Do landlords sometimes discriminate against tenants who want to rent?

2. Are tenants protected by the law?

3. What are some of the ways in which landlords discriminate? For instance, do they discriminate on the basis of language, religion, disability, or other?

B. Culture talk. Compare and contrast information about housing rights in your home country and your classmates' countries.

Review

(For general suggestions, see *Introduction*, page Txii.)

Procedure:

A. Pair work or group work.

➤ Have students take turns pointing to and naming as many things as they can in the picture.

Ask and answer questions.

➤ Point out the two questions asked in the directions. Point to one of the three numbered buildings on High Street. Ask *What are the people doing?* (301: repairing a problem with the cable; 303: talking about renting one of the three available apartments; 305: The tenant is complaining to the building manager.) Ask *What is the problem?* (301: The cable is out; 303: There may be discrimination against the family because of their children, pets, color, religion, or national origin; 305: There's a flood in the kitchen.)

Option: Working in pairs, students can write their own questions about the picture. Elicit example questions before they begin, such as *Who is the man in the apartment at 301 High Street? What does the sign in the window of 303 High Street say?*) Create a game by separating the students into two teams. Teams take turns asking the questions team members have created. Give points for each correct answer.

Option: Give students one minute to study the picture, trying to remember all they can about it. Remind them of some of the memory strategies you discussed earlier. Then have students close their books and form small groups. Ask questions about the picture and keep a record of the correct answers. After each question, allow the groups time to discuss and record the group's answer on a sheet of paper. Possible questions include *How many people are walking on the other side of the street?* (two) *How many dogs are in the picture?* (two) *What street are the three apartment buildings on?* (High Street) *Who is crossing the street?* (a woman pushing a child in a stroller) *Is there a parking lot in the picture?* (yes)

Create conversations.

➤ Hold up the book and point to the tenant and the manager in the lobby of 305 High Street. Play the role of the tenant and say *I've got an emergency in my apartment.* Elicit from the class an appropriate response for the manager, such as *What's the problem?* Respond, and then elicit an appropriate next line for the manager. Continue playing the role of the tenant and eliciting responses for the manager from the class.

➤ Put students in pairs and have them choose two people in the picture and create a conversation for them. Ask volunteers to role-play their conversations for the class.

Option: After students have created the conversations suggested by the picture, give them a new task. Have them imagine conversations between different pairs, such as the two tenants in the lobby of 305 High Street, or the parents of the family in front of 303 High Street.

Tell a story.
Option: Create a character. Point to one person in the picture and relate the details or his or her life. For example, for the woman crossing the street with a child in the stroller, say *Her name is Maria Arenas. She's from Chile. She's been living in the neighborhood for five years. She's been studying English since 2001 . . .* Then have students tell the story of at least one person in the picture to a partner. Explain that they will need to make up the information they relate.

Option: Describe the family. Have students describe the family members in front of 303 High Street. Students should include details such as a description of their clothing, their ages, and how long they have been looking for an apartment. They will need to make up some of the information.

Option: How's it going? Point to one person in the picture and give his or her extended response to the question. For example, for the tenant getting her mail at 305 High Street, say *Not so hot. My air conditioning's out again. And I've had a problem with my phone for a week . . .* Circulate through the room, encouraging students to make up as much as possible about each person's situation.

🎧 B. Listening comprehension . . .

➤ Tell students they are going to listen to five different conversations, one corresponding to each number in Exercise B. The task is to decide which problem is being discussed and fill in the oval.

➤ Ask students to read the options for item 1. Brainstorm terms related to an electrical problem that they might listen for, such as *outage, circuit, fuse, wire*.

➤ Read the first conversation or play the cassette.

➤ To model item 1, write out the two choices and have students choose the correct problem. Model how to select an answer by filling in the oval with the correct answer.

➤ Have students read the options for items 2 through 5.

➤ Read conversations 2 through 5 or play the cassette. Students fill in the correct ovals according to what they hear.

➤ Have students check answers with a partner. Then review as a class.

C. Read each sentence . . .

➤ Students work individually to complete the exercise.

➤ Have students check answers with a partner. Review answers as a class.

Challenge: Have partners create a statement or question that would require the alternate response. For example, for item 1, a student might write *The landlord wouldn't rent to me because I'm in a wheelchair.* This sentence might lead to the response *That's a violation of the Fair Housing Act!*

Tapescript

Conversation 1

A: Oh, no! Not again.

B: What?

A: I blew a fuse. It's this ridiculous hair dryer.

B: Better get a new one. Meanwhile, I'll call the super.

Conversation 2

A: Hello?

B: Hello, Mr. Cramden? This is Mrs. Norton in 3B. There's no hot water. And the cold water is dark brown.

A: You're kidding. I'll be right up to have a look.

Conversation 3

A: I can't believe the cable's out. I wanted to see the fight tonight.

B: Maybe it'll be back on by then. Did you call?

A: Sure. But it always takes a day or two until they get out to *this* neighborhood.

Conversation 4

A: Let's check the cabinets under the sink before we sign the lease.

B: Good idea. Hey, what's *this*?

A: What?

B: These boxes with blue stuff . . . I don't know what it is . . . Oh. Rat Resort? What???

A: Well, that's that. They've had rats. Forget this dump!

Conversation 5

A: We're here to see the apartment.

B: Certainly, Mr. . . . ?

A: Sirinivatsu.

B: Serina-who?

A: Sirinivatsu. It's a Chappaquakian name. We're from Chappaqua.

B: I see . . . Oh, your wife has a wheelchair? Well, I think you'd be happier in a different building. This apartment is in the basement.

B. Listening comprehension. Listen to the conversations. Then decide what the problems are. Fill in the ovals.

1. **(a)** an electrical problem   (b) a flood
2. (a) a security problem   **(b)** a plumbing problem
3. **(a)** a cable outage   (b) a gas outage
4. (a) a safety problem   **(b)** pest infestation
5. **(a)** housing discrimination   (b) a lease problem

C. Read each sentence or question. Underline your response.

1. "The cable's out."

   YOU <u>But my favorite show is on tonight!</u>   **YOU** That's a violation of the Fair Housing Act!

2. "Have you checked all the burners?"

   YOU Yes, and there's a pest problem.   **YOU** <u>Yes, the stove is fine.</u>

3. "What are the terms of the lease?"

   YOU <u>It's for two years, and it permits sublets.</u>   **YOU** It's out again.

4. "But how secure is the apartment?"

   YOU <u>Well, there's a dead-bolt lock on both doors.</u>   **YOU** Well, I didn't see any traps or sprays.

5. "Do you think you were discriminated against?"

   YOU I'm not sure. I'll call the manager.   **YOU** <u>I'm not sure. I need to check the Fair Housing Act.</u>

6. "Do you know which utilities are included?"

   YOU <u>Not off the top of my head.</u>   **YOU** Plumbing and electrical problems, I think.

7. "Who's at fault for this water damage?"

   YOU It has a no-pet policy.   **YOU** <u>The tenant.</u>

D. Complete each sentence with the present perfect or the simple present tense.

1. Last year I _____ tried _____ to rent an apartment in this building.
    tried / have tried

2. This morning, the landlord _____ told _____ me that I need a new lease.
    told / has told

3. I _____ have never lived _____ in such a terrible apartment.
    never lived / have never lived

4. The locks are broken. I called the manager, but he _____ hasn't called me back _____ yet.
    didn't call me back / hasn't called me back

5. I _____ have already looked _____ for another apartment.
    already looked / have already looked

6. It's hard to move. I _____ have lived _____ here for a long time.
    lived / have lived

E. Choose one or more of the questions. Find the information in the unit and write the answer in your own words.

1. What is an outage? (Answers will vary.) _____

    _____

2. What is a lease? _____

    _____

3. What is a disability? _____

    _____

4. What is illegal discrimination?

    _____

F. Composition. On a separate sheet of paper, write about the picture on page 26. Say as much as you can.

> **Now I can**
> ❑ describe a housing emergency.
> ❑ ask for housing repairs.
> ❑ know what to look for in a potential rental.
> ❑ understand tenant rights.
> ❑ understand the Fair Housing Act.
> ❑ act on housing discrimination.

D–E.

➤ Students work individually to complete the review exercises.

➤ Circulate to offer help as needed.

➤ Have students check answers with a partner. Review answers as a class.

➤ Identify any areas of difficulty that may require additional instruction and practice.

Option: Review the vocabulary from the unit. You should include the terms for housing emergencies on page 16, utilities on page 17, the vocabulary items from Exercise E on page 22 and from Exercise B on page 24. Divide the class into two teams. Ask the members of Team A to define the first word. Give students a couple of minutes to prepare their definition. Teams get 1 point for each correct definition. If a team can't give an acceptable definition, the other team can try. Ask Team B to define the second word. Continue playing until all the words have been defined.

F. Composition . . .

➤ Provide students with concrete approaches to writing about the picture on page 26. Use one of the following options, give students a choice of options, or assign options based on students' level of proficiency. Model what is expected of students for each option.

➤ Advise students to look back through the unit for help and ideas as they write.

➤ Circulate to offer help as needed.

Option: Have students choose one of the pairs of people who are talking to each other in the picture, label them *A* and *B*, and write an extended conversation for them. Students can later role-play their conversations for the class.

Option: Have students number the people in the picture and then write two sentences about each one. To reinforce the grammar points in the unit, one sentence can tell something about the person using the present perfect with *for* or *since*. For example, for the cable repairperson, students might write *He's been repairing the cable since 2:00, He's been working for an hour.*

Option: Have students use sequential or chronological connectors to write a story about a situation in the picture. They should write each sentence on a different line and skip lines between sentences. Then ask students to cut up their papers so that each sentence is on a different strip. Have students scramble the strips and exchange them with a partner to reorder. Students can read aloud the reordered story to a group or the class.

Now I can

➤ Read the first item in the box out loud: *Now I can describe a housing emergency.* Elicit from the class an example of a housing emergency, such as *A broken pipe is a housing emergency.*

➤ In pairs, students take turns reading each item in the box and giving an example of what they have learned. When students can provide an example, they should check that box. For the items students weren't able to check, they should look back through the unit for ideas.

➤ When students have finished reviewing with their partners, read each item out loud and elicit an example from the class.

Oral test (optional)

You may want to use the *Now I can* box as an informal evaluation. While students are working on the *Composition* activity, you can call them up individually and check their ability with two or three objectives.

Your equipment and machines

Note: For the *Discussion* on page 31, have students bring in articles from the newspaper about traffic accidents.

 Preview

(For general suggestions, see *Introduction*, page Tviii.)

Warm up. Do you have all the "should haves" in your car? Have you ever needed to use this equipment?

Procedure:

➤ Ask students to read the title of the magazine article: "The Responsible Driver." Have them close their books. Put them in small groups to discuss what being a responsible driver means.

➤ Ask for students' reactions and write their ideas on the board. The list may include *having a driver's license, registration, and insurance; obeying the traffic laws; not drinking and driving; being considerate of other drivers; maintaining the car properly; having the proper safety equipment.* If students have not included proper safety or emergency equipment, elicit by asking *What should a responsible driver do in an emergency? If the car breaks down?* Keep the students' list on the board.

➤ Tell students that scanning is a necessary academic skill. Remind them that scanning involves reading quickly to find specific information. Ask students to open their books and scan the article to find the five pieces of equipment that they should have in their car (a flashlight, a spare tire, a jack, flares, jumper cables). If necessary, remind students that formatting—headings, subheadings, boldfaced words, bullets, check boxes, pictures, etc.—can help with scanning.

➤ Some terms in the article may be unfamiliar to students. If necessary, review the meanings of *a moment's notice, better safe than sorry, ASAP, common sense, spare.* Point out that *spare* can be both a noun (*a spare*) and an adjective (*a spare tire, a spare battery*).

➤ Have students read the article silently. Ask questions such as *Can we plan for emergencies?* (No, but we can be equipped to handle them.) *When do drivers need these five pieces of equipment?* (in a breakdown or to help other drivers) *Why should drivers keep a jack in their car?* (to change a flat tire)

➤ Point out the use of exclamation marks in the article. Exclamation marks are used to emphasize a particular point or to convey emotion. Exclamation marks also make written text seem more like spoken English. Have students find the phrases that end with exclamation marks *(Better safe than sorry! keep some spares!)* and repeat them after you for proper emphasis and intonation.

Unit 3 objectives

Procedure:

➤ Have students read the objectives. Ask them to put a check next to the objectives that they can do now and circle those they want to work on most.

➤ Ask students to underline any words they do not understand. Write any unfamiliar terms on the board. Some students may not be familiar with the terms *road rage* and *Golden Rule.* Give a quick explanation of these terms. Students will find out more about road rage in the listening comprehension exercise on page 36. Students will read about driving by the Golden Rule in the advice column on page 38.

➤ Focus students' attention on the issues in the unit. Ask *Have you ever been stopped by a police officer because of a traffic violation? Have you ever been in a traffic accident?* Have students share their experiences. Tell students they will learn more about these topics in the unit.

➤ Refer to the students' list on the board about responsible driving. If the students listed anything that now appears in the objectives, put a check mark next to it. Point out that meeting these objectives will help students be more responsible drivers.

Your equipment and machines

Preview

Warm up. Do you have all the "should haves" in your car? Have you ever needed to use this equipment?

Road Talk Magazine / July 2004
67

THE RESPONSIBLE DRIVER

Emergencies can happen at a moment's notice and can turn deadly in an instant. We can't plan for emergencies, but we can be equipped to handle them. This month, the Responsible Driver examines what you should have in your car at all times. Better safe than sorry!

"Should haves" self-check

Check the items you have in your car right now. Then get the ones you don't have ASAP! Common sense requires that you have these items in your car in case of a breakdown or in case you have to assist another driver in need.

- ❑ a flashlight with working batteries—keep some spares!
- ❑ a spare tire—to replace a flat tire
- ❑ a jack—to change the tire
- ❑ flares—to warn oncoming traffic that you are stopped
- ❑ jumper cables—to start a car with a dead battery

Unit 3 objectives

- Respond appropriately to a police officer in a traffic stop.
- Describe an accident.
- Understand traffic violations.
- Avoid aggressive driving and road rage.
- Drive by the Golden Rule.
- Understand what equipment is needed in a car.

Practical conversations

A. Listen and read.

A: I'm going to have to give you a ticket for speeding.

B: You're right. I'm sorry, officer.

A: License and registration, please.

B: Here you go.

A: I'll be back in a few minutes. Please turn off your engine.

B: OK.

B. Pronunciation and intonation practice.

Vocabulary

Traffic violations

speeding

not stopping at a stop sign

not yielding at a yield sign

tailgating

not signaling

talking on a hand-held cell phone

C. Pair work. Get a ticket for a traffic violation.

A: I'm going to have to give you a ticket for _____.

B: You're right. I'm sorry, officer.

A: License and registration, please.

B: _____.

A: I'll be back in a few minutes. Please turn off your engine.

B: _____.

30   Unit 3

Practical conversations

(For general suggestions, see *Introduction*, page Tviii.)

Model 1

Content: responding appropriately in a traffic stop, apologizing for a traffic violation, traffic violations, gerunds

Procedure:

🎧 A–B.

➤ To set the scene for the conversation, ask questions about the photo and the inset, such as *Who is in the picture?* (a police officer and a driver) *What is happening?* (The police officer has stopped the driver, and the driver is giving her his license.) *What documents are in the inset?* (a car registration, a driver's license)

➤ Ask students about their own experiences with questions such as *Have you ever been stopped by a police officer while driving? How does an officer stop a motorist? What did you do when the officer flashed the lights?*

➤ After students listen to the conversation, check comprehension by asking questions such as *What was the traffic violation?* (speeding) *What does the driver say when the officer tells him that he is getting a ticket for speeding?* (You're right. I'm sorry.) *What documents does the officer ask for?* (the driver's license and registration)

➤ Play the cassette or read the conversation again. Encourage students to imitate the rhythm, stress, and intonation of the conversation as closely as possible. Correct where necessary.

Option: Play the role of the police officer and have the class respond chorally as the driver. Tell students that it is important to show the correct attitude through their voices, so they should be serious and respectful.

🎧 Vocabulary

➤ Play the cassette or read the traffic violations. Ask students to point to each picture as the caption is read.

➤ Call students' attention to the form of the verb in each violation. Tell students that the *-ing* form is called a gerund. Point out that the negative form of a gerund is *not* in front of the gerund.

➤ Play the cassette or read the traffic violations again and have students repeat.

➤ Ask questions about the pictures, such as *How fast is the driver going?* (70 mph) *What does the abbreviation "mph" mean?* (miles per hour) *What is the speed limit?* (55 miles per hour) *In the second picture, why is the pedestrian upset?* (Not stopping at a stop sign is dangerous, could cause an accident, is illegal.)

Option: Ask pairs of students to write descriptions or definitions to clarify each violation. For instance, *Speeding is going faster than the speed limit. Tailgating is following another car very closely.* Ask each pair to join another pair and compare explanations. Share explanations as a class to make sure students understand all the terms.

Option: Tell students that talking on a hand-held cell phone while driving is illegal in some states. Even if it is not a violation, it can be dangerous to talk on cell phones while driving. Tell students or elicit information about cell phone regulations in your state. Ask *Do you think talking on a cell phone should be a traffic violation? Why or why not?*

C. Pair work ...

➤ Before students practice the conversation, direct their attention to B's second response, *Here you go.* Ask students to brainstorm other possible responses: *Here they are; Here; OK; I have them here.* Direct attention to B's last response. Make sure students understand that they must give an affirmative response such as *Yes, officer; Sure; Of course.*

➤ Model the conversation with a more advanced student. Play the role of Student A to demonstrate substituting a traffic violation from the *Vocabulary* box for *speeding.*

➤ Have students practice the conversation in pairs, using different violations from the *Vocabulary* box and switching roles so each student plays the part of the driver.

If your students are ready . . .

Culture / Civics note: In this culture, a traffic stop can sometimes lead to misunderstandings. It is important for drivers to stay in the car until told otherwise and to let the officer begin the interaction. Drivers should not do anything that the officer has not asked for, including taking out their license or registration. Sudden moves may be interpreted by the officer as threatening. If a driver receives a ticket, he or she must either pay it by the date specified or go to court to challenge the ticket. Failure to do either of these things can lead to more serious charges.

T30

Model 2

Content: describing an accident, reactions to accidents, car accidents

Procedure:

🎧A. Listen and read.

➤ Set the scene for the conversation by asking questions about the photo, such as *Who do you see in the picture?* (a man and a woman, a husband and wife) *Where do you think they are?* (at home) Have students look at the man's expression and speculate about how he feels and what problem he has.

➤ After students listen to the conversation, check comprehension by asking questions such as *What happened?* (The man had a car accident.) *Was anyone hurt?* (no) *Was the accident serious?* (No, it was just a fender bender.) *How will he pay for the car repair?* (The insurance will cover it.)

➤ Explain that a *fender bender* is an accident that causes minor damage. A fender is the part of a car that covers the wheels. A fender bender is a collision that bends or dents the fender but doesn't damage the rest of the car.

➤ After students listen to *Reactions to accidents*, direct their attention to the conjunctions *but* and *and* used in the two sentences. Ask the students how the two conjunctions are used. Elicit or point out that *and* is used to add information that is similar, and *but* is used to add information that is contradictory. The first sentence presents two pieces of information: the damage is minor, the driver is upset. We expect the driver not to be upset about minor damage, so *but* is used to add information that contradicts our expectation.

🎧B. Pronunciation and intonation practice.

Option: Play the cassette or read the conversation again, stopping after the formulaic expressions that indicate emotion: *Oh, no; thank goodness; take it easy.* Ask students to repeat just these expressions.

🎧Vocabulary

➤ Play the cassette or read the captions, and have students repeat the different car accidents.

➤ Explain that *sideswipe* means to brush or swipe against the side of another car. Sideswiping usually scratches or dents the side panels of one or both cars.

Option: Point out the verb forms in the second and fourth sentences. The past continuous (*was following, wasn't paying attention*) is used to describe a past action in progress, and the simple past tense (*rear-ended, hit*) is used to describe a past action that interrupted the action in progress.

Challenge: Brainstorm other car accidents (*bumped into another car, hit a sign, scratched the door*). Begin sentences in the past continuous and have students describe car accidents in the simple past: *I was following too closely, and I bumped into another car; I wasn't paying attention, and I hit a stop sign.*

C. Pair work . . .

➤ Ask students what information should go in the first slot (a type of car accident) and in the second (a reaction to the accident).

➤ Brainstorm other sympathetic responses for Student B if Student A says *But there was a lot of damage, and I'm really upset.* Responses might include *That's really too bad, I'm so sorry to hear that, Don't worry.*

➤ Model the conversation with a more advanced student. Play the role of Student A to demonstrate substituting a car accident from the *Vocabulary* box and a reaction.

➤ Do it yourself!

(For general suggestions, see *Introduction*, page Txiii.)

Procedure:

A–B.

➤ Have students read the example in the chart. Ask them to complete the second line of the chart with their own information. Prompt students by asking *Have you been in an accident recently? Has anyone you know been in an accident recently? What caused it?*

➤ Pair students to talk about the information in their charts.

C. Discussion . . .

➤ If you or the students have brought in articles about traffic accidents, have students take them out. On the board, write the following questions: *What type of accident was it? What was the cause? What happened? Was anyone hurt?* Working individually, students scan the article and underline the answers to the questions on the board.

➤ Put students in small groups to discuss the accidents. Have them report the answers they underlined as well as any other important details.

🎧 **A. Listen and read.**

A: I had an accident. I sideswiped another car.

B: Oh, no. Was anyone hurt?

A: No, thank goodness. It was just a fender bender, but I'm really upset.

B: Well, take it easy. The insurance will cover it.

🎧 **B. Pronunciation and intonation practice.**

🎧 **Reactions to accidents**

It was just a fender bender, but I'm really upset.
But there was a lot of damage, and I'm really upset.

🎧 **Vocabulary**

Car accidents

I **sideswiped** a parked car.

I was following too closely, and I **rear-ended** another car.

I **totaled** the car.

I wasn't paying attention, and I **hit** another car.

C. Pair work. Discuss an accident.

A: I had an accident. I _____.

B: Oh, no. Was anyone hurt?

A: No, thank goodness. _____.

B: ___1___. The insurance will cover it.   [1]It's OK, Don't worry, etc.

❯ Do it yourself!

A. True story. Describe an accident you had or an accident you know about. What was the cause?

Accident	What was the cause?
a fender bender	The driver was talking on a cell phone.

B. Pair work. Compare information with your partner.

C. Discussion. Bring in an article describing an accident from a newspaper. Discuss the accident with your classmates. What happened? What was the cause?

Practical grammar

Using gerunds

A gerund is the *-ing* form of the verb, used as a noun. Gerunds can be used in a variety of ways.

as a subject of a sentence:

Passing on the right is dangerous.

as an object of a verb:

I don't like **honking** at another driver.

as an object of a preposition:

Even if you're in a hurry, that's no excuse for **speeding**.

as a complement:

My favorite way to get places is **driving**.

See page 146 for a list of verbs followed by gerunds. See page 147 for how to spell the gerund and the present participle.

A. Complete the sentences with gerunds.

1. We got a ticket for not _____stopping_____ at the stop sign.
   stop

2. _____Leaving_____ the scene of an accident is a serious crime.
   Leave

3. The officer stopped us for not _____yielding_____ to the car in the rotary.
   yield

4. _____Parking_____ is not permitted in a bus stop.
   Park

5. I get angry at drivers for _____tailgating_____.
   tailgate

6. I'm not used to _____driving_____ at night.
   drive

7. The worst traffic offense is _____speeding_____.
   speed

8. _____Talking_____ on a hand-held cell phone while driving is very distracting
   Talk
   to a driver.

9. I'm tired of _____getting_____ tickets. I'd better stop _____driving_____ so
   get   drive
   fast!

10. Instead of _____observing_____ the speed limit, he just kept _____looking_____
    observe   look
    for radar traps.

Practical grammar

(For general suggestions, see *Introduction*, page Tix.)

Using gerunds

Procedure:

➤ Write three sentences on the board:

1. She is smiling.
2. She is the smiling woman.
3. Smiling is a sign of friendliness.

➤ Ask the students which word is repeated in all three sentences (smiling). Tell them that this –ing word has a different use in each sentence. In one, it is an adjective; in another, it is a noun; and in the other, it is part of the verb. Ask students to tell you how this –ing word is used in each sentence. Elicit that it is part of the verb in sentence 1, an adjective in 2, and a noun in 3.

➤ Tell students that, in this section, they will be focusing on –ing words when they act as nouns. Mention that these –ing words are called gerunds. This term was introduced earlier in the Vocabulary section on page 30.

➤ Direct students' attention to the box. Have volunteers read the information aloud. Make sure that students know what a complement is (it completes sentences that have linking verbs such as the verb be).

Option: Point out the gerund (speeding) in the model conversation on page 30. Note that all the traffic violations in the *Vocabulary* box are gerunds.

Option: To help students practice using gerunds as objects of verbs or prepositions and as complements, have them play a game. Read aloud the following incomplete sentences or create your own. Students should complete each sentence with a single word—a gerund. Model the activity by completing the first two sentences yourself. Brainstorm gerunds for the third sentence to make sure students understand that they should use a gerund and not another kind of noun. Move up and down the rows, reading the incomplete sentences and having students answer. Change the sentence frequently.

1. I really enjoy ___.
2. I don't like ___.
3. I appreciate ___.
4. I am afraid of ___.
5. I am excited about ___.
6. My favorite activity is ___.
7. One thing that really annoys me is ___.
8. Most people are worried about ___.
9. Everyone is hurt by ___.
10. Police will stop you for ___.

A. Complete the sentences ...

➤ Model the activity by writing the sentence on the board. Point to the word *stop* below the line. Ask students to supply the correct verb form and write it in the blank.

➤ Review the spelling rules for gerunds. Remind students to double the last consonant in one-syllable verbs that end in a consonant-vowel-consonant pattern (stop ➠ stopping), and to drop the –e from the simple form before adding –ing (hope ➠ hoping). Refer to page 147 for additional rules.

➤ After students have completed the sentences individually, have them compare answers, including spellings, with a partner. Review as a class.

➤ The word *rotary* in item 3 may be unfamiliar to students. In some areas it is called a circle, a traffic circle, or a roundabout. If necessary, draw a picture on the board.

Challenge: Ask students how the gerund is used in each sentence—as subject (s), object of a verb (ov), object of a preposition (op), or complement (c). Elicit the following: 1 (op); 2 (s); 3 (op); 4 (s); 5 (op); 6 (op); 7 (c); 8 (s); 9 (op), (ov); 10 (op,) (ov).

Infinitives of purpose

Procedure:

➤ Ask a series of *why* questions like the ones following, or create your own. Answer the first two questions yourself to demonstrate the use of the infinitive. *Why did you turn on the TV?* (to watch the news) *Why did you buy the newspaper?* (to read the news) *Why did you go to the supermarket?* (to buy bread) *Why did you go to the drugstore?* (to buy aspirin) *Why did you go to the post office?* (to buy a money order) Write down the infinitives that students use in their answers.

➤ Remind students that *to* plus the simple form of the verb is an infinitive. Refer to the list of infinitives on the board and add the heading *Infinitives*.

➤ Tell students that, like gerunds, infinitives are used in several ways. Explain that infinitives of purpose often answer the question *why*.

➤ Create a series of example sentences on the board that show the use of infinitives after the verbs *forget, need, plan,* and *want*. Use the following sentences or create your own. Ask volunteers for additional sentences that follow the pattern. *I forgot to stop at the stop sign, He needs batteries, She didn't plan to total the car, The officer wanted to see my license and registration.* Tell students that another use of infinitives is after certain verbs.

➤ Have students read the information in the grammar box. Point out that a list of verbs followed by infinitives appears on page 146.

B. Read...

➤ Ask students if they ever make "to-do" lists, lists of chores or errands that they need to accomplish on a certain day or at a certain time. Elicit examples of what kinds of things they write on their lists. Write a few items on the board, beginning each one with the simple form of the verb. For example, students may say *do the laundry, buy pet food, pay the car insurance bill.*

➤ Have students read Dr. Jamie Greene's "to-do" list. Students then answer the questions individually. Correct as a class.

➤ Point out that students have to convert the wording of some of the tasks in their answers. For example, the list says *renew my driver's license,* but the answer for item 1 is *her driver's license.* In item 4, students have to change *pay my parking ticket* to *her* (or *a* or *the*) *parking ticket.*

Option: On a separate sheet of paper, students write their own "to-do" lists with at least five items. Have students exchange lists with a partner and make up an appropriate *why* question for each item. The writer of the list then answers, using an infinitive of purpose. The task, question, and answer might look like this: *do the laundry. Why did you go to the laundromat? to do the laundry*

C. Complete each answer...

➤ Model the exercise by writing the question on the board. Write the first part of the answer, *They stop speeders,* and ask the class for possible answers. List students' suggestions on the board, using an infinitive of purpose for each idea.

➤ Students work individually to answer the questions and then compare answers with a partner.

If your students are ready...

Language note: The verbs *remember* and *forget* can be followed by either an infinitive or a gerund, but each choice produces a very different meaning. *I remembered to get new tires* means that I didn't forget, I accomplished my task. *I remembered getting new tires* means I have a memory of doing it. *I forgot to get new tires* means I didn't accomplish my task, whereas *I forgot getting new tires* means that I bought the tires, but I forgot that I did so. Refer students to the list of verbs that are followed by gerunds or infinitives on page 146.

➤ Do it yourself!

(For general suggestions, see *Introduction,* page Txiii.)

Procedure:

A. Make a list...

➤ Direct students' attention to the example and ask *Why did I go to the ATM yesterday?* (to get money for groceries)

➤ Have students write down one activity they did yesterday and the purpose of the activity. On a separate sheet of paper, have students write down three or four more actions they completed yesterday with the purpose for each one.

B. Pair work...

➤ Put students in pairs. Student A says where he or she went yesterday, and Student B asks why. Student A answers with an infinitive of purpose. Students take turns reading their activities until all the items on their lists have been discussed.

Infinitives of purpose

An infinitive is *to* and the simple form of the verb. Infinitives are used after certain verbs: *decide, forget, need, plan, remember, want.*

   Remember **to pass** on the left, not on the right.

You can use an infinitive to explain the purpose of an action. Statements using an infinitive of purpose often answer questions with *why*.

   A: And why did the officer stop you?
   B: **To give** me a ticket.

See page 146 for a list of verbs followed by infinitives.

B. Read Dr. Jamie Greene's "to-do" list for tomorrow. Then answer the questions with an infinitive of purpose.

renew my driver's license

make an appointment with the guidance counselor about college visits for Sam

buy new tires

pay my parking ticket

pick up cookies for the office party

1. Why did she drive to the Department of Motor Vehicles? _to renew her driver's license_

2. Why did she call the guidance counselor?
   to make an appointment about college visits for Sam

3. Why did she drive to Discount Tire World?
   to buy new tires

4. Why did she go to the municipal courthouse? to pay her parking ticket

5. Why did she drive to the bakery? to pick up cookies for the office party

C. Complete each answer. Use an infinitive of purpose.

1. Why do police officers stop speeders? They stop speeders _to give them tickets._

2. Why do people speed? They speed (Answers will vary.)

3. Why did you get a driver's license? I got a driver's license (Answers will vary.)

➤ Do it yourself!

A. Make a list of where you went yesterday and why. Use infinitives of purpose.

Activity	Purpose
I went to the ATM	to get money for groceries

B. Pair work. Ask your partner what he or she did yesterday. Ask why.

Appropriate behavior with a police officer

A. Read the picture story again. Answer the questions.

1. Why did the officer pull the driver over? for going too fast

2. What did the officer ask for? the driver's license and registration

3. How fast was the driver driving? 74 miles per hour

B. Vocabulary. Choose one of the words or phrases to complete each sentence.

1. Uh-oh! There's a cop behind us with her lights flashing. I think she's going to
   _____ pull us over _____!
   let us off / pull us over

2. I'm sorry, _____ officer _____. I didn't realize how fast I was going.
   cop / officer

3. Are you aware that I _____ clocked _____ you going over 80?
   warned / clocked

4. Be sure to look both ways before you _____ pull out _____. There's a lot of traffic.
   are wise / pull out

5. This time I'm going to _____ let you off _____. Next time it'll be more serious.
   pull you over / let you off

Authentic practice

(For general suggestions, see *Introduction*, page Tx.)

Appropriate behavior with a police officer

Procedure:

➤ To set the scene, have students look at the picture story. Ask *Who are the people in the story?* (a police officer and a driver) *What are they doing?* (talking) *What does the sign say?* (Speed Limit 65) *What do you think their conversation is about?* (how fast the man was driving)

➤ Have students listen with their books closed for answers to the following questions: *Why did the police officer stop the driver? What explanation does the driver give?*

➤ After students have listened to the picture story once, ask *Why did the police officer stop the driver?* (He was speeding.) *Why was the driver speeding?* (to get to the bank before it closed)

➤ Have students open their books and read along as you read the picture story or play the cassette again.

➤ Ask comprehension questions such as *How fast was the driver going?* (74 miles per hour) *How fast does he think he was going?* (about 65, maybe 70) *Why is it a good idea to leave yourself a little extra time?* (to avoid having to speed) *What will happen the next time the driver speeds?* (He'll get a ticket and points.)

➤ Some terms may be unfamiliar to students but can be inferred from the context. Make sure they understand the meanings of *hand over, pull over, clocked, a big hurry, let off,* and *pull out.* Point out that the speed limit is given in miles on the sign. The officer and the driver also discuss how fast the driver was going in miles. Give the speeds in kilometers if necessary (65 mph = 105 kilometers; 70 mph = 113 kilometers; 74 mph = 119 kilometers).

➤ Ask the students to describe the driver's behavior and give supporting examples from the story. If necessary, prompt with questions such as *Why does the driver say "Yes, officer" and "Thank you very much, officer"? What does the sentence "I'll be more careful in the future" express about the driver's attitude?* You may want to discuss whether students think the driver's behavior and attitude are appropriate.

Option: In pairs, students read the picture story, playing the roles of the police officer and the driver.

A. Read the picture story again...

➤ Point out that item 1 is a *why* question. Write the question on the board and ask students for possible answers. Model the answer (*to give the driver a warning about his speeding*) to demonstrate the use of an infinitive of purpose and write it on the board.

➤ Have students complete the exercise individually and then check answers with a partner. Review as a class.

B. Vocabulary...

➤ Working individually, students complete the sentences and check answers with a partner.

➤ Review the answers as a class before having students read their completed sentences out loud.

➤ Discuss the choices in item 2 and elicit or point out that *cop* and *officer* have the same meaning but are very different in tone. Make sure students understand that *cop* is an informal term. It is not appropriate to address a police officer as *cop*.

Challenge: Assign one sentence to each pair of students. Have partners work together to create a conversation that contains that sentence. Ask volunteers to read their conversations in front of the class.

Challenge: Ask pairs of students to create sentences for each of the unused phrases or words. Have them share their sentences with another pair or small group.

If your students are ready...

Culture / Civics note: In some areas, drivers who commit moving violations earn points. In a point system, each moving violation is assigned a certain number of points. If a driver gets more than a certain number of points in a given time (typically eight to twelve points over three years), the driver's license is suspended for a period of time. Moving violations are assigned different numbers of points, depending on the severity of the violation. Students need to be aware of how moving violations can result in the loss of their licenses. If appropriate, help students get information from your state's Department of Motor Vehicles.

T34

Procedure:

🎧 C. Listen...

➤ Read each item in the tapescript out loud or play the cassette as many times as necessary for students to complete the exercise. If students have difficulty, prompt them by reading the response yourself.

➤ Review the answers before having students read their responses out loud.

Challenge: Use the items in the tapescript as a dictation. Have students listen to the items and write what they hear. Allow students to listen as many times as necessary. Ask volunteers to write the questions on the board. Make corrections as a class. Students can then practice the prompts and responses with a partner.

D–E.

➤ Students complete the exercise individually and then compare responses with a partner.

➤ Partners read the items and responses, switching roles for more practice.

Option: After both students have practiced reading the items and responses in Exercise D, have Partner B in each pair close his or her book. Partner A then reads each item, and Partner B responds from memory.

Challenge: Have pairs of students work together to write a statement or a question for each unused response in Exercise D. For example, in item 2, a question that could elicit the response *To get to the bank* might be *Why were you speeding?* Have students take turns reading their new items and responses.

➤ Do it yourself!

(For general suggestions, see *Introduction*, page Txiii.)

Procedure:

A. Write your own response...

➤ Tell students to imagine that the police officer in the pictures has just pulled them over for a traffic violation. Have students read the speech balloons and write an appropriate response to each one.

➤ Remind students that they can refer to the model conversation on page 30 or to the picture story on page 34 for help in responding.

➤ Before students practice with a partner, have a volunteer play the part of the police officer and read each speech balloon aloud. Respond to each statement for yourself, giving students an opportunity to check the appropriateness of their responses. Remind students of the importance of appropriate, respectful behavior in a traffic stop.

➤ Have students interview each other in pairs to check their responses.

B. Culture talk...

➤ Put students in small groups, trying to include people from different cultures in each group.

➤ Ask one student in each group to be the facilitator, one to be the recorder, and one to be the reporter. Elicit or tell students what each role involves: the facilitator asks questions and encourages everyone to talk, the recorder takes notes of the group's discussion, and the reporter tells the class about the discussion. When students have an active role in the discussion, they are more likely to be involved.

➤ Circulate and offer help as necessary.

➤ Have reporters tell the class about the discussions.

Option: Write the names of the countries represented in the class across the top of the board. Down the left side write *traffic violations, penalties, appropriate responses.* Have one student from each group fill in the columns on the board. You may have a chart like this one following:

	Mexico	**Somalia**	**Vietnam**	**Russia**
Traffic violations				
Penalties				
Appropriate responses				

Tapescript

1. Hand over your license and registration, please.

2. Are you aware how fast you were going?

3. Are you in a big hurry to get somewhere?

4. I'll let you off easy with just a warning this time. Next time it's a ticket and points.

🎧 **C.** Listen. Read each response out loud from the text on page 34.

D. Read each sentence or question. Underline your response.

1. "Do you know why I pulled you over?"

   YOU <u>Yes, officer. I was speeding.</u>   **YOU** Yes, officer. To clock me.

2. "Are you aware how fast you were going?"

   YOU To get to the bank.   **YOU** <u>Actually, no. I'm sorry.</u>

3. "Being in a hurry is no excuse."

   YOU <u>I know. You're right.</u>   **YOU** As a matter of fact.

4. "I'm going to let you off easy this time."

   YOU <u>I really appreciate it, officer.</u>   **YOU** It was just a fender bender.

5. "Be careful when you pull out. "

   YOU I sideswiped the car.   **YOU** <u>I will. Thanks for the warning.</u>

E. Pair work. Take turns reading the items and responses in Exercise D.

➤ Do it yourself!

A. Write your own response. Then read the conversation out loud with a partner.

 I'm going to have to see your license and registration.   **YOU** _____

 You were tailgating, and then you didn't signal your right turn.   **YOU** _____

 You got off easy this time. Next time you might not be so lucky.   **YOU** _____

B. Culture talk. In the country you come from, what are some traffic violations? What are the penalties for committing them? What do you say to a police officer who stops you? Compare cultures with your classmates.

Authentic practice

Aggressive driving and road rage

🎧 **A.** Listening comprehension. Listen to the panel discussion.

B. Discussion. Answer the question. Then discuss with the class.

What's the difference between aggressive driving and road rage? _(Answers may vary.)_

_____

🎧 **C.** Listen to the panel discussion again. Check the advice given to help people avoid the consequences of road rage.

1. ☐ Get angry.
2. ☑ Step back from your anger.
3. ☐ Go to the Behavior Management Institute.

4. ☐ Control others.
5. ☑ Recognize you can't control others.
6. ☑ Don't take things personally.

D. Look at the examples of aggressive driving.

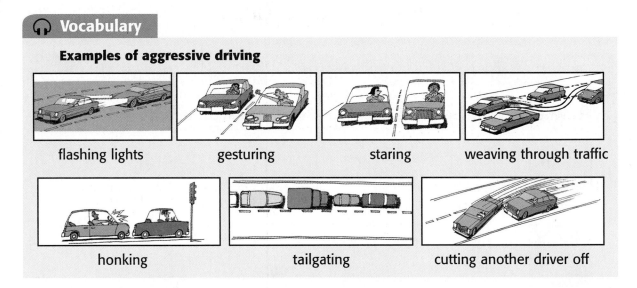

🎧 **Vocabulary**

Examples of aggressive driving

flashing lights　　gesturing　　staring　　weaving through traffic

honking　　tailgating　　cutting another driver off

E. Discussion. What's your reaction to aggressive driving?

I honk back!

I don't do anything. It's not worth looking for trouble.

I don't take it personally.

Authentic practice

(For general suggestions, see *Introduction*, page Tx.)

Aggressive driving and road rage

Procedure:

➤ Have students read the bar. Brainstorm ideas about the two terms. Write ideas on the board.

➤ Lead a discussion about the students' experiences with aggressive driving and/or road rage by asking questions such as *Have you ever been in a situation where another driver did something that made you angry? What did the other driver do? How did you respond?*

A–B.

➤ Have students read the question.

➤ Read the tapescript out loud or play the cassette as many times as necessary for students to complete the exercise.

➤ Students work individually to write an answer to the question. When students have finished, elicit the difference between the two terms according to the selection. (*Aggressive driving* is cutting other drivers off, excessive honking, and other behaviors that can be dangerous. *Road rage* is a driver's behavior that purposely results in injury to another driver, to a pedestrian, or to another driver's car.)

➤ Refer to the list of students' ideas about the two terms that you wrote on the board earlier. Check how closely their ideas resemble the descriptions in the selection.

C. Listen to the panel discussion...

➤ Read the six pieces of advice. Tell students to listen to the advice the panel gives and check the advice the panelists offer.

➤ Read the tapescript or play the cassette again so students can check the advice as they hear it.

➤ Read the tapescript or play the cassette again so students can confirm their responses. Have students compare answers with a partner.

D. Look at the examples...

Vocabulary

➤ Put students in pairs or small groups. Make sure they know the examples of aggressive driving given in the panel discussion. Brainstorm other examples and write them on the board.

➤ Read the examples of aggressive driving or play the cassette, and ask students to point to the pictures.

➤ Read the examples or play the cassette again and have students repeat the phrases.

➤ Refer to the list of examples students brainstormed earlier and check those that are included in the *Vocabulary*.

Option: To review gerunds as subjects and as objects of verbs, ask students to use the examples of aggressive driving in the *Vocabulary* box to complete these sentences.

1. _____ really annoys me.
2. I really hate _____.

Ask volunteers to share their sentences with the class.

E. Discussion...

➤ If necessary, review the examples of aggressive driving given in the panel discussion, in the list on the board, and in the *Vocabulary*. Ask students which of the speakers at the bottom of the page best express their own reactions.

➤ Have students discuss their reactions with a partner or a group. Students can use these questions as discussion starters: *Which behavior makes you angry? How do you respond?*

Tapescript

Jessica: This is Jessica Mondale. Welcome to "Driving Smart." Today's segment deals with a serious subject that many of us have to confront on a daily basis: Aggressive driving and road rage. Today's panel of experts includes Dr. James Levin, senior administrator of the Behavior Management Institute. The institute specializes in teaching drivers to stay cool when traffic gets hot. Welcome, Dr. Levin.

Levin: Thanks, Jessica.

Jessica: Next is Jane Taylor, author of *When Good Drivers Go Bad,* a self-help encyclopedia of coping skills for driving in heavy traffic. Hello, Jane.

Jane: Hello, Jessica.

Jessica: And our third expert today is Detective Clarence Breen of the Rapid City Traffic Enforcement Department. Welcome to all of you. Let's start with Detective Breen. Detective Breen, has Rapid City been experiencing a rise in aggressive driving incidents recently? It seems that everyone has a terrible story to tell.

Breen: Yes, Jessica, I'm afraid so. Just yesterday, we had two complaints, one quite serious, that I would describe more as road rage than as aggressive driving.

(Tapescript is continued on page T37.)

Tapescript (*continued from page T36*)

Jessica: What exactly is the difference between aggressive driving and road rage?

Breen: Aggressive driving is just that: cutting other drivers off, excessive honking, pulling out in front of another driver, cutting into a lane too close to the front of another car, et cetera. Aggressive driving is also the cause of a lot of accidents. Aggressive drivers get too close to other drivers, *and* they're unpredictable. Especially in heavy, fast traffic, the consequences of aggressive driving can be catastrophic.

Jessica: And road rage? Dr. Levin, I'll let you tackle that one.

Levin: Road rage describes a driver's behavior that purposely results in injury to another driver, to a pedestrian, or to another driver's car. These are the cases we read about in the newspaper and see on the nightly news. A driver gets angry at another driver or a pedestrian for some real or imagined cause and then yells, or worse, purposely slams into the other driver's back bumper. There's actually been a case of an argument between two drivers leading to one driver's running over another driver. We've even heard of shootings and stabbings. People need to step back from their anger and control themselves.

Jessica: Ms. Taylor, what can drivers do to avoid getting carried away with their anger when faced with other drivers who are aggressive or incompetent?

Taylor: I'm glad you asked me that question, Jessica, since that's the subject of my book, *When Good Drivers Go Bad,* published by Lyman and Bluster, and which you can receive by calling 1-800-DRIVERS, and …

Jessica: Ms. Taylor. What can an angry driver do to calm down?

Taylor: Yes, of course. Well, in my book, I have a three-step program for avoiding the road rage trap.

First: Recognize that you have no control over other drivers, only over yourself.

Second: Don't take others' driving personally. They don't even know who you are.

Third: Get a life. Driving is not life: It's just a way to get somewhere.

Breen: And if I might break in—don't forget the serious legal consequences of road rage. Assault is a felony, and the law takes it very seriously.

Jessica: That's very good advice. And that's all for today's segment of "Driving Smart." This is Jessica Mondale, wishing you happy driving and saying thank you to today's panelists. Until next week!

➤ Do it yourself!

(For general suggestions, see *Introduction*, page Txiii.)

Procedure:

A–B.

➤ Have students read the survey introduction and directions silently. Ask volunteers to read each of the 12 "hot-button" behaviors aloud. Explain *"hot-button" behaviors* and any other unfamiliar terms.

➤ Model the activity by writing the first item on the board, followed by numbers 1, 2, 3. Read the item aloud and circle the number that corresponds to your reaction: 1 for not bothered, 2 for annoyed, 3 for very angry. Tell students *Tailgating to make others go faster or get out of the way doesn't bother me (or annoys me or makes me very angry).*

➤ Students work individually to complete the survey about their attitudes. If students are not drivers, let them answer as passengers. Have students total their score.

➤ Write the numbers 12 through 36 on the board. Beginning with 12, read each number out loud. Ask students to raise their hands when they hear the number that represents their score. Put the corresponding tally mark or marks next to each number. Group the scores into three categories (12–23, 24–29, 30–36).

➤ Have students read the box at the bottom of the page. Make sure students understand the expression *cool as a cucumber.* Ask which students are "cool as a cucumber," "let others have power," or need to "calm down."

Note: The list of commonly misspelled words on page 144 warns students not to make the word *behavior* plural. This word is rarely seen in the plural. It is almost always used as a non-count noun.

C. Culture talk...

➤ Put students in small groups to answer the questions. Try to have students from different cultures in each group.

Option: Call a local police station and ask if a community or public relations officer is available to talk to your class about driving issues. Have pairs or groups of students prepare questions in advance and take notes during the officer's visit.

A. Complete the magazine survey about driver attitudes.

What's your driving anger quotient?

The National Highway Transportation Safety Administration estimates that aggressive driving has caused **2.28 million accidents** and **27,935 deaths** in the past five years. Aggressive driving is often a response to feeling stress and getting angry at the driving of others.

How do these behaviors affect you?
Rate each behavior on a scale of 1 to 3.

1 = not bothered	2 = annoyed	3 = very angry

Circle the number after each behavior.

HOT-BUTTON BEHAVIORS

		1	2	3
1.	Tailgating to make others go faster or get out of the way	1	2	3
2.	Flashing lights to signal others to move to another lane	1	2	3
3.	Making hand gestures at others	1	2	3
4.	Weaving in and out of traffic	1	2	3
5.	Honking excessively	1	2	3
6.	Driving too slowly in the passing lane so no one can pass	1	2	3
7.	Staring angrily at another driver	1	2	3
8.	Cutting people off	1	2	3
9.	Slowing down after passing someone	1	2	3
10.	Trying to beat a yellow light that's about to turn red	1	2	3
11.	Not making a right turn in the right-hand turn lane	1	2	3
12.	Not reacting quickly after the red light turns green	1	2	3

Total your score.

What your score means	
30-36:	Calm down. Life is shorter than you think.
24-29:	Don't let the behavior of others have power over you.
12-23:	You're cool as a cucumber.

B. **Collaborative activity. Compile the scores of all the students in the class.**

C. **Culture talk. How do people feel about these behaviors in the country you come from? Does driving behavior differ from country to country? Compare cultures.**

Driving by the Golden Rule

🎧 A. Read and listen to the letters.

Ask Joan

Culture tips for newcomers

Dear Joan:
The other day I was driving out of a parking lot and my baby was in the back seat. She threw down her bottle, and for a second I was distracted. I reached back to get her bottle and I bumped a little into another car. It was just a soft bump, but I was afraid to stop to look, Joan, so I drove away. I don't have a lot of money and every little scratch and dent costs so much to fix. My wife said I did the wrong thing. She told me to think how angry I would be if someone hit my car and caused damage and didn't leave a name and phone number for me to call. What do you think?

Clarence in Claremont

Dear Clarence:
I'm with your wife on this one. And so is the law. It's against the law to leave the scene of an accident, even a small one, if there is any property damage. But over and above the law, put yourself in the shoes of the owner of the car and you will understand why leaving was wrong. There's nothing you can do now, but let this be a lesson to you and to all my readers.

Joan

Dear Joan:
Last week I saw a car parked on the shoulder of the road and it looked like the driver might be sick. I wanted to stop to help him, but a passenger in my car said I would just be looking for trouble. He told me that if I stopped to help and the man died or something else bad happened, that his family could go to court to sue me. Joan, it seems like everybody in this country wants to go to court to sue someone! I didn't stop, but I still feel bad about it.

Lucille from Louisiana

Dear Lucille:
If you see a person in imminent danger of dying, and your actions could save that person's life, you should not be afraid to stop and help.

The laws everywhere protect "Good Samaritans" from being sued under such circumstances. Under more normal circumstances, however, where there is no immediate danger of death, the best advice is to call 911 from a car phone or from the most convenient public or emergency phone. In that way, trained medical personnel will arrive quickly.

Remember, though, the courts expect people to behave with common sense. No one expects you to be a doctor or to have medical training. It's always best to drive (and live!) by the Golden Rule: Treat others as you wish others to treat you.

Joan

B. Read the letters again. Then answer the questions.

1. Why didn't Clarence stop? _It might cost money to fix the other car._

2. What did Lucille see? _a car parked on the shoulder, driver might be sick_

3. Why didn't she stop? _She didn't want to be sued._

4. What is the Golden Rule? _Treat others as you wish others to treat you._

C. Pair work. What advice would you give to each driver? Compare advice with a partner.

Uh-oh. I might have sideswiped that parked car. I don't think anything happened, though. And anyway, the owner isn't there.

Look at the woman in that parked car over there. Do you think there's something wrong? She's got her head down on the wheel.

YOU _____

YOU _____

Authentic practice

(For general suggestions, see *Introduction,* page Tx.)

Driving by the Golden Rule

Procedure:

⌒A–B.

➤ Have students read along silently while you read the letters or play the cassette.

➤ Some words and phrases may be unfamiliar to students: *I'm with your wife, over and above, put yourself in the shoes, let this be a lesson to you, common sense, Golden Rule.* Make sure students understand how these expressions are used.

➤ Working individually, students answer the questions and then compare answers with a partner.

Option: Have students practice focused listening by doing this activity. Write the following list of words from the advice letters on the board: *baby, parking lot, court, bottle, bumped, threw, leave, scratch, dent, damage, wife, law, shoes, shoulder, passenger, family, life, advice, phone, doctor, reached, think, understand, stop, help, behave, sick.* Draw a four by four grid and tell students to create their own grids on a separate sheet of paper. Ask students to choose 16 words from the list and write one word in each of the 16 boxes in their grid, in any order they choose. Tell students that they will not use every word. Have students listen to the letters with books closed. Every time they hear a word in their grid, they should put a check in that box. The goal is to check all of their boxes. After students have listened to the letters once, find out who checked the most boxes.

Option: To boost academic skills, have students express Joan's advice in their own words.

C. Pair work...

➤ Have students read the speech balloons and work individually to write advice.

➤ Put students in pairs and ask them to take turns reading the speech balloons and responding with their advice.

➤ Circulate and offer help as needed. If students are having trouble, model the exercise with a student. The student reads the driver's speech balloon and you give the driver advice.

➤ Have volunteers read their advice aloud. Ask the class which advice is best and why.

D. Read...

➤ Remind students of the magazine article they read at the beginning of the unit. Review the equipment responsible drivers should have in the car (a flashlight with working batteries, a spare tire, a jack, flares, jumper cables).

➤ Elicit from students the other items that they now know they should have in the car. If necessary, prompt by asking *What do you need to show if you are stopped by a police officer?* (the car registration, your driver's license) *What else do you need if you have an accident?* (an insurance card)

➤ Have students open their books and read the entire article, paying special attention to the section headed "Must haves." Explain that *damages* is a legal term meaning an amount of money. It is not used here as an ordinary non-count noun. Tell students that they already know the information presented in the article.

➤ Be sure students observe the infinitives of purpose in the "should haves" and "must haves" sections of the article.

Challenge: Discuss the difference between *should* (advisable, a good idea) and *must* (necessary, a requirement). Ask students to make a chart of things they should do and things they must do as good drivers or responsible community members. Have them explain why they must do these things using an infinitive of purpose. Their chart may look like the following:

I should	(because)	I must	(because)
pay my bills on time	to avoid a late fee.	get a driver's license	to drive here legally.

When students have completed their charts, have them read their sentences to a partner.

E. Critical thinking...

➤ Students should first identify the objects in each trunk and then decide what equipment is missing based on the "should haves" self-check in the article in Exercise D. Then have them work individually and write the missing equipment on the line.

➤ Put students in pairs to compare answers and make sure that each list includes all five "should have" items mentioned in the article. If any items are still missing, have students scan the article again.

➤ Do it yourself!

(For general suggestions, see *Introduction*, page Txiii.)

Procedure:

A–B.

➤ Have students read the list of topics and choose one that they would like to talk about.

➤ Put students in small groups. Tell them to make sure their true stories include answers to the questions *What was the problem? What happened? What was the solution?* Give them a few minutes to plan what they're going to say. Encourage them to make notes of specific details they want to include.

➤ Circulate and offer help as needed. If students are having difficulty, you may want to model the activity by telling a true car story of your own.

Challenge: Have students write their true car story. They should explain the problem and what happened but not write the solution. Students exchange papers with a partner who then writes advice about how to solve the problem.

D. Read the car equipment safety checklist from *Road Talk Magazine*.

THE RESPONSIBLE DRIVER

Emergencies can happen at a moment's notice and can turn deadly in an instant. We can't plan for emergencies, but we can be equipped to handle them. This month, the Responsible Driver examines what you should have in your car at all times. Better safe than sorry!

"Should haves" self-check

Check the items you have in your car right now. Then get the ones you don't have ASAP! Common sense requires that you have these items in your car in case of a breakdown or in case you have to assist another driver in need.

- ❑ a flashlight with working batteries—keep some spares!
- ❑ a spare tire—to replace a flat tire
- ❑ a jack—to change the tire
- ❑ flares—to warn oncoming traffic that you are stopped
- ❑ jumper cables—to start a car with a dead battery

"Must haves"

And don't forget these! The law requires that you have these items in your car in case of an accident or a police stop.

- ❑ car registration—to establish the name of the owner of the car and the state the car is registered in
- ❑ insurance card—to provide to any driver whose car you might have damaged, to show who to contact about the damages
- ❑ your valid driver's license—of course!

E. Critical thinking. Look in the trunk of each car. What should the driver get?

Get today: _____   Get today: _____

➤ Do it yourself!

A. True story. Tell a true car story to your partner or your group. Choose one of these topics:

- an accident
- a ticket
- an experience with an aggressive driver or road rage
- a problem with a car
- car equipment

B. Discussion. What was the problem? What happened? What was the solution?

Review

A. Pair work or group work.

- What is happening?
- What are the people doing?

Ask and answer questions.

Create conversations.

Tell a story.

Say as much as you can.

Review

(For general suggestions, see *Introduction*, page Txii.)

Procedure:

A. Pair work or group work.

Ask and answer questions.

➤ Ask general questions about the picture, such as *What is the police officer doing?* (writing a ticket) *What is the driver doing?* (giving the officer her license and registration) *What's the problem with the yellow car on the left?* (a flat tire, no spare tire or jack)

➤ Ask *What examples of aggressive driving do you see in the picture?* (flashing lights, weaving, honking, gesturing, using a cell phone while driving, tailgating)

Option: Have students write a question about the picture and its answer on two separate slips of paper. Collect all the slips and distribute either a question or an answer to each student. Have students walk around the room, asking and answering questions until they have their match.

Create conversations.

➤ Have the students look at the two people in the traffic stop at the top of the page. Play the role of the police officer and have a more advanced student come to the front of the class and play the role of the driver. Initiate a conversation; for example, say *I'm going to have to give you a ticket for not stopping at a stop sign.* If necessary, the class can help the student playing the role of the driver to respond. Continue the conversation as long as possible, with each of you making a tally mark on the board every time you speak. When finished, count the marks.

➤ In pairs, have students create conversations for the people with a flat tire and keep track of how many times they speak. Explain that the goal is to say as much as they can. Have pairs count their tally marks and report how many times they spoke.

Option: Have pairs create a third conversation between one of the drivers in the picture and a friend. In the conversation, the driver should tell the friend about a problem they had on the road. The friend should ask questions, express concern, and give advice.

Tell a story.

➤ Have a student time you while you talk about the picture for one minute. Then, put students in pairs or small groups and have each student talk about the picture for one minute. Encourage students to describe each of the scenes in the picture and to say as much as they can. Tell students to continue talking until you say *Stop,* indicating that the minute is up.

B. Listening comprehension ...

➤ Tell students that they are going to hear a conversation between a father and his teenage daughter. Have students read the list of equipment and identify the "should have" items (items 4 through 8). Ask students to speculate which items they think the daughter's car has and which she needs.

➤ After students listen to the conversation the first time, ask questions such as *Where is the daughter going?* (to a concert) *Does the daughter have a spare tire?* (no) *Why doesn't she have a spare?* (The tires are new, nothing's going to happen to them.) *Why does she carry jumper cables?* (One of her friends always needs a jump.)

➤ Have students read the list of equipment and listen again to complete the exercise. Discuss whether students' speculations were accurate.

Challenge: Divide the class into two teams. Ask the teams to listen to the conversation again and then to create comprehension questions. The two teams alternate asking and answering questions. Keep score on the board of the correct answers for each team.

C–D.

➤ Students work individually to complete the review exercises.

➤ Circulate to offer help as needed.

➤ Have students check answers with a partner. Review answers as a class.

➤ Identify any areas of difficulty that may require additional instruction and practice.

Tapescript

Father: I don't believe you're going to drive all the way to the concert in this car!

Daughter: What's wrong?

Father: What's wrong? What *isn't* wrong? Didn't you take driver's ed? Didn't you pass the driver's test? Doesn't it occur to you that something can go wrong? You're just looking for trouble.

Daughter: Calm down. You're ridiculous. What's going to go wrong?

Father: Did you ever hear of a flat tire?

Daughter: But these tires are brand new. Nothing's going to happen to them!

Father: It's just common sense to have a spare. And what about a jack? Of course, if you have no tire, you certainly don't need a jack.

Daughter: You are *so* ridiculous. Nothing's going to go wrong. Take it easy!

Father: You wait until you have children. Then you'll understand. Let's go through the checklist.

Daughter: Oh, come *on*. I've got to go.

Father: Young lady, you're not going anywhere until I'm sure you have the minimum of equipment in case there's a problem. Ready?

Daughter: Oh, all right.

Father: License?

Daughter: Yup.

Father: Registration and insurance card?

Daughter: Yup, yup.

Father: Spare tire? Get that from the garage, ASAP. And we have a spare jack in Mom's car. Get that too.

Daughter: Yes, *sir*.

[pause, door slamming]

Daughter: OK. Bye, Dad. See you on Sunday.

Father: What about a flashlight?

Daughter: Yes.

Father: Flares?

Daughter: You are paranoid. You need help.

Father: Flares?

Daughter: Yes. What else? I'm going to be late.

Father: I saw the jumper cables. Congratulations!

Daughter: Yeah. Well, one of my friends always needs a jump.

B. Listening comprehension. Listen to the conversation between a father and his teenage daughter. Check the equipment they have and the equipment they need.

	They have	They need
1. License	☑	☐
2. Registration	☑	☐
3. Insurance card	☑	☐
4. Spare tire	☐	☑
5. Jack	☐	☑
6. Flashlight	☑	☐
7. Flares	☑	☐
8. Jumper cables	☑	☐

C. Read each sentence or question. Underline your response.

1. "Do you know why I pulled you over?"

   YOU No, thank goodness.   **YOU** I think I was tailgating.

2. "You were speeding. I clocked you at 84."

   YOU You're right. I was going a little fast.   **YOU** Take it easy.

3. "You're getting off easy this time. Next time it's a ticket and points."

   YOU That's no excuse.   **YOU** I appreciate it, officer.

4. "Leave yourself a little extra time so you won't have to speed."

   YOU That's a good idea.   **YOU** Be careful when you pull out.

D. Complete each sentence with the name of the equipment.

jumper cables	spare	jack	registration	flare

1. You need a _____jack_____ to change a flat tire.

2. If you have a flat tire, you need to replace it with a _____spare_____.

3. When you have an accident and are stopped on the side of the road, protect yourself from other motorists by lighting a _____flare_____.

4. Be sure to carry _____jumper cables_____ to help start a car that has a dead battery.

5. Two important documents that you should always have with you when you drive are an insurance card and the car's _____registration_____.

E. Read about the equipment. Then complete each sentence with a phrase using an infinitive of purpose.

> 🎧 **Vocabulary**
>
> **Emergency use of equipment**
>
> a flashlight—**helps you look under the hood in the dark**
>
> a blanket—**keeps you warm if you break down on a cold night**
>
> a cell phone—**enables you to call for service in an emergency**
>
> a map—**helps you find places when you don't have directions**
>
> an auto club membership—**provides free or inexpensive emergency road service**

1. I have a flashlight _to help me look under the hood in the dark_ .

2. I have a blanket _to keep me warm if I break down on a cold night_ .

3. I have a cell phone _to call for service in an emergency_ .

4. I have maps _to help me find places when I don't have directions_ .

5. I belong to an auto club _to provide (or to get) free or inexpensive emergency road service_ .

F. Complete the sentences with gerunds.

1. I got a ticket for not _____stopping_____ at the light.
                              stop

2. I can't stand aggressive _____driving_____ .
                              drive

3. The subject of the magazine article is _____avoiding_____ road rage.
                                            avoid

4. _____Controlling_____ others' behavior is impossible.
     Control

G. Composition. On a separate sheet of paper, write about the picture on page 40.

> **Now I can**
> ❏ respond appropriately to a police officer in a traffic stop.
> ❏ describe an accident.
> ❏ understand traffic violations.
> ❏ avoid aggressive driving and road rage.
> ❏ drive by the Golden Rule.
> ❏ understand what equipment is needed in a car.

E–F.

⌒Vocabulary

➤ Read aloud the items in *Vocabulary* box or play the cassette. Have students repeat each item.

➤ Model item 1 in Exercise E to demonstrate that students will have to modify the phrases in the *Vocabulary* when they write infinitives of purpose, changing the pronoun *you* to *me.* Write on the board *I have a flashlight* and ask students what purposes it might serve. Answers may include *to read a map, to look in the glove compartment, to find something under the seat.* List the answers on the board, underlining the infinitives of purpose. Complete item 1: *to help me look under the hood in the dark.*

➤ Students work individually to complete the review exercises.

➤ Circulate to offer help as needed.

➤ Have students check answers with a partner. Review answers as a class.

➤ Identify any areas of difficulty that may require additional instruction and practice.

G. Composition . . .

➤ Provide students with concrete approaches to writing about the picture on page 40. Use one of the options that follow, give students a choice of options, or assign options based on students' levels of proficiency. Model what is expected of students for each option.

➤ Advise students to look back through the unit for help and ideas as they write.

➤ Circulate to offer help as needed.

Option: Have students choose one of the pairs of people who are talking to each other in the picture, label them *A* and *B,* and write an extended conversation for them. Students can later role-play their conversations for the class.

Option: Have students look at the traffic violations in the picture and then write two sentences about each driver's dangerous behavior. To reinforce the grammar in the unit, one sentence should tell something about the violation using a gerund.

Option: Tell students to focus on the equipment shown in the scenes with the police officer and the flat tire. Have them create a car safety equipment checklist and add any missing equipment. To reinforce the grammar in the unit, have students write about car equipment using infinitives of purpose.

Challenge: Have students write an *Ask Joan* letter from the driver receiving the ticket. Advise students to include the driver's name, length of time in this country, the reason for the traffic stop, and how drivers would respond to such a traffic stop in their home countries.

Now I can

➤ Read the first item in the box out loud: *Now I can respond appropriately to a police officer in a traffic stop.* Elicit from the class an example of how to respond appropriately; for example, a student could say *I should be polite and apologize for my mistake.*

➤ Put students in pairs and have them take turns reading each item in the box and giving an example of what they have learned. When students can provide an example, they should check that box. For the items students weren't able to check, they should look back through the unit for ideas.

➤ When students are finished reviewing with their partners, read each item out loud and elicit an example from the class.

Oral test (optional)

You may want to use the *Now I can box* as an informal evaluation. While students are working on the *Composition* activity, you can call them up individually and check their ability with two or three objectives.

UNIT 4

Your customers

 Preview

(For general suggestions, see *Introduction*, page Tviii.)

Note: For the activity on page 51, students should bring in phone books and travel ads. If possible, you should also bring in travel ads.

Warm up. Do you believe this offer is true? Explain your answer.

Procedure:

➤ Direct students' attention to the illustration and encourage critical thinking by asking questions such as *Is the envelope sent by a business or an individual?* (business) *How can you tell?* (There is a printed message in the return address space, the postage is metered, the envelope has an address window.) *What is the letter about?* (a dream vacation) *How does the letter get people interested in the offer?* (by saying the recipient has been specially selected, by promising a spectacular luxury vacation)

➤ Point out that offers for vacation packages often use exaggerated adjectives such as *spectacular*.

➤ Ask students if they think the offer is true. Have them explain their reasoning in small groups.

➤ Access students' experience by asking *Have you ever received an offer like this one?* Ask students to use their personal experience in their answer to the *Warm up* question.

Option: Point out the ways this vacation offer tries to capture the consumer's interest. The flyer uses all capital letters and an exclamation mark to emphasize the message. The picture is designed to make the recipient think of a luxurious pampered vacation. In small groups, have students discuss ways that a flyer can attract business. Then have students draft the text for a special vacation offer and think of an appropriate picture.

Option: Working in pairs, students sort pairs of adjectives into two classes, plain and more exaggerated. Use this list or create your own: *funny, hilarious; interesting, exciting; great, stupendous; unusual, phenomenal; big, gigantic; happy, ecstatic; unexpected, incredible*. Ask what kind of adjectives they used in their group's vacation offer and why.

Unit 4 objectives

Procedure:

➤ Read the objectives. Discuss any unfamiliar vocabulary.

➤ Point out the word *service* in the first two objectives. Ask students *What is service?* (doing something to help others) *What are some service industries?* (hospitality, food, health care, retail) *Do any of you work in service industries? What kinds of qualities are necessary in a service worker?* (courtesy, responsibility, people skills, attention to detail, trying to please the customer)

➤ Have students read the objectives again. Ask *What service industry do you think this unit will focus on?* (hospitality, hotel, travel) Ask students to put a check next to the objectives that they can do now and circle those they want to work on most.

Your customers

➤ **Preview**

Warm up. Do you believe this offer is true? Explain your answer.

Unit 4 objectives

- Request service and respond to requests for service.
- Make and respond to complaints about bad service.
- Make and guarantee hotel reservations.
- Check in at a hotel.
- Evaluate offers for vacation packages.
- Protect yourself against travel fraud.

Practical conversations

A. Listen and read.

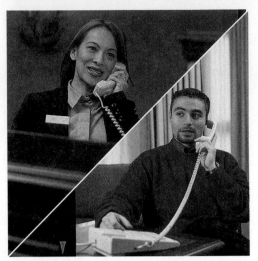

A: Front desk. May I help you?

B: Hello. This is Mr. Hasan in Room 403.
    Would it be possible to get an ironing board?

A: Absolutely, Mr. Hasan. Right away. Is there
    anything else?

B: Actually, I could use some extra towels too.

A: Sure, no problem.

B. Pronunciation and intonation practice.

Vocabulary

Hotel room amenities

an ironing board   a pillow   hangers   towels

a sewing kit   a shower cap   glasses

C. Pair work. Ask the front desk to send you something you need. Use the items in the vocabulary and in the box, or other items you would like.

shampoo	conditioner	a sewing kit	washcloths
soap	lotion	a shower cap	glasses

A: Front desk. ____1____?

B: Hello. This is _____ in Room _____. Would it be possible to get _____?

A: Absolutely, _____. Right away. Is there anything else?

B: Actually, I could use _____ too.

A: ____2____.

[1]Can I help you?

[2]OK, no problem, Of course, Right away

Practical conversations

(For general suggestions, see *Introduction*, page Tviii.)

Model 1

Content: asking for service, responding to a request, hotel room amenities, *some* to describe an indefinite number

Procedure:

⌒A–B.

➤ To set the scene for the conversation, direct students' attention to the split photo on the right and ask questions such as *Who do you see in the picture?* (a man and a woman on the phone, a hotel worker and a hotel guest on the phone) *Who is the hotel employee? How do you know?* (the woman, she is wearing a uniform and a name plate) *What is her expression?* (She is smiling.)

➤ After students listen to the conversation, check comprehension by asking *What is the guest's name?* (Mr. Hasan) *What does he need?* (an ironing board and some extra towels) *What are some expressions of politeness and helpfulness that the hotel employee uses?* (May I help you? Absolutely. Right away. Is there anything else? Sure, no problem.)

➤ Point out that *extra* means additional. The ironing board is not extra because there is none in the room.

Option: Tell students that intonation is very important in conveying meaning and emotion. Read the hotel employee's first line to convey polite helpfulness, as it was said on the cassette. Then read it again in a bored, monotonous way. Put students in pairs to read the conversation again, with each student alternating in the role of the employee. The first time, students should read in a bored, monotonous tone. The second time, they should read with expression. Have them exaggerate both styles. Ask volunteers to read in front of the class.

⌒Vocabulary

➤ After students listen to and repeat the hotel room amenities, explain *skirt hangers*, if necessary.

➤ Brainstorm other amenities found in a hotel room or offered at the front desk, such as *a hairdryer, toothpaste, an ice bucket, paper, a pen, a toothbrush, a razor, tea bags.* Write students' ideas on the board.

C. Pair work ...

➤ Have students read the items in the box. Remind them of the list of other amenities on the board.

➤ Model the conversation with a more advanced student. Play the role of Student B to demonstrate substituting any of the items in the box or on the board for *an ironing board* and *some extra towels*.

➤ Have students practice the conversation in pairs, using any of the items in B's two requests.

If your students are ready ...

Language note: The words *may* and *can* are often used interchangeably when offering help: *May I help you? Can I help you?*, although *may* is perhaps seen as a little more polite. We also use both *may* and *can* in making requests: *Can I have some more towels? May I have some more towels?* The most formal way to make a request is *Would it be possible to have some more towels?*

Model 2

Content: complaining about service, responding to complaints about service, hotel services

Procedure:

🎧 A–B.

➤ To set the scene for the conversation, point to the picture and ask questions such as *Who is in this picture?* (a hotel desk clerk and a guest) *Look at the guest's expression. How do you think she is feeling?* (not happy, mad, upset)

➤ After students listen to the conversation, check comprehension by asking questions such as *What is the guest's complaint?* (Her breakfast never came.) *What does the guest want the hotel to do?* (make sure the breakfast doesn't appear on her bill) *What does the hotel employee do?* (apologize)

➤ Note that hotel employees may say *Please accept our apologies* because they are speaking on behalf of the hotel staff. If necessary, explain the meaning of the expression *make that up to you* (repair the damage, set something right).

🎧 Vocabulary

➤ Ask students why people go to hotels. Elicit examples such as *for lodging on trips, for meetings or conferences, for special events, to go out to eat.* In small groups, have students discuss the features that might be important for each function. Have them create a chart like the one following.

Note: This discussion can serve as an introduction to the *Do it yourself!* activity, or it can take place later as part of that activity.

Lodging	Meetings	Special events	Dining
Comfortable beds	Good equipment	Large rooms	Good food

➤ Play the cassette or read the hotel services and have students repeat the items.

➤ If students are unfamiliar with the audiovisual equipment, explain as necessary.

C. Pair work . . .

➤ Have students read the hotel departments in the box. Brainstorm some service that is provided by each department, such as extra blankets from the housekeeping department. Point out the use of the article with hotel departments: *the gift shop, the front desk,* but *room service* (no article).

➤ Ask students to work in pairs to create sentences with complaints like the one in the conversation; for example, *I ordered <u>a newspaper from the gift shop</u>, and <u>it wasn't delivered</u>.* Review the sentences and ask volunteers to put examples on the board.

➤ Still in pairs, students create a resolution for their complaint sentences; for example, *Please make sure I get one tomorrow.* Elicit resolutions and write them on the board next to the complaints.

➤ Model the conversation with a more advanced student. Play the role of Student A to demonstrate how to complain about a problem and suggest a resolution.

➤ Have students practice the conversation in pairs. Refer them to the complaints and resolutions on the board.

➤ Do it yourself!

(For general suggestions, see *Introduction*, page Txiii.)

Procedure:

A–B.

➤ Ask students to identify their reason for going to a hotel. (Refer to the discussion and chart in the *Vocabulary* section above.)

➤ Read the list of variables. Make sure students understand that a rating of 1 means that the item is least important to them, while a rating of 5 means it's most important. It is possible for students to give the same rating to more than one variable. Model the activity and give your own rating for each item.

➤ Read aloud the speech balloon. Point out that the man stresses location and explains why it's important to him.

➤ Put students in pairs to discuss their ratings and explain their opinions.

Challenge: To review infinitives of purpose (Unit 3), ask students to hold the following conversation. First have Student A tell which factor is most important in choosing a hotel. Student B then asks why, and Student A responds with an infinitive of purpose. Note that students may have to use their ingenuity to find an appropriate infinitive of purpose. Students' conversations may look like the following:

A: I choose a hotel based on its <u>price</u>.

B: Why?

A: <u>To save money</u>.

T45

A. Listen and read.

A: I have a complaint. I ordered breakfast from room service, and it never came.

B: I'm so sorry. Is there some way we can make that up to you?

A: Well, just make sure it's not on my bill.

B: Of course. And please accept my apology.

B. Pronunciation and intonation practice.

Vocabulary

Hotel services

an overhead projector

a screen

an LCD projector

a VCR

audiovisual equipment

photocopies

a meal

a newspaper

beverages

C. Pair work. Complain about service. Use the hotel departments in the box.

| room service | the business center | the catering department |
| the front desk | the gift shop | the housekeeping department |

A: I have a complaint. I ordered _____ and ____1____.

B: I'm so sorry. Is there some way we can make that up to you?

A: ____2____.

B: ____3____. And please accept my apology.

[1] it was terrible, it was broken, etc.
[2] Please get me another one, etc.
[3] Right away, No problem

➤ Do it yourself!

A. What's important to you in a hotel or motel? Rate the following items from 1 (least important) to 5 (most important).

- price _____
- location _____
- service _____
- amenities _____

I like a hotel near the center of the city because I don't want to spend a lot on taxis.

B. Discussion. Explain your opinions to your partner or your group.

Some and any

> Use *some* and *any* to describe an indefinite amount or number (exact amount or number not known).
> Use *some* in affirmative statements.
>
> They brought us **some** extra soap.
>
> Now we have **some**.
>
> Use *any* in negative statements.
>
> We don't want **any** lotion, and we don't need **any** towels.
>
> They don't have **any**. (*Any* could refer to the lotion or the towels.)
>
> Use *some* or *any* in questions.
>
> Do you need **some** extra cups or shampoo?
>
> Do you need **any** extra cups or shampoo?

A. **Rewrite the affirmative sentences in the negative.**

1. There is some ice in the bucket.

   There isn't any ice in the bucket.

2. There are some towels in the housekeeper's closet.

   There aren't any towels in the housekeeper's closet.

3. We have some extra shampoo for you.

   We don't have any extra shampoo for you.

4. The women need some skirt hangers.

   The women don't need any skirt hangers.

5. She left some luggage at the bell desk.

   She didn't leave any luggage at the bell desk.

6. There's some problem with the phones in their suite.

   There isn't any problem with the phones in their suite.

7. He has some laundry to pick up.

   He doesn't have any laundry to pick up.

8. I need some help with the audiovisual equipment.

   I don't need any help with the audiovisual equipment.

9. Please send some butter up with my breakfast.

   Please don't send any butter up with my breakfast.

Practical grammar

(For general suggestions, see *Introduction*, page Tix.)

Some and *any*

Procedure:

➤ Write on the board *The housekeeping department brought us some extra towels*. Brainstorm other hotel amenities that the housekeeping department might supply, such as *some extra soap, lotion, conditioner; some extra pillows, blankets, glasses*. Write the examples on the board in two lists, one using *some* with non-count nouns and one with count nouns. Underline the word *some* in each sentence.

➤ Ask *How many towels are "some towels"? How much soap is "some soap"?* Elicit or point out that *some* describes an indefinite amount or number. The exact amount or number is not known.

➤ Put the following sentences on the board: *I don't need any lotion, No one has any shampoo, I never use any conditioner, We don't have any towels*. Underline the word *any* in each sentence. Point to the sentences on the board with the word *some*. Elicit from the class or tell students that *some* is used in affirmative statements and *any* is used in negative statements.

➤ Read the information in the box. Have volunteers read the example sentences. Stress that *any* is used with negatives (*not, no one, never*).

Option: Note that *some* and *any* are used with both count and non-count nouns. Have students change the first example sentence in the box to a sentence using a count noun. Refer to the list of hotel amenities generated above.

A. Rewrite the affirmative sentences ...

➤ If necessary, review the formation of the negative in the simple present tense and the simple past tense. Practice with the verb *to be* and other verbs. Make sure students use *do / does / did* where necessary.

➤ Model item 1 of the exercise. Write on the board *There is some ice in the bucket*. Elicit the negative statement and write it on the board: *There isn't any ice in the bucket*. Note that some students will produce *There's no ice in the bucket*. That's also acceptable.

➤ Have students complete the exercise individually and then check answers with a partner. Review as a class and ask volunteers to write the sentences on the board.

Option: Review how to express a polite complaint in a hotel. Write on the board *This is _____ in Room _____ and I don't have any _____*. Play the role of a front desk clerk and say *Front desk. May I help you?* Call on individual students to respond with the completed sentence.

Challenge: Practice the use of *some* and *any* by playing a riddle game. Tell students that they should think of something and give clues about its identity using only sentences with *some* or *any*. Model the activity by describing something yourself: *It has some keys, but it doesn't have any wheels. It has some letters, but it doesn't have any mail. It has some pictures, but it doesn't have any paper. It has some memory, but it doesn't have any feelings.* Have students guess: *a computer*. Give students a few minutes to think of their own object and create *some* and *any* statements, and then ask volunteers to present their riddles to the class.

B. Complete each statement . . .

➤ Have pairs of students read each statement in the exercise and decide if it is affirmative or negative. Ask them to write *A* for affirmative or *N* for negative next to each item.

➤ Elicit from the students or remind the class to use *some* in affirmative statements and *any* in negative statements. Review that questions such as item 5 can use either *some* or *any*.

➤ Have the pairs complete the exercise and then review as a class.

Challenge: In pairs, students create mini-conversations using the items from the exercise as responses or prompts. For example, item 1 could be the response to the question *Would you like some more coffee?* Remind students to use *some* or *any* in their questions. Have volunteers perform their conversations for the class.

C. Write *yes–no* questions . . .

➤ Model the first item. Write the sentence elements on the board and elicit the *yes-no* question from the class. Write *Is there some / any cold food on the menu?*

➤ Have students work individually to complete the exercise and check questions with a partner.

➤ After you review the questions as a class, have volunteers write them on the board.

Option: Have partners take turns reading the questions and answering them.

Challenge: Play the game "Create a character." Ask pairs of students to create a character and imagine a monologue that might end with one of the questions in Exercise C. Model this activity with a character and monologue of your own: *I am an elderly man, and what teeth I have left are very sensitive. I cannot eat any warm or hot food. If I eat hot food, I get a terrific pain in my tooth that shoots up into my head, and I have to lie down. So what I'm asking is . . .* Stop and elicit the question in item 1: *Is there some / any cold food on the menu?* Encourage students to create an interesting character and a detailed monologue. Have students read their characters' monologues and ask the rest of the class to fill in the appropriate question from the exercise.

➤ Do it yourself!

(For general suggestions, see *Introduction*, page Txiii.)

Procedure:

➤ Working individually, students look at the picture and create questions using *Is there, Are there*, and *some* and *any*. Tell students that their questions can elicit *yes* or *no* answers. Give them one minute.

➤ Ask students to close their books. Put students in pairs and have them take turns asking and answering their questions.

Option: Have pairs write all their *yes* answers as a connected paragraph describing the picture. Pairs can then exchange paragraphs and see which pair has included the most details.

Option: After students have created questions and committed the picture to memory, divide the class into two teams. A member of Team A asks a question of a member of Team B. The game continues, with teams alternating questions. A correct answer earns a point for that team.

B. Complete each statement with *some* or *any*.

1. I don't want ___any___ more coffee, thank you.

2. There isn't ___any___ soap in the bathroom.

3. They asked for ___some___ assistance with their luggage.

4. The business center is making ___some___ copies of this flyer.

5. You didn't order ___any___ dessert?

6. It's a shame that there isn't ___any___ cable service in the room.

7. I don't see ___any___ request for breakfast for Room 203.

8. There are ___some___ phone messages for you on the desk.

C. Write *yes–no* questions with *some* or *any*.

1. there is / cold food on the menu / ?

   Is there some / any cold food on the menu?

2. there are / newspapers in the gift shop / ?

   Are there some / any newspapers in the gift shop?

3. you / need / extra towels / ?

   Do you need some / any extra towels?

4. they / want / milk with their coffee / ?

   Do they want some / any milk with their coffee?

5. Ms. Banks / need / help with her luggage / ?

   Does Ms. Banks need some / any help with her luggage?

6. the housekeeping department / have / more hangers / ?

   Does the housekeeping department have some / any more hangers?

➤ Do it yourself!

Pair work. Look at the picture of the kitchen for one minute. Then close the book and ask questions about the things in the room. Use *Is there*, *Are there*, and *some* and *any* in your questions. Answer from memory.

Is there any fruit?

The hotel check-in

A. Read the picture story again. Then check *True* or *False* for each statement.

	True	False
1. Ms. Thompson is checking out of the hotel.	☐	☑
2. Ms. Thompson is paying her hotel bill.	☐	☑
3. Ms. Thompson asked for a key to the mini-bar.	☐	☑
4. Ms. Thompson has luggage.	☑	☐

B. Check the information the clerk requests.

1. ☐ length of stay
2. ☐ check-out date
3. ☐ check-in time
4. ☑ need for bellman assistance

C. Listen. Read each response out loud from the text.

Authentic practice

(For general suggestions, see *Introduction*, page Tx.)

The hotel check-in

Procedure:

🎧

➤ To activate students' prior knowledge, ask *What happens when you check in at a hotel?* Write students' answers on the board. They may include what the clerk does (checks the reservation, asks about room preference, asks about length of stay, asks about the number in the party) and what the guest does (gives his or her name, gets keys, gets help with baggage, asks about check-out time and airport shuttle service).

➤ After students have read and listened to the picture story, have volunteers come to the board and put a check mark next to each item that was actually covered in the story. Have students add any activities in the story that are not written on the board.

➤ Some words or expressions may be unfamiliar to students. Check for understanding of *imprint, mini-bar, bellman, stay.* Point out that the gender-neutral term *bellhop* is often preferred to *bellman.* Other gender-neutral terms in current use include *police officer* (not *policeman*), *fire fighter* (not *fireman*), and *chairperson* (not *chairman*). Ask students if they can add any others.

➤ Remind students that some expressions are used frequently in service industries because they demonstrate politeness. Ask them to identify such phrases in the picture story: *Certainly, Is that satisfactory?, That's no problem at all, Will you be needing any . . .?* Write these expressions on the board and ask students to express them in more casual speech: *Sure, Is that OK?, No problem, Do you need any . . .?*

➤ Point out that the question in picture 5, *Will you be needing any assistance with your luggage?*, conflicts with the rule presented in Unit 1 not to use the present continuous with non-action verbs. This regionalism is gaining acceptance, however, and students may hear non-action verbs used with continuous forms.

A–B.

➤ Working individually, students complete the exercises and then check answers with a partner.

➤ Note that it is sometimes difficult to tell the difference between requesting and confirming. For example, when the clerk says *I see you'll be with us for three nights, checking out on Saturday*, he is confirming information he already has.

Option: Have pairs of students make up additional *true-false* questions. They can then take turns asking and answering questions with another pair.

🎧 C. Listen . . .

➤ Read each item in the tapescript out loud or play the cassette as many times as necessary for students to complete the exercise. If students have difficulty, prompt them by reading the response yourself.

➤ Review the answers before having students read their responses out loud.

Challenge: Use the items in the tapescript as a dictation. Have students listen to the items and write what they hear. Allow students to listen as many times as necessary. Ask volunteers to write the questions on the board. Make corrections as a class. Students can then practice the prompts and responses with a partner.

If your students are ready . . .

Culture / Civics note: It is common to tip for services provided in the hospitality industry. Such services include serving in a restaurant, room cleaning, and carrying a guest's luggage to the room. In a restaurant, customers usually tip between 15 percent and 20 percent. The amount given to the housekeeping staff depends on the guest's length of stay and is usually from $1 to $2 per day. Bellmen usually receive from $1 to $2 per bag. Anyone who provides a special service—for example, a room-service waiter who brings breakfast or a member of the housekeeping staff who brings extra pillows—usually receives a 15-percent tip.

Tapescript

1. Good afternoon. Are you checking in?
2. I see you'll be with us for three nights, checking out on Saturday.
3. Can I make an imprint of your credit card?
4. Will you be needing any assistance with your luggage?
5. Let me call the bellman for you.

T48

D. Vocabulary...

➤ Have students work individually to complete the exercise. If necessary, let them refer to the picture story to use the context to infer meaning.

➤ Have students check answers with a partner, and then review as a class.

Option: Put students in pairs to create sentences that use the words not selected in the exercise (*imprint, available, bellmen, single*). Have volunteers read their sentences aloud.

E–F.

➤ Remind students of the punctuation mark used for questions. Looking for question marks will help them scan the picture story and locate the questions.

➤ Have volunteers present their role plays to the class.

Option: To give students additional ideas for the hotel clerk's questions, create a list of appropriate topics and write it on the board. Look at the hotel reservations form on page 50 for ideas. Your list might include the guest's name and address, the guest's date of departure, the number of people checking in, the guest's preference in room type and bed size, the name of the guest's credit card. You may also want to refer to the answers generated in the discussion before the first reading of the picture story.

G. Reread the picture story...

➤ Tell students that sometimes information is stated directly and sometimes it is implied. Making correct inferences about implied information is an important academic skill.

➤ Put a chart on the board like the one following. Ask students first to write down what they know about Ms. Thompson. Then, in either the column headed *Direct* or the one headed *Implied*, have them write down the quotation from the picture story that supplies the information. Students' charts may include the following:

What is known	Direct	Implied
She's married.	"My husband will be joining me tomorrow."	
She doesn't smoke.	"I need to be certain that's a non-smoking room."	
She arrives on Wednesday.		"...three nights, checking out on Saturday."

➤ Do it yourself!

(For general suggestions, see *Introduction*, page Txiii.)

Procedure:

A. Read...

➤ Point out that there are three speakers and, therefore, three separate conversations. Have three volunteers each read aloud one of the speech balloons. Ask *Who are the speakers?* (hotel guests) *What do their statements have in common?* (The guests all have problems that need resolution.)

➤ If necessary, review bed sizes (single or twin, double, queen, king). You may want to refer to hotel room features in the *Vocabulary* on page 51.

➤ Tell students to imagine that they are hotel employees responding to the hotel guests. They should propose a solution to each problem and apologize when appropriate.

➤ Remind students that they can refer to the model conversations on pages 44 and 45 or to the picture story on page 48 for help in responding.

➤ Before students practice with a partner, have volunteers read each speech balloon aloud. Respond to each statement yourself, giving students an opportunity to check the appropriateness of their responses. Remind students of the importance of polite behavior toward hotel guests.

➤ Have students practice the conversations in pairs to check their responses. Ask volunteers to read their responses to the class.

B. Discussion...

➤ Brainstorm problems that the front desk can help resolve. Write students' ideas on the board. Problems may include needing local transportation, wanting a restaurant recommendation, needing a rollaway bed, having to replace forgotten toiletries, needing the address of a 24-hour pharmacy.

➤ Put students in small groups to discuss the problems and think of new problems to share with the class.

D. Vocabulary. Choose one of the words or phrases to complete each sentence.

1. Would it be possible to make _____a reservation_____ for a non-smoking double
   facing the ocean?
   a reservation / an imprint

2. That room won't be _____satisfactory_____. I requested a non-smoking room.
   satisfactory / available

3. I have a lot of _____luggage_____. I'm going to need some help.
   luggage / bellmen

4. I'm traveling with my daughter, so I need a _____double_____.
   single / double

E. Find and write the four questions the clerk asked when Ms. Thompson checked in.

Are you checking in? Can I make an imprint of your credit card? Is that satisfactory? Will you be needing

any assistance with your luggage?

F. Role play. Role-play a conversation between a traveler checking in and a front desk hotel clerk. Use the questions you wrote in Exercise E and your own questions.

G. Reread the picture story on page 48. Write what you know about Ms. Thompson.

She's married. She has luggage. She's staying three nights. She doesn't want a smoking room.

➤ Do it yourself!

A. Read the hotel guests' statements. Write your own responses. Then read each conversation out loud with a partner.

I have a lot of audiovisual equipment to carry.

YOU _____

I wanted a double room, but the key you gave me is for a single.

YOU _____

The key to the mini-bar doesn't work.

YOU _____

B. Discussion. What other problems can the front desk help travelers with?

Authentic practice

Reserving a hotel room

A. Listening comprehension. Listen to the telephone conversation.

B. Discussion. Answer the questions. Then compare your answers.

1. Who made the phone call and why? <u>Adam Stern, to make a reservation</u>

2. Why does the man give his credit card number to the woman? _____

   <u>to guarantee the room for late arrival</u>

C. Look at the hotel reservations form on the computer screen. Then listen to the conversation again. Fill out the reservations form with information you hear. Listen several times if necessary.

Authentic practice

(For general suggestions, see *Introduction*, page Tx.)

Procedure:

Reserving a hotel room

🎧**A–B.**

➤ To set the scene for the conversation, have students read the bar. Then direct their attention to the pictures and ask questions such as *Who do you see on the left?* (a hotel clerk) *Who is on the right?* (a man calling the hotel) *Why do you think he is calling?* (to make a hotel reservation)

➤ Read the tapescript out loud or play the cassette.

➤ Before students listen again, have them read the questions. Read the tapescript or play the cassette again and have students answer the questions individually.

➤ Review answers as a class.

Option: Discuss when it's OK to give your credit card information over the phone and when it isn't. Elicit from students or tell them that it's OK if it's a real place and you make the call.

🎧**C. Look at the hotel reservations form ...**

➤ Have students look at the reservations form, and then ask them what information is required. Elicit *arrival date, departure date, occupancy, room type, bed size, traveler's name and address, payment information.* Tell students to listen for this information and write it on the reservations form as they listen to the conversation again.

➤ Have students check their information with a partner, and then review as a class.

Challenge: Have students listen to the conversation a third time and create their own questions. If necessary, you may want to suggest questions such as *Who answers the phone?* (Lauren) *Where does the man want a room?* (on a high floor, on the quieter side of the hotel) *Who will be traveling with him?* (his wife) *What time does their flight arrive?* (5:15 p.m.) Have students write the questions on slips of paper and take turns asking and answering questions with a partner. Or collect the slips and read the questions to the class, calling on individuals to answer.

Tapescript

A, female: Skyview Suites Conference Center. This is Lauren. How may I direct your call?

B, male: I'm calling to make a reservation.

A: Certainly. Let me put you through to our reservations department.

B: Thanks.

[Recorded music]

C, female: Reservations. Melanie speaking. Can I assist you with a reservation?

B: Yes, thanks. I need a reservation for two nights, arriving on September 5th.

C: Let me confirm those dates for you, sir. Night of the 5th, departing on the 7th.

B: Yes, that's right.

C: And what type of accommodations will you be needing?

B: I'd like a double room, non-smoking, on a high floor, on the quieter side of the hotel, that is, if there's a lot of street noise.

C: Double, non-smoking, quiet.

B: And on a high floor.

C: Right . . . Will you be traveling alone?

B: No, actually, my wife will be traveling with me.

C: And would you prefer a king-size bed or two queens?

B: We'll take the queens.

C: OK. I'll check availability for you. Just one moment, please.

[Recorded music]

C: Good. I can confirm that for you. Can you please give me your name and address?

B: Adam Stern, 10 Bank Street, White Lanes, Louisiana 70822.

C: Let me see if I've got that right: Adam Stern, 10 Bank Street, White Lanes, Louisiana, zip 70822. Would you like to guarantee that for late arrival, Mr. Stern?

B: What do you mean?

C: Ordinarily, if you don't arrive by 6 p.m., we give your room away. But if you'd like to protect your reservation in case your flight is delayed, or if you just come in after 6, we'll hold the room for you. Of course, if you don't arrive at all, we'll charge your credit card for one night.

B: Actually, that sounds like a good idea. Our flight isn't coming in until 5:15. We might not get there until after 6. What do you need to guarantee the room?

C: A major credit card will be fine.

(Tapescript is continued on page T51.)

Tapescript (continued from page T50)

B: OK. Just a minute while I get my card. [pause] Here you go: It's the MultiCard, number 1242-5674-3200-081.

C: And the expiration date?

B: 4/6/05.

C: And is the card in your name, Mr. Stern?

B: Yes. Adam J. Stern.

C: Let me give you a reservation number, just in case you need to change your reservation. We require 48 hours notice. Do you have a pen?

B: Yes.

C: It's 2345 J, as in "John."

B: Thanks.

C: Good-bye, Mr. Stern. See you on the 5th.

➤ Do it yourself!

(For general suggestions, see *Introduction*, page Txiii.)

Procedure:

➤ Make sure you have phone books and/or travel ads for this activity. Have pairs of students choose the name of a hotel to use in their role play.

➤ After students listen to and repeat the hotel room features, have them point to the pictures as you read the items in random order.

➤ Read the directions for the hotel guest and the reservations clerk. Make sure students understand that Student A will play the reservations clerk and use the questions in the box as a guide. Student B will play the role of a hotel guest making a reservation. Before students begin their conversation, the guest must decide when he or she is arriving and departing, who is in the party, what type of bed is needed, and what other features he or she desires.

➤ Model the role play with a more advanced student. Play the role of Student B to demonstrate appropriate answers to the clerk's questions.

➤ Have students practice their role play, switching roles for more practice.

Option: Before pairs practice their conversations, divide the class in half. Have one half play the role of the reservations clerk and read the questions in the box together. Ask individual volunteers from the other half to answer the questions.

Option: Tell students to draw a line across the last picture in the *Vocabulary* box to separate the TV and fax machine from the mini-bar and safe. They now have a "Bingo" board with nine spaces. The object of this game is to mark off all nine spaces. As you read the following story, students mark off each space when you mention one of the hotel room features. At the end of the story, ask how many students marked all the spaces.

Optional read-aloud story

I worked a double shift yesterday. What a nightmare! I had several guests make complaints about their reservations. Mr. Stern had requested <u>a double room</u>, but he ended up with <u>a king</u>. That was a problem because he said he and his wife needed separate beds. Well, I found a room with <u>two queens</u>, but it was a smoking room, so I couldn't really make him happy. He decided to stay in the king but asked for a <u>rollaway</u> too. I wonder who ended up in which bed! Then Ms. Thompson came down. She said the key to the <u>mini-bar</u> didn't work. I finally had to go up to her room myself to show her how the key worked. Her husband was trying to get some work done, but he complained that the <u>fax machine</u> and the <u>data port</u> weren't working properly. The problem is that guests in the double rooms can't use the fax and the data port at the same time, so I had to switch the Thompsons to <u>a suite</u>. The suites have a much better setup for business work. Then it turned out that Ms. Thompson's co-worker arrived at the last minute to bring some papers for her big presentation tomorrow. Fortunately, we had <u>a single room</u> left—the last one—so I got that problem solved.

➤ Do it yourself!

Role play. Choose the name of a hotel from the phone book or from a travel ad in the newspaper. Then make reservations for a stay.

Hotel guest: Use the hotel room features from the vocabulary.

Reservations clerk: Use some of these questions plus some of your own questions.

What's your arrival date?

- What's your departure date?
- What type of accommodations do you need?
- Will you be traveling alone?
- Would you prefer a king-size bed or two queens?
- Would you like to guarantee that for late arrival?
- Credit card number? And the expiration date?
- Is the card in your name?

🎧 Vocabulary

Hotel room features

a single room

a double room

a suite

a king-size bed *or* a king

two queen-size beds *or* two queens

a TV

a fax machine

a mini-bar

an in-room safe

a rollaway bed

a data port

Vacations

🎧 **A.** Read and listen to the letters.

Ask Joan
Culture tips for newcomers

Dear Joan:

I have been working as a medical biller at a large HMO, and I get two weeks of vacation after one year. Joan, this is a *paid* vacation! I feel so lucky. I would like to plan a wonderful driving trip for my family. My family has been in this country for three years, and this is the first time we will be taking a real vacation away from the city! We'd like to see something beautiful in our new country. Any suggestions?

Edward from Bedford

Dear Edward:

Congratulations on your upcoming anniversary! You don't give me much information about your budget, your family's tastes, or how far you want to go. So here are three rules for a good vacation.

- Plan ahead: If you will be staying in a hotel or a motel, it's a good idea to make reservations. There's

nothing worse than not finding a place to sleep after a long day driving or enjoying the outdoors.
- Be cash smart: Carry traveler's checks, credit cards, or an ATM card. It's not a good idea to carry around a lot of cash. Better safe than sorry.
- Shop around: If you have Internet access, surf the travel sites for bargains and package deals. It's possible to save a lot of money on rental cars, plane fares, and hotels if you book in advance and are willing to be flexible about travel dates and times.

Have fun. There's a beautiful country out there to see, wonderful sights, and friendly people.

Joan

Dear Joan:

Last week I got a phone call telling me that I had won a free vacation!!! All I have to do is choose one of three holiday packages and overnight a deposit in cash. Then the company will send me the tickets. The airfare and the taxis are free. The only thing I have to pay for is the hotel. But I have to hurry,

because the offer is good for only one week. Joan, you know this country, so my question to you is this: Which would be the best package—"Aloha, Hawaii," "Star-Studded Hollywood," or "Hot Salsa New York"? Please answer soon!

Gullible Gus

Dear Gullible:

WHOA! Slow down. That free vacation offer sounds too good to be true. And you know when something sounds too good to be true, it usually is. While some package deals are legitimate, don't fall for one that claims to be free. Pressuring you to send cash is also a red flag. More and more readers are writing to me about travel scams that turned their travel dreams into travel nightmares. So, before you send any money, get the details and any refund policy in writing so you can be sure you know what the final costs really might be.

There's an old American saying: "There's no such thing as a free lunch."

Joan

B. Choose an answer to each question. Fill in the ovals.

1. How can you save money on a vacation?

   ⓐ plan ahead and shop around   ⓑ send cash

2. How can a traveler be cash smart?

   ⓐ carry enough cash to pay for all expenses   ⓑ use traveler's checks, credit cards, and ATM cards

3. Where can you find good deals and discounted tickets?

   ⓐ on the Internet   ⓑ in star-studded Hollywood

Authentic practice

(For general suggestions, see *Introduction*, page Tx.)

Vacations

Procedure:

A. Read and listen to the letters.

➤ Play the cassette or read the letters. Students listen and read silently. Pause after Edward's letter and make sure students know what an *HMO* is (health maintenance organization). Explain as necessary *better safe than sorry* and *surf*, which refers to researching on the Internet.

➤ Have students continue to listen and read silently. After Joan's letter to Gus, check comprehension of the following terms: *overnight*, *too good to be true*, *red flag*, *scams*, and *nightmares*. Note that *overnight* is used as a verb meaning to send overnight. Tell students that the saying *There's no such thing as a free lunch* means that all offers come with conditions or obligations. We don't get anything without paying for it in some way.

➤ Check comprehension with questions such as *What does Edward want to do?* (take a wonderful driving trip with his family) *What three pieces of advice does Joan give?* (plan ahead, be cash smart, shop around) *What offer did Gus get over the phone?* (a free vacation) *What does Gus have to do to get this "free" vacation?* (overnight a cash deposit and pay for the hotel) *What is a warning sign that an offer might not be legitimate?* (pressuring the person to send cash)

Option: Summarizing is an important academic skill. Have pairs of students work together to summarize Joan's advice to Edward.

Option: Ask students if there is an expression in their language similar to *There's no such thing as a free lunch*. Write any such expressions on the board and discuss. Ask students to give their reasons for agreeing or disagreeing with the expression.

Challenge: Have students do the following sentence completion task as a dictation. Before students read and listen to the letters, write these incomplete sentences on the board:

1. I would like to plan _____.
2. Congratulations on _____!
3. Surf the travel sites for _____.
4. That free vacation offer _____.
5. There's no such thing _____.

Play the cassette or read the letters and have students complete the sentences according to what they hear. Let students listen several times if necessary. Have pairs of students check their answers by comparing their sentences with the sentences in the text.

B. Choose an answer . . .

➤ Students complete the exercise individually and then compare answers with a partner.

➤ To practice scanning for information, students can underline the sentences in the text where they found the answers.

If your students are ready . . .

Culture / Civics note: In North America, full-time employees usually get a paid vacation as one of their benefits. This paid vacation time is usually two weeks. In some workplaces, the amount of paid vacation leave increases with the length of time the person is employed by the company.

C. Read the information ...

➤ Review the terms of Gus's "free" vacation offer (He had to overnight a deposit in cash, pay for the hotel, decide quickly) and Joan's advice (Get details in writing). Tell students to keep this information in mind as they read about travel fraud. Ask them to look for information that is similar to Gus's situation and to Joan's response.

➤ Check comprehension and encourage key reading skills by asking questions such as *What is the topic of this reading?* (protecting yourself against travel fraud, vacation scams) *How many tips does the Web site give?* (five) *What's a good way to locate these tips?* (look at the bullets)

➤ Make sure students understand *unsolicited fax*, *legitimate businesses*, *a scam operator* or *artist*. Explain the meaning of *snap decisions* by snapping your fingers to indicate speed.

➤ Note that quotation marks are used in two ways in this reading: to indicate actual speech (say "no") and to suggest that a term is being used in an unusual or deceptive way (a "free" trip). Have students find additional terms that are used in deceptive ways and explain their meaning ("trip trap," "won").

➤ Direct students' attention to the Hello message at the top of the screen. Ask them to find the three adjectives that describe the vacation (spectacular, luxury, dream). Tell them that these exaggerated adjectives can be a clue that the offer is a scam.

➤ Remind students that they saw this message in the unit preview on page 43. Ask the *Warm up* question again: *Do you believe this offer is true?*

Option: On the board, create a chart of do's and don'ts. Ask students to divide the tips they read into these two categories. Write their suggestions on the board. Your list should include the following:

Do's	Don'ts
•Be careful.	•Be pressured into buying.
•Ask detailed questions.	•Give your credit card
•Say "no" if you have any doubt.	number over the phone.
	•Send money by messenger.

D. Warn this consumer ...

➤ Have students look at the picture and read the letter that the woman received. Ask *What has the woman won?* (a vacation prize, a space at a time-share) *Look at the woman's expression. How do you think she feels?* (surprised, excited, pleased) *Which exaggerated adjectives are used in the letter?* (all inclusive, exclusive) *What other words are red flags?* (extravaganza, hurry, limited)

➤ Ask students what problems they can identify in this situation. Remind students to think about the lists of do's and don'ts they prepared. They can also reread Joan's advice to Gus on page 52.

➤ Model the activity. On the board, write a warning to the woman, such as *Be careful. The vacation you've "won" probably isn't "free."* Brainstorm other warnings.

➤ Have students complete the activity individually. In pairs, students compare warnings.

➤ Do it yourself!

(For general suggestions, see *Introduction*, page Txiii.)

Procedure:

A. True story ...

➤ Model the activity for the class. Choose one of the three topics and tell a true story of your own. Include details about transportation, accommodations, and travel companions, and add two to three additional sentences. Focus students' attention on the verb forms you use.

➤ Brainstorm other details students could include in their stories in addition to information about transportation, accommodations, and travel companions. Write students' suggestions on the board to be used for additional prompts.

➤ Put students in pairs. To practice the simple past tense, ask them to talk about their best or worst vacations. They can use these questions as prompts: *What kind(s) of transportation did you take? What kind of accommodations did you have? Who did you travel with? What made the vacation memorable?* Have students add details based on the suggestions on the board. Tell students to try to talk for one minute.

➤ To practice future and conditional forms, partners can talk about a vacation they would like to take. They can use these questions as prompts: *Where would you like to go? Why? What kind of transportation will you use? What kind of accommodations do you want? Who will you travel with?*

B. Culture talk ...

➤ Ask each pair of students to join another pair to create small groups of four. Have them discuss travel destinations and travel dangers in their home countries.

➤ Lead a class discussion. Explore common patterns by asking *What are some of the dangers or difficulties that tourists face? What are some of the warnings you might give a tourist?*

C. Read the information about travel fraud from the FTC Web site.

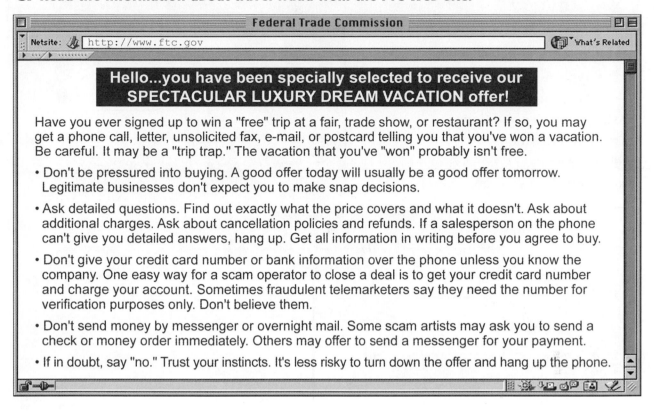

Federal Trade Commission

Netsite: http://www.ftc.gov — What's Related

Hello...you have been specially selected to receive our SPECTACULAR LUXURY DREAM VACATION offer!

Have you ever signed up to win a "free" trip at a fair, trade show, or restaurant? If so, you may get a phone call, letter, unsolicited fax, e-mail, or postcard telling you that you've won a vacation. Be careful. It may be a "trip trap." The vacation that you've "won" probably isn't free.

• Don't be pressured into buying. A good offer today will usually be a good offer tomorrow. Legitimate businesses don't expect you to make snap decisions.

• Ask detailed questions. Find out exactly what the price covers and what it doesn't. Ask about additional charges. Ask about cancellation policies and refunds. If a salesperson on the phone can't give you detailed answers, hang up. Get all information in writing before you agree to buy.

• Don't give your credit card number or bank information over the phone unless you know the company. One easy way for a scam operator to close a deal is to get your credit card number and charge your account. Sometimes fraudulent telemarketers say they need the number for verification purposes only. Don't believe them.

• Don't send money by messenger or overnight mail. Some scam artists may ask you to send a check or money order immediately. Others may offer to send a messenger for your payment.

• If in doubt, say "no." Trust your instincts. It's less risky to turn down the offer and hang up the phone.

D. Warn this consumer about travel fraud. Then compare warnings with your classmates.

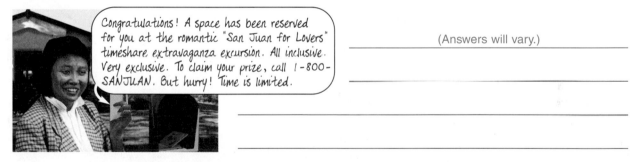

Congratulations! A space has been reserved for you at the romantic "San Juan for Lovers" timeshare extravaganza excursion. All inclusive. Very exclusive. To claim your prize, call 1-800-SANJUAN. But hurry! Time is limited.

(Answers will vary.)

❯ Do it yourself!

A. True story. Tell a true vacation or travel story. Choose one of these topics:

• your best vacation
• your worst vacation
• the vacation you would like to take

Include information about transportation, accommodations, and travel companions.

B. Culture talk. Is your home country a travel destination for foreign tourists? What are some things tourists there should be careful of? Compare information.

> **Review**

A. Pair work or group work.

• What is happening?
• What are the people doing?

Ask and answer questions.

Create conversations.

Tell a story.

Say as much as you can.

54   Unit 4

➤ Review

(For general suggestions, see *Introduction*, page Txii.)

Procedure:

A. Pair work or group work.

Option: Create questions. Put students in pairs. Ask them to create questions about the pictures. Questions for scene 4, for example, might include *Who is going to help with their luggage?* (the bellman) *What do you think the clerk is giving the woman?* (the room key, the mini-bar key, a voucher for a free breakfast) Pairs then exchange questions with another pair and take turns answering them.

Ask and answer questions.

➤ Ask general questions about the picture, such as *Who are the people in these scenes?* (a husband and wife, hotel employees) *What is this picture about?* (a couple going on a trip) *Where do they go?* (New Orleans, the New Orleans Farley Hotel) *What does the woman request from the front desk?* (some hangers and towels)

➤ Have pairs of students take turns pointing to and describing different events in the story.

Create conversations.

➤ Point to the first scene. Play the role of the husband and say *You know, I'd really like to go to Paris. This brochure looks great.* Elicit the wife's possible responses: *That sounds wonderful, but too expensive, Let's go somewhere closer to home, Here's an ad for a hotel in New Orleans.* Put students in pairs to finish the conversation.

➤ Have pairs of students choose one of the four other scenes and create an extended conversation for the speakers. Remind students to refer to the conversation on page 44 for help and ideas.

➤ Have pairs number the speech balloons and, on a separate sheet of paper, write one line of conversation for each person in the picture.

Tell a story.

Option: One-minute stories. Have a student time you while you model the activity and talk about the picture for one minute. Then, in pairs or small groups, each student talks about the picture for one minute. Encourage students to describe each of the five scenes and to say as much as they can. Tell students to continue talking until you say *Stop*, indicating that the minute is up.

Option: Chronological order. Write the following sentences on the board. Have students rewrite them, putting them in chronological order. Have students check the order with a partner (4, 1, 8, 3, 2, 6, 5, 7).

- "Would you like to guarantee your room for late arrival?"

- Last May, Mr. and Mrs. Swenson talked about going on a trip.

- "Absolutely. I'll send them right up," the clerk replied.

- Mr. Swenson called the hotel and made a reservation.

- About a week later, Mrs. Swenson received an offer in the mail for a travel discount package.

- The bellman helped them with their luggage.

- They checked in at the Farley Hotel before dinner.

- Mrs. Swenson called the front desk to ask for some hangers and towels.

Option: Travel warnings. Have students look at scene 2. They should then imagine a conversation between the husband or wife and a friend. The friend gives warnings about the travel offer the wife received. The friend's warnings might include *Don't overnight any money, Ask for details in writing, What's "free"?*

Option: Newspaper articles. Pairs of students choose one of the headlines in scene 2 and create the rest of the article. Volunteers can read their articles to the class.

Challenge: When journalists report a story, they write a very brief summary in the headline. A headline usually focuses on nouns and verbs and leaves out articles and adjectives. Ask students to write headlines for each scene. Headlines for scene 1 might include *Man reads travel brochure, Wife sees hotel ad.* Elicit examples and write them on the board. Ask students to judge the headlines based on length, accuracy, and active language.

⌕B–C.

➤ Play the cassette or read the conversation out loud while students listen with books closed.

➤ Have students open their books. Read the questions in Exercise B out loud. Play the cassette or read the conversation again. Have students complete the exercise.

➤ Ask students to read the room service order slip in Exercise C. Play the cassette or read the conversation as many times as necessary for students to complete the exercise.

➤ Have students check Exercises B and C with a partner. Review as a class.

Challenge: After students have completed Exercise C, put students in pairs. Students should create the room service person's questions that elicited the filled-out order slip. For example, the room service person might ask *Would you like to start with a shrimp cocktail? How many? Small or jumbo?* Have students practice the conversation, playing the roles of the order taker and the guest in Room 306. Then have students switch roles for more practice.

D. Read each sentence or question . . .

➤ Students work individually to complete the review exercise.

➤ Have students check responses with a partner. Review as a class.

Challenge: Pairs of students create extended conversations that include each item and its response.

Tapescript

Male: Claire? Could you check the other closet? There aren't any hangers in this one.

Female: Sure. Just a minute. Here you go. They must have put them all in here. I've got a ton of them. Are these enough?

Male: Yeah. That's great. [pause] What's this? Oh, no. Can you believe it? There are three ironing boards in this closet. No wonder there wasn't any room for hangers! . . . You know what? Let's order room service.

Female: But room service is so expensive.

Male: I know. But it's our anniversary. Let's make this like a second honeymoon. [pause] Hello. Room service? I'd like to order dinner. I'm in Room 306. For two people. [pause] Excuse me? How long did you say? Claire, he says it'll be forty-five minutes to an hour. Can you hold out?

(Tapescript is continued.)

Tapescript *(continued)*

Female: Well, actually, I'm not that hungry. It's only 5 o'clock. It isn't any problem for me. What about you?

Male: I'm OK. That'll give us a little time to finish unpacking. Why don't I just order for both of us? [pause] Room service? That'll be OK. We're not in a hurry. . . . We'll start with two jumbo shrimp cocktails. Then we'll have one broiled chicken with a salad and one steak. Medium. Do you have any fresh vegetables? Good. I'll have some broccoli with that steak. [pause] Dressing? Just a minute. Claire, any dressing with your salad?

Female: Yes. Italian, please.

Male: That'll be Italian dressing on the salad. Thanks.

Female: Mmm. Sounds great!

---

1. Where are the husband and wife? <u>in a hotel room</u>

2. Who does the husband call on the telephone? <u>room service</u>

☊ **C.** Listen again and check the items on the room service order slip.

Fawlty Suites

Room Service Order Slip   Room No. <u>306</u>   Time <u>5 pm</u>

☑ shrimp cocktail	☐ small	☑ jumbo	
soup	☐ consomme	☐ tomato bisque	
☑ sirloin steak	☐ rare	☑ medium	☐ well done
☑ chicken	☐ fried	☑ broiled	☐ barbecued
vegetables	☑ broccoli	☐ corn	
salad dressing	☑ Italian	☐ Ranch	☐ Thousand Island ☐ French

(Note: shrimp cocktail box shows "2")

D. Read each sentence or question. Underline your response.

1. "I asked the bellman to pick up my luggage, but he never came."

   YOU <u>Please accept my apology.</u>   **YOU** Will you be traveling alone?

2. "Would you like to guarantee that reservation for late arrival?"

   YOU No, thanks. I travel cash smart.   **YOU** <u>Sure. What do you need—
   a credit card?</u>

3. "When will you be checking in?"

   YOU I'd prefer to charge that on this card.   **YOU** <u>Pretty late. Maybe I'd better
   guarantee the room.</u>

4. "Can I make an imprint of your card?"

   YOU <u>Of course. Here you go.</u>   **YOU** I never give my card number
   over the phone.

E. Complete each statement with *some* or *any*.

1. We don't have _____any_____ bellmen available right now.

2. The guest in Room 566 ordered ____some____ audiovisual equipment for a meeting.

3. This hotel doesn't have ____any____ room service. Let's go out.

4. We have ____some____ nice doubles facing the ocean.

5. There isn't ____any____ noise from the street.

F. Choose one of the words or phrases to complete each sentence.

1. If you have a lot of cash or valuables, you should request _____an in-room safe_____.
   a mini-bar / an in-room safe

2. Mr. Martin is traveling with his wife and son. He reserved a double room and a
   _____rollaway bed_____.
   rollaway bed / data port

3. They have some memos to send, so they need a room with a _____fax machine_____.
   fax machine / suite

4. Ms. Thompson is on a business trip and needs to check her e-mail. She reserved
   a room with _____a data port_____.
   a data port / two queens

G. Composition. On a separate sheet of paper, write about the picture on page 54. Say as much as you can.

> Now I can
> ❑ request service and respond to requests for service.
> ❑ make and respond to complaints about bad service.
> ❑ make and guarantee hotel reservations.
> ❑ check in at a hotel.
> ❑ evaluate offers for vacation packages.
> ❑ protect myself against travel fraud.

E–F.

➤ Students work individually to complete the review exercises.

➤ Circulate to offer help as needed.

➤ Have students check answers with a partner. Review answers as a class.

➤ Identify any areas of difficulty that may require additional instruction and practice.

G. Composition . . .

➤ Provide students with concrete approaches to writing about the picture on page 54. Use one of the options that follow, give students a choice of options, or assign options based on students' levels of proficiency. Model what is expected of students for each option.

➤ Advise students to look back through the unit for help and ideas as they write.

➤ Circulate to offer help as needed.

Option: Have students write an extended conversation for one of the pairs in the picture. Students can later role-play their conversations for the class.

Option: Have students number the different people in the picture and then write two sentences about each one.

Option: Have students write a letter to the manager of the Farley Hotel, complaining about the service.

Now I can

➤ Read the first item in the box out loud: *Now I can request service and respond to requests for service.* Elicit from the class an example of how to request and respond to service, such as *Would it be possible to get more hangers?* and *Of course. How many would you like?*

➤ Put students in pairs. Tell the students to take turns reading each item in the box and giving an example of what they have learned. When students can provide an example, they should check that box. If there are items students aren't able to check, have them look back through the unit for ideas.

➤ When students are finished reviewing with their partners, read each item out loud and elicit an example from the class.

Oral test (optional)

You may want to use the *Now I can* box as an informal evaluation. While students are working on the *Composition* activity, you can call them up individually and check their ability with two or three objectives.

Your time

Note: For the plan-ahead project on page 67, divide the students into four topic groups: registering a child at a day-care center, voter registration, community college registration, and immunizations for schoolchildren. Students should get information about deadlines for each topic. Assist students by giving them the names of local day-care centers and community colleges. The number of the central office of the public school system can be found in the telephone book. Libraries and the League of Women Voters are good sources of information about voter registration. Provide local phone books for reference.

 Preview

(For general suggestions, see *Introduction*, page Tviii.)

Warm up. What do these documents have in common?

Procedure:

➤ Ask *What documents do you see?* (a computer-generated "card" for a library book, a driver's license, information about voter registration) *What information is circled on each document?* (the due date, the expiration date, the dates by which voter registration requirements must be met) Elicit that these are all deadlines. If necessary, clarify the meaning of *deadline*: the time by which you must finish something.

➤ Elicit students' experience by asking questions such as *Is anyone registered to vote? Who has a library card? What materials can you borrow with your library card? How long can you check materials out? Who has a driver's license for this state? How often do licenses have to be renewed?*

➤ Note that Joan Manners's driver's license expires on her birthday. Many states match the license expiration date with a driver's birthday.

➤ Ask *What is the difference between a due date and an expiration date?* Elicit that a *due date* is a date on which something must be returned or paid. Sometimes a late fee is charged if a payment or return is late. An *expiration date* is the date after which something is no longer good, or effective.

➤ Write *Due date* and *Expiration date* on the board. Brainstorm things that have due dates or expiration dates and write them under the appropriate heading. Your list may include the following items:

Due date	Expiration date
Library books	Licenses
Videos from the video store	Parking permits
Bills	Student IDs

Option: Ask additional questions related to voter registration: *Do you have to be a citizen to vote? Is anyone in the class a citizen? What do you have to do to become a citizen?* Broaden the discussion by asking *Why is it important to vote? What are other ways of being a good citizen or community member?*

Option: Elicit information about your local library's policy on length of loans and amount of fines. Write this information on the board. Your list may look like the one following:

Material	Length of loan	Late fine per day
Book	Three weeks	$.15
Cassette	Three weeks	$.15
Video or DVD	Two days	$1.00

Unit 5 objectives

Procedure:

➤ Have students read the objectives. Ask them to put a check next to the objectives that they can do now and circle those they want to work on.

➤ Ask students to underline any words they do not understand. Define any words that are unfamiliar, such as *prioritize* (to put in order of importance).

➤ As a class, choose one of the objectives. Find out what related information students already know. For the objective *Manage time,* for example, ask *What does "manage" mean?* (direct, handle, control) *Can we really control time?* (no) Point out that when we talk about managing time, we really mean using our own time with positive results. Then brainstorm questions students have related to the objective. These may include *How can I do my job and also take care of my family? I can't get used to the attitude that people in this country have about time. What can I do? How can I do things at the time people in this country want them done?* Write the questions on a large sheet of paper for students to answer at the end of the unit.

Your time

 Preview

Warm up. What do these documents have in common?

GREEN GABLES PUBLIC LIBRARY
8/30/2004
05:28 PM

GREEN GABLES PUBLIC LIBRARY
TO RENEW, REQUEST, OR RESERVE
Call 696-4212 during business hours

Mon., Wed., Fri. 1 – 5:30
Tues., Thurs. 10 – 8; Sat. 10 – 5:30

Title: The night of the hunter
Author: Grubb, Davis
Item ID: 0011400823826
Due: 09/13/2004

FLORIDA
DRIVER LICENSE
ID: 215 776 536
DOB: 03-08-44
MANNERS, JOAN
87 CROSS CREEK RD
COCONUT CITY, FL 33146
SEX: F EYES: BL HT: 5-05 CLASS: D
ISSUED: 7-16-02 EXPIRES: 03-08-10
Joan Manners
05205844

To Make Application to Register to Vote, You Must:

• Be **a citizen of the United States** for
  at least one month before the next election;
• Be **a resident of Pennsylvania** and your election district for
  at least 30 days before the next election; and
• Be **at least 18 years of age** on the day of the next election.

Do you meet these qualifications?

Unit 5 objectives

- Understand the consequences of missing deadlines.
- Apologize for missing an appointment.
- Manage time.
- Prioritize.
- Anticipate and plan actions necessary to make deadlines.

Practical conversations

A. Listen and read.

A: Oh, no. I don't believe it!

B: What?

A: I was supposed to return these books by the 14th. I'll have to pay a fine.

B: Can I give you some advice?

A: Sure. What?

B: Write everything down. That way you won't forget.

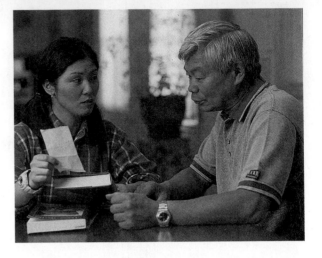

B. Pronunciation and intonation practice.

Vocabulary

Consequences of missing a deadline

pay a credit card bill
"You'll have to pay a late fee and interest."

return a library book
"You'll have to pay a fine."

register to vote
"You'll have to wait for the next election."

register for a class or training
"You'll have to wait until the next term."

renew a driver's license
"You'll get a ticket."

C. Pair work. Express dismay. Offer advice.

A: Oh, no. I don't believe it!

B: ____1____?

A: I was supposed to _____. I'll _____.

B: Can I give you some advice?

A: _____?

B: Write everything down. That way you won't forget.

[1]What's wrong, What's the matter

Practical conversations

(For general suggestions, see *Introduction*, page Tviii.)

Model 1

Content: expressing dismay, offering advice, consequences of missing a deadline

Procedure:

🎧 A–B.

➤ To set the scene for the conversation, ask questions about the photo, such as *Who do you think the people are?* (friends or family) *Why do you think so?* (They're informally dressed, sitting at a table together.) *What is their mood?* (serious, upset)

➤ After students listen to the conversation, check comprehension by asking questions such as *What was the young woman supposed to do?* (return the books by the 14th) *What is the consequence of returning the books late?* (She'll have to pay a fine.) *What advice does the man give?* (Write everything down so you won't forget.)

➤ Point out that the young woman says *the 14th*. Remind students that we use ordinal numbers when talking about dates.

➤ Note that the young woman says *by the 14th*. Point out that the preposition *by*, not *on*, is used with deadlines, since we have the opportunity to pay a bill or return a library book up until the deadline.

Option: If necessary, review ordinal numbers and the abbreviations (first) *-st*, (second) *-nd*, (third) *-rd*, (fourth through ninth) *-th*. Have students stand and form a line. Have them use ordinal numbers to give their position on line. Model by standing at the front of the line and saying *I'm first*. Give additional examples by changing your place in line and saying *I'm fourth, I'm ninth,* and so on. Ask questions such as *When is Independence Day? Christmas?* Write students' answers on the board and underline the ordinal numbers: July 4th, December 25th. Have the class repeat the dates. For more practice, draw or tape a large calendar for the current month on the board. Tell students that if we are talking about a date in the current month, we can just say *the [10]th*, without the month. Ask questions such as *When is our next class? When does the weekend begin? When do we return to school?* Make sure students answer with *the* + an ordinal number.

🎧 Vocabulary

➤ Point out that this *Vocabulary* section includes obligations that must be met by a certain deadline and the consequences of missing that deadline. For example, in the first item, the obligation is to pay a credit card bill by a certain deadline. The consequence of missing that deadline is "You'll have to pay a late fee and interest."

➤ Note that there is a deadline printed on the credit card bill, the library slip, the Board of Elections envelope, and the driver's license. The information circled in red has been enlarged to make it easier to read the deadline.

➤ Have students listen to and repeat the obligations and the consequences of missing a deadline.

Option: Write the heading *Obligation* on the board. Brainstorm other obligations that involve deadlines and write them under the heading. In pairs, students predict the consequences of not meeting the deadlines. Elicit students' ideas and write them on the board. Your list may look like this one:

Obligation	Consequences of missing a deadline
renew a visa	You'll have to leave the country.
pay a utility bill	Your phone service will be cut off.
pay the rent	You'll be charged a late fee.
file tax returns	You'll have to pay a fine.

C. Pair work . . .

➤ Point out that the consequences expressed in the *Vocabulary* are addressed to the reader: *You'll*. In the *Pair work*, students will have to say *I'll*, as in *I'll get a ticket*.

➤ Direct students' attention to Student A's second line. Point out that Student A must first state a missed obligation and a date: for example, *I was supposed to renew my driver's license by the 23rd.* The consequence of missing the deadline goes in the next slot: *I'll get a ticket.*

➤ Model the conversation with a more advanced student. Play the role of Student A to demonstrate choosing an obligation, stating the date of the deadline, and expressing the consequence of missing the deadline.

➤ Have students practice the conversation in pairs, using the *Vocabulary* or the ideas on the board for obligations and consequences.

Challenge: If appropriate for your class and community, assign students to interview someone outside the class about work deadlines. As a class, brainstorm possible interview questions: *What kind of work do you do? What happens if you miss a deadline?* Students report their findings about deadlines to the class.

Model 2

Content: notifying someone about missing an appointment, apologizing for missing an appointment, asking about rescheduling, agreeing to reschedule, types of appointments

Procedure:

🎧 A–B.

➤ To set the scene for the conversation, point to the photos and ask *Who is on the left?* (a woman on the phone) *How do you think she is feeling?* (upset) Point to the inset and ask *What is this?* (a schedule of appointments) *Who do you think is on the right?* (a receptionist in an office, a woman who is reading the schedule)

➤ After students read and listen to the conversation, check comprehension by asking questions such as *Who calls Mrs. Martin?* (Paula in Dr. Paine's office) *Why is she calling?* (to tell Mrs. Martin she missed an appointment and to reschedule) *Is Mrs. Martin surprised that she missed the appointment?* (yes) *How do you know?* (She is upset, she says "Oh, no! You're right!")

➤ Practice choral reading of the conversation. Play the role of Student A, Mrs. Martin, and have the class play the role of Student B, the receptionist Paula. Read Student A's second and third lines with exaggeration, emphasizing Mrs. Martin's dismay *(Oh, no! You're right!)* and then her apology *(I'm so sorry)*. Switch roles. Remind students to exaggerate their dismay and apology.

🎧 Vocabulary

➤ After students listen to and repeat the appointments, brainstorm other appointments that they might have. Suggestions may include a meeting at a child's school, a job interview, a business meeting. Write the appointments on the board and have students repeat them after you.

C. Pair work . . .

➤ Model the conversation with a more advanced student. Play the role of Student B, demonstrating how to notify someone of a missed appointment. To complete Student B's line, *This is _____,* give both your name and location; for example, This is Max at Grove Street Auto or This is Ms. Perry at Ridge Elementary School.

➤ Before students practice the conversation in pairs, remind them to choose a name for Student A, a name and location for Student B, and to decide what kind of appointment Student A has missed.

If your students are ready . . .

Culture / Civics notes: Note that the receptionist in Dr. Paine's office calls the patient Mrs. Martin. According to current social usage, a woman is usually addressed as Ms. rather than Mrs., even if the speaker knows she is married. Note too that the caller identifies herself by her first name, Paula, rather than as Ms. plus her last name. It is common for a receptionist to use only his or her first name.

➤ Do it yourself!

(For general suggestions, see *Introduction*, page Txiii.)

Procedure:

A. Write your appointments . . .

➤ On the board, make a chart like the one on page 59. Model the activity by writing your own appointment and a consequence for missing it in the Monday slot; for example, *a haircut appointment / I'll have to reschedule for sometime later in the week.* Point out the use of the future *will* to express the consequence. Fill in the rest of the chart with appointments and consequences suggested by volunteers.

➤ Tell students to open their books and complete the charts for themselves. They should write down at least one appointment or deadline for each weekday next week. Have them write down a consequence of missing the appointment or deadline in the column on the right.

➤ Remind students to use the future *will* or *won't* to express the consequence.

➤ Have students share their schedules in pairs.

B. Discussion . . .

➤ Put the following questions on the board: *What appointment or deadline did you miss? Why did you miss it? What was the consequence of missing it? Did you reschedule?*

➤ Model the activity by telling about an appointment or deadline you missed in the past. Refer to the questions on the board and include the reason for missing the appointment and the consequence. Tell students whether you rescheduled.

➤ In pairs or small groups, students tell about their own missed appointments.

A. Listen and read.

A: Hello?

B: Mrs. Martin? This is Paula in Dr. Paine's office. You had a 2:00 appointment.

A: Oh, no! You're right! I missed it.

B: Would you like to reschedule?

A: Yes, I would. I'm so sorry.

B. Pronunciation and intonation practice.

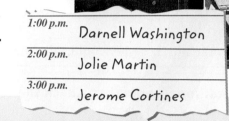

1:00 p.m.	Darnell Washington
2:00 p.m.	Jolie Martin
3:00 p.m.	Jerome Cortines

Vocabulary

Appointments

a doctor's appointment

a dentist's appointment

an orthodontist's appointment

a car service appointment

a hairdresser's appointment

a music lesson

C. Pair work. Apologize for missing an appointment. Use one of the appointments above or your own appointment.

A: Hello?

B: _____? This is _____. You had a _____.

A: Oh, no! You're right! I missed it.

B: Would you like to reschedule?

A: ___1___.

[1]Yes, please, No, thank you

➤ Do it yourself!

A. Write your appointments, deadlines, and other plans for the next week in this chart.

Appointment or deadline	Consequence of missing it
Monday: car service appointment	The car won't pass inspection.
Monday:	
Tuesday:	
Wednesday:	
Thursday:	
Friday:	

B. Discussion. Tell your classmates about an appointment you missed in the past. What was the reason? What was the consequence?

Practical grammar

Conditional sentences

Use *if* in conditional sentences for both real and unreal conditions.

Real conditions (facts)

             if clause   result clause

    If you miss an appointment, you have to reschedule.

    If I miss one more appointment, I'll have to pay.

Unreal conditions

    If she knew the number, she would call. (unreal: She doesn't know it.)

A. Read the conditional sentences. Check the ones that describe an unreal condition.

1. ☐ If you return a library book after the due date, you have to pay a fine.

2. ☑ If Carl took music lessons, he would be a better pianist.

3. ☐ If your teeth are crooked, the orthodontist can straighten them.

4. ☐ If you don't register before the deadline, you won't be able to vote.

5. ☐ If my mother doesn't wear her glasses, she's not allowed to drive.

6. ☑ If I were you, I'd write everything down.

7. ☑ If they registered for the class today, they would get a discount.

8. ☑ If we always paid on time, we wouldn't have to pay a late fee.

Verb forms in conditional sentences

Real conditions

Use *if* and the simple present tense in the *if* clause, even if the result is in the future.

        if clause   result clause

    If I **return** this book late, I'll pay the fine.

Don't use a future form (*will, be going to*) in the *if* clause.

    ~~If I will return this book late, I'll pay the fine.~~

Unreal conditions

Use *if* and the simple past tense or *were* to state an unreal condition. Use *would* or *could* and a verb in the result clause. *Could* is less certain than *would*.

    If Paul **wore** his glasses, he **could see** better. (unreal: He doesn't wear them.)

    If I **were** in your shoes, I**'d return** that book on time.

    If she **were** a doctor, she**'d be** a pediatrician.

Don't use *would* or *could* in the *if* clause.

    ~~If she would be a doctor, she would be a pediatrician.~~

Practical grammar

(For general suggestions, see *Introduction*, page Tix.)

Conditional sentences

Procedure:

➤ Review the consequences of missing a deadline from the *Vocabulary* box on page 58. Ask students questions using *if* and have them respond with the quoted statements from the text; for example, *What happens if you pay a credit card bill late?* (You'll have to pay a late fee and interest.) Write the questions and answers on the board as conditional sentences: *If you return a library book late, you'll have to pay a fine.* Underline the *if* clauses.

➤ Tell students that the sentences on the board represent real possibilities: If you miss a deadline, certain consequences are likely to occur. A sentence with an *if* clause and a consequence, or a result clause, is called a conditional sentence.

➤ Write on the board *If I paid my bills on time, I wouldn't have to pay interest.* Underline the *if* clause. Write a series of unreal conditions on the board; for example, *If I were you, If I wanted to save money.* Brainstorm result clauses and write students' ideas on the board, making sure to use *would.* Ask *Are these real situations?* (no) Tell students that unreal conditional sentences express hypothetical or imaginary situations.

➤ Have students read the information in the box. Answer any questions.

A. Read the conditional sentences ...

➤ Model item 1. Write the sentence and the check box on the board, and underline the *if* clause. Ask *Is this a real situation?* (yes) Continue with item 2. Ask *Does Carl take music lessons?* (no) *Is this a real situation?* (no) Put a check in the box.

➤ Tell students to look at the *if* clauses in the remaining sentences and ask themselves if they describe real or unreal conditions. Working individually, students check the boxes next to unreal conditions.

Option: After the class has reviewed Exercise A, read the *if* clauses out loud in random order and call on individual students to respond with the consequences in the result clauses.

Verb forms in conditional sentences

Procedure:

➤ Write on the board the first example sentence from the box. Include the blue brackets and labels. Ask *Does this sentence describe a real condition or an unreal condition?* (real, it represents a real possibility) *How many clauses are there in this conditional sentence?* (two) *What are they?* (the *if* clause, the result clause) Have volunteers read aloud the two clauses.

➤ Remind students that an *if* clause states a condition that leads to the consequence in the result clause. Tell students that we use *if* and the simple present tense to state a real condition. We can use the simple present tense or the future in the result clause. Illustrate the correct use of verb forms in several examples. Write on the board items 1, 3, 4, and 5 from Exercise A or your own examples. Point to each verb form and elicit what it is.

➤ Write on the board the first unreal conditional sentence from the box and add blue brackets and the labels *if clause* and *result clause*. Ask *Does this sentence describe a real condition or an unreal condition?* (unreal, Paul doesn't wear his glasses) *How many clauses are there in this conditional sentence?* (two) *What are they?* (the *if* clause, the result clause) Read aloud the two clauses.

➤ Tell students we use *if* and the simple past tense to state an unreal condition. We can also state unreal conditions using *if* and *were.* We use *would* or *could* + the base form of the verb in the result clause. Illustrate the correct use of verb forms in several examples. Write on the board items 2, 6, 7, and 8 from Exercise A or your own examples. Point to each verb form and elicit what it is.

➤ Have students read the information in the box. Direct attention to the unreal conditions and ask questions such as *Does Paul wear his glasses?* (no) *Is she a doctor?* (no). Answer any questions and give additional examples if necessary.

Challenge: Give students an example of a possible condition (you pay the phone bill early) and an obviously imaginary one (you won a million dollars). Working in pairs, students create a list of five possible conditions and five imaginary or impossible ones. Students use their lists to write real and unreal *if* clauses. Have pairs exchange their lists and add a result clause to each one to form complete sentences (If you pay the phone bill early, you won't have to pay a fine. If you won a million dollars, you could travel).

Order of clauses in conditional sentences

Procedure:

➤ On the board, write pairs of conditional sentences. In the first sentence of each pair, write the *if* clause first and circle the comma. In the second sentence, write the result clause first. You can use the example sentences from the grammar boxes on page 60 or your own sentences. If necessary, remind students that *I'd* is a contraction for *I would*.

➤ Read the sentence pairs out loud. Ask *Is there any difference in meaning between the two sentences?* (no) Ask *What is different in the two sentences?* Elicit the response that there is a comma between the two clauses in the first sentence. Tell students that when the *if* clause comes first, there is a comma before the result clause.

B. First complete . . .

➤ Focus students' attention on item 1. Read the first sentence aloud. Ask *Is this a real or an unreal condition?* (real) *How can you tell?* Elicit or tell students that the use of the future and the simple present tense provides a clue. Read the second sentence aloud. Ask *Is this a real or an unreal condition?* (unreal) *How can you tell?* Elicit or tell students that the use of *would* and the simple past tense provides a clue.

➤ Working individually, students complete the exercise.

➤ Students compare answers with a partner.

➤ Have volunteers write their pairs of sentences on the board.

Option: If possible, bring in the children's book *If You Give a Mouse a Cookie.* Read it aloud to provide extended examples of real conditions. (Other related books by author Laura Nemeroff are *If You Give a Moose a Muffin, If You Take a Mouse to School, If You Take a Mouse to the Movies, If You Give a Pig a Pancake.*)

Challenge. Tell students that you are going to tell a group story. Each person will contribute an unreal conditional sentence. Begin the story with an idea of your own or use this one: *If I were a movie star, I would live in Hollywood.* The next person must continue *If I lived in Hollywood, I would* or *could . . . .* If necessary, prompt students with the correct beginning.

➤ Do it yourself!

(For general suggestions, see *Introduction*, page Txiii.)

Procedure:

A–B.

➤ On the board, write a chart like the one on page 61 but with several more rows. Read aloud the heading in the first column *If I had more time,* and point out the comma. Fill in the first row for yourself; for example, *I could read more.* Write *What could you do if you had more time?* on the board and underline the word *could* to remind students to use it in their answer. Ask several students the question and write their responses in the first column.

➤ Read aloud the heading in the second column *If I had more money,* and fill in the first row for yourself. Continue, following the same procedure as before.

➤ Put students in small groups to compile their ideas. Elicit any new examples from the class. Make sure students are using *would* or *could* with the base form of the verb.

Order of clauses in conditional sentences

> In all conditional sentences, the clauses can be reversed with no change in meaning.
> If you don't return the book on time, you'll pay a fine.
> You'll pay a fine if you don't return the book on time.

B. First complete each conditional sentence as a real condition. Then write the sentence as an unreal condition.

1. He ___*will go*___ back to school if he ___*has*___ enough time.
    go   have

    He would go back to school if he had enough time.

2. If I ___get___ my electronics certification, I ___'ll get___ a better job.
    get   get

    If I got my electronics certification, I would / could get a better job.

3. If the library ___is___ open this afternoon, I ___'ll return___ these books.
    be   return

    If the library were open, I would / could return these books.

4. If she ___misses___ the deadline, she ___won't vote___ in this election.
    miss   not vote

    If she missed the deadline, she wouldn't vote in this election.

5. ___Will___ you ___register___ for English classes at work if they ___are___ offered?
             register   be

    Would you register for English classes at work if they were offered?

➤ Do it yourself!

A. Write what you would or could do if you had more time and more money.

If I had more time,	If I had more money,
I could learn to play the guitar.	I would take a great vacation.

B. Collaborative activity. Write all your sentences on the board in two lists. Then compare with your group or class.

Juggle commitments

❶ Mrs. Gebert, how nice to see you. How's Ronald?

He's fine, Ms. Fun. And how are you?

Fine, thanks.

❷ Please accept my apology again about the last appointment. I can't believe I missed it.

Co-payment expected at time of service.

Don't worry about it. I know you have a lot on your plate right now.

❸ I guess so. Ever since my husband went back to school, I'm just on total overload.

It's no picnic having to juggle everything. You're working right now, aren't you?

Yes. I have no choice if we want to make ends meet. I don't know what I'd do if I didn't have my mom to help out.

❹ Let me give you a little tip. If I were in your shoes, I'd write everything down—in one place. And make a habit of checking the list every morning.

That's good advice. I'll start that tomorrow. Better late than never!

A. Read the picture story again. Answer the questions.

1. Why is Mrs. Gebert apologizing? <u>She missed the last appointment.</u>

2. Why is Mrs. Gebert having a problem? <u>She has too much on her plate.</u>

3. What advice does Ms. Fun give her? <u>Make a list and check it every morning.</u>

B. Vocabulary. Choose one of the words or phrases in the box to complete each sentence.

make ends meet	better late than never	juggle
total overload	no picnic	

1. Many people have to _____<u>juggle</u>_____ parenthood and career. It's a time management problem.

2. When a mother or a father goes back to school, it's hard to _____<u>make ends meet</u>_____ if the other parent doesn't work.

Authentic practice

(For general suggestions, see *Introduction*, page Tx.)

Juggle commitments

Procedure:

➤ Point to the sign on the wall in the second picture. Ask *Where do you usually see this sign?* (at a doctor's or dentist's office) *How else can you tell this is a doctor's or dentist's office?* (The receptionist or nurse is wearing a white uniform.) *Why do you think the woman with the baby is here?* (She has an appointment.)

➤ Read the conversation out loud or play the cassette. With books open, students read and listen. Then ask students to underline all the idioms in the picture story: *juggle* (handle, balance), *have a lot on your plate* (have too many things to do), *I'm on total overload* (I'm overwhelmed, dealing with too much), *it's no picnic* (it's not easy), *make ends meet* (have enough money to pay for expenses), *if I were in your shoes* (if I were in your situation), *better late than never* (even if it is late to get started, it's a good idea to do it). Make sure students understand the meanings.

➤ Note that *better late than never* is similar in structure to another expression students know: *better safe than sorry.*

➤ Have students talk about the pressures and responsibilities that Mrs. Gebert is handling right now. Elicit examples: *her husband went back to school, she's on total overload, she's working, she has a young child.*

➤ Then have students find and circle two pieces of advice that Ms. Fun gives Mrs. Gebert (write everything down in one place, make a habit of checking the list every morning).

A. Read the picture story again . . .

➤ Working individually, students answer the questions and then compare answers with a partner. Review answers as a class.

➤ To support their answers, have students underline the appropriate lines in the text.

Option: In pairs, have students offer additional advice to Mrs. Gebert.

B. Vocabulary . . .

➤ Students read the items in the box and then find and circle each one in the picture story. To reinforce context as a way of getting meaning, have students reread the speech balloons in which the items occur.

➤ Note that the exercise continues on page 63. Have students complete the entire exercise individually. Then review the five sentences as a class.

Challenge: After reviewing the answers, have students use each idiom in an original sentence. Have students check their sentences with a partner before reading them aloud.

If your students are ready . . .

Culture / Civics note: Many of your students may come from cultures where extended families are the norm. Our North American culture is a mobile one, and often nuclear families are separated geographically from grandparents, aunts and uncles and cousins, and other family members. Mrs. Gebert is fortunate to have her mother close by to help her. Many families in this culture turn to social service agencies or private organizations for help in difficult times. These may include day-care arrangements, federal food stamp programs, and government loans to students.

🎧 C. Listen . . .

➤ Students listen to two statements and read the correct responses from the picture story. If students have difficulty, prompt them by reading the response yourself.

➤ Review the answers before having students read their responses out loud.

Challenge: Use the items in the tapescript as a dictation. Have students listen to the statements and write what they hear. Allow students to listen as many times as necessary. Ask volunteers to write the questions on the board. Make corrections as a class. Students can then practice the prompts and responses with a partner.

D–E.

➤ Students complete the exercise individually and then compare responses with a partner.

➤ Partners read the items and responses, switching roles for more practice.

Option: After both students have practiced reading the items and responses in Exercise D, have Partner B in each pair close his or her book. Partner A then reads the item, and Partner B responds from memory.

Option: After students have practiced reading the items and responses, have them close their books. They then respond chorally when you read the items in random order.

Challenge: Have pairs of students work together to write a statement or a question for each unused response in Exercise D. For example, in item 1, a statement that could elicit the response *I don't believe it!* might be *You missed another appointment.* Have students take turns reading their new items and responses.

➤ Do it yourself!

(For general suggestions, see *Introduction*, page Txiii.)

Procedure:

A. Write your own response . . .

➤ Students read each speech balloon and speculate who the person might be. (a close friend or colleague, a family member)

➤ Model this activity with a more advanced student. Ask the student to read the first speech balloon so that you can demonstrate an appropriate response. Note that there are three different speakers, so the conversations do not have to be linked.

➤ Students read the speech balloons and complete the activity individually.

➤ Review as a class. Have a volunteer read each speech balloon and elicit a variety of appropriate responses.

➤ Students read their conversations out loud with a partner and then change roles to practice both parts.

B. Culture talk . . .

Option: Put students in groups. Ask them to create a Venn diagram illustrating the similarities and differences between their home cultures and this culture. Prompt them with questions such as *What stresses did you have in your home country? What stresses do you have here? What stresses are the same in both cultures?* Elicit some examples and model a Venn diagram on the board.

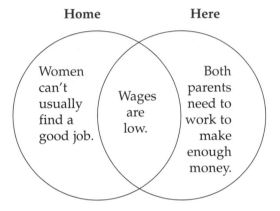

Home   Here

Women can't usually find a good job. | Wages are low. | Both parents need to work to make enough money.

Tapescript

1. Please accept my apology again about the last appointment. I can't believe I missed it.

2. Let me give you a little tip. If I were in your shoes, I'd write everything down—in one place. And make a habit of checking the list every morning.

3. When you have too many commitments, you feel like you're on ___total overload___.

4. Start organizing your day beginning right now: _Better late than never_

5. Another way to say something is really hard is "It's ___no picnic___."

🎧 **C. Listen. Read each response out loud from the text on page 62.**

D. Read each sentence or question. Underline your response.

1. "Please accept my apology."

   YOU <u>Don't worry. It's OK.</u>   **YOU** I don't believe it!

2. "Why did you miss the appointment?"

   YOU I just couldn't make ends meet.   **YOU** <u>I just have too much on my plate.</u>

3. "It's really hard to make ends meet."

   YOU <u>You're working right now, aren't you?</u>   **YOU** Thank goodness.

4. "I'm on total overload!"

   YOU Better late than never.   **YOU** <u>I know—it's no picnic.</u>

5. "What would you do if you were in my shoes?"

   YOU <u>I'd ask my mother to help.</u>   **YOU** That's good advice.

E. Pair work. Take turns reading the items and responses in Exercise D.

➤ Do it yourself!

A. Write your own response. Then read each conversation out loud with a partner.

You look like you're on total overload. What's the matter?

YOU _____

What are you going to do to avoid missing so many appointments?

YOU _____

If you don't mind my advice, I think you should make a list. That way you'll remember everything.

YOU _____

B. Culture talk. In the country you come from, is juggling family and work more complicated or less complicated than it is here? Compare cultures with your classmates.

Time management

🎧 **A.** **Listening comprehension. Listen to the lecture on time management. Then listen again. As you listen, take notes on what Dr. Gutentag says.**

> _NOTES_   (Notes will vary.)
>
> _____
>
> _____
>
> _____
>
> _____

B. **Discussion. Answer the question. Then discuss with a partner.**

According to the lecture, what can we do to help manage our time? _____

prioritize responsibilities
_____

C. **Vocabulary. Choose one of the words from the box to complete each sentence.**

perfectionism	procrastination	prioritization

1. Doing the most important things before doing the least important things is
   _____prioritization_____.

2. Putting off until tomorrow what you can do today is _____procrastination_____.

3. Expecting yourself to do everything well is _____perfectionism_____.

D. **Read about Ramon Cruz's and Wendy Del Aguila's time management problems. Then choose advice from the list below or give your own advice.**

> _Ask someone else to help._
>
> _Reschedule a less important commitment._
>
> _Prioritize—you've got too much on your plate._
>
> _Just say no._

1. Ramon Cruz works from 9:00 to 5:00. His wife just had foot surgery. She can't walk or drive for a week. His daughter has a doctor's appointment on Tuesday at 4:00. His son has soccer practice at 3:30 on Tuesday and Thursday. His wife agreed to help at voter registration on Wednesday, and they have books due at the library.

   Your advice to Ramon Cruz: _____

Authentic practice

(For general suggestions, see *Introduction*, page Tx.)

Time management

Procedure:

A. Listening comprehension ...

➤ Ask students to read the bar. Check understanding of the term *time management.* Elicit that it means using our time effectively to get done what we need to do.

➤ Read the directions and brainstorm possible time management tips. Based on the picture story, answers may include *Ask someone to help out, write all obligations down in one place.* Tell students that in this selection they will hear some additional suggestions to help them manage time.

➤ Tell students that they should first listen for the main ideas of the lecture. Play the cassette or read the tapescript.

➤ Write on the board *perfectionism, procrastination, prioritization.* Elicit brief definitions based on the information in the selection.

➤ Understanding a lecture and taking notes are important academic skills. Tell students to take notes as they listen a second time.

Option: Using a graphic organizer can help with taking notes. Put the following outline on the board, and ask students to complete it in their notebook.

Time Management Problems

A. Causes	B. Remedy
1.	1.
Explanation:	Explanation:
2.	
Explanation:	

B–C.

➤ Working individually, students complete the exercises. Have them refer to their notes.

➤ In pairs, students compare answers. Check exercises as a class and have volunteers read their answers to Exercise B aloud.

Option: Is your class full of perfectionists, procrastinators, or prioritizers? Have students rate their perfectionism, procrastinating, and prioritizing on a scale of 1 (least) to 5 (most). For example, someone who is content with things that are less than perfect might be rated as a 1 on perfectionism. Someone who is not happy unless everything is done absolutely perfectly might be rated as a 5. A person who never procrastinates, who always does things on time or ahead of time would get a 1 rating on procrastination. Tally the results on the board.

D. Read about ...

➤ Note that this exercise continues on page 65.

➤ Ask students to quickly read Ramon Cruz's and Wendy Del Aguila's time management problems. Make sure students understand the following terms: *bit off more than she can chew, Girl Scouts, den mother, carpools.*

➤ Read the list of possible advice aloud.

➤ Put students in groups of three. Designate one member in each group as reader, one as facilitator, and another as reporter. The reader reads both time management problems to the group, the facilitator encourages everyone to contribute advice, and the reporter tells the group's ideas to the class.

➤ When the small groups are finished, elicit their advice for Ramon and for Wendy.

Tapescript

Woman: This is Business Today, a service of KKCC Radio, Kalamazoo Public Radio, being brought to you today direct from the business management school of Kalamazoo Community College. This lecture was recorded on September 12 and is replayed here for our radio audience. [pause]
    Good morning. Today's lecture is on time management. Our guest lecturer is Professor Heinz Gutentag, visiting KCC from the University of Gutenberg. Professor Gutentag, good day.

Man: Good day to you and to the listeners. Today I'd like to discuss the two most important causes of time management problems and offer a simple, effective solution.
    First: Perfectionism. Now, no human being can be perfect. In today's busy world, almost everybody has too much to do and not enough time to do it in. And somewhere in our childhood, we are given the message that we have to do everything perfectly.
    Take a moment to step back from your commitments and evaluate whether it's realistic to try to accomplish them all. You may have bitten off more than you can chew. But, if you need two jobs to make ends meet, if you want to go back to school to train for a better job, if you have children who need your care and a house that needs keeping, you may have no choice. If that's the case, then forgive yourself for your mistakes, for the work undone, for the occasional missed appointment and deadline. If you forgive yourself, then others will too.

(Tapescript is continued on page T65.)

Tapescript (*continued from page T64*)

The second major contributor to time management problems is procrastination. When we have too much to do, and when we are perfectionistic, we tend to procrastinate. Procrastination is putting off until tomorrow what we should do today. Sometimes we procrastinate because we're afraid that if we don't have enough time to do something, we won't do it well. But when you're on overload, you just have to roll up your sleeves, put one foot in front of the other, and forgive yourself if what you do isn't perfect. Others will forgive you too.

Now for the remedy. Since most people are perfectionistic, and most people procrastinate, the solution is to prioritize. Prioritization is deciding which of your responsibilities are essential and which are not essential. Make a list of the things you absolutely have to do. Call that list the A list.

Next, make another list of what you'd like to do if you had enough time. Call that list the B list.

Finally, make a list of things you don't really have to do or that you can get someone <u>else</u> to do. Call that the C list. Then put your day in order. Don't spend time on tasks from the B and C lists until you're sure the A list is taken care of. Another way to say this is don't procrastinate on the A list.

A final thought: Some lives are just too difficult to prioritize. Sometimes the only way to manage a busy life is to learn to say no. If someone asks you to work the booth at the school book fair and you've promised yourself you would pay all your bills on time, just say no . . . politely.

So, to review. We all have too much to do and too little time. This causes unhappiness because we cling to the idea that we must do everything perfectly, with no mistakes. We procrastinate and make the problem worse by putting things off. We can help ourselves by prioritizing our tasks. And, when all else fails, we can learn to politely say no.

Option: Draw a blank "to-do" list for the next week on the board. Ask students to complete a list for Ramon and one for Wendy. The list for Ramon might include the following items:

Ramon's "to-do" list

Monday	Tuesday	Wednesday	Thursday	Friday
Work until 5:00	3:30: Take son to soccer practice			

Note: Keep the list on the board as a reference for the *Do it yourself!* activity on this page.

E. Discussion . . .

➤ In pairs or small groups, students list the week's responsibilities for Ramon and for Wendy. Next to each responsibility, they write a consequence of missing the appointment, deadline, or obligation. Ramon's list might include the following:

Responsibility	Consequence of missing it
• Return library books • Help at voter registration	• Pay a fine • They'll have to get someone else

➤ Have groups share the consequences of each missed deadline.

➤ Do it yourself!

(For general suggestions, see Introduction, page Txiii.)

Procedure:

A–C.

➤ Working individually, students make "to-do" lists for themselves including their obligations and responsibilities for tomorrow or for the week. Refer students to Ramon's "to-do" list that they completed in the Option for Exercise D above.

➤ To help students understand how to prioritize their lists, ask *What should you write A next to?* (the most essential things, things they have to do no matter what) Elicit examples such as go to work and take care of the children. Ask *What items are B items?* (things they might do, things they'll do if they have time) Elicit examples such as go to the library and drop clothes off at the cleaners. Finally ask *What items on your list can be classified as C?* (least essential things, things they don't have to do or that someone else can do) Elicit examples such as help with the bake sale and go to the movies with a friend.

➤ Students write A, B, or C next to each item on their list and then explain to a partner the reasons for their prioritization.

2. Wendy Del Aguila bit off more than she can chew. She's a Girl Scout den mother, a volunteer at the hospital, the mother of three children, and a single parent. Wendy works until 3:00 in the office of her children's school and then carpools three days a week. On Tuesday, Wendy hears about a Girl Scout bake sale. She'd like to bake cookies with the girls in her kitchen on Wednesday, but her driver's license will expire on Thursday.

Your advice to Wendy Del Aguila: _____

E. **Discussion. Describe the consequences of missing each deadline in Exercise D. Use *if*.**

> If he doesn't return the library books, he'll have to pay a fine.

➤ Do it yourself!

A. **Make your own "to-do" list for tomorrow or for this week.**

To do! _____

_____

_____

_____

B. **Prioritize your list.**

- A for things you have to do no matter what
- B for things you'll do if you have the time
- C for things you don't really have to do or that you can get someone else to do

C. **Discussion. Discuss your list and your priorities with a partner or a group.**

> If I don't do the laundry today, the kids won't have anything to wear!

> If I don't buy groceries today, I could buy them tomorrow.

The importance of time sensitivity

A. Read and listen to the letters.

Ask Joan

Culture tips for newcomers

Dear Joan:

I just can't get used to one thing in this country. I think people here are very nervous about time. And they are making me nervous too!

At work I have to punch a time clock, and if I'm five minutes late from my break, my manager gives me a dirty look. If I come late to someone's house for a party, they are unfriendly to me.

I think this is silly, and I think people should just relax! What would happen if someone brought a book back to the library a couple of days late? What would the big deal be? Sometimes it takes a little longer to finish the book. And if the people who are giving the party are my friends, why do they mind if I'm not right on time? And what's so terrible if I pay my rent a day or two late? The landlord has a lot of money. Believe me, he won't starve!

Please explain to me, Joan: Why are the people here so crazy about schedules and time? I think it's very unfriendly.

Deborah in Dallas

Dear Deborah:

You don't say where you come from, but it is true that each culture has its own ideas about the importance of schedules, times, and dates. Adjusting to a different concept of time can be very difficult, even more difficult than adjusting to other customs such as food or clothing styles.

It's very hard to explain why one culture has one idea and another culture sees things differently. In every culture, though, "rules" have developed in order to prevent conflicts and misunderstandings between people.

If you think about this a little, you will realize that in some ways time is important to you too. I'm sure you don't like to wait a long time when you have an appointment to see a doctor or a dentist. Remember, Deborah, that no matter how different our cultures may seem, people all over the world are basically the same: friendly, fun-loving, hardworking, but in ways that may look different from the outside.

Joan

B. Culture talk. Discuss the following questions.

1. What do you think about the attitudes toward time in this country? Do they make you uncomfortable? Have you adjusted? Give examples.

2. If someone from this culture went to live in your country, what cultural rules would be difficult to understand or adjust to? Give examples so your classmates will understand.

3. Where do you think Deborah comes from originally? Why do you think that?

Authentic practice

(For general suggestions, see Introduction, page Tx.)

The importance of time sensitivity

Procedure:

A. Read and listen to the letters.

➤ Before playing the cassette or reading the letters . . . ask *How important is being on time at work? How important is being on time for social activities?*

➤ As students listen to and read the letters, pause at the end of each paragraph and ask volunteers to retell the main information in their own words.

Option: Have students find and underline all the conditional sentences in the letters. Remind students to look for the word *if* as they scan the letters. Have students determine which sentences express real conditions and which unreal conditions.

Option: After students have read and listened to the letters, have students close their books. Write the following sentences on the board. Ask students to number the sentences from 1 to 6, according to their order in the letters. Let the students listen again so they can check their answers (4, 1, 5, 3, 2, 6).

_____ It's very hard to explain why one culture has one idea and another culture sees things differently.

_____ I think people here are very nervous about time.

_____ I'm sure you don't like to wait a long time when you have an appointment to see a doctor or a dentist.

_____ I think it's very unfriendly.

_____ Sometimes it takes a little longer to finish the book.

_____ People all over the world are basically the same: friendly, fun-loving, hard-working.

Challenge: Joan tries to respond to Deborah's argument point by point. Have pairs of students find Joan's answer to each of Deborah's concerns. They can also add their own answers.

1. I think people here are very nervous about time.
2. What would the big deal be if (something) were late?
3. I think (being crazy about schedules and time) is unfriendly.

B. Culture talk . . .

➤ Read the questions aloud and elicit examples from the class. Write them on the board.

➤ Remind students that generalizations and stereotypes are often unfair to individuals. Encourage students to talk about other cultures with respect.

C. Collaborative activity...

➤ Put students in groups of four. Tell students that when completing a group project, it is often a good idea to divide up the tasks. To register Grace for kindergarten, the group must first understand the document. Each student should take one of the bulleted items and read the document to find information that relates to the item: *If you don't have a family doctor you can go to a clinic; Grace can get the booster at one of the clinics; she is eligible for kindergarten this year;* and *Grafton School registers students on Tuesday, May 7.* Students report their findings to their group.

➤ The groups create two lists: documents to prepare and things to do. The list of things to do should be chronological, beginning with tasks that must take place early in the process and ending with the deadline of kindergarten registration. Suggest that students work backwards from the registration date. Ask questions such as *What day will Grace register?* (Tuesday, May 7) *What immunizations does she need to have to register?* Elicit that she needs a polio booster. *How can she get the booster?* (by going to one of the Clark County Health Department clinics)

➤ Remind students to read the entire document carefully to create their lists.

➤ While groups are working on their lists, circulate and offer help as necessary.

Option: Have the groups create calendars that begin with April 1 and run through May 7. Note that the document states that May 7 is a Tuesday. Students can use that information to write in the dates. Have students decide when they will do each task and write it on the calendar. For example, students might write "Pick up registration packet at Grafton School Office" in the calendar box for Tuesday, April 9.

Challenge: Ask students to write 10 *if* statements using the information on the document about Denton Area City Schools. The statements can give the consequences of missing deadlines (*If Grace doesn't get her booster before May 7, she won't be able to register*) as well as explanations of the policies (*If a student turns five in October, he or she will have to wait until next year to enter kindergarten*).

D. Discussion...

➤ Ask representatives from each group to come to the board and write down their "to-do" list in chronological order.

➤ Have different representatives write down the list of documents.

➤ Have the class look at the lists on the board. Ask questions such as *What differences do you see? Did everyone do the same thing first? Is there anything missing from the lists?*

➤ Do it yourself!

(For general suggestions, see *Introduction*, page Txiii.)

Procedure:

➤ Have students work in the four topic groups that were created at the beginning of the unit (see page T57). Ask students to get out the information that they researched.

➤ Have the four topic groups compare information.

➤ Create new groups of four, consisting of one student from each of the four topic areas. Ask them to discuss the following questions: *Which process is the simplest? Which is the most complicated? Which one has the most requirements? Which one takes the longest? Which one is the most important to your family?*

C. **Collaborative activity. With a group, make a list of things to do and documents to prepare to register a child named Grace Lukin for kindergarten in September. Decide together when to do each activity. Today's date is April 1.**

- Grace has no family doctor.
- She needs a polio booster.
- Her fifth birthday is September 10.
- She lives in the Grafton School attendance area.

Denton Area City Schools

Kindergarten Registration

Denton Area City Schools will hold kindergarten registration during the week of May 6 through May 9. Each elementary school building will register students in its attendance area as follows:

Monday, May 6	**Tuesday, May 7**	**Wednesday, May 8**	**Thursday, May 9**
Smith School	Grafton School	Denton School	Ennis School
(426-0572)	(265-5372)	(466-0224)	(486-0705)

Students whose last names begin with A through L will register between 8:30 and 11:30 a.m., while M through Z will register between 12:30 and 3:30 p.m.

Registration packets will be available at each elementary school office after April 8. Parents are asked to pick up and complete the registration forms prior to registration day.

To be eligible for kindergarten, students must be five years old by September 30. Children whose birthday falls after September 30 will not enter kindergarten until the following year.

PLEASE BRING YOUR CHILD, and the following information, as required by law, with you for registration:

1. Birth Certificate
2. Social Security Number
3. Registration Form
4. Written Proof of Immunization:
   * DPT (diphtheria, pertussis, tetanus) — minimum of 4 (including 1 booster)
   * Polio — minimum of 3 or 4 (including 1 booster)
   * MMR (measles, mumps, rubella) — 2 doses of each
   * Hepatitis B — 3 doses
5. Proof of Legal Guardianship

If you do not have a family doctor to complete the necessary immunizations, the Clark County Health Department sponsors the following clinics:

* Every Tuesday, 10:00 a.m. – 12:00 noon, Denton Community Center
* Every Monday and Friday, 9:00 a.m. – 3:00 p.m., Denton Health Department

D. **Discussion. Write your lists on the board and compare.**

➤ Do it yourself! A plan-ahead project

Choose one of these subjects and get information about deadlines. Compare information with your classmates. Make a "to-do" list.

- registering a child at a day-care center
- voter registration
- community college registration
- immunizations for schoolchildren

Review

(For general suggestions, see *Introduction*, page Txii.)

Procedure:

A. Pair work or group work.

Ask and answer questions.

➤ Have students take turns asking each other questions about the picture. Model the activity with a more advanced student. Hold up the textbook and point to the woman on the phone. Ask *Who is she talking to?* (someone at the dentist's office) The student answers and then asks you a question such as *Why did the office call?* (The woman missed her appointment.) Model one more question and answer and then have students ask and answer questions with a partner.

➤ Point out the two questions asked in the directions and suggest that students ask who the different people in the picture are and what the problems are. Begin by pointing to the man reading in the background. Ask *Who do you think he is?* (the father) *What is he doing?* (reading, listening to music on his headphones) *Why isn't he helping?*

Create conversations.

➤ In pairs, students create conversations between the mother with the baby and the receptionist, and between the woman at the door and the boy doing homework.

➤ Have pairs number each person in the picture and, on a separate sheet of paper, write one line of conversation for each one.

➤ Remind students to refer to the model conversations on pages 58 and 59 for help and ideas. Circulate to offer help as necessary.

➤ Ask volunteers to role-play their conversations for the class.

Tell a story.

Option: Put yourself in another's shoes. Have students tell what they would do if they were the mother, the receptionist, the woman at the door, the boy doing homework. Give students an example such as *If I were the mother, I would ask my husband to come and get the baby. Then I would ask him to do the laundry and . . .*

Option: Prioritize. Tell students to read the "to-do" list on the refrigerator. In pairs, have them prioritize the list, using A for things that must be done no matter what, B for things that the mother will do if she has enough time, and C for things someone else can do. Then imagine what advice the mother's best friend might give her.

Challenge: Tell students that sometimes stories have morals or lessons. Ask them to look at the people in the picture and imagine one lesson each might have learned from their experience. They should then express this lesson in a sentence beginning with *If*. Model the activity for students by pointing to the woman at the door and saying *If it's my turn to carpool, I'm going to call first.*

🎧 B-C.

➤ Have a volunteer read the document out loud. Ask the class to predict the topic of the listening exercise.

➤ After students listen to the conversation the first time, have students read the statements so they will know what to listen for. Allow students to listen to the conversation as many additional times as necessary to complete the exercise.

Option: Have partners rewrite the false statements in Exercise C to make them true.

D-E.

➤ Students work individually to complete the review exercises.

➤ Circulate to offer help as needed.

➤ Have students check answers with a partner. Review answers as a class.

➤ Identify any areas of difficulty that may require additional instruction and practice.

Tapescript

Male: Good morning. DMV. This is Manolo. How can I direct your call?

Female: I'd like some information about a driver's license.

Male: Is this a new license or a renewal?

Female: A new license.

Male: What's the age of the applicant?

Female: She's 15. Her birthday is June 24th.

Male: Is she planning to take driver's education in school?

Female: I'm not sure. Sometimes the classes fill up.

Male: Well, if she doesn't take driver's education, then she can't have a senior license until she's 18.

Female: That's too bad.

Male: The law is that if she wants a senior license with no restrictions before her eighteenth birthday, then she has to have completed a full three-months driver's ed course and received her certificate before she takes her driver's test.

Female: Can't she just take lessons at a driving school?

Male: No. She has to have state-certified driver's ed through a public school. I'm sorry. That's the law.

Female: OK. Well, I guess there's still time. It's only February. I'll check whether there are openings in the course.

Male: You know, if the classes are filled up at her high school, there are public adult education driver's ed courses that are given at night for adults who work during the day. You can pick that list up at the DMV or log onto our Web site for the list. That's www.dmv.st.gov.

Female: Thanks. I'll go to the Web site.

Male: OK, then. Is there anything else I can help you with?

Female: No, thanks.

Male: OK. Bye.

> If you are under the age of 18 and hold a junior driver's license, you can bring proof of completion of a driver education course approved by the

🎧 **C.** **Read the statements and listen to the conversation again. Then check *True* or *False* for each statement.**

		True	False
1.	The caller wants to renew her daughter's driver's license.	☐	☑
2.	The girl will be sixteen in June.	☑	☐
3.	You can only take driver's ed at your own high school.	☑	☑
4.	If you are seventeen, you have to take driver's ed to get a senior license.	☐	☐

D. **Read each sentence or question. Underline your response.**

1. "Do you mind if I give you a tip?"

   YOU How much?   **YOU** <u>Not at all.</u>

2. "What would you do if you were in my shoes?"

   YOU I'd <u>prioritize.</u>   **YOU** I'd procrastinate.

3. "It sounds like you're on total overload."

   YOU <u>Yes. I've got too much on my plate.</u>   **YOU** Better late than never.

4. "What would you do if you couldn't make ends meet?"

   YOU I would have no choice.   **YOU** <u>I'd get a night job.</u>

E. **Read the conditional sentences. Check the ones that describe an unreal condition.**

1. ☐ If you take driver's ed, you can get a license earlier.
2. ☑ If Pete got some more training, he could get a promotion.
3. ☑ If I worked a second job, I could make ends meet.
4. ☐ If you don't have three DPT shots, you can't register for kindergarten.

F. Complete each real conditional sentence with a result clause.

1. If you pay a credit card bill after the due date, _____(Answers will vary.)_____ .

2. If you have an overdue library book, _____ .

3. If you forget to renew your driver's license, _____ .

4. If you don't register to vote, _____ .

G. Complete each unreal conditional sentence with the correct form of the verb.

1. He __would take__ driver's ed if he __were__ in a hurry to get a license.
   take   be

2. If I __went__ back to school, I __would need__ a part-time job.
   go   need

3. If the DMV __were__ open on weekends, I __could / would take__ my driver's test sooner.
   be   take

4. What do you think he __would do__ if he __were__ in your shoes?
   do   be

H. Read the overdue policy from the Milwaukee, Wisconsin, public library system. Then compute the overdue charges on this book. Today's date is June 1.

Charges: ____$5.00_____

TITLE: **Overload! It's not the end of the world.**

DUE: **03/15**

Milwaukee Public Library

Address: @ http://www.mpl.org/File/libcard_about.htm   › go

Overdue charges

- The fee is 10 cents per item per day, including Sundays and holidays. For most items there is a three-day grace period during which no fines are charged. On the fourth day the overdue charges total 40 cents.
- The maximum overdue charge is $5 per item.
- There are no fines on overdue materials checked out on children's library cards, except videos, DVDs and puppets.
- Rental books may be checked out for $1 per week. When rental books are not returned in one week, cardholders are charged $1 for each additional week (or portion of a week) the books are out.
- The Milwaukee Public Library accepts Master Card and Visa.

Web zone

I. Composition. On a separate sheet of paper, write about the picture on page 68. Say as much as you can.

> **Now I can**
> ❑ understand the consequences of missing deadlines.
> ❑ apologize for missing an appointment.
> ❑ manage time.
> ❑ prioritize.
> ❑ anticipate and plan actions necessary to make deadlines.

F–G.

➤ Students work individually to complete the review exercises.

➤ Circulate to offer help as needed.

➤ Have students check answers with a partner. Review answers as a class.

➤ Identify any areas of difficulty that may require additional instruction and practice.

H. Read the overdue policy...

➤ Have students read the information on overdue charges from the Milwaukee Public Library.

➤ Make sure students understand the meaning of a *grace period* (time during which no fines are charged).

➤ Ask *What's the title of the overdue book? (Overload! It's Not the End of the World) When was the due date?* (March 15) *What is today's date?* (June 1) *How many days overdue is this book?* (78) Then have students figure out the amount of the fine ($5.00).

I. Composition...

➤ Provide students with concrete approaches to writing about the picture on page 68. Use one of the options that follow, give students a choice of options, or assign options based on students' levels of proficiency. Model what is expected of students for each option.

➤ Advise students to look back through the unit for help and ideas as they write.

➤ Circulate to offer help as needed.

Option: Have students imagine they are the woman with the baby. They should write to Joan, telling her they are on total overload, and ask for advice.

Option: Have students write a sentence beginning with *If* about each item on the "to-do" list on the refrigerator. The sentences should include a consequence of not meeting the obligation. For example, *If I don't do the laundry, the baby won't have any clean clothes.*

Option: Have students write an extended conversation for one of the pairs in the picture on page 68. Have students refer to the model conversations on pages 58 and 59 for an example of the form to use.

Challenge: Have students write a story like the group story they told on page T61. Model a beginning such as *If you miss your dental appointment, the office is going to call. If the office calls at dinner time . . .* Tell students to write at least six connected sentences based on the picture on page 68.

Now I can

➤ Read the first item in the box out loud: *Now I can understand the consequences of missing deadlines.* Elicit from the class an example such as *If I forget to return a library book, I will have to pay a fine.*

➤ Put students in pairs. Tell the students to take turns reading each item in the box and giving an example of what they have learned. When students can provide an example, they should check that box. If there are items students aren't able to check, have them look back through the unit for ideas.

➤ When students are finished reviewing with their partners, read each item out loud and elicit an example from the class.

➤ Refer to the piece of paper on which you wrote the students' questions about one of the objectives (from page T57). Ask what questions students answered as they worked on this unit.

Oral test (optional)

You may want to use the *Now I can* box as an informal evaluation. While students are working on the *Composition* activity, you can call them up individually and check their ability with two or three objectives.

Your supplies and resources

Note: Have students bring envelopes to class for the *Do it yourself!* activity on page 75. You will also need telephone books for this activity. For an activity on page 79, ask students to bring in newspaper or magazine articles that discuss damage to homes, especially damage caused by bad weather such as tornadoes, hurricanes, and ice storms.

 Preview

(For general suggestions, see *Introduction*, page Tviii.)

Warm up. What is the purpose of an estimate? Which painter would you hire? Why?

Procedure:

➤ Draw on students' prior experience by asking questions about their own home and car repairs, such as *Have you ever had your house painted? Have you ever needed car repair service? How did you decide which painter or repair person to hire? Did you get an estimate?*

➤ Point to the word *estimate* in the first illustration. Ask *What does it say next to the word "estimate"?* ($4,500, including labor and supplies) *What do you think an estimate deals with?* (the cost of something) Ask *What is an estimate?* Elicit or tell students that *an estimate* is someone's best guess about something, often referring to cost. Tell students that the word *estimate* can be either a noun or a verb. Point out the two different pronunciations (an "est<u>imit</u>," to est<u>imate</u>). Ask *What does the verb "estimate" mean?* (guess, approximate)

➤ To encourage critical thinking, ask *Why is an estimate important for the consumer?* (It tells the cost of a service in advance.) *Why is an estimate important for the service provider?* (It spells out exactly what the provider will do for a certain price.)

➤ Have students read the two estimates in the *Warm up* section. Check comprehension by asking questions such as *What service is the estimate for?* (painting a house) *Whose house is it?* (Mr. and Mrs. Paul Mitchell's) *Where do they live?* (45 Plainview Court, Milton, Colorado) Point out that both estimates are on company stationery, or letterhead, with the company name, address, and (for Velela Household Painting) phone number.

➤ Point to the two logos. Make sure students understand the word *logo* (a design that is a company's official sign). Ask students *What do the logos tell you about the companies?* (The paintbrush suggests painting, and the KBS logo suggests a house or building.)

➤ Put students in small groups to discuss what factors they would consider in hiring a painter. Have them list and rank these factors from 1 to 5 by importance, with 1 the least important. Write the groups' ideas on the board. The list might include these factors: *cost, time, reputation, personal knowledge of the company, friendliness, size.*

➤ Still in groups, students make a list of the differences between the two estimates. Elicit ideas and write them on the board. You may have a table like the following:

Velela	Konstantanides
• Located in Denver	• Located in Milton
• Hand-written estimate	• Typed estimate
• States the brand of paint	• No brand specified
• Includes labor and supplies	• Labor will be additional
• Cost is estimated as $4,500	• Cost is estimated as $3,600

➤ Ask students which company they would choose to paint their house. Have them explain the reasons for their choices. Ask *Which estimate do you think is most accurate?* Elicit that Velela's is more accurate because it includes the cost of labor, which is often hard for consumers to estimate. In fact, the labor cost can exceed the cost of supplies.

Unit 6 objectives

Procedure:

➤ Have students read the objectives. Ask *What do you think this unit will help you do?* (be a better consumer, know how to decide on a service provider, know about different kinds of insurance) Tell students to write down any questions they may have about the three types of insurance.

➤ Collect the questions and save them to discuss at the end of the unit.

Your supplies and resources

> **Preview**

Warm up. What is the purpose of an estimate? Which painter would you hire? Why?

Velela Household Painting
15678 E. Dakota Avenue, Denver, CO 80232
(303) 555-7838

Mr. and Mrs. Paul Mitchell
45 Plainview Court, Milton, CO 80231
Paint all sides of house with Silas Morton paints, 2 coats
Estimate: $4,500, including labor and supplies

Konstantanides Building Services
4597 Brenner Avenue, Milton, CO 80211

For Paul Mitchell, 45 Plainview Court
Paint house, 2 coats, $3,600 + labor

Unit 6 objectives

- Ask for a recommendation of a person who provides a service.
- Ask for an estimate and get it in writing.
- Make an agreement.
- Understand homeowner's, car, and life insurance.

Model 1   Ask for an estimate. Get it in writing.

A. Listen and read.

> A: Can you give me an estimate?
> B: Yes. It'll be about $500.
> A: How long will it take?
> B: Three or four days.
> A: Will you put that in writing?
> B: Of course. No problem.

B. Pronunciation and intonation practice.

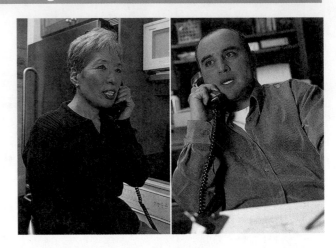

Vocabulary

Services you should get an estimate for

a paint job

dental work

an auto repair

construction

plumbing

electrical work

C. Pair work. Ask for an estimate. Get it in writing.

> A: Can you give me an estimate?
> B: _____1_____. It'll be about $_____.
> A: How long will it take?
> B: _____2_____.
> A: Will you put that in writing?
> B: _____3_____.

[1]Of course, Sure
[2]Three hours, a week, etc.
[3]Sure, No problem

Practical conversations

(For general suggestions, see *Introduction*, page Tviii.)

Model 1

Content: asking for an estimate, getting an estimate in writing, services you should get an estimate for

Procedure:

A–B.

➤ Have students first cover the conversation. Ask them to read the bar and then look at the photos. Ask *What do you think the people are talking about?* (an estimate) *Who do you think the customer is?* (the woman) *Who's the service provider?* (the man)

➤ Tell students that they are going to listen for the answers to the questions *How much?* and *How long?* With books closed or with the text still covered, students listen to the conversation.

➤ Then ask *How much will it cost?* ($500) *How long will it take?* (three or four days)

➤ Have students read the conversation silently. Check comprehension by asking questions such as *What does the caller want?* (an estimate) *Will the man write down the cost and the time it will take?* (yes) *What kind of job or service is the estimate for?* (We don't know.)

➤ Play the cassette or read the conversation again. Have students repeat the lines in the pauses.

Vocabulary

➤ Play the cassette or read the items and have students repeat.

➤ Read the services one at a time in random order and have students point to the pictures.

➤ Ask questions about the services, such as *Which services might you have done at your house or apartment?* (a paint job, construction, plumbing, electrical work) *Which ones are done at the service provider's place of business?* (an auto repair, dental work) *Which service do you think the people in the conversation were talking about? Why is it important to get an estimate for these services?* (The cost of the service varies from job to job.)

➤ Brainstorm other services for which consumers should get an estimate. Write the ideas on the board. Students' ideas might include *a decorating job, mowing the lawn, cutting down a tree.*

C. Pair work ...

➤ Model the conversation with a more advanced student. Play the role of Student B, the service provider, to demonstrate how to give cost and time estimates.

➤ Have the students practice the conversation in pairs, switching roles to play both parts. Tell students to choose a service from the *Vocabulary* or the list on the board in order to give more realistic estimates.

Option: Write on the board *Can you give me an estimate on the _____ we talked about yesterday?* Ask a volunteer to read the line using one of the services from the *Vocabulary* or the list on the board; for example, *Can you give me the estimate on the paint job we talked about yesterday?* Note that students will have to change *a* or *an* to *the.* Students practice this modified conversation in pairs. Ask volunteers to present their conversation to the class.

Model 2

Content: asking for a recommendation, benefiting from word of mouth, descriptions of good workers, service people

Procedure:

🎧 A–B.

➤ To set the scene for the conversation, point to the photo and ask questions such as *Who do you see in the picture?* (a man and a woman) *Where are they?* (outside, talking over a fence) *What do you think their relationship is?* (friends, neighbors) Point to the illustration and ask *What do you think they're talking about?* (a painter, a paint job)

➤ Have a volunteer read the bar above the conversation. Ask *What is word of mouth?* (information that one person tells another, information we get from talking about something rather than reading about it or seeing it on TV)

➤ After students listen to the conversation and read along silently, check comprehension by asking *What does the woman want?* (a good painter) *What is the description of the painter?* (He's reasonable and does a really good job.) *How is the neighbor going to help?* (He's going to give the woman the name of a painter.)

➤ Point out that *reasonable* can mean sensible or showing good judgment, but in this case it means not expensive.

➤ Play the cassette or read the conversation again. Have students repeat the lines in the pauses.

🎧 Vocabulary

➤ After students listen to and repeat the descriptions of good workers, ask questions about the items, such as *What does "reliable" mean? What is a word that means doesn't waste time?* Make sure students understand *commitments* and *delivers on promises*.

➤ Ask students to read the list of service providers in the box in Exercise C and think about the qualities these people should have. Brainstorm other good qualities for a service provider and write them on the board. The list might include *thorough, neat, friendly, careful,* and *responsible*.

Option: Note that using a dictionary is an important academic skill. Have students compare the definitions in the *Vocabulary* box with those in their dictionaries. Ask volunteers to read aloud the dictionary definitions.

C. Pair work . . .

➤ Model the conversation with a more advanced student. Play the role of Student A to demonstrate choosing a service provider from the box and a description from the *Vocabulary*.

➤ Point out that both Student A and Student B must be careful to use appropriate subject pronouns and possessive adjectives (for example, *his* name, *Is she reliable?*) when talking about the service provider.

Option: Have students work in pairs to match at least one desirable quality with every service person. Have them use this question as a guide: *What is the most important quality that [a painter] should have?* Students might reply *A painter should be honest and efficient.*

Option: In pairs, students decide how important each of the five descriptions of good workers is for each of the eight service people. For example, students might rank honesty as the number-one quality in a mover but reliability as the number-one quality in a dentist.

➤ Do it yourself!

(For general suggestions, see *Introduction*, page Txiii.)

Procedure:

➤ On the board, write the service people from the box in Exercise C. Ask *Which service people have you used? Which one can you recommend? Did you have a problem with any of the service people? Which one?*

➤ Read the directions above the chart. Then point to the examples and ask questions such as *What kind of service is in the first example?* (painting) *What's the name of the company?* (Powell Company) *Was using this service provider a good experience or a bad one?* (good—Pete is reliable and does good work.) *What kind of service did Pincus Pipes provide?* (bad—The workers left a mess and were late.)

➤ Tell students to complete the chart with two experiences they have had with service providers.

➤ Have students share their experiences with a partner.

Challenge: Ask students to jot down notes about a good or bad experience they had with a service provider. Have partners take turns timing each other and trying to talk for one minute about their experience. Students can refer to their notes but should not read. Partners who are timing can also help by asking questions that will elicit more details.

🎧 **A. Listen and read.**

    A: Do you know a good painter?

    B: As a matter of fact, I do. Would you
        like me to give you his name?

    A: Is he reasonable?

    B: Yes. And he does a really good job.

    A: Thanks. That sounds like a good reference!

🎧 **B. Pronunciation and intonation practice.**

> 🎧 **Vocabulary**
>
> **Descriptions of good workers**
>
> **reasonable:** doesn't charge too much   **efficient:** doesn't waste time
>
> **fast:** completes the job quickly   **reliable:** delivers on promises
>
> **honest:** is truthful and meets commitments

C. Pair work. Ask for a recommendation. Use the people in the box or your own service people.

painter	dentist	hairdresser	babysitter
mover	doctor	plumber	electrician

    A: Do you know a good _____?

    B: As a matter of fact, I do. Would you like me to give you _____ name?

    A: Is _____ _____?

    B: Yes. And _____ does a really good job.

    A: ___1___. That sounds like a good reference!   [1]That's great, Terrific, etc.

➤ Do it yourself!

True story. Recommend a service provider you have used and explain why. Or describe a bad experience you have had with a service provider.

Type of service	Recommendation or problem
painting: *Powell Company*	*Pete is reliable and does good work.*
plumbing: *Pincus Pipes*	*The workers left a mess and were late.*

Practical grammar

The sentence: Definition

A sentence is a group of words with a subject and a verb that expresses a complete idea.

    subject   verb

The Johnsons know a good painter.

A. Check the groups of words that are sentences.

1. ☐ Four old houses.
2. ☐ The insurance policy is.
3. ☑ The insurance policy is paid.
4. ☑ They called the FTC to make a complaint.
5. ☐ Seven houses in the neighborhood but no more than eight.
6. ☑ They volunteered.
7. ☑ The painter said he would finish in a week.
8. ☑ We didn't volunteer.
9. ☑ He's an aggressive driver.
10. ☑ She's great.
11. ☐ An estimate.

B. Pair work. Explain your answers in Exercise A.

"Four old houses" has no verb.

"The insurance policy is" is not a complete thought.

The sentence: Punctuation and capitalization

Always capitalize the first word of a sentence. Always use a period or a question mark at the end.

She's the president of the insurance company.
Is he a claims adjuster?

C. Rewrite the sentences and questions with correct capitalization and punctuation.

1. where is the exit   Where is the exit?
2. whose policy is this   Whose policy is this?
3. is Mr. Sutherland here   Is Mr. Sutherland here?
4. there's something wrong with it   There's something wrong with it.
5. it's hard to know all the terms   It's hard to know all the terms.

74   Unit 6

Practical grammar

(For general suggestions, see *Introduction*, page Tix.)

The sentence: Definition

Procedure:

➤ Ask *How can we recognize a sentence?* Discuss students' ideas. Write on the board any relevant key words that students supply, such as *verb, subject, complete thought, capital letter*.

➤ Read aloud the definition of a sentence in the box. Write the example sentence on the board and ask *What is the subject?* (The Johnsons) *What is the verb?* (know) As students answer each question, circle the subject and underline the verb.

➤ Write additional sentences on the board and have students identify the subject and verb in each one. Make sure students understand what a complete idea is. Use these sentences or write your own.

1. I have homeowner's insurance.
2. Paul Mitchell recommended a good painter.
3. The plumber will give us an estimate for the job tomorrow.
4. This estimate is too high.
5. The painters weren't reliable.

A–B.

➤ Remind students that a sentence must have a subject and a verb. Have students circle the subjects and underline the verbs in each numbered item in Exercise A.

➤ Working individually, students put a check mark in the box next to each item that is a sentence.

➤ Read aloud the speech balloons in Exercise B. Ask *Is "Four old houses" a sentence?* (no) *Why not?* (It has no verb, It's not a complete idea.) *Is "The insurance policy is" a sentence?* (no) *Why not?* (It's not a complete idea.)

➤ Students compare answers for items 3 through 11 with a partner, explaining why each item is or is not a sentence.

Option: Discuss different kinds of verbs, including *be*, action verbs, and non-action verbs. Make sure students understand that *be* is contracted in Exercise A, items 9 and 10.

Option: Have students create complete sentences for items in Exercise A that do not express a complete idea (1, 2, 5, and 11). Give an example such as *Four old houses fell down in the storm.*

Challenge: On a separate sheet of paper, students write five items, either sentences or groups of words that do not express a complete idea. They exchange papers with a partner, and either write *S* next to the sentences or rewrite the groups of words to express a complete idea. Review as a class.

The sentence: Punctuation and capitalization

Procedure:

➤ On the board, write sentences from Exercise A (items 3, 4, 6, 7, 8, 9, 10), or ask volunteers to write sentences from the Challenge activity above. Review the key words students supplied in the earlier discussion of how to recognize a sentence. Elicit or point out that a sentence begins with a capital letter and ends with a period or a question mark. Read aloud the sentences on the board and circle the initial capital letters and end punctuation.

➤ Ask *How can we recognize a question?* Elicit the response that a question may begin with a question word such as *who* or *why*. A question may also have a verb before the subject, as in *Did she find a reliable painter? Is he also efficient?*

➤ Summarize by reading aloud the rules in the box. Have volunteers read the two examples. Point out that the capital letters and end punctuation marks have been written in red for emphasis.

Option: Note that some sentences end in another type of punctuation—the exclamation point. The exclamation mark is used to express strong emotion. Write on the board item 10 from Exercise A: *She's great.* Write it a second time with an exclamation mark: *She's great!* Elicit or point out that the second sentence is stronger and more emphatic.

C. Rewrite the sentences ...

➤ Working individually, students rewrite the sentences. After you review the sentences as a class, have volunteers write them correctly on the board.

Option: Write items 4 and 5 on the board using an exclamation mark as the final punctuation. Ask students what difference the exclamation mark makes (the sentences are more emphatic and stronger).

D. Pair work...

➤ Have pairs of students review the decisions they made in capitalizing and punctuating the items in Exercise C.

Other capitalization rules

Procedure:

➤ Tell students your full name and then spell it aloud. Begin with the word *capital* before the first letter of your first and last name; for example, *capital K-A-T-E capital M-U-R-P-H-Y.* As you spell your full name, write it on the board using a capital for the first letter in each name. Circle the capitals.

➤ Ask students why you began your first and last name with a capital letter. Elicit the response that we capitalize the first letter of a person's names.

➤ Have students work in pairs to practice asking each other's names and how to spell them.

➤ Write on the board and tell students your title together with your last name; for example, *capital M-S period capital M-U-R-P-H-Y.* Ask students why you began the title *Ms.* with a capital letter. (We capitalize the first letter of titles.)

➤ Brainstorm other titles, including *Dr., Mr.,* and *Mrs.* and write them on the board. Point out that these titles are abbreviations and therefore end with a period. Write the title *Miss* and elicit from students that it has no period because it is not an abbreviation. Point out that we do not use titles with first names; for example, we say *Dr. Svesko* or *Dr. Caroline Svesko* but not *Dr. Caroline.*

➤ Summarize the discussion of capitalization rules by having volunteers read aloud the rules and examples in the box.

➤ Point to the envelope and ask questions such as *Who is this envelope addressed to?* (Dr. Caroline Svesko) *What information goes on the line under the name?* (the street number and street name) Introduce the term *return address.* Make sure students understand that the return address is the name and address of the sender. Ask *Who is the sender?* (Solange Phillips) *What is Ms. Phillips's zip code?* (10514)

➤ Still pointing to the envelope, ask questions about capitalization and punctuation, such as *Why is the D capitalized?* (It's the first letter of the title Dr.) *Why is there a period after Dr.?* (It's an abbreviation.) Tell students that *NY* is a U.S. postal abbreviation and is written without periods. Elicit and write on the board other state postal abbreviations.

Option: Tell students that other common abbreviations are found in street addresses; for example, *St., Ave., Rd.* Point out the abbreviation *Pl.* in the return address on the envelope.

E. Write your name and address...

➤ Have volunteers come to the board and write their names and addresses, including street number and name, city, state, and zip code. If necessary, help students with the abbreviation for *apartment* (Apt.) and *floor* (Fl.). Review with the class, asking questions such as *What is capitalized in the name? What is capitalized in the address? Why?*

➤ Have students complete the exercise individually and then work in pairs to ask and answer questions such as *What is your address? What is your zip code? Do you have an apartment number?*

F. Rewrite the sentences...

➤ While students are working individually to rewrite the sentences and questions, have five volunteers rewrite the items on the board.

➤ Review as a class, referring to the sentences and questions on the board and correcting them as necessary.

➤ Do it yourself!

(For general suggestions, see *Introduction,* page Txiii.)

Procedure:

➤ Have students get out their envelopes, or distribute those you brought in.

➤ Students write their return address in the upper left-hand corner on the front of the envelope, as shown on page 75. Point out that the return address can also be written on the back flap.

➤ Have students look up the name of a service provider in the telephone book and address the envelope to that person. If students have their own service provider, they can use that person's name and address.

➤ If necessary, remind students of the format for addressing an envelope. Review rules for capitalization and punctuation of names and addresses as well.

➤ In small groups, have students read aloud the service provider's name and address and their own return addresses. Have students exchange envelopes for correcting.

D. **Pair work. Explain your punctuation and capitalization decisions in Exercise C.**

Capitalize the first letter of a person's names.
    Roberto Lopez
Capitalize the first letter of titles: *Mr., Ms., Mrs., Miss, Dr.* (Don't capitalize the word *doctor* unless it's a title.)
    Dr. Roberts can see you now.   She's a doctor.
Capitalize the first letter of names of streets, cities, states, and countries.
When you write an address, use a comma between the city and the state.

Solange Phillips
6301 Victoria Pl.
Perry, NY 10514

Dr. Caroline Svesko
99 Main Street
Perry, NY 10514

E. **Write your name and address.**

Name: _____

Address: _____

F. **Rewrite the sentences and questions with correct capitalization and punctuation.**

1. ms laura brown lives in chicago   Ms. Laura Brown lives in Chicago.

2. the address is 78 haights cross road   The address is 78 Haights Cross Road.

3. mr mitchell asked two companies to give him an estimate   _____
    Mr. Mitchell asked two companies to give him an estimate.

4. were they born in peru   Were they born in Peru?

5. when did you move to casper wyoming   When did you move to Casper, Wyoming?

_____

➤ Do it yourself!   A do-ahead project

Bring an envelope to class. Find the name of a plumber, a painter, or another service provider (such as a doctor, dentist, lawyer) in the Yellow Pages. Address an envelope to him or her. Include your return address (your own name and address) on the envelope.

Make an insurance claim

A. Discussion. Answer the questions in your own words. Then discuss with your group.

1. What happened? _A storm caused a tree to fall on the house._

2. Why is the woman talking to the man? _She is from the insurance company._

3. What does he want to know? _if he is insured_

4. What advice does she give him? _to ask around and get a couple of quotes for the tree removal_

B. Check the subjects the homeowner and the insurance adjuster talk about. Listen again if necessary.

1. ☐ painting
2. ☐ contacting the police
3. ☑ tree removal
4. ☑ storm damage
5. ☑ insurance coverage

Authentic practice

(For general suggestions, see *Introduction*, page Tx.)

Make an insurance claim

Procedure:

➤ To prepare students for the picture story, have them look at the different scenes. Ask questions such as *What is the woman holding?* (a homeowner's insurance policy) *Who do you think she is?* (She could be the homeowner or the insurance agent.) Note the man's gesture in the first scene. Ask *What do you think the people are talking about?* (the fallen tree, the damaged roof)

➤ Ask a volunteer to read aloud the bar above the picture story. Ask *What is an insurance claim?* Elicit that it is a request from the person who has the insurance policy to get money to pay for an expense covered by the policy.

➤ Play the cassette or read the text and have students read along silently.

➤ Ask students to identify the idioms used in the picture story. Write them on the board: *thank your lucky stars, you can say that again, run into a lot of money, word of mouth.*

➤ In pairs or small groups, students discuss what they think these expressions mean. Remind students that they saw the phrase *word of mouth* in Model 2 on page 73.

➤ Lead a class discussion about the meaning of the idioms using students' ideas as a springboard.

➤ Point out that *some* in *some tree* and *some storm* does not refer to an unknown amount as in *I need some milk*. Instead, it is used to emphasize the amount of damage caused by the falling tree and to express the severity of the storm. Have students express *some tree* and *some storm* in their own words. Elicit or suggest such phrases as *What a big tree! That tree certainly did a lot of damage! That was quite a storm! That was a really serious storm.*

A. Discussion ...

➤ Working individually, students answer the questions. They can compare answers with a partner or in a small group.

➤ Let students read or listen to the story again if necessary.

Option: Ask comprehension questions such as *What is the problem?* (A big storm caused a tree to fall on the roof of the house and damage it.) *Who is the man?* (the homeowner) *What does he want to know?* (if the insurance policy covers damage to the house and tree removal) Have students create additional questions about the story to ask their partners.

Challenge: Making inferences is an important academic skill. Have students give examples of information that was stated in the story and examples of information that can be inferred. Students should include the statement from the story that supports each inference. See the example:

Information that was stated	Information that can be inferred
No one was killed.	Many homes were damaged. ("I've had dozens of claims already.")

B. Check the subjects ...

➤ Working individually, students check the topics discussed. Play the cassette or read the story again if necessary. Make sure students know what an *insurance adjuster* is (an agent from an insurance company who investigates claims and decides how much the company will pay).

➤ Have students underline the subjects in the picture story. Point out that being able to cite sources is an important academic skill.

➤ Review students' answers with questions such as *Do they discuss painting?* (no) *Do they discuss tree removal?* (yes) *Where can you find evidence in the story?* (In picture 2, the insurance adjuster says, "I have to check the terms of your policy about <u>the tree removal</u>.")

Option: Have students read the story out loud in pairs. Student A reads the role of the insurance adjuster and Student B reads the role of the homeowner. Have students switch roles for more practice.

T76

C–D.

➤ Working individually, students complete the exercises.

➤ In Exercise D, make sure students understand the terms in item 2. Have student define *run out of money* (spend all your money so you don't have any left) *and run into a lot of money* (cost or add up to a great deal of money).

➤ Review the exercises as a class.

Option: Have students write sentences using the words in Exercise C that were not chosen. For Exercise D, have pairs of students create a statement or question that would elicit the response that was not underlined.

Option: Ask pairs to create an extended conversation that includes each item and response in Exercise D. Have volunteers read their conversations aloud.

E. Pair work ...

➤ In pairs, students practice reading the items and responses in Exercise D aloud.

Option: Student B closes the book. Student A reads each item and Student B responds appropriately. Then partners switch roles.

➤ Do it yourself!

(For general suggestions, see *Introduction*, page Txiii.)

Procedure:

A. Write your own response ...

➤ Point to the first photo. Ask a volunteer to read the speech balloon out loud. Ask *What do you think she is talking about?* Point to the other photos, have volunteers read the speech balloons, and ask questions such as *Who do you think this person is talking to? Who do you think this person is?*

➤ Working individually, students complete the activity. Circulate to offer help as needed.

➤ Students read their conversations out loud with a partner and then change roles to practice both parts.

B. Culture talk ...

➤ Put students in small groups. Try to include students from different countries or cultures in each group.

➤ Using the questions as prompts, students complete a table like the one following. Write this model on the board and explain any unfamiliar kinds of insurance.

Country	Types of insurance individuals carry
United States	car, homeowner's, life, health, malpractice

C. Vocabulary. Choose one of the words or phrases to complete each sentence.

1. A _____policy_____ is a written agreement with an insurance company.
   policy / removal

2. Insurance doesn't _____cover_____ all costs of the policyholder.
   damage / cover

3. Another way to say "covered" is _____insured_____.
   insured / claimed

4. The _____terms_____ describe who is responsible for repairing damage.
   terms / words of mouth

5. Another way to say "an estimate" is a _____quote_____.
   quote / deal

D. Read each sentence or question. Underline your response.

1. "Do you know the terms of the policy?"

   YOU As a matter of fact, I don't.   **YOU** I think you should ask around.

2. "How much will it cost?"

   YOU We've run out of money.   **YOU** It can run into a lot of money.

3. "This is some policy. It doesn't cover anything!"

   YOU You can thank your lucky stars.   **YOU** You can say that again.

4. "Do you know how to get the best deal?"

   YOU Check the policy.   **YOU** Get more than one quote.

E. Pair work. Take turns reading the items and responses in Exercise D.

➤ Do it yourself!

A. Write your own response. Then read each conversation out loud with a partner.

What a mess! Can you recommend someone to help me clean this up?

YOU _____

I had fire damage in my kitchen, and I need to make a claim. Do you know what's covered?

YOU _____

Look at that house. That was some fire!

YOU _____

B. Culture talk. In the country you come from, do people have insurance? What kinds? Compare cultures with your classmates.

Competitive bids for service

🎧 **A.** Listening comprehension. Listen to the conversations.

🎧 **B.** Listen to the conversations again. Complete the chart.

Speedy Tree Removal	The Chapman Chipmunk
can start: *tomorrow*	can start: now
price: $980	price: $700
will finish: Wednesday	will finish: Thursday

🎧 **C.** Discussion. Talk about these questions with your classmates. Listen again if necessary.

- What happened?
- What does Mr. Adams want?
- Which company got the job?
- Why?

D. Role play. Mr. Adams's tree was removed. Now he has to repair the roof, paint the house, and replace the fence that was destroyed by the tree. All the repairs are covered by his homeowner's insurance policy.

Read the questions Mr. Adams asked the contractors. Then role-play conversations between Mr. Adams and a roofer, a painter, and a person who builds fences. Fill in the estimates on page 79.

So you say $___, plus $___ for tips? Day and a half?

Can you put that all in writing?

When could you start?

So, you think you'll be finished by ___?

Authentic practice

(For general suggestions, see *Introduction,* page Tx.)

Competitive bids for service

Procedure:

🎧 A–C.

➤ To set the scene for the listening activity, point to the picture and ask *What happened?* (A tree fell on the house.) Then point to the business cards and ask *What kind of service do these companies provide?* (tree removal, tree service) *What are the names of the companies?* (Speedy Tree Removal, The Chapman Chipmunk) Have students look at the logo on The Chapman Chipmunk card. Make sure students understand what a chipmunk is (a small, striped ground squirrel).

➤ Have students read the bar. Ask *What do you think the conversations will be about?* (The companies will talk about their services and prices.) Play the cassette or read the tapescript.

➤ Have students look at the chart. Ask *What three pieces of information do you need to listen for?* (when each company can start, the price, when the company will finish)

➤ Have students listen again and complete the chart individually. In pairs, students answer the discussion questions.

➤ If students have difficulty, let them listen again.

➤ Review the information on students' charts and go over the questions as a class.

Challenge: In pairs or small groups, have students discuss the advantages and disadvantages of a one-person company such as The Chapman Chipmunk vs. a larger company such as Speedy Tree Removal. Put the following chart on the board and ask students to complete it with their ideas. Compare advantages and disadvantages as a class.

How many employees?	Advantages	Disadvantages
One	Lower overhead	The jobs take longer.
Several	They may finish jobs faster.	Higher overhead

D. Role play . . .
➤ Read the directions for Exercise D.

➤ Have volunteers read the questions in the speech balloons on the bottom of page 78. Brainstorm other questions a homeowner might want to ask the contractors and write them on the board.

Challenge: Have students work in pairs to write a description of the damage to the house. Tell students to look at the picture at the bottom of page 78.

Tapescript

Conversation 1

A: You Mr. Adams?

B: Yes. Are you Hernan?

A: Yes, sir. From Speedy Tree. Here's my card. That's some tree fell on you. Anyone hurt?

B: Luckily, no.

A: Thank goodness.

B: You can say that again! Let's go take a closer look. [pause] Well, what do you think?

A: Whew! This job's going to take three guys a day and a half. The truck's over on the north side right now. We can start first thing tomorrow morning. It'll run you $950, plus tips for the guys, about ten bucks each.

B: So you say $950, plus $30 for tips? So that makes $980. Day and a half?

A: Give or take a few hours. We're never absolutely sure something won't go wrong.

B: And you can start tomorrow?

A: That's right. First thing.

B: And you'll finish by Wednesday, right?

A: Yes. That's right.

B: I'm going to need a written estimate for the insurance. Could you put that and your completion date in writing, on your letterhead?

A: Sure. [pause] Is this OK?

B: Yes, thanks. That's fine. I'll let you know before noon. Is that OK?

A: Sure. Just call the number on this sheet.

(Tapescript is continued on page T79.)

Tapescript *(continued from page T78)*

Conversation 2

B: Oh, hi. Are you the Chapman Chipmunk?

C: Yes, sir. Here's my card.

B: My brother Terry recommended you. Have you had a chance to see the damage?

C: Yes. You can't miss it! Everyone OK?

B: Yes, thankfully.

C: This is a big job. I work alone. It'll take me two or three days, depending. I'll charge you $700.

B: When could you start?

C: Now. My equipment's right outside.

B: And you say it'll take you two or three days?

C: Yes. Give or take.

B: So, you think you'll be finished by Thursday?

C: Yes. Thursday at the latest.

B: Can you put that all in writing? I need it for the insurance—the cost, start time, estimated completion time, number of workers. You know.

C: Sure. No problem. I have my invoices out in the truck. I'll be back in a minute.

Conversation 3

A: Hello. Speedy Tree. Hernan speaking.

B: Hernan? Mr. Adams. I'm sorry, but I've decided to go with someone else for the tree job… But thanks so much for coming out so fast.

A: No problem, Mr. Adams. Good luck with the tree.

B: Thanks. Bye.

➤ Divide the class into groups of four students each. Let students decide who will play each role: Mr. Adams, a contractor at Tip Top Roofing, a contractor at Odessa Painting, and a contractor at Universal Fencing. "Mr. Adams" should talk to each contractor in turn, asking questions such as those in the speech balloons on page 78 and others that the class brainstormed.

➤ After students have completed their role-plays, have all students fill out the contractors' estimates on page 79.

Option: To provide more practice, have the groups change parts so that each student has a chance to play all four roles.

➤ Do it yourself!

(For general suggestions, see *Introduction,* page Txiii.)

Procedure:

A–B.

➤ On the board, draw a chart like the one on page 79. Ask *Did you ever have damage to your home? What was the damage? When did it happen? What was the cause?* Fill in the first line of the chart with an example from the class.

➤ Have students open their books and read the questions. Point to the chart and ask *What happened?* (broken windows) *When did it happen?* (May 19, 2001) *What caused the damage?* (an earthquake)

➤ Working individually, students complete the chart according to their own experiences.

➤ In pairs or small groups, students share their stories.

Option: Collect magazine or newspaper articles that students have brought in and distribute them. After reading the accounts of natural disasters such as floods, tornadoes, or hurricanes, pairs of students take turns asking questions about the stories, such as *What kind of damage was there? When did it happen? What caused the damage?*

TIP TOP
ROOFING
102 Shanley Avenue
Newark, NJ 07045

Estimate

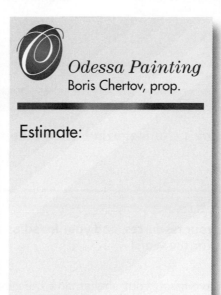

Odessa Painting
Boris Chertov, prop.

Estimate:

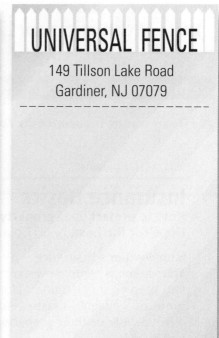

UNIVERSAL FENCE
149 Tillson Lake Road
Gardiner, NJ 07079

➤ Do it yourself!

A. True story. Did you ever have damage to your house or apartment? Or have you read about such damage? What happened? What was the cause? Complete the chart.

Damage	Date	Cause
broken windows	May 19, 2001	earthquake

B. Discussion. Tell the class your story.

Insurance basics

A. Read about insurance in *Today's Life* Magazine. Then take the insurance self-test.

Today's Life Magazine   November 2004   **41**

Insurance Basics
**How to protect your property, your resources, and your loved ones
Hope for the best. . . BUT plan for the worst**

Homeowner's Insurance
Your home is your most expensive asset, your shelter, and the place you keep your belongings. Homeowner's insurance provides financial protection against disasters—damage to your property and injury to other people or their property. If you own a house or an apartment, you need it.

Auto Insurance
Auto insurance protects you against financial loss if you have an accident. It generally covers damage to or loss of your car and injury or property damage to others. Most states require you to carry some car insurance coverage.

Life Insurance
Life insurance pays your beneficiaries in case of your death. If other people depend on your income, then you need life insurance. Life insurance helps pay short-term expenses, such as funeral costs, medical bills, debt, and taxes, and long-term expenses, such as college expenses, mortgage payments, etc.

Health Insurance
Health insurance coverage comes in many forms and combinations. One form is a health maintenance organization, or HMO. Some policies pay all or part of your medical costs, doctor's bills, and prescription drug costs. See next month's issue for a complete presentation of the pros and cons of different types of health insurance.

INSURANCE SELF-TEST. Check the statements that are true for you.

❑ I need homeowner's insurance.   ❑ I need life insurance.

❑ I need auto insurance.   ❑ I need health insurance.

Key Insurance Terms

insurance A contract between you and an insurance company to make payments to you or another person in case of injury, damage, or death

premium The amount you pay the insurance company for coverage

liability Your legal responsibility to pay the victim of injury or damage you cause either directly or indirectly

beneficiary A person who receives payments from an insurance company

claim A report you make to an insurance company in order to receive payments you are entitled to under the terms of your policy

B. Pair work. Explain your answers in the insurance self-test to a partner.

FYI. For consumer information about insurance, log on to the following Web sites:

Better Business Bureau
www.bbb.org/bureaus

Coalition Against Insurance Fraud
www.insurancefraud.org

Federal Trade Commission
www.ftc.gov or call (202) 382-4357

Insurance Information Institute
www.iii.org or call (800) 331-9146

Authentic practice

(For general suggestions, see *Introduction*, page Tx.)

Insurance basics

Procedure:

A. Read about insurance . . .

➤ Review how to scan a reading. Ask *What features should you look at before you begin to read?* Elicit or remind students of headings, subheads, boldface words, bulleted items, items in the margin.

➤ Check comprehension of these features by asking *What kinds of insurance are discussed in this article?* (homeowner's, auto, life, health) *What are some key terms?* (insurance, premium, liability, beneficiary, claim)

➤ After students have read the article, ask comprehension questions such as *What does homeowner's insurance provide? Who needs it? What does auto insurance usually cover? Who needs life insurance?*

➤ Have students complete the insurance self-test.

➤ Point out that householder's insurance covers the contents of a renter's house or apartment.

Challenge: Team questions. Divide the class into two teams. Each team creates questions on the article to pose to the other team. Each correct answer earns a point.

Challenge: Game. Divide the class into two or more teams to play this game. Write the names of the types of insurance on the board for reference. Your chart will look something like the one below. Teams take turns choosing a category and point value. Read the questions and give the teams a point for each correct answer. The team with the highest score wins.

B. Pair work . . .

➤ Have students discuss their choices on the insurance self-test with a partner. Model the activity by giving a reason of your own, such as *I need auto insurance because it is a law in this state.*

FYI . . .

➤ Remind students that *log on* means to type in a Web site address and visit that Web site on the Internet.

Option: If your students don't have access to computers, print out some of the information available at these sites.

Value	Homeowner's	Auto	Life	Health	Key terms
100	When do you need this insurance?	What requirement do most states have about auto insurance?	When does this insurance get paid?	What is one form of health insurance?	Define *insurance*.
200	What does it protect against?	What does it protect against?	Who benefits?	What does HMO stand for?	Define *premium*.
300	What is covered by this insurance?	What is covered by this insurance?	What are three short-term expenses covered?	What are three things often covered by health insurance?	Define *liability*.
400	In what three ways is your home defined?	Define *claim*.	What are two long-term expenses covered?	Who needs health insurance?	Define *beneficiary*.

C. Read how to prepare...

➤ Have students read what it is necessary to include in an insurance claim. Ask for clarification of each bulleted item, such as *What is an example of road conditions?*

➤ Note that the past continuous is used in items *(you and the other driver were going)*. Remind students that we often use the past continuous to talk about what actions we were engaged in when something else—such as an accident—happened.

Option: A group story. Begin a story about a car accident with one line such as *I had a terrible accident last night.* Each student adds to the story with a line that includes a piece of information required on an insurance claim. For example, the next line might be *It was around 8 p.m.* All students take notes on the "monitor screen" as the story unfolds.

Challenge: Put students in pairs. Student A is an insurance adjuster who asks questions based on the bulleted items; for example, *What time was it?* Student B is the driver who had the accident recounted in the group story above. Student B answers the questions using the information in the group story.

D. Betsy Harris had an accident...

➤ Have students cover the notes on the right side of the page. Ask questions about the picture, such as *What were the weather conditions?* (It was raining hard.) *Where was the accident?* (at the corner of Stanley Road and South Orange Avenue) *What are the people doing?* (exchanging license plate numbers and insurance information)

➤ Have students read the notes. Check comprehension by asking questions about new information, such as *How was the visibility?* (poor) *What time was the accident?* (7:30 p.m.) *What state was the accident in?* (New Jersey)

➤ Do it yourself!

(For general suggestions, see *Introduction*, page Txiii.)

Procedure:

➤ Tell students that they are going to write a description of Betsy Harris's accident for her insurance claim. As they write, they should imagine that they are Betsy Harris. They will use her notes in Exercise D as a basis for the description, but they will have to expand the notes into a narrative using complete sentences.

➤ Ask the class how to start the description. Refer students to the first bulleted item in Exercise C: time and date of the accident. Write on the board *I had an accident on November 27 at 7:30 p.m.* Point out that students will use *I* in their descriptions since they are writing as Betsy Harris. Remind them to use complete sentences and correct capitalization and punctuation in their description.

➤ Have students complete the activity individually. Review as a class.

Challenge: Telephone. In this variation on the telephone game, send several students out of the room. Have two or more volunteers come to the front of the room. Tell a story about an auto accident that you had (real or imagined). Include the date, time, location, weather and road conditions, and a brief description of what happened. During your story, students seated at their desks should take notes, but the volunteers at the front of the room should only listen. Call in one of the students who is waiting outside the class. One volunteer listener retells the story of the accident. The rest of the class adds any missing details. Repeat this process with each remaining student outside the class.

C. Read how to prepare the information on an insurance claim after a car accident.

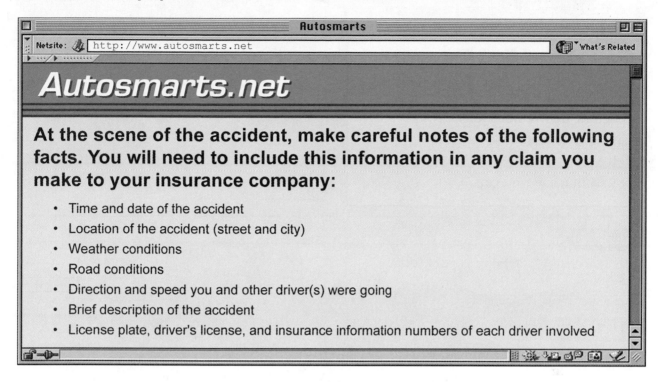

Autosmarts

Netsite: http://www.autosmarts.net

What's Related

Autosmarts.net

At the scene of the accident, make careful notes of the following facts. You will need to include this information in any claim you make to your insurance company:

- Time and date of the accident
- Location of the accident (street and city)
- Weather conditions
- Road conditions
- Direction and speed you and other driver(s) were going
- Brief description of the accident
- License plate, driver's license, and insurance information numbers of each driver involved

D. Betsy Harris had an accident. Read the notes she took at the scene of the accident.

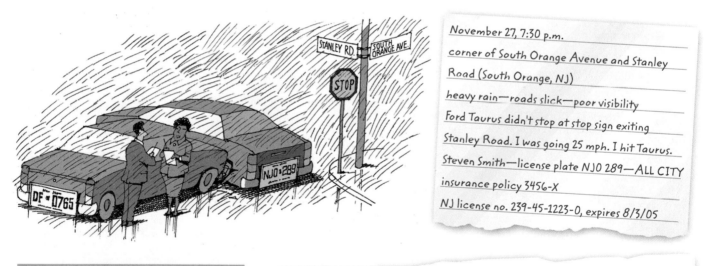

November 27, 7:30 p.m.

corner of South Orange Avenue and Stanley Road (South Orange, NJ)

heavy rain—roads slick—poor visibility

Ford Taurus didn't stop at stop sign exiting Stanley Road. I was going 25 mph. I hit Taurus.

Steven Smith—license plate NJO 289—ALL CITY insurance policy 3456-X

NJ license no. 239-45-1223-0, expires 8/3/05

▶ Do it yourself!

Fill out the accident description on Betsy Harris's claim form. Use her notes. Write complete sentences. Capitalize and punctuate correctly.

Describe the accident. Include time, date, and weather conditions.

_____

_____

_____

_____

Review

A. Pair work or group work.

- What happened?
- What are the people doing?

Ask and answer questions.

Create conversations.

Tell a story.

Say as much as you can.

June 12

June 13

June 14

NORDIC TREE SERVICE

ATHENS PAINTING

RELIABLE ROOFING

June 16

Homeowner's Policy

Review

(For general suggestions, see *Introduction*, page Txii.)

Procedure:

A. Pair work or group work.

Ask and answer questions.

➤ Ask the class general questions about the pictures, such as *What happened on June 12?* (A tornado caused some damage.) *What happened to the house?* (The roof was torn off.) Ask at least one question about each day. Include questions about who the people are and what they're doing.

➤ In pairs, students take turns asking their partners about what happened on each day.

➤ Make sure students understand what a tornado is and what kinds of problems it can cause.

Challenge: Working individually, students list all the services the homeowner will need to take care of the problems caused by the tornado. Then have students compare lists by asking questions such as *Who does the homeowner need to talk to first? What kinds of repairs are needed? Who did she call?*

Create conversations.

➤ In pairs, students create a conversation for either the homeowner and the neighbor (June 13), the homeowner and a contractor (June 14), or the homeowner and the insurance adjuster (June 16). Have the students label the pair they chose *A* and *B*. Students write their conversations in the same format as the model conversations.

➤ Pairs copy each line of their conversations onto a slip of paper, mix up the order of the slips, and give them to another pair. The other pair must then put the conversation back in the correct order.

➤ Each pair reads the conversation they put in order to the pair who wrote the conversation. Together, the pairs add additional lines of dialogue.

Tell a story.

Option: Play a part. Have students play the role of one of the characters in the picture who is narrating the events in chronological order. Students can portray the insurance adjuster who must explain the claim to a supervisor, the homeowner talking to a friend in another town, the neighbor talking to a co-worker, or a contractor reporting to a supervisor. Encourage students to say as much as they can.

Option: One-minute stories. Have a student time you while you talk about the picture for one minute. Then, in pairs or small groups, each student talks about the picture for one minute. Encourage students to describe each of the four scenes and to say as much as they can. Tell students to continue talking until you say *Stop,* indicating that the minute is up.

Option: Insurance claim. Have students tell the story of the tornado damage from the point of view of the homeowner. Students will need to include the time and date of the accident, the location (street, city, and state), the weather conditions, and a brief description of the damages.

⌒B–C.

➤ Tell students they are going to listen to three telephone conversations about some damage to a home.

➤ After students listen the first time, have them answer the questions in Exercise B.

➤ Have students read the statements in Exercise C before they listen again so that they will know what to listen for.

➤ Make sure students know that ? means that the information was not included in the conversations.

➤ Allow students to listen to the conversations as many times as necessary to complete the exercise. Review the answers as a class.

Option: In pairs, students rewrite the false statements to make them true.

D–E.

➤ Students work individually to complete the review exercises.

➤ Circulate to offer help as needed.

➤ Have students check answers with a partner. Review answers as a class.

➤ Identify any areas of difficulty that may require additional instruction and practice.

Tapescript

Conversation 1

Ralph: Hello. Rubin Roofing. No job too big. No job too small. This is Ralph. How can I help you today?

Woman 1: I need to discuss an emergency roof repair. My roof flew off in the storm last night.

Ralph: That was some humdinger, wasn't it?

Woman 1: Well, yes. This is kind of an emergency. Can you come out and have a look and give me an estimate today?

Ralph: Not before about three, three-thirty.

Woman 1: That'll be fine. I'm at 78 Hunter Street, on the south side of town.

Ralph: 78 Hunter Street. Let's say 4 o'clock.

Conversation 2

Woman 2: Hello. Arbor City Roof.

Woman 1: Hello. My roof got blown off in the storm last night.

Woman 2: Oh, my goodness. Was anyone hurt?

Woman 1: Luckily, no. Thanks for asking. Can you come by and give me a price quote on replacement?

Woman 2: Certainly. Where are you?

Woman 1: Hunter Street. South side. Number 78.

Woman 2: I can have someone there right away, about 20 minutes. He'll give you an estimate this morning.

Woman 1: Thanks. I'll be waiting outside. You can't miss it!

Conversation 3

Todd: Hello?

Woman 1: Todd? I'm sorry to call so early. But this is kind of an emergency.

Todd: Sure. What's up?

Woman 1: My roof. It blew off in the storm.

Todd: Oh, no. Are you OK?

Woman 1: Yes. We're all fine. But I need a good roofer in a hurry. You just had your roof repaired. Can you recommend the roofer?

Todd: Actually, yes, I can. I used Arbor City Roof. They're great. Fair, reasonable, efficient.

Woman 1: Thanks. As a matter of fact, they're on their way over to give me an estimate.

Todd: Tell them I recommended them. That way, you'll get a good deal.

1. What happened? The woman's roof flew off in a storm.

2. Why does the woman call her friend Todd after she speaks to the roofers?

   to get a recommendation for a roofer

🎧 **C.** Read the statements. Then listen to the conversations again and check *True*, *False*, or *?* *(No information)* for each statement.

	True	False	?
1. A tree fell on the roof.	☐	☑	☐
2. No one was hurt.	☑	☐	☐
3. A car caused the damage.	☐	☑	☐
4. The caller got the names of the companies from the Yellow Pages.	☐	☐	☑
5. The caller asked the roofers to put their estimates in writing.	☐	☑	☐

D. Answer the questions.

1. Which roofer did the caller choose, Arbor City or Rubin? Arbor City

2. Why did she make that choice? Todd recommended them.

E. Read each sentence or question. Underline your response.

1. "Can you recommend a good plumber?"

   YOU He's reliable.   **YOU** <u>As a matter of fact, I can.</u>

2. "That sounds like a good reference."

   YOU Personally, no.   **YOU** <u>It is.</u>

3. "That is some mess!"

   YOU <u>You can say that again.</u>   **YOU** Thank you very much.

4. "What's a good way to find a reliable painter?"

   YOU <u>Ask around.</u>   **YOU** That's a relief.

5. "Will you put that in writing?"

   YOU <u>Sure. No problem.</u>   **YOU** That can run into a lot of money.

F. **Choose one of the words or phrases to complete each sentence.**

1. This policy looks great. How much are the _____premiums_____?
   terms / premiums

2. Before you make a claim, you have to ask for _____an estimate_____.
   an estimate / a deal

3. A worker who doesn't charge too much is _____reasonable_____.
   fast / reasonable

4. Someone who doesn't waste time is _____efficient_____.
   honest / efficient

5. A worker who does what is promised is _____reliable_____.
   reasonable / reliable

G. **Rewrite the sentences and questions with the correct capitalization and punctuation.**

1. mr benson is a reliable and efficient painter _____

   Mr. Benson is a reliable and efficient painter.

2. we live at 45 elm street in stony creek _____

   We live at 45 Elm Street in Stony Creek.

3. who wrote this description of the accident in colorado _____

   Who wrote this description of the accident in Colorado?

4. ms laura linden is in texas right now _____

   Ms. Laura Linden is in Texas right now.

H. **Guided composition. Look at the picture on page 82. Complete the story. Use correct capitalization and punctuation.**

On June 12, _____

_____

Then on June 13, _____

_____

Finally, _____

_____

> **Now I can**
> ❑ ask for a recommendation of a person who provides a service.
> ❑ ask for an estimate and get it in writing.
> ❑ make an agreement.
> ❑ understand homeowner's, car, and life insurance.

F–G.

➤ Students work individually to complete the review exercises.

➤ Circulate to offer help as needed.

➤ Have students check answers with a partner. Review answers as a class.

➤ Identify any areas of difficulty that may require additional instruction and practice.

Option: In Exercise F, have students create original sentences using the words that were not selected.

H. Guided composition ...

➤ Have students write a summary of the picture on page 82. Remind them to check capitalization and punctuation.

➤ Allow students to continue their story on a separate sheet of paper, if necessary.

Now I can

➤ Read the first item in the box out loud: *Now I can ask for a recommendation of a person who provides a service.* Elicit from the class an example of how to do this, such as *Do you know a good babysitter?*

➤ Put students in pairs, tell the students to take turns reading each item in the box and giving an example of what they have learned. When students can provide an example, they should check that objective. If there are items students aren't able to check, have them look back through the unit for ideas.

➤ When students are finished reviewing with their partners, read each item out loud and elicit an example from the class.

➤ Have students refer to the questions about insurance they had at the beginning of the unit. Ask them what answers they learned during their work on the unit.

Oral test (optional)

You may want to use the *Now I can* box as an informal evaluation. While students are working on the *Guided composition* activity, you can call them up individually and check their ability with two or three objectives.

Your relationships

 Preview

(For general suggestions, see *Introduction*, page Tviii.)

Warm up. What do you know about the Constitution of the United States?

Procedure:

➤ Activate prior knowledge by asking *What do you know about the beginnings of the United States?* Write students' ideas on the board. If necessary, prompt with questions such as *Who originally lived in the area now called the United States?* (Native Americans) *When did Europeans first start settling in the United States?* (16th century) *What country did the settlers of the thirteen colonies come from?* (England) *When did the United States become independent?* (1776, late 18th century) *What document established the government of the new United States?* (the Constitution)

➤ Read the *Warm up* question. Brainstorm ideas the class has about the Constitution.

➤ Tell students that they are going to read three excerpts from the Constitution. Note that they will find some of the language old fashioned and perhaps difficult to understand. Reassure students that they do not have to understand every word of the document at this time.

➤ Point out the use of *shall* in the article and amendments. *Shall* is still commonly used in British English but rarely in American English. In this case, *shall* is a stronger form of *will*.

➤ Check comprehension with questions such as *According to Article I, what are the two parts of the Congress?* (the Senate and the House of Representatives) *What freedoms or rights are mentioned in Amendment I?* (religion, speech, press; the right to assemble peaceably) *What right does the accused have under Amendment VI?* (a speedy and public trial by an impartial jury)

Unit 7 objectives

Procedure:

➤ Read the objectives and discuss the meaning of any unfamiliar words. Elicit examples from students. For example, for *Agree and disagree respectfully*, students might say *I don't agree* or *Absolutely*. When the class can't think of an example, provide one; for example, for pros and cons of controversial issues, say *Capital punishment is a controversial issue. What are some reasons to support it? What are some reasons to be against it?*

➤ Have students underline the two objectives that are the most useful or interesting to them. Have students tell a partner why they chose those two objectives.

Challenge: Put students in small groups to brainstorm everything they already know about the Constitution, the Bill of Rights, and the U. S. justice system. Have students organize their thoughts in a K-W-L chart like the one following. Have students write their ideas in the K (what I know) column and their questions in the W (what I want to know) column. Save the chart until the end of the unit so students can complete the L (what I learned) column.

K What I know	W What I want to know	L What I learned
The first amendment gives me freedom of speech.	What rights do I have if I am accused of a crime?	

Your relationships

 Preview

Warm up. What do you know about the Constitution of the United States?

THE CONSTITUTION OF THE UNITED STATES

We the People of the United States, in order to form a more perfect union, establish justice, insure domestic tranquility, provide for the common defense, promote the general welfare, and secure the blessings of liberty to ourselves and our posterity, do ordain and establish this Constitution for the United States of America.

Article I

Section 1. All legislative powers herein granted shall be vested in a Congress of the United States, which shall consist of a Senate and House of Representatives.

Amendment I

Congress shall make no law respecting an establishment of religion, or prohibiting the free exercise thereof; or abridging the freedom of speech, or of the press; or the right of the people peaceably to assemble,

Amendment VI

In all criminal prosecutions, the accused shall enjoy the right to a speedy and public trial, by an impartial jury of the state and district wherein the crime shall have been committed, which district shall have been previously

---

Unit 7 objectives

- Discuss pros and cons of controversial issues.
- Agree and disagree respectfully.
- Report what other people say.
- Understand the importance of the U.S. Constitution and the Bill of Rights.
- Understand the elements of the U.S. justice system.

Practical conversations

Model 1   Discuss pros and cons of controversial issues.

A. Listen and read.

> **A:** Are you in favor of capital punishment?
> **B:** Yes, I am. I believe in "an eye for an eye." What about you?
> **A:** Actually, I'm against it. I think it's wrong to take a life, no matter what.
> **B:** Well, I guess we'll have to agree to disagree!

B. Pronunciation and intonation practice.

Opinions

I'm in favor of it.   I'm against it.
It's wrong.   It's OK under some circumstances.
It's right.   It's wrong no matter what.

Vocabulary

Sample pros and cons of controversial ideas

Capital punishment
pro I feel that some crimes are so bad that the criminal doesn't have a right to live. If you kill someone, then you should be killed.
con I think it's morally wrong to take a life. If we execute criminals, then we are doing the same thing the criminal did. Also, sometimes innocent people are executed.

Government censorship of books and movies
pro I think some books and movies are too violent and offensive. They can cause crime.
con I don't think government has the right to tell us what we can read or watch.

Organized prayer in public schools
pro I think students would behave better if they prayed in school. Prayer reminds people of what is right and wrong.
con I feel religion is private. Some children are uncomfortable if they are of a different religion or if they have no religion.

C. Pair work. Disagree about a controversial issue. Use an issue above or your own issue.

> **A:** Are you in favor of _____?
> **B:** _____, I _____. What about you?
> **A:** Actually, I'm _____ it. I _____.
> **B:** Well, I guess we'll have to agree to disagree!

86   Unit 7

Practical conversations

(For general suggestions, see *Introduction*, page Tviii.)

Model 1

Content: discussing pros and cons of controversial issues; expressing opinions; arguing for and against capital punishment, government censorship of books and movies, and organized prayer in public schools

Procedure:

A–B.

➤ To set the scene for the conversation, ask questions about the photo such as *Where are the women?* (sitting on a bench in or near a playground) *Is this a formal or informal setting?* (informal) *What does the women's body language tell you?* (They are facing each other, talking, receptive, engaged.)

➤ After students listen to the conversation, check comprehension by asking questions such as *What is the topic of the conversation?* (capital punishment) *Are the two speakers in agreement?* (no)

➤ Ask students what they think "an eye for an eye" means. Elicit or explain that it means people should receive a punishment that is like the wrong they committed. This means that the punishment for killing is being killed or that the punishment for theft is taking the same things from the thief.

➤ Make sure students know that the expression "agree to disagree" is a polite way to acknowledge a difference of opinion that probably cannot be resolved.

➤ Students read and listen and then repeat after each line of the conversation.

Option: Have students listen with books closed. Read each line at a native rate of speed. Encourage students to imitate the rhythm, stress, and intonation of the conversation as closely as possible.

Opinions

➤ Play the cassette or read the opinions. Have students repeat.

➤ Ask individual students what they think about different issues such as public transportation, discrimination, or bilingual education. Tell other students to respond with an opinion.

Vocabulary

➤ Have students read the text silently before you play the cassette or read the sample pros and cons.

➤ If necessary, explain the concepts of capital punishment, government censorship, and organized prayer in public schools. Make sure that students understand prayer is allowed; the issue is whether it can be an organized student activity.

➤ After students listen, check comprehension by asking questions such as *What is one argument people might make against capital punishment?* (The punishment is as bad as what the criminal did.) *What is one argument in favor of government censorship?* (Some books and movies are too violent for people to read or see.)

➤ Brainstorm other controversial issues and write them on the board. Elicit arguments for and against each idea and write them down.

Option: Note that many of the arguments are phrased as conditional sentences. Have students underline each conditional sentence and then say which are real conditions (*If you kill someone . . . , If we execute criminals . . . , Some children are uncomfortable . . .*) and which are unreal conditions (*I think students would behave better . . .*).

Challenge: Put students in pairs. Give each pair an issue and a stance to prepare; for example, for capital punishment, against organized prayer in public schools. Make sure that each side of each controversial idea in the *Vocabulary* box is covered by at least one pair of students. Have students prepare additional arguments in support of their position. Students can also use the list of issues and arguments on the board. When students have prepared their arguments, ask students from both sides of an issue to present their arguments to the class.

C. Pair work . . .

➤ Model the conversation with a more advanced student. First play the role of Student A to demonstrate choosing a controversial issue. Then switch roles and play Student B.

➤ Note that in the second line, Student B must first give a positive or negative response and then give an argument to support that position. Student A's responding argument depends on whether Student B chooses a position for or against the issue. Remind students that they can begin arguments with *I believe, I think,* or *I feel.*

Model 2

Content: agreeing and disagreeing respectfully, rules, discussing a rule you don't like

Procedure:

🎧 A–B.

➤ To set the scene for the conversation, point to the photo and ask questions such as *Where are the people?* (in the back of a car) *How do you think the woman on the left feels?* (upset, mad) *What is she doing?* (putting on a seat belt)

➤ After students listen to the conversation, check comprehension by asking *What is the woman upset about?* (wearing a seat belt) *Does the man think that wearing a seat belt is ridiculous?* (No, he says it saves lives.) *What do they agree about?* (There are too many rules.)

➤ Before students repeat, note that the first line is a question although it is written in statement form. The question is conveyed by the use of a question mark and a rising intonation at the end of the line. The complete form of the reduced question is <u>Do</u> *you want to know what I think?*

➤ Also point out that the phrase *You want to know* is almost always reduced in native speech to *You wanna know.*

➤ Listen again to the conversation and have students repeat during the pauses. Then have them practice the conversation in pairs.

🎧 Vocabulary

➤ After reading and listening, students repeat the rules.

➤ Tell students that a rule can be a law, or it can be a regulation in a school or workplace. For example, a school might have a rule that no one is allowed in a classroom until 15 minutes before the class is scheduled to begin.

➤ Point out that some of these rules apply to everyone in the United States (license requirements for gun ownership, voting age) and some vary according to state law (legal drinking age, seat belt and helmet requirements). Restrictions on smoking depend on local laws.

➤ Brainstorm other rules that people in your city must follow. Write students' ideas on the board. Ideas may include parking restrictions, pet cleanup rulings, and home window-guard restrictions.

➤ Have students fill in their own rule in the *Vocabulary* box.

Challenge: Have pairs of students work together to research local rules on smoking indoors in public places. Have them also find out your state's legal drinking age and whether seat belts and helmets are required. With the class, brainstorm how to find this information. Elicit or suggest the public library, a search engine on the Internet, the local newspaper.

C. Pair work ...

➤ Write *Pro* and *Con* on the board. For each rule in the *Vocabulary*, brainstorm reasons in favor of the rule and reasons against it. Write the reasons on the board under the appropriate heading.

➤ Model with a more advanced student. Play the role of Student B. If necessary, prompt Student A to choose a rule from the *Vocabulary*. In response to the rule that Student A doesn't like, state one of the reasons listed on the board under *Pro*. Student A's rejoinder should be one of the reasons listed under *Con*.

➤ Have students choose a rule that they don't like, and practice the conversation in pairs.

➤ Do it yourself!

(For general suggestions, see *Introduction*, page Txiii.)

Procedure:

A–B.

➤ Read aloud the directions for Exercise A. Tell students they can choose a rule from the *Vocabulary* box, including their own rule, or one on the board. Have students reread the controversial issues in the *Vocabulary* box on page 86.

➤ Tell the students to write the rule or the issue they have chosen. They should then write an argument supporting that rule or issue and an argument against it.

➤ On a separate sheet of paper, students write their opinions about the rule or issue, beginning with *I think, I believe,* or *I feel*. If necessary, have students review the yellow note on page 86 on how to express opinions.

➤ Have students share their opinions with a partner or a group.

➤ Students may not feel comfortable discussing what they have written about a controversial topic or one they feel is too sensitive. If they are uncomfortable sharing, invite them to choose another topic to discuss.

A. Listen and read.

A: You want to know what I think?

B: What?

A: I think it's ridiculous that you have to wear a seat belt.

B: But seat belts save lives.

A: You have a point. But I just think there are way too many rules.

B: Actually, I agree with that.

B. Pronunciation and intonation practice.

Vocabulary

Rules

You have to wear a seat belt / a helmet.

You can't smoke indoors in a public place.

You have to have a license to own a gun.

You can't drink until you're twenty-one, but you can vote and join the Army at eighteen.

Your own rule: _____

C. Pair work. Discuss a rule you don't like.

A: You want to know what I think?

B: _____?

A: I think it's ridiculous that _____.

B: But _____.

A: You have a point. But _____.

B: Actually, I agree with that.

➤ Do it yourself!

A. Choose a rule you don't agree with or a controversial issue people disagree about. Then write an argument for and an argument against.

Issue: _____

pro _____

con _____

B. Discussion. Write your opinion on a separate sheet of paper. Begin with "I think" or "I feel." Then discuss.

Reporting a person's words: Direct speech

Use quotation marks to write a person's exact words.
    Martin said, "Censorship is wrong."
Put the period or the question mark before the quotation mark at the end of the quoted words.
    Nicole asked, "Why are there so many rules?"

A. Write quotation marks around the quoted speech.

1. They asked, "Are you in favor of prayer in the schools?"

2. We answered, "Not in the public schools."

3. Maria said, "Actually, I'm for capital punishment under some circumstances."

4. Senator Smith asked, "Are you in favor of a constitutional amendment outlawing capital punishment in all circumstances?"

5. We said, "We'll have to think about that."

B. Write quotation marks and a period or a question mark at the end of the quoted speech.

1. Jessica asked, "Do you want to know what I think?"

2. Terry answered, "Yes, please tell me."

3. Jessica answered, "I think it's ridiculous that we have to wear a seat belt."

4. Terry said, "I do too, but I'm in favor of the law that children have to wear them."

5. Jessica responded, "To tell you the truth, I agree with that."

Use of a comma in quotations

Use a comma after the verb that introduces the quoted speech.
Begin the quoted statement or question with a capital letter.
    The advertisement says, "Seat belts save lives."

C. Insert a comma and a period or a question mark in each quoted statement and question.

1. Marcia said "I'm against capital punishment in all circumstances . "

2. Then Paul said, "I disagree. I think some crimes are so bad that capital punishment is justified . "

Practical grammar

(For general suggestions, see *Introduction*, page Tix.)

Reporting a person's words: Direct speech

Content: quotation marks and end punctuation in quoted speech

Procedure:

➤ Ask students to repeat an opinion about a rule or an issue that the class has already discussed. You may choose to begin with a statement such as *I think it's a good idea for a cyclist to wear a helmet.*

➤ Write students' ideas on the board in two ways: first give the student's exact words, and then add the student's name and the verb *says*. For example, you might write *I'm against capital punishment* and *Maria says, "I'm against capital punishment."* Include quotation marks, commas, and end punctuation.

➤ Point to the quotation marks in several examples and ask *Why do we use quotation marks?* Elicit the response that quotation marks are used to write a person's exact words. Note that the period or question mark goes inside the quotation marks.

➤ Tell students that when we use someone's exact words, we are quoting them. The quotation marks show that the exact words are a quote. Quoting someone's exact words is also called direct speech.

➤ Ask a volunteer to read the first example in the box. Then point to another student and say *You are Martin. What did you say?* Make sure the student says *Censorship is wrong.* If necessary, give the response yourself. Now ask a volunteer to read the second example. Then point to another student and say *You are Nicole. What did you ask?* Make sure the student says *Why are there so many rules?* If necessary, give the response yourself.

➤ Write Martin's and Nicole's sentences on the board with quotation marks. Ask *Why do we need quotation marks here?* Elicit the response that the sentences give Martin's and Nicole's exact words.

➤ To summarize, have students silently read the bar at the top of the page and the rule and examples in the box.

A–B.

➤ Write the first item in Exercise A on the board. Ask a volunteer to come to the board and add quotation marks. If necessary, have the class offer corrections. Point out that the quotation marks at the end of the question follow the question mark.

➤ Working individually, students complete Exercises A and B.

➤ Students compare answers with a partner. Review as a class.

Use of a comma in quotations

Content: capitalization and use of a comma in quoted speech

Procedure:

➤ Write on the board the two example sentences from the box at the top of the page. To focus students' attention on the punctuation and capitalization, ask questions such as *Why is the M in Martin capitalized?* (It's the first letter of his name.) *Is this a statement or a question?* (a statement) *How can you tell?* (It includes the word *said* and not *asked*. It ends with a period and not a question mark.) *What kind of punctuation follows the word "said"?* (a comma) *Why do you think there's a comma there?* Elicit or tell students that we use a comma after the verb that introduces the quoted speech.

➤ Have students look again at Exercise A at the top of the page. Point to item 1 and ask *What kind of punctuation follows the word "asked"?* (a comma) *Why do you think there's a comma there?* (to separate the verb from the quoted speech) Continue asking questions about the items.

➤ Read the information in the second box. Focus students' attention on the rules by asking questions about the example, such as *What punctuation mark comes after the word "says"?* (a comma) *What letters are capitalized and why?* (T—first word in the sentence; S—first word in the quoted speech)

C. Insert a comma ...

➤ Have students read the direction line and then work on the exercise individually.

➤ Tell students that the exercise continues on page 89. They should complete all five items.

➤ Have students compare answers with a partner. Review as a class.

Reporting a person's words: Indirect speech

Procedure:

Note: This section avoids the back shift in reported speech as this is too challenging for most students of this level.

➤ Write the first two examples from the box on the board. Do not include the parenthetical labels. Circle the pronouns *I* and *he* as well as the comma and quotation marks in the first sentence.

➤ Have volunteers read each sentence aloud. Then ask *Which sentence has quotation marks?* (the first one) *Which sentence has a comma?* (the first one) Ask what other differences students notice. Elicit that *I disagree* in the first sentence changes to *he disagrees* in the second.

➤ Tell students that the first sentence reports Paul's speech using his exact words. Elicit from the class that this is called quoted or direct speech. Then tell students that the second sentence reports Paul's speech without using his exact words. This is called indirect speech.

➤ Review the differences between direct or quoted speech and indirect speech. Write on the board a chart with the headings *Direct speech* and *Indirect speech*. Have students suggest how to fill in each column. Your completed chart should include the following:

Direct speech	Indirect speech
Quotation marks and a comma	No quotation marks or comma
A person's exact words	Not the exact words

➤ To summarize, have students read the information in the box silently. Then ask *Does using "that" to introduce the indirect speech change its meaning?* (no) Have a volunteer say the sentence without *that: Paul says he disagrees with that law.*

D. Report what each person says.

➤ Write the first item on the board. Ask *How can we rewrite Adam's words in direct speech?* Elicit from students and write on the board *Adam says, "I don't agree."* Ask *How can we rewrite Adam's words in indirect speech?* Elicit from students and write on the board *Adam says (that) he doesn't agree.* Remind students that indirect speech does not use quotation marks or a comma.

➤ Working individually, students rewrite items 2 through 5 as reported speech.

➤ In pairs, students compare answers. Review as a class and then have volunteers write their sentences on the board.

Note: Make sure students use *says* in this exercise and not *said*, which will require back shift in some items.

Option: Working in pairs, students rewrite the items in Exercise D as direct speech. Review as a class.

➤ Do it yourself!

(For general suggestions, see *Introduction*, page Txiii.)

Procedure:

A–B.

➤ Ask students to turn to page 87 and review the opinion they wrote. Have them write their opinion on the board and sign their name. Remind students to begin their opinion with *I think, I believe,* or *I feel;* for example, *I think censorship is a bad thing.*

➤ Students copy the opinions from the board as direct speech; for example, *Kristin said, "I think censorship is a bad thing."* They should then rewrite each quoted speech as indirect speech; for example, *Kristin said (that) she thinks censorship is a bad thing.* Then have volunteers read Ellen's opinions expressed in both direct and indirect speech.

➤ Circulate to offer help as needed. Then review the written opinions as a class.

Challenge: Opinion chain. Have students continue changing direct speech to indirect speech. Begin by expressing an opinion such as *I think non-smoking areas are very rude.* Student A reports your opinion in indirect speech: *Ms. Murphy said (that) she thinks non-smoking areas are very rude.* Student A then expresses a personal opinion, and Student B reports it in indirect speech. Continue until every student has reported someone else's opinion and has expressed his or her own opinion.

3. She answered, "Well, I think it's morally wrong to take a life . "

4. Finally Paul asked, "What do you think society should do with terrible criminals ? "

5. Marcia answered, "Lock them up and throw away the key . "

Reporting a person's words: Indirect speech

Sometimes we report a person's speech without using the exact words the person said. This is called indirect speech. Don't use quotation marks for indirect speech. Don't use a comma in indirect speech.

Paul says, "I disagree with that law." (direct speech)

Paul says he disagrees with that law. (indirect speech)

Sometimes we use *that* to introduce the indirect speech. There's no change in meaning.

Paul says **that** he disagrees with that law.

D. **Report what each person says.**

1. **Adam:** I don't agree. *Adam says he doesn't agree.*

2. **Laura:** I'm against censorship. Laura says (that) she's against censorship.

3. **Richard:** I'll have to think about it. Richard says (that) he'll have to think about it.

4. **Martina:** I read about that in the paper. Martina says (that) she read about that in the paper.

5. **Mr. Lewis:** Mary has it. Mr. Lewis says (that) Mary has it.

➤ Do it yourself!

A. **Look at the opinion you wrote on page 87. Write that opinion on the board and sign your name.**

B. **On a separate sheet of paper, write your classmates' opinions in direct speech. Then write them in indirect speech.**

Ellen says, "It's silly that you have to be twenty-one to buy cigarettes."

Ellen says that it's silly that you have to be twenty-one to buy cigarettes.

A mistake about shoplifting

A. Read the picture story again. Answer the questions.

1. What are Dan and Paul shopping for? <u>Mother's Day presents</u>

2. What does Dan buy? <u>a watch</u>

3. Why doesn't Paul buy the same thing for his mom? <u>It's too expensive.</u>

4. What does the guard want to see? <u>the receipt</u>

Authentic practice

(For general suggestions, see *Introduction*, page Tx.)

A mistake about shoplifting

Procedure:

➤ Before students open their books, read the bar out loud. Ask students what *shoplifting* means. Elicit that it means taking something from a store without paying for it. Tell students that shoplifting is a crime.

➤ Access students' knowledge and experience by asking *How do stores try to discourage shoplifting?* (by using scanning machines at the exits, having guards patrol the store, watching shoppers) *How can you show you are not shoplifting?* (keep merchandise out in the open before purchase and in the store's bag after purchase, have the receipt available, observe rules about trying things on)

➤ Have students open their books and look at the pictures. Help them anticipate the story by asking questions such as *Who are the shoppers in this story?* (two teenage boys, Paul and Dan) *What kind of merchandise are they looking at?* (expensive watches)

➤ Have the students read along silently while they listen to the story.

➤ Some terms may be unfamiliar to students, but meanings can be inferred from the context. Check understanding of *awesome, out of my price range, I'll pass, pricey, piggy bank,* and *later.* Make sure students understand that *later* here is a reduction of *I'll see you later.* Ask *Why does Dan say, "Just my luck"?* Elicit the response or tell students that this is an ironic comment: Dan doesn't really feel lucky.

A. Read the picture story again ...

➤ After students read the story again, they work individually to write answers to the questions.

➤ While students are comparing answers with a partner, circulate and offer help as needed.

➤ Making inferences is an important academic skill. Tell students that sometimes information is stated directly, and sometimes it is implied. We have to make inferences from implied or unstated information. Ask students *What can we infer when Dan asks where the gift-wrapping department is?* (He wants to have the watch gift-wrapped.) *What can we infer from the security guard's question to Dan?* (The guard thinks Dan might be shoplifting.)

B–C.

➤ Working individually, students underline the appropriate response.

➤ Students compare answers with a partner.

➤ Partners then take turns reading and responding to each item.

Option: Ask students to close their books. Read each item and elicit appropriate responses. For example, the question *Do you like this robe?* might elicit these responses: *Yes, it's beautiful; No, it doesn't look good; Sure, it's great;* or *I don't think so. It's a funny color.*

Option: Choral reading. Divide the class into two groups. The two groups take turns reading and responding to each item chorally.

D. Guided composition . . .

➤ Tell students to look at the picture story on page 90 again. Ask *What are Dan and Paul doing?* Note students' responses on the board. Tell students that they are going to write a composition using their answers to a series of questions. As a class, decide on one answer to use as the start of the composition. Write the answer on the board, indenting the sentence and using appropriate capitalization and punctuation.

➤ Have students read the list of questions silently. Make sure students understand the questions and can answer them. You may want to ask each question and elicit answers before students begin writing.

➤ Remind students to answer the seven questions in complete sentences, using capital letters and periods where necessary. Student can start their composition with the sentence the class chose above, or they can use the example in the text. Point out that their answers should use the same verb forms as the questions, either the present continuous or the simple present tense.

➤ When students have completed their compositions, have them exchange papers with a partner. Have students check compositions for correct information, indentation, capital letters, and periods.

➤ Review compositions as a class, having students in turn read one line of their work.

E. Discussion . . .

➤ In small groups, students discuss the consequences of not getting a receipt for a purchase from a store. Each small group should list the consequences.

➤ Remind students of *if* clauses in real conditional sentences: *If you don't get a receipt, . . .* Review with students the verb forms that can follow *if* clauses in real conditions. (the simple present tense, the future)

➤ Call on each group, asking students to list one consequence such as *you may get stopped by a clerk, an alarm will go off.* Write the consequences on the board.

➤ Do it yourself!

(For general suggestions, see *Introduction*, page Txiii.)

Procedure:

A–B.

➤ Have students read the speech balloons. Ask *Where do you think these people are?* (in a store) *Who do you think they're talking to?* (a friend, someone they're shopping with)

➤ Read the first speech balloon. Elicit a response such as *You're right* or *Let's look at something else.* Ask another student to respond in disagreement; for example, *I don't think so* or *It's worth it.*

➤ Working individually, students write their responses. Then they practice the conversations in pairs.

➤ Prediction is an important academic skill. In pairs or small groups, students predict what will happen next in the story. Ask students to give reasons for their predictions.

Challenge: In pairs, students discuss and then write continuations of the picture story on page 90. Have them use these questions as prompts: *Does Dan have the receipt? If so, what happens? If not, what happens?* Tell students to write at least three sentences that continue the story.

B. Read each sentence or question. Underline your response.

1. "Do you like this robe?"

   YOU <u>Yes. It's awesome.</u>   **YOU** Actually, I'm against it.

2. "That's out of my price range."

   YOU I have exact change.   **YOU** <u>Mine too. But I've been saving up.</u>

3. "I've got to go now."

   YOU <u>OK. Later.</u>   **YOU** I guess we'll have to agree to disagree.

4. "I'm sorry. There are no more watches."

   YOU I think I'll pass.   **YOU** <u>Just my luck. That's what I wanted.</u>

C. Pair work. Take turns reading the items and responses in Exercise B.

D. Guided composition. Read the story again. Then answer these questions in paragraph form on a separate sheet of paper. Indent the first sentence. Use capital letters and periods where necessary.

- What are Dan and Paul doing?
- What do they look at?
- What does Dan think of it?
- How can Dan afford it?
- How does Dan pay?
- Does he get a receipt from the cashier?
- What happens when he's leaving the store?

Dan and Paul are shopping for Mother's Day presents.

E. Discussion. What can happen if you don't get a receipt? Make a list of consequences.

➤ Do it yourself!

A. Write your own response. Then read each conversation out loud with a partner.

I think I'll pass on that robe. It's a little too pricey.

YOU _____

Later!

YOU _____

This store is way out of my price range!

YOU _____

B. Discussion. What do you think is going to happen next to Dan? Explain your idea.

An arrest for shoplifting

Hernan Guzman
Attorney at Law

A. Listening comprehension. Listen to the conversation. Then answer the questions.

1. Who are Mr. Guzman and Mrs. Ochoa? a lawyer and Dan's mother

2. Why are they having this discussion? Dan was arrested and has to go to court.

3. What will happen after this conversation? Make a list.

   Dan will meet with Mr. Ochoa at 3.

B. Read the statements. Listen to the conversation again. Then check *True*, *False*, or *?* (No information) for each statement.

	True	False	?
1. The conversation is in a courtroom.	☐	☑	☐
2. Dan Ochoa needs a lawyer.	☑	☐	☐
3. The cashier went to the cafeteria.	☐	☐	☑
4. Dan was arrested for shoplifting.	☑	☐	☐
5. Dan won't go to college in September.	☐	☐	☑

C. Vocabulary. Choose one of the words or phrases to complete each statement.

1. Taking something from a store without paying for it is _____shoplifting_____.
   an arrest / shoplifting

2. A notice to appear in court is a _____summons_____.
   receipt / summons

3. A person who accompanies you to court to help you when you are arrested is a _____lawyer_____.
   police officer / lawyer

4. A person who didn't break the law is _____innocent_____.
   guilty / innocent

Authentic practice

(For general suggestions, see *Introduction*, page Tx.)

An arrest for shoplifting

Procedure:

➤ Help students anticipate the topic of the conversation by reading the bar aloud.

➤ To set the scene for the conversation, have students look at the picture. Ask questions such as *Where are the people in the picture?* (in an office) *Whose office is it?* (the man's, Hernan Guzman's) *What does the sign on the wall say?* (Hernan Guzman, Attorney at Law) *Who do you think the woman might be?* (Dan's mother)

⌒A–B.

➤ To focus their attention, have students read the three questions in Exercise A before listening to the conversation.

➤ After listening, students work individually to write answers to the questions.

➤ Note that Dan's mother and the lawyer both call him Danny. It is not unusual for someone to have a childhood name that the family and close friends still use. More recent friends such as Paul call him Dan, an older-sounding nickname for Daniel. You may want to ask students to give personal examples of childhood names and older-sounding versions of the same name.

➤ Before listening again, students read the statements in Exercise B.

➤ After listening, students check the appropriate boxes. Review both exercises as a class.

➤ Discuss what students think will happen after the conversation between Mr. Guzman and Mrs. Ochoa. Make a list on the board of students' suggestions. Ideas should include the events mentioned in the listening (Dan's appointment with the lawyer at 3:00 p.m. on Saturday, the trial on Tuesday) and any other predictions students have.

Challenge: Have students support their answers in Exercise B by taking notes while they listen to the conversation. For example, to support their *False* answer for item 1, students should write *What brings you here on a Saturday?*

C. Vocabulary . . .

➤ Working individually, students complete the exercise.

➤ In pairs, students compare answers.

Option: Have students use all the choices in original sentences.

Option: Have students work in pairs to write definitions for all the choices.

If your students are ready . . .

Culture / Civics note: In most localities, it is up to the police whether to release an arrested person or to detain him or her. In this case, Dan was released and given a bench warrant, sometimes referred to as a summons to appear in court. Sometimes the arrested person must stay in jail until the hearing unless he or she gives a certain amount of money called bail. Bail insures that the person will appear in court for the trial. If the person shows up in court, the bail money is returned; if not, the money is forfeited. If an arrested person doesn't have enough money for the bail, he or she can get a loan from a bail bondsman. Local regulations and customs may differ in your area.

Tapescript

Mr. Guzman: Good morning, Mrs. Ochoa. What brings you here on a Saturday?

Mrs. Ochoa: Thank you for seeing me on such short notice, Mr. Guzman, but this is an emergency. My Danny was arrested for shoplifting yesterday, and we need help.

Mr. Guzman: Danny? Shoplifting? That's ridiculous. He's such a good kid.

Mrs. Ochoa: I know. Don't worry. He didn't do it, but he has to be in court on Tuesday, and he needs a lawyer. Mr. Guzman, Danny's innocent.

Mr. Guzman: Tell me what happened, Mrs. Ochoa. From the beginning.

Mrs. Ochoa: OK. Danny was at Larson's Department Store. He was looking for a Mother's Day present for me. He picked out a watch and bought it.

Mr. Guzman: OK. So far so good.

Mrs. Ochoa: Danny wanted to get the watch gift-wrapped for me, but I guess he was in a hurry or something. So he just put the watch in his backpack. He figured he would wrap it himself.

Mr. Guzman: M-hmm. Then what happened?

(Tapescript is continued on page T93.)

Tapescript (continued from page T92)

Mrs. Ochoa: Well, when he was leaving the store, an alarm went off and a guard at the door asked Danny to show him the backpack. It turns out the cashier didn't cut off that electronic sensor thing. When the guard saw the watch, he asked to see the receipt. And Danny didn't have a receipt.

Mr. Guzman: So, that shouldn't be a problem. The cashier could have backed Danny up.

Mrs. Ochoa: Right. But when they went back to the cashier, she was gone. So Danny couldn't prove he paid for the watch. He paid cash. So the store manager called the police and they took Danny to the station. They gave him a summons for shoplifting and told him to appear in court on Tuesday with a lawyer. That's why I called you. Mr. Guzman, how serious is this? He's innocent, not guilty! My Danny never stole anything in his life. And he's going to college in September. This could ruin his whole life!

Mr. Guzman: Mrs. Ochoa, tell Danny to be here this afternoon at 3. I'll see what we can do.

D. Read Dan Ochoa's arrest record.

➤ Direct students' attention to the arrest record. Have them read all 23 visible headings. Make sure students understand all the terms. If necessary, explain the difference between an alias and a nickname. (An *alias* is an assumed name that is intended to deceive people. A *nickname* is a familiar or shortened form of a name, such as Dan or Danny for Daniel.) Elicit or explain that a *common-law marriage* is an agreement between a couple who live together but who have not gone through a religious or civil marriage ceremony. Ask *What does "Unk" mean?* (It's an abbreviation for Unknown.)

➤ Check comprehension by asking questions such as *What is Dan Ochoa's full name?* (Daniel Michael Ochoa) *Is he a U.S. citizen?* (yes) *What is his birth date?* (September 17, 1987)

Option: Your students may want to discuss the categories under the headings Race and Ethic (group) on the arrest record. They may choose other categories to describe their own ethnicity or race. Remind students to express their opinions respectfully.

E–F.

➤ Have volunteers read each of the bulleted items aloud. After each item, elicit examples if appropriate. Following the first item, students might suggest saying "*Yes, officer*" and not saying anything like "*You made a stupid mistake.*"

➤ Ask *What does "ASAP" mean?* (As Soon As Possible) Answer any questions students may have about language. Help students rephrase any difficult items in their own words.

➤ Then have students read the description of Dan's behavior. When students read a description indicating appropriate behavior, have them check the corresponding bulleted item in Exercise E.

➤ Ask students to identify the bullets that they did not check. Ask *Did Dan do the right things? What else should he do?* Write a list on the board of students' ideas about what Dan should do now.

Challenge: If your students have access to a computer, have them do an Internet search of the following topics: arrest rights, Miranda rights, what to do when you are arrested. One useful Web site for more information is www.infoline.org. Ask students to share their findings with the class.

➤ Do it yourself!

(For general suggestions, see *Introduction*, page Txiii.)

Procedure:

A–B.

➤ Ask students to think about a true story or a story from a book or movie about a person who was arrested.

➤ On a separate sheet of paper, students make notes about the events in the story. Have students use the key words *who, what, when,* and *where* as prompts for details. Have students note whether the person followed the advice on the Web site shown above. Ask students to think about the outcome of the story as well.

➤ Model the activity by telling a story about a person who was arrested. Use a movie or a newspaper article for facts. Put the words *who, what, when,* and *where* on the board and check each one as you provide details that answer that question.

➤ In pairs or small groups, students tell the story, using their notes to provide details.

Challenge: Students answer the bulleted questions to write a guided composition about someone who was arrested.

D. Read Dan Ochoa's arrest record.

New Castle Police | CHARGE *Shoplifting*

DEFENDANT INFORMATION						
1. Name (Last, First, Middle) *Ochoa, Daniel, Michael*				**2. Alias / Nickname** *Dan*		**3. Phone number** *287-5065*

4. Date of Birth *9* Mo *17* Day *1987* Yr **5. Age** *17* **6. Sex** ☑M ☐F ☐U **7. Race** ☑White ☐Black ☐Asian ☐Indian ☐Other ☐Unknown **8. Ethnic** ☑Hispanic ☐Non-Hispanic ☐Unknown

9. Skin ☐Dark ☐Light ☑Medium ☐Other ☐Unknown **10. Height** *5* Feet *10* Inches **11. Weight** *158* **12. Hair** *Brown* **13. Eyes** *Brown* **14. Glasses** ☑No ☐Yes ☐Contacts

15. Build ☐Small ☑Med ☐Large **16. Marital Status** ☐Married ☑Single ☐Common Law ☐Separated ☐Divorced ☐Widowed ☐Unk **17. U.S. Citizen** ☑Yes ☐No ☐Unknown

18. Social Secuity No. **19. Education** **20. Religion** **21. Occupation** **22. Employed** **23. Scars / Marks / Tattoos (Describe)**

E. Read the advice from a civil liberties Web site.

In Case of an Arrest

Address: @ http://yourrights.org › go

In case of an arrest

- Be polite and respectful. Never bad-mouth a police officer. Don't get into an argument.
- Stay calm and in control of your words, body language, and emotions.
- Remember, anything you say or do can be used against you.
- Keep your hands where the police can see them. Don't touch any police officer.
- Don't run. Don't resist even if you believe you are innocent.
- Don't complain on the scene or tell police they're wrong or say you're going to file a complaint.
- Don't make statements about the incident. Ask for a lawyer immediately upon your arrest.
- Remember officers' badge and patrol car numbers. Write down everything you remember ASAP.
- Try to find witnesses and their names and phone numbers.

Web zone

F. Now read about Dan Ochoa's behavior. Compare his behavior with the advice on the Web site. Did Dan do the right things? What else should he do?

Dan didn't argue when he was arrested. He understood that it looked like he was guilty. He was polite and totally in control of his behavior. He went to the police station and quietly accepted the summons and agreed to appear in court. As soon as he got home, he wrote down everything that happened before and after the arrest. The next day his mother called an attorney to represent him at his trial.

➤ Do it yourself!

A. **True story. Do you know a true story or a story from a book or a movie about a person who was arrested? Make notes.**

- Who?
- What?
- When and where?
- Did the person follow the advice on the Web site?

B. **Discussion. Use your notes to tell the story to your partner or your group.**

Authentic practice

A. Read the excerpt from a textbook of U.S. history.

The U.S. Constitution

In May 1787, the early leaders of this country met in Philadelphia to design the government of the United States. The document they created is called the Constitution. All the laws in this country are based on the Constitution. All new and old laws are examined to be sure they are "constitutional."

The Constitution tells us how the government is organized. It clearly lists and explains the powers of the government. It also explains the limits of the powers of the government.

> *We the People* of the United States, in order to form a more perfect union, establish justice, insure domestic tranquility, provide for the common defense, promote the general welfare, and secure the blessings of liberty to ourselves and our posterity, do ordain and establish this Constitution for the United States of America.

The Bill of Rights

The Constitution gives the government power to make laws. Citizens have the responsibility of obeying those laws or facing punishment. But in order to protect citizens from unfair punishment, the Constitution also gives citizens certain rights. Those rights and protections are described in an important addition to the Constitution called the Bill of Rights. Below are a few of those rights that relate to the protections given citizens accused of crimes:

- The government or the police cannot search a house without permission. If the police think someone has committed a crime, they have to convince a judge of the court that the person is probably guilty. And if the judge believes the police, he or she will give the police a letter of permission to search the person's house. That permission is called a "warrant." Warrants protect citizens from unfair searches.
- A citizen accused of a crime is called a "defendant." Defendants have a right to a trial by a jury of impartial people, people who don't have an opinion yet about the facts. Defendants have the right to call witnesses who know the facts to help prove they are not guilty. Defendants also have the right to have a lawyer to help them at the trial.

One of the most important principles of our justice system is the "presumption of innocence." In every state, jurors are given instructions like these: The defendant enters this courtroom as an innocent person, and you must consider him or her to be an innocent person until the State (or the "government") convinces you beyond a reasonable doubt that he or she is guilty. The defendant does not have to prove his or her innocence. It is the State's responsibility to prove guilt.

42 *Our United States History*

Our United States History **43**

See page 148 for the complete Bill of Rights.

🖥 **FYI. For the complete Constitution and all its amendments, go to this Web site:**

http://www.access.gpo.gov/congress/senate/constitution/toc.html

Authentic practice

(For general suggestions, see *Introduction*, page Tx.)

The elements of the U.S. justice system

Procedure:

A. Read the excerpt . . .

➤ Have students preview the reading. Remind them that previewing includes skimming the first lines of each paragraph, looking at headings, sub-headings, bulleted material, visuals, and specially formatted words or phrases.

➤ Ask questions about what they learned from pre-viewing, such as *What topics are covered in this excerpt?* (the Constitution and the Bill of Rights) *In the Bill of Rights, what protections are given to people accused of crimes?* (no search without per-mission, a trial by jury, the right to witnesses and a lawyer)

➤ Point out that significant words or phrases are often indicated by boldface, italics, or, in this case, quotation marks. Elicit examples of impor-tant terms in quotation marks in this reading (constitutional, warrant, defendant, presumption of innocence, government). Write these terms on the board.

➤ Tell students that specially formatted terms are often defined in the sentence or paragraph. Ask students to find the definitions in the reading for the terms in quotation marks. Elicit the defini-tions and write them on the board next to the terms. Your board might look like this:

1. "constitutional": from or based on the Constitution

2. "warrant": permission to search an accused person's house

3. "defendant": a citizen accused of a crime

4. "presumption of innocence": jurors must consider a defendant to be innocent until the state convinces them beyond a reasonable doubt that he or she is guilty

5. "government": the state

➤ Have students read the excerpt thoroughly. Check comprehension after each paragraph or section by asking questions such as *When was the Constitution written?* (in 1787) *What does the Constitution talk about?* (how the U.S. government is organized, the limits of the powers of the gov-ernment) *Why does the Constitution give citizens certain rights?* (to protect citizens from unfair punishment) *What are some rights that defendants have?* (a trial by jury of impartial people, a lawyer)

➤ Point out that the reading is very simplified and meant to be an introduction to the topic. The complete Bill of Rights appears on page 148 of the student's book.

Option: To succeed academically, students need to be able to anticipate questions that might be asked about a text. To practice this skill, have students cre-ate questions based on the reading. Put students in small groups to create 10 questions. When all the groups have finished, have them exchange and answer each other's questions.

FYI . . .

➤ Tell students that they can find information about the U.S. government and how it works online. The Web site given here includes the complete Constitution and all the amendments.

➤ Make sure students know that the amendments are changes and additions to the Constitution that have been made over time. The Bill of Rights is the first 10 amendments to the Constitution. They were added in 1791 to protect certain rights of citizens.

Option: Have students go to the Web site and print out other amendments, or do it yourself. Put stu-dents in small groups to read different amendments, and ask each group to explain its amendment to the class. Some amendments that concern criminal pros-ecutions are the 4th (protection against unreason-able search and seizure), the 6th (rights of the accused in criminal prosecutions), the 8th (protec-tion against cruel and unusual punishment), and the 14th (right to equal protection and due process).

B. Vocabulary . . .

➤ Scanning is an important academic skill. Tell students that they should go back and scan the excerpt to find the answers, if necessary.

➤ Have students check answers by reading the completed statements out loud to a partner. If students are not sure of the answers, have partners identify the sentence in the excerpt that contains each definition.

FYI . . .

➤ Print out the glossary of legal terms from the Web site. Assign terms to pairs or groups to read and rephrase in their own words. Have students present the terms to the class.

Note: Students may find the definitions challenging and need help processing the information. The terms will be useful in preparing the role play below.

Option: Have individuals log on to the Web site and choose three to five words. They should study the definitions and make notes in order to present the information to the class or a group.

Option: Make flashcards with the term on one side and the definition on the other. Have pairs or groups study the terms and then quiz each other.

C. Culture talk . . .

➤ With the class, brainstorm questions for students to use as prompts. You may want to use the text-book excerpt on page 94 as a basis for the questions. Suggestions may include *Does your country have a document like the U.S. Constitution? When was it written? Are defendants entitled to a trial by jury?*

➤ Have students suggest additional questions that are not based on the textbook excerpt.

➤ Have students work in small groups to compare and contrast justice systems in their home countries.

➤ Do it yourself!

(For general suggestions, see *Introduction*, page Txiii.)

Procedure:

➤ Tell the students that there are two attorneys at a trial. One is the defense attorney (in this case, Hernan Guzman) who represents the person accused of the crime (Dan Ochoa). The other is the prosecutor or state's attorney (Marion Wilkens) who tries the case for the government.

➤ Brainstorm with the class the important information that must be presented at the trial. Ask students to think of movies or television shows they have seen that include courtroom scenes. Write students' ideas on the board. Elicit that we need to know the following: Dan's story, what Paul saw and heard before he left Dan, what the cashier remembers, and what the guard saw. Students may also suggest that evidence should be presented about Dan's character, the day's receipts from the register at the watch counter, the fact that Dan had money before the sale and not after, and so on.

➤ Put students in small groups to make two lists of questions, one for the prosecutor to ask and one for the defense attorney.

➤ Collect the questions. Assign every student a role. There are eight non-juror roles, so everyone else can be jurors or assistants to the two attorneys. Other possible roles are the manager of Larson's Department Store, the arresting officer, and the officer who gave Dan the summons to appear in court. Give the attorneys the questions provided by the small groups. If you think it would help organize the role play, play a role yourself, such as that of the judge.

➤ Give all the students a few minutes to think about what they need to do in their roles. Tell jurors that they can take notes at this trial, although this is not permitted at a real trial. Remind the class that the jury verdict must be unanimous.

➤ After the role play, discuss the court proceedings and the verdict.

Challenge: Trial witnesses often have to make a written statement. Tell students to imagine that they are one of the witnesses (Paul Yon, the cashier, or the guard). Have them write a brief report about what happened from that person's perspective. Collect the reports and read them aloud.

B. **Vocabulary. Complete each statement with a word or phrase from the textbook excerpt on page 94.**

1. The document that describes the organization and powers of the government is the _____Constitution_____.

2. Protections for citizens are contained in the _____Bill of Rights_____.

3. A person who is innocent of a crime is not _____guilty_____.

4. The _____government_____ has the power to make laws.

5. The police cannot search a private house without a _____warrant_____.

6. Only a _____judge_____ can give the police permission to search a house.

7. A _____defendant_____ is a person accused of a crime.

8. A _____trial_____ is the process in which a person is judged guilty or not guilty.

9. Defendants have a right to a trial by a _____jury_____.

10. Jurors have to be _____impartial_____. They haven't yet formed an opinion.

11. A person who knows the facts and can bring that information to the trial is a _____witness_____.

12. It is the state's responsibility to prove _____guilt_____.

FYI. For a simple and understandable presentation of vocabulary that relates to the U.S. system of justice, go to this Web site:

http://www.usdoj.gov/usao/eousa/kidspage/glossary.html

C. **Culture talk. How does the justice system in your home country differ from the justice system here? Compare and contrast cultures with your classmates. Give examples.**

➤ Do it yourself!

Role-play. Role-play the trial of Dan Ochoa. First write questions that the attorneys might ask the defendant and the witnesses. Then role-play the trial.

Possible roles: Daniel Ochoa, the defendant
　　　　　　 Paul Yon, the defendant's friend, a witness
　　　　　　 Other witnesses: the cashier and the guard at Larson's Department Store
　　　　　　 Julia Ochoa, the defendant's mother
　　　　　　 Hernan Guzman, the defendant's attorney
　　　　　　 Marion Wilkens, the state's attorney
　　　　　　 Oliva Fernandez, the judge
　　　　　　 Jurors

Review

A. Pair work or group work.

Tell the story of Dan Ochoa's arrest and trial.

Ask and answer questions.

Create conversations.

Say as much as you can.

Review

(For general suggestions, see *Introduction*, page Txii.)

Procedure:

Note: The format of this exercise is somewhat different from those in other *Review* sections. There are no general questions about who the characters are or where they are, and the task requires students to summarize and synthesize information from the *Authentic practice* sections on pages 90 through 95.

A. Pair work or group work.

Ask and answer questions.

➤ Ask the class general questions about the pictures, such as *What is Dan doing in the first scene?* (paying for the watch) *Where is Dan in the third scene?* (at the police station) *What are the people talking about in the fourth scene?* (Dan's arrest for shoplifting, his need for a lawyer) *What is happening in the last scene?* (Dan's friend Paul Yon is answering questions on the witness stand.) In pairs, students take turns asking and answering questions about what happened on each day.

➤ Point to the jurors in the jury box. Ask *How many people are on this jury?* (12) Tell students that a jury may include one to two additional jurors called alternates. They are present during the entire trial in case one of the regular jurors gets sick.

Option: Working in pairs, students write factual questions that can be used by the trial lawyers. An example of a factual question about the first scene is *Who saw Dan give the cashier the money?* (Paul Yon) Then have one pair of students join another pair to ask and answer the questions they have written.

Create conversations.

➤ Assign pairs of students one of the scenes and have them create a conversation for the characters. Have five pairs read their conversations in order to the class.

Option: Have pairs number the speech balloons and, on a separate sheet of paper, write one line of conversation for each person.

Option: Each student assumes the role of a character in the story (Dan, Paul, the cashier, the guard, the police officer, Mr. Guzman, or Mrs. Ochoa). Students say as much as they can about what happened from their character's point of view. They should keep talking until you say *Stop*.

Challenge: Remind the class about capitalization and punctuation. In pairs, students write one of the conversations using quoted speech. Then have pairs take turns reading aloud each part.

Challenge: Have students report one of the conversations using indirect speech. For scene 1, students might report *Dan says he has the exact change, even the pennies.* If necessary, refer students to Exercise D on page 89.

🎧B–C.

➤ Tell students they are going to listen to Paul Yon's testimony. Make sure students understand that a *testimony* is evidence presented orally by a witness during a trial.

➤ After students listen the first time, have them read the six statements in Exercise B so they will know what to listen for. Allow students to listen to the conversation as many additional times as necessary to complete the exercise individually.

➤ Have students check answers with a partner. Then have pairs change the false statements to make them true.

➤ Tell students to read Mr. Guzman's questions in Exercise C. As students listen again, they should take notes, focusing on Paul Yon's answers.

➤ Working individually, students report Paul's answers in indirect speech.

➤ In pairs, students check their statements. Review as a class.

D. Read each sentence...

➤ Students work individually to complete the review exercise.

➤ Circulate to offer help as needed.

➤ Have students check answers with a partner. Review answers as a class.

➤ Identify any areas of difficulty that may require additional instruction and practice.

Tapescript

Mr. Guzman: Now, Paul, could you please tell me where you were on Friday afternoon at about 4:45?

Paul: I was at Larson's Department Store, Mr. Guzman.

Guzman: Who, if anyone, were you with?

Paul: I was with my friend, Dan Ochoa.

Guzman: And could you please tell me in your own words what happened on that occasion?

Paul: Everything?

Guzman: Just the facts.

Paul: Sure. Well, we were shopping for Mother's Day presents and Dan picked out a watch. We went to the cashier and Dan paid for the watch.

Guzman: How did he pay for the watch?

Paul: What do you mean, "How did he pay?"

Guzman: Did Dan charge the watch? Did he pay by check? Cash?

Paul: He paid cash. I remember that because he had exact change. He said, "I have exact change, even the pennies."

Guzman: Did he get a receipt?

Paul: I don't know.

Guzman: You don't remember?

Paul: No, it's not that. I left to look for a robe for my mom. I didn't see if he got a receipt or not.

Guzman: But you're sure he paid for the watch?

Paul: Absolutely sure. Dan paid for the watch.

Guzman: No further questions.

Female: You may step down, Mr. Yon. Thank you for your testimony.

Listening comprehension. Listen to Paul Yon's testimony. Then check *True, False,* or *?* (No information) for each statement.

	True	False	?
1. Mr. Guzman asks how much the watch cost.	☐	☑	☐
2. Mr. Guzman asks how Dan paid for the watch.	☑	☐	☐
3. Paul doesn't remember how Dan paid.	☐	☑	☐
4. Paul didn't see a receipt.	☑	☐	☐
5. Paul is sure Dan paid for the watch.	☑	☐	☐
6. The cashier went to the restroom.	☐	☐	☑

ᑫᑭ **C.** **Listen to the first part of Paul Yon's testimony again. Then report Paul's answer in indirect speech.**

1. Mr. Guzman asked, "Now, Paul, could you please tell me where you were on

    Friday afternoon at about 4:45?" What did Paul say? _____

    <u>He said he was at Larson's Department Store.</u>

2. Mr. Guzman asked, "Who, if anyone, were you with?" What did Paul say?

    <u>He said he was with his friend, Dan Ochoa.</u>

D. **Read each sentence or question. Underline your response.**

1. "Are you in favor of censorship of books and movies?"

    YOU <u>Under some circumstances.</u>   **YOU** If it's not too pricey.

2. "I don't have any coins in the register."

    YOU <u>That's OK. I have exact change.</u>   **YOU** We'll have to agree to disagree.

3. "I could use a new watch."

    YOU <u>Great. Let's go shopping.</u>   **YOU** I think I'll pass.

4. "Here's another one for $59. What do you think?"

    YOU <u>Awesome!</u>   **YOU** I think it's morally wrong.

5. "This robe is $129. It's beautiful."

    YOU Just my luck.   **YOU** <u>That's way out of my price range.</u>

E. Punctuate each sentence or question. Use correct capitalization.

1. Mrs. Ochoa said, "My Danny never stole anything."

2. Dan said, "I paid for the watch but I didn't get a receipt"

3. Mr. Guzman asked Paul, "Did you see Dan pay for the watch?"

4. Paul said, "He paid cash."

F. Reread the excerpt on page 94. Then complete each statement with the correct word.

1. The _____Constitution_____ is a document that describes the organization of government and the rights of citizens.

2. In a trial, the person arrested for a crime is the _____defendant_____.

3. The presumption of _____innocence_____ ensures that defendants get a fair trial.

4. A letter of permission that allows the police to search a person's house is a _____warrant_____.

G. Composition. On a separate sheet of paper, write about the picture on page 96. Say as much as you can.

> **Now I can**
> ❑ discuss pros and cons of controversial issues.
> ❑ agree and disagree respectfully.
> ❑ report what other people say.
> ❑ understand the importance of the U.S. Constitution and the Bill of Rights.
> ❑ understand the elements of the U.S. justice system.

E–F.

➤ Students work individually to complete the review exercises.

➤ Circulate to offer help as needed.

➤ Have students check answers with a partner. Review answers as a class.

➤ Identify any areas of difficulty that may require additional instruction and practice.

G. Composition...

➤ Provide students with concrete approaches to writing about the picture on page 96. Use one of the options that follow, give students a choice of options, or assign options based on students' levels of proficiency. Model what is expected of students for each option.

➤ Advise students to look back through the unit for help and ideas as they write.

➤ Circulate to offer help as needed.

Option: Students tell the story of Dan Ochoa's arrest and trial in chronological order. They can refer to the guided composition they wrote in Exercise D on page 91 to begin the story and add details to complete the story.

Option: Have students choose any scene on page 96 and write an extended conversation between the characters. Students should refer to the model conversations on pages 86 and 87 for an example of the format to use.

Option: Have students write an extended conversation for any two characters on page 96. Tell students to use direct speech. Remind them to use correct capitalization and punctuation.

Challenge: Have students write an *Ask Joan* letter from Mrs. Ochoa, who wants advice following her son's arrest.

Now I can

➤ Read the first item in the box out loud: *Now I can discuss pros and cons of controversial issues.* Elicit from the class an example of how to discuss an issue, such as *I'm against capital punishment.*

➤ Put students in pairs, tell the students to take turns reading each item in the box and giving an example of what they have learned. When students can provide an example, they should check that objective. If there are items students aren't able to check, have them look back through the unit for ideas.

➤ When students are finished reviewing with their partners, read each item out loud and elicit an example from the class.

➤ Have students take out the K-W-L charts they created at the beginning of the unit. Ask them to complete the L section with what they have learned.

Oral test (optional)

You may want to use the *Now I can* box as an informal evaluation. While students are working on the *Composition* activity, you can call them up individually and check their ability with two or three objectives.

UNIT 8

Your health and safety

Note: For a discussion on page 105, have students bring in ads from newspapers or magazines for miracle products.

Note: If you are interested in educator materials related to food and nutrition, go to the home page for the food and nutrition information center at www.nal.usda.gov.fnic. You can click on the Food Guide Pyramid for information on this specific topic, or go to teacher resources for other materials.

 Preview

(For general suggestions, see *Introduction*, page Tviii.)

Warm up. Do you know what this chart is? What can you use it for?

Procedure:

➤ Introduce the topic of the Food Guide Pyramid by asking questions about the illustration, such as *What shape is this chart?* (a pyramid) *What is pictured in each section of the pyramid?* (different kinds of food) *What kind of food is in the biggest section?* (grains) *What kind of food is in the smallest section?* (fats, oils, and sugars)

➤ Read the first question and elicit or tell students that it is the Food Guide Pyramid. Ask *What can you use it for?* (identifying foods in each group, making food choices)

➤ Put students in pairs or small groups to identify all the categories of food and the examples shown in the chart. Elicit students' ideas and create a table on the board like the one following. At the left, write foods from the section at the top of the pyramid. Continue with foods from the remaining sections, ending with foods from the bottom of the pyramid.

Unit 8 objectives

Procedure:

➤ Have students read the objectives. Explain any unfamiliar terms, such as *quackery* (practices or treatments that pretend to cure an illness).

➤ Working individually, students rank the objectives from 1 to 5, with 1 being the objective that is most important to them.

➤ Have students form groups based on which objective they ranked as 1. So, for example, all students who ranked "Suggest a remedy" as the most important objective form one group. Students then brainstorm questions they have about the objective.

Fats, oils, sweets	Milk products	Meats, poultry	Vegetables	Fruits	Grains
oil sugar cookies	milk yogurt cheese	egg fish meat poultry nuts beans	carrots celery eggplant onion pepper Brussels sprout potato	apple bananas orange pear grapes watermelon	bread cereal rice pasta crackers

Your health and safety

Preview

Warm up. Do you know what this chart is? What can you use it for?

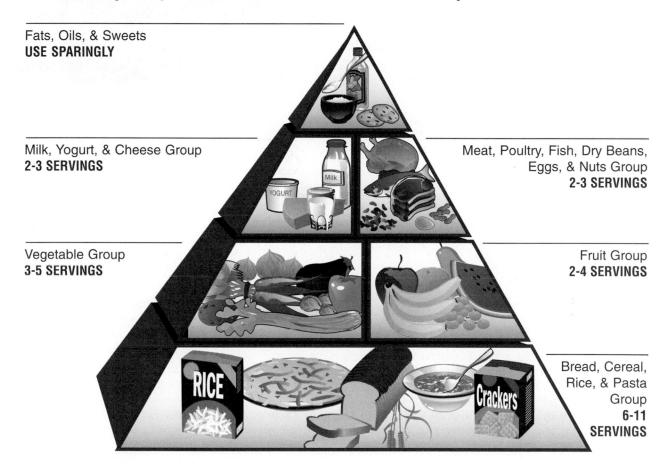

Fats, Oils, & Sweets
USE SPARINGLY

Milk, Yogurt, & Cheese Group
2-3 SERVINGS

Meat, Poultry, Fish, Dry Beans,
Eggs, & Nuts Group
2-3 SERVINGS

Vegetable Group
3-5 SERVINGS

Fruit Group
2-4 SERVINGS

Bread, Cereal,
Rice, & Pasta
Group
**6-11
SERVINGS**

Unit 8 objectives

- Express regret.
- Suggest a remedy.
- Avoid quackery.
- Separate weight-loss facts from myths.
- Make daily food choices based on the Food Guide Pyramid.

Practical conversations

🎧 **A.** Listen and read.

A: I shouldn't have eaten those pretzels.

B: Why not? Didn't you like them?

A: Are you kidding? Of course I did. But I have to limit my salt. I have high blood pressure.

B: Oh, really? That's too bad.

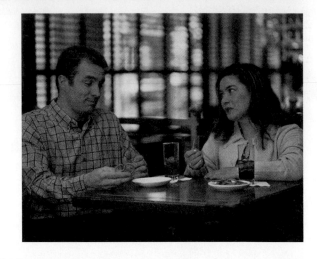

🎧 **B.** Pronunciation and intonation practice.

🎧 **Vocabulary**

Ways to take care of health problems

I have to **watch my weight**. I'm overweight.

I have to **limit my salt**. I have high blood pressure.

I have to **stay away from fatty foods**. I have high cholesterol.

Another health problem and what you have to do: _____

C. Pair work. **Make a list of fattening, salty, or fatty foods. Express regret about having eaten them.**

fattening foods: _candy_____

salty foods: _pretzels_____

fatty foods: _meat_____

A: I shouldn't have eaten _____1_____.

B: Why not? Didn't you like _____?

A: Are you kidding? Of course I did. But _____. I _____.

B: _____2_____.

[1] that cheese, that candy, those chips, etc.

[2] I'm sorry to hear that, I'm sorry, etc.

Practical conversations

(For general suggestions, see *Introduction*, page Tviii.)

Model 1

Content: expressing regret; *shouldn't have*; expressing sympathy; ways to take care of health problems; fattening, salty, and fatty foods

∩A–B.

➤ To set the scene for the conversation, point to the photo and ask questions such as *Where are the people?* (in a restaurant) *What have they been eating and drinking?* (pretzels, soft drinks) *What expression does the man have on his face?* (regretful, a little upset)

➤ To access students' experience, ask *Have you ever eaten something and then wished you hadn't?* Elicit examples or give one of your own: *I was eating cookies and watching TV. All of a sudden, I realized I'd eaten the whole bag! I was sorry I had eaten so much fat and sugar!*

➤ After students listen to and read the conversation, check comprehension by asking questions such as *What did the man regret eating?* (pretzels) *Why?* (He has to limit his salt.) *What is his health problem?* (high blood pressure)

Option: Before students listen to and read the conversation, have them cover the conversation and look at the photo. Read the first line of the conversation. Then ask students *Why not? Why shouldn't he have eaten the pretzels?* Elicit reasons he might not want to eat pretzels.

Option: Play the role of Student A and have the class respond chorally with Student B's lines. Then switch roles.

∩Vocabulary

➤ Have students read and listen to *Ways to take care of health problems.*

➤ Check students' understanding of the relationship of ideas by asking questions such as *Why does the man have to watch his weight?* (because he is overweight) The woman has high blood pressure. *What does she have to do?* (limit her salt)

➤ Make sure students understand that *watch one's weight* means to keep one's weight low, not to gain weight. Also, *fatty foods* are foods that contain a lot of fat.

➤ Have students write down another health problem, such as having diabetes, and what the person has to do (not eat foods with sugar).

Option: Begin a chart on the board with the headings *Health problem, Contributing food,* and *Solution / advice.* Begin with the information in the *Vocabulary* section and elicit ideas from the class to fill in the chart.

Health problem	Contributing food	Solution / advice
Overweight	Fattening foods (desserts, fast food, junk food)	Watch your weight, avoid fattening foods
High blood pressure	Salty foods (chips, fries)	Limit salt intake
High cholesterol	Fatty foods (fast food, junk food, meats)	Avoid fatty foods

Brainstorm other health problems that certain kinds of foods can exacerbate, and continue completing the chart. You may have examples like the following:

Health problem	Contributing food	Solution / advice
Diabetes	Foods with sugar (sweets)	Lose weight, avoid sweets
Ulcers	Spicy foods (chili peppers)	Avoid spicy food food
Lactose intolerance	Dairy products (milk, ice cream)	Reduce dairy intake
Migraines	Caffeine (coffee, tea, colas)	Cut down on coffee, tea

C. Pair work ...

➤ Point out that *fatty foods* contain a lot of fat such as butter, lard, or oil. *Fattening foods* contain a lot of calories. Elicit some examples of fattening foods that may not be fatty foods, such as soda and candy. There will be some overlap between these two categories.

➤ Give students time to brainstorm foods that fit into the three categories in the box. Opinions will vary and conversation will be lively. Allow discussion.

➤ When students have completed their lists, model the conversation with a more advanced student. Play the role of Student A to demonstrate how to express regret for eating a certain food and how to give a reason for the regret. Make sure the class understands that Student A states both a way to take care of the health problem and the health problem.

➤ In pairs, students practice making the appropriate substitutions. Have volunteers read their conversations aloud.

T100

Model 2

Content: asking about ailments, negative *yes-no* questions, suggesting a remedy

Procedure:

🎧 A–B.

➤ To set the scene for the conversation, point to the photo and ask *Where are the women?* (sitting at a table) *What are the women doing?* (drinking tea or coffee, talking, looking at a magazine)

➤ After students listen to the conversation, check comprehension by asking questions such as *What problem does the woman in red have?* (migraines) *What is the remedy that the woman on the left suggests?* (Rackinusha)

➤ Play the cassette or read aloud the conversation. Have students repeat the lines in the pauses and then practice reading the conversation in pairs.

➤ Circulate, correcting students' pronunciation if necessary.

C. Pair work . . .

➤ Have students read the ad for Rackinusha. Ask questions such as *Have you ever heard of this remedy?* (no) *Do you need a prescription to buy it?* (No, it's an over-the-counter medication.) *Does it sound too good to be true?* (yes) *Why?* (It says it cures many ailments, probably too many.)

➤ Write the conversation with substitution slots on the board. Walk the students through each line, eliciting a word or phrase that could go in each slot. You may get a conversation like this:

A: Don't you have *(name of an ailment, possibly from the Rackinusha ad)?*

B: Yes, I do. *(follow-up question such as "Why?" or "What's up?")*

A: They say *(a remedy, possibly Rackinusha)* cures *(a pronoun, or repeat name of the ailment).*

B: *(questions about the information)?*

A: *(source of information).* It couldn't hurt to give *(the pronoun or the remedy)* a try.

➤ Brainstorm other ailments. Write examples on the board. Next to each ailment, write the names of remedies (real or fictitious) that students suggest.

➤ Have pairs practice the conversation, using an ailment and a remedy from the board or the ad.

➤ Do it yourself!

(For general suggestions, see *Introduction*, page Txiii.)

Procedure:

A–B.

➤ Remind students that a remedy can be a medicine, a supplement, a food, or another treatment that they have used.

➤ Have students complete the charts individually.

➤ When students have finished their charts, have pairs or small groups discuss the remedies. Have them use these questions as a guide for discussion: *Did you list ailments in common? Which ones? What remedies do you use? Which remedies are the most effective?*

Option: Have pairs of students create an ad for one of their remedies. Remind them to include what the product is for, good things about it, and a picture or other visual.

A. Listen and read.

A: Don't you have migraines?

B: Yes, I do. Why?

A: They say Rackinusha cures them.

B: Really? Where did you hear that?

A: Right here. It couldn't hurt to give it a try.

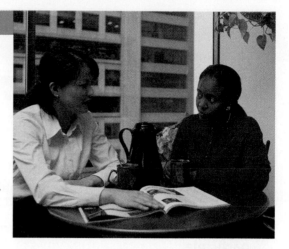

B. Pronunciation and intonation practice.

C. Pair work. Choose an ailment from the ad or a real ailment. Suggest a remedy.

A: Don't you have _____1_____?

B: Yes, I do. _____?

A: They say _____ cures _____.

B: _____?

A: _____. It couldn't hurt to give _____ a try.

¹backaches, stomachaches, allergies, etc.

The miracle secret of the ancient Middle East—

Recently rediscovered in forgotten pyramid!

RACKINUSHA

Cures migraines, arthritis, insomnia, nail fungus, psoriasis, and much much more!

➤ Completely natural

➤ Absolutely safe

➤ Available at drugstores everywhere

Stop suffering. Throw out all those useless medicines and get **RACKINUSHA** today!

OTC. No prescription necessary.

➤Do it yourself!

A. Complete the chart with remedies you use.

Ailment	Remedy	Prescription required?	Effective?
colds	vitamin C	no	yes

B. Pair work. Compare remedies with a partner. Which is most effective?

Practical grammar

Should have / shouldn't have

> Express regret for behavior with *should have* or *shouldn't have* and a past participle.
>
> past participle   past participle
>
> I **shouldn't have** eaten that cake! I **should have** ordered fruit. It's much healthier.

A. Complete each sentence with a regret. Use *should have* or *shouldn't have* and a past participle.

1. You ___shouldn't have bought___ all that candy. It's too hard to resist!

not buy

2. We ___should have ordered___ the soup. It looked great.

order

3. You ___should have taken___ aspirin for that headache. It would be gone by now.

take

4. They ___should have read___ the fine print before spending all that money.

read

5. I ___should have called___ the doctor for a new prescription.

call

6. He ___shouldn't have eaten___ the whole cake! He has to watch his weight.

not eat

Negative *yes–no* questions

> Use a negative question to confirm information you think is correct or to ask for agreement.
> >Don't you have migraines?
> >Isn't that ad ridiculous?
> >Didn't you taste the chocolate cake?
> Sometimes the question also expresses surprise or disbelief.

B. Complete each negative *yes–no* question.

1. ___Didn't you see___ the ad on TV last night?

you / see

2. ___Isn't it___ better yet?

it / be

3. ___Don't the stores have___ Rackinusha yet?

the stores / have

4. ___Didn't the pharmacist say___ some herbal remedies were dangerous?

the pharmacist / say

5. ___Doesn't she___ usually ___take___ something for her back pain?

she / take

Practical grammar

(For general suggestions, see *Introduction*, page Tix.)

Should have / shouldn't have

Procedure:

Note: If students have difficulty with past participles, refer them to the list of irregular verbs on page 145.

➤ Refer students to the model conversation on page 100. Read aloud the first line: *I shouldn't have eaten those pretzels.* Ask *How does the man feel?* (regretful, sorry) *Why?* (He shouldn't have eaten all the pretzels.) *Have you ever done something you wish you hadn't?* Elicit students' experience or tell your own, such as *I shouldn't have gone to that movie. It got a terrible review; I shouldn't have left the house so late. I missed my bus.*

➤ Tell students that we use *shouldn't have* plus a past participle to talk about regrets—when we've done something but wish we hadn't. Tell them that we can also express regret with *should have: I should have gone to the new movie across the street, I should have left the house at 7:30.* We use *should have* when we haven't done something but wish we had. Elicit students' regrets with *should have* plus a past participle.

➤ Point out that in speech both *should have* and *shouldn't have* are usually contracted, or reduced. It sounds like the speaker is saying *should of* and *shouldn't of.*

➤ Write on the board *You shouldn't have* and *You should have.* To check that students understand how these expressions are used, tell them that you will make some statements about behavior you regret. They will comment either *You shouldn't have* for things you did or *You should have* for things you didn't do. Create your own or use these statements: *I didn't call my mother on her birthday! I just ate the whole pie. I quit my job. I didn't ask my boss for a raise. I didn't study for the test.*

A. Complete each sentence ...

➤ Write the first item on the board. Include the blank and the words *not buy* below the line. Read the directions aloud and ask the class to suggest the completion of the first item.

➤ Working individually, students complete sentences 2 through 6.

➤ In pairs, students compare answers. Review as a class and answer any questions.

Negative *yes–no* questions

Procedure:

➤ Refer students to the model conversation on page 101. Read aloud the first line: *Don't you have migraines?* Point out that the speaker believes that the other woman does have migraines and is seeking confirmation. In fact, her belief is confirmed: *Yes, I do.* Note that the response is a short answer and stands for *Yes, I do have migraines.*

➤ Ask a series of negative *yes-no* questions to confirm information you think is correct and elicit short answers from the class. Use these questions or create your own: *Didn't you drive here today? Wasn't it beautiful yesterday? Didn't I see you on the street the other day?*

➤ Tell students that negative *yes-no* questions are used both to get confirmation or agreement and to express surprise or disbelief. When expressing disbelief, a negative question can sound accusatory: *Can't they turn down their TV?*

➤ Read each of the examples in the box and have volunteers answer the questions.

B. Complete each negative *yes–no* question.

➤ Write the first item on the board. Include the blank and the words *you / see* below the line. Read the directions aloud and ask the class to suggest the completion of the first item.

➤ Tell students that they should complete the exercise using the simple present tense or the simple past tense. As a class, go over the items and decide whether the verb should be written in the simple present tense or the simple past tense. Have students point out the words that helped them decide. (1: simple past tense, "last night"; 2: simple present tense, "yet"; 3: simple present tense, "yet"; 4: simple past tense, "were"; 5: simple present tense, "usually")

➤ Working individually, students complete sentences 2 through 5.

➤ In pairs, students compare answers. Review as a class and answer any questions.

➤ In item 5, students may ask about the word *anything*. Tell them that either *anything* or *something* is appropriate in the question: *Doesn't she usually take something for her back pain?*

C. Complete each conversation . . .

➤ Write the first item on the board. Include A's blank line and the words *cake / be delicious* under the blank.

➤ Tell students that they will use the words *cake / be delicious* to create a negative *yes-no* question that leads to B's answer, *Yes, it is.*

➤ Remind students that a short answer follows a *yes-no* question. The verb used in the answer can help students identify the auxiliary verb they will need to form the question. B's answer in item 3, for example, *Yes, I do*, tells students to use a form of *do* in the question. Remind them that they need a negative form: *Don't you have insomnia?*

➤ Working individually, students write questions.

➤ Have students check answers with a partner and then review as a class.

Option: After correcting the exercise, students work in pairs to practice asking and answering the questions in the exercise.

Challenge: Have students work in pairs to create conversations that include one of the items in the exercise. They must use both question and answer in the conversation, which should be at least six lines long.

Challenge: Although a negative *yes-no* question usually seeks confirmation or agreement, sometimes the listener disagrees. Have students write negative responses to the questions. For item 1, for example, the response might be *Actually, I don't really like cake.*

➤ Do it yourself!

(For general suggestions, see *Introduction*, page Txiii.)

Procedure:

A–B.

➤ On the board, write the two headings *I should have* and *I shouldn't have*. Under the first heading, write *I should have bought milk yesterday. Now we're out.* Under the second heading, write *I shouldn't have drunk all that coffee after dinner!* Read the sentences and tell students they are both regrets about your recent behavior. Ask students for examples of regrets they have about their recent behavior. Write two or three students' ideas under the appropriate heading.

➤ Tell students to look at the chart in their books. Working individually, students write down two regrets about something they didn't do (*I should have*) and two regrets about something they did (*I shouldn't have*).

➤ Working in pairs, students take turns telling each other about their regrets.

Challenge: After Student A expresses a regret, Student B asks a negative question about the behavior. For example, if Student A says *I should have bought milk yesterday*, Student B might ask *Didn't you write it on your list?* Or if Student B says *I shouldn't have drunk all that coffee after dinner*, Student A might ask *Didn't you have trouble sleeping later?*

C. Complete each conversation with a negative question.

1. **A:** *Isn't the cake delicious*   ?
    cake / be delicious

    B: Yes, it is. But it's too fattening for me.

2. **A:** Isn't he a nurse   ?
    he / be a nurse

    B: Yes, he is. He works at General Hospital downtown.

3. **A:** Don't you have insomnia   ?
    you / have insomnia

    B: Yes, I do. I never get enough sleep.

4. **A:** Wasn't that article on vitamins great   ?
    that article on vitamins / be great

    B: Yes, it was. I learned a lot.

5. **A:** Didn't you try that new herbal remedy   ?
    you / try that new herbal remedy

    B: Yes, I did. It didn't work.

6. **A:** Didn't you ask your doctor about it   ?
    you / ask your doctor about it

    B: Yes, I did, but he didn't know the answer.

7. **A:** Didn't your sister tell you about it   ?
    your sister / tell you about it

    B: Yes, she did. But I didn't believe it.

8. **A:** Didn't it work   ?
    it / work

    B: No, actually, it didn't.

➤ Do it yourself!

A. Complete the chart with two regrets about your recent behavior.

I should have	I shouldn't have
I should have bought milk yesterday. Now we're out.	*I shouldn't have drunk all that coffee after dinner!*

B. Pair work. Compare regrets with a partner.

Avoid quackery.

A. Discussion. Answer the questions. Then discuss with your classmates.

1. What's Sophie's problem? _She wants to lose weight._

2. What is she planning to do about her problem? _buy Fat-B-Gone_

3. Does Helen think Sophie has a good plan? _no_

4. What does Helen think Sophie should do instead? _cut down on food and exercise more_

➤ Authentic practice

(For general suggestions, see *Introduction*, page Tx.)

Avoid quackery.

Procedure:

➤ To set the scene for the picture story, point to the pictures and ask general questions such as *Where are the two women?* (sitting outside on a bench) *What are they doing?* (talking, looking at magazines)

➤ Have students read along silently as they listen to the picture story.

➤ Some terms may be unfamiliar to students, but the meaning can be inferred from the context. Elicit the meanings of *breakthrough, a thing of the past, gullible, pass up, couch potato, don't fall for that, take my word for it, there's no free lunch, no pain, no gain.*

➤ Explain that *my word* is used to represent *my statement* or *my promise*, so *take my word* means *believe me, believe what I say.*

➤ Check understanding by asking questions such as *What is Sophie reading about?* (Fat-B-Gone) *What is Fat-B-Gone?* (a new weight-loss product, perhaps a pill) *Why might Sophie have a weight problem?* (She can't pass up food and she doesn't exercise.) *Does Sophie believe the claims for Fat-B-Gone?* (yes) *Does Helen believe the claims?* (no)

Option: Write *Fat-B-Gone* on the board. Tell students that this is the name of a new weight-loss product and that you're going to dictate portions of an ad that tells all about its benefits: *It makes dieting a thing of the past. Eat what you want, when you want. Fat-B-Gone goes to work when you go to sleep . . . Does the dieting for you. No annoying exercise. Guaranteed. Lose up to 30 pounds the first week, or your money back! Completely natural. Made from the bark of the ancient chinchona tree, found only in the La Mancha region of Spain.* While students are writing individually at their desks, have volunteers write the sentences on the board. Read each sentence aloud again as students look at the board. After each claim, ask *Does this sound too good to be true?* If students say *yes*, put a check mark next to the statement.

Option: Have pairs of students read the conversation between Sophie and Helen.

A. Discussion . . .

➤ Working individually, students write answers to the questions.

➤ Being able to give support for answers is an important academic skill. Have students underline the information in the story that supports their answers. For example, if students answer the question *What's Sophie's problem?* by saying that she wants to lose weight, they might underline *I'm going to send away for this miracle weight-loss breakthrough* or *I just can't pass up food. And I'm a real couch potato.*

➤ In pairs, students compare answers.

➤ Review answers as a class. Note that Sophie might have two problems: wanting to lose weight (or being overweight) and being gullible.

Option: Read the part of Sophie and have students respond chorally with Helen's lines.

Challenge: Have students write an *Ask Joan* letter from Helen about Sophie's problem and her plan to buy Fat-B-Gone. Remind students to use indirect speech or quoted speech where appropriate in describing the product claims and Sophie's statements. Students can exchange letters and write responses from Joan giving advice.

B. Vocabulary ...

➤ Have students read the statements in Exercise B.

➤ Then have them reread the picture story, scanning for the underlined words or phrases. Remind students to use the context to check meaning.

➤ Working individually, students check *True* or *False* for each statement.

➤ Review answers as a class. Ask students to explain their answers, giving support from the text.

Challenge: Have students create original *True-False* statements using other words or phrases from the picture story. Make sure statements demonstrate the meaning of the words. An example might be *"No free lunch" means Sophie will have to buy her lunch today.* (False) Have volunteers write their sentences on the board. Have students copy the sentences and write *True* or *False* next to each one.

C. Read each sentence or question ...

➤ Point out that *Come on!* can have different meanings: to encourage someone to go with you or to express disbelief.

➤ Working individually, students select a response. In pairs, they compare answers.

Option: Read each item and have students respond chorally with the correct response.

Option: Have pairs of students take turns reading the items and responses.

D. Reread the picture story ...

➤ Tell students to reread the story on page 104.

➤ Tell them to write down on a separate sheet of paper at least five claims made for the product.

➤ Elicit the claims and write them on the board.

E. Discussion ...

➤ Have students read the questions. Put students in small groups to discuss the answers.

➤ Elicit examples of products that make exaggerated claims, such as weight-loss, memory improvement, better muscle tone, or baldness remedies. Ask *Where might you find out about a product like Fat-B-Gone?* (ads on TV or radio or in magazines or newspapers, word of mouth, direct mail ads)

➤ Point out that the answer to the second question is not given in the picture story. Students will have to come up with their own ideas to discuss as a group.

Challenge: Out-of-class assignment. Ask students to watch television or listen to the radio for ads. They should take notes on product claims that may be too good to be true. After a few days, ask students to report on products they discovered, claims they heard, and any other information they would like to share.

➤ Do it yourself!

(For general suggestions, see *Introduction*, page Txiii.)

Procedure:

A. Write your own response ...

➤ Have a volunteer read the first speech balloon out loud. Model an appropriate response such as *Don't be so gullible* or *The only way to build muscle is to exercise.*

➤ Have volunteers read the other speech balloons aloud. Point out that, like Sophie, the three speakers sound as though they believe the product claims they're talking about. Have students decide whether they want to respond sympathetically or take the opposite attitude toward the claims.

➤ Point out that *cream* in the second speech balloon may also be written as *crème* when referring to cosmetics.

➤ Working individually, students write responses to the speech balloons.

➤ In pairs, students compare answers and practice their conversations.

Challenge: Have students write a response to each speech balloon using a negative *yes-no* question; for example, *Don't you think this ad sounds ridiculous?*

B. Discussion ...

➤ Ask students to take out the ads they collected, and supply some of your own.

➤ If possible, put students in small groups according to the type of product represented in their ads, such as weight-loss programs, muscle development, or health promotion. In small groups, students list the different claims made for the products.

➤ In each group, have students classify the claims as believable or unbelievable. Ask students to be prepared to give reasons for their classifications.

➤ Have groups share examples of products and claims with the class.

T105

B. Vocabulary. **Find the underlined phrases in the picture story. Then check *True* or *False*.**

		True	False
1.	A <u>gullible</u> person believes everything he or she hears.	☑	☐
2.	When you <u>send away</u> for something, you don't have it yet.	☑	☐
3.	When you <u>pass up</u> food, you eat everything offered.	☐	☑
4.	A <u>couch potato</u> doesn't exercise much.	☑	☐
5.	When you <u>take someone's word</u>, you believe what he or she says.	☑	☐

C. **Read each sentence or question. Underline your response.**

1. "I just sent away for a miracle breakthrough."

   YOU <u>You shouldn't have done that.</u>   **YOU** Is it a couch potato?

2. "You can lose up to 30 pounds in the first week."

   YOU <u>Come on!</u>   **YOU** That's too bad.

3. "Don't you take my word for it?"

   YOU <u>Are you kidding? Of course I do.</u>   **YOU** I shouldn't have.

D. **Reread the picture story. What are some of the claims the ad makes about Fat-B-Gone?**

It says it works while you sleep. It says it does the dieting for you, you can lose up to 30 pounds the first week, and it's completely natural.

E. Discussion. **Discuss your answers to these questions with a partner or a group.**

1. Have you ever heard of a product like Fat-B-Gone? Explain your answer.
2. What is a healthful diet? How much exercise is necessary or good?

➤ Do it yourself!

A. **Write your own response. Then read each conversation out loud with a partner.**

Look at this ad for a muscle-building machine! You don't have to exercise!   **YOU** _____

This cream is made from an ancient recipe, and it cures cancer!   **YOU** _____

Isn't it safe? It says it's completely natural.   **YOU** _____

B. Discussion. **Find an ad for a miracle product. What claims does it make? Do you think it works?**

Authentic practice

Nutrition, diet, and health

A. Take the self-test from *Body Wonderful* Magazine.

Body Wonderful Magazine

Self-Test
Dieting Facts and Myths

Test yourself on these common beliefs about diet and weight control.

FACT or MYTH? Check Fact or Myth next to each statement.

	FACT	MYTH
1. Skipping meals is a good way to lose weight.	☐	☑
2. Eating after 8 p.m. causes weight gain.	☐	☑
3. A good way to lose weight is to eat small meals throughout the day.	☑	☐
4. You need to use more calories than you eat to lose weight.	☑	☐
5. Certain foods, like grapefruit, celery, and cabbage, can burn fat and make you lose weight.	☐	☑
6. A "low-fat" label means the food has no calories.	☐	☑

B. Listening comprehension. Listen to the report on nutrition and health.

C. Listen to the report again. Then check your answers on the self-test. (The answers are at the bottom of the page.)

D. Discussion. Compare answers with your classmates. Did the information surprise you? Which diet myths did you believe?

FYI. More information on overweight can be found at this U.S. government Web site:

http://www.niddk.nih.gov/health/nutrit/pubs/statobes.htm

1. myth 2. myth 3. fact 4. fact 5. myth 6. myth

Authentic practice

(For general suggestions, see *Introduction*, page Tx.)

Nutrition, diet, and health

Procedure:

A. Take the self-test . . .

➤ Make sure students understand that a *myth* is a story or an idea that is widely believed but not actually true.

➤ Working individually, students check whether each statement is a fact (true) or a myth (false).

➤ Tell students that they will check their answers after listening to the report on nutrition and health.

⌒B–D.

➤ Students listen to the report twice. After the second listening, they check their answers on the self-test according to the information they heard in the report. The answers are at the bottom of the page.

➤ Working in small groups, students discuss their answers.

➤ Elicit examples of information that students found surprising and write them on the board.

Option: Determining meaning from context is an important academic skill. Sometimes a definition for an unfamiliar term appears as an appositive—it's next to the word it explains. In written material, an appositive may be set off by commas, parentheses, or dashes (as it is in the previous sentence). In the listening comprehension, there are two appositives; they define the words *obese* and *myths*. Have students listen to the report again and note the definitions.

FYI . . .

Option: If your students have access to computers, assign each student or pair one or more of the following questions. Ask them to find the answers on the Web site listed on page 106.

1. How has the prevalence of overweight and obesity in adults changed over the years?

2. What is the prevalence of overweight and obesity in minorities?

3. What is the prevalence of overweight and obesity in children and adolescents?

4. What is the prevalence of overweight and obesity in people with diabetes?

5. What is the prevalence of overweight and obesity in people with hypertension (high blood pressure)?

6. What is the prevalence of overweight and obesity in people with high cholesterol?

7. What is the prevalence of overweight and obesity in people with cancer?

8. What is the mortality rate associated with obesity?

9. What is the cost of overweight and obesity?

10. What is the cost of hypertension (high blood pressure) related to overweight and obesity?

11. How much do we spend on weight-loss products and services?

12. How physically active is the U.S. population?

Tapescript

Sinclair: Good evening, viewers. I'm Martin Sinclair with tonight's nutrition update.

More than half the U. S. population is overweight, and about 25 percent are obese—very overweight. This evening's guest is Dr. Prunella Kazan, nutritionist and expert on healthy weight control and weight loss. [pause] Good evening, Dr. Kazan. What's tonight's subject?

Kazan: Good evening, Martin. Tonight we turn our attention to common myths about diet and weight loss.

Sinclair: Myths?

Kazan: Yes. There are a lot of myths, or misconceptions, about how to lose weight. Since so many people are always trying to lose weight, I thought I would talk about four common myths many people think are facts.

First: Many people think that an effective way to lose weight is to skip meals.

Sinclair: Isn't it? That's what I do.

Kazan: No. Not a good idea. If you skip meals during the day, you are likely to eat more at the next meal. Studies show that people who skip breakfast tend to be heavier than those who eat a nutritious breakfast.

Sinclair: No kidding! I'm never hungry at breakfast, so I thought skipping it was a painless way to cut down on calories. What else do you have on your list?

(Tapescript is continued on page T107.)

Tapescript *(continued from page T106)*

Kazan: The second myth is that eating at night makes you gain weight.

Sinclair: You mean that's not true either?

Kazan: Nope. It doesn't matter what time of day you eat—it's how much you eat during the whole day and how much exercise you get that make you gain or lose weight. The best way to lose weight is to eat many small meals throughout the day and to exercise. The secret is just using more calories than you eat, and exercise burns calories.

Sinclair: Hmm. That's interesting.

Kazan: Three. Many people believe that some foods burn fat and make you thin. Certain foods, such as grapefruit, celery, and cabbage, have the reputation as fat burners, but there is absolutely no truth in this. It's possible that these myths were created by people marketing products that include grapefruit or other foods. Don't believe it.

Sinclair: Are you sure?

Kazan: Yes. Grapefruit, celery, and cabbage are great low-calorie foods that fill you up so you don't want to eat high-calorie things. But they don't have any magical powers to "burn" fat.

Sinclair: And what's myth number 4?

Kazan: This one's my favorite. People think that when they see a label that says "Low fat" or even "No fat" that the food has no calories. People need to understand that they are fooling themselves if they fill up on low-fat cookies, cakes, or candies. Those foods often have lots of sugar, and they are often as fattening as foods with fats. It's important to educate yourself about both the concepts and the vocabulary of diet and weight loss.

Sinclair: Well, that's really interesting. Unfortunately, our time is up. See you next week at the same time. This is Martin Sinclair, thanking Dr. Prunella Kazan for tonight's nutrition update.

➤ Do it yourself!

(For general suggestions, see *Introduction,* page Txiii.)

Procedure:

A. Study the food classes.

🎧**Vocabulary**

➤ Play the cassette or read the classes of foods. Have students repeat.

➤ Call out classes of foods and have students point to the pictures. Ask students to identify the items they see in each category.

Challenge: Classification Game. Divide the class into two or more teams. Members on each team brainstorm as many examples as they can of each class of foods. Then have a member of Team A call out a food. A member of Team B must state the food class it belongs to. Each correct classification earns 1 point for the team.

Challenge: Alphabet Game. Divide the class into two or more teams. Members on each team brainstorm foods that begin with each letter of the alphabet. Then teams take turns stating foods for all the letters in the alphabet. When stating a food, the team member must say the letter, the food, and the class it belongs to: *A, artichoke, vegetable.* If Team A names a food beginning with a letter and Team B cannot, Team A gets 1 point. When teams come to the end of the alphabet, the team with the highest number of points wins.

B. Classification...

➤ Working individually, students complete the chart with the names of single-ingredient foods that they like.

➤ Circulate and offer help as needed.

➤ Have students put a check mark next to the foods they listed that they think are healthful.

C. Discussion...

➤ With the class, brainstorm criteria for healthful foods. Criteria might include the following considerations: low in fat, high in vitamins, high in fiber, protein-rich, and so on. Write students' ideas on the board.

➤ In small groups, students discuss which of the foods they listed that they consider healthful. Have students explain why they consider a particular food healthful.

Challenge: Have students work in pairs to list the ingredients of a recent meal they ate at a restaurant. Remind them to list all the ingredients in each dish. Circulate to offer help as necessary. Then have students refer to the criteria for healthful foods on the board and rate their restaurant meals on a scale of 1 to 5, with 1 being most healthful and 5 being least healthy. Have students compare their findings.

A. Study the food classes.

🎧 Vocabulary

Classes of foods

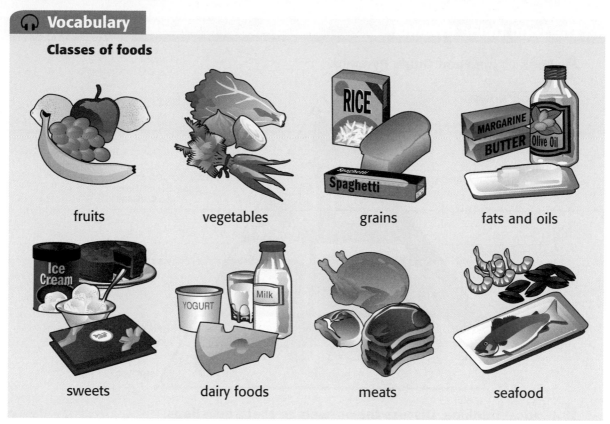

fruits   vegetables   grains   fats and oils

sweets   dairy foods   meats   seafood

B. Classification. Now complete this chart with foods you like. (Don't include prepared foods, like pizza, because it belongs to several categories.)

Fruits	Vegetables	Grains	Fats/Oils

Sweets	Dairy foods	Meats	Seafood

C. Discussion. In your opinion, which foods are healthful? Which foods are not healthful? Explain your reasons.

The Food Guide Pyramid

A. Look at the Food Guide Pyramid.

Fats, Oils, & Sweets
USE SPARINGLY

Milk, Yogurt, & Cheese Group
2-3 SERVINGS

Meat, Poultry, Fish, Dry Beans,
Eggs, & Nuts Group
2-3 SERVINGS

Vegetable Group
3-5 SERVINGS

Fruit Group
2-4 SERVINGS

Bread, Cereal,
Rice, & Pasta
Group
**6-11
SERVINGS**

B. Critical thinking. Discuss the answers to these questions.

1. What do you think is the purpose of the Food Guide Pyramid?

2. Can you explain why some foods are in the large bottom section of the Pyramid and other foods are in the small top section?

C. Write all the foods you ate yesterday.

Breakfast / Quantity	Lunch / Quantity	Dinner / Quantity	Snacks / Quantity
toast – 2 slices			

D. Discussion. Which part or parts of the Pyramid did most of your foods come from?

Authentic practice

(For general suggestions, see *Introduction*, page Tx.)

The Food Guide Pyramid

Procedure:

A–B.

➤ Have students look at the Food Guide Pyramid and read the name of each group. Have them also read the number of recommended servings for each group.

➤ Put students in groups of three. Assign one the role of facilitator, one the role of recorder, and one the role of reporter. The facilitator asks the questions and makes sure everyone responds. The recorder takes notes on the answers, and the reporter tells the class about the discussion.

➤ When groups have finished their discussion, elicit the answers to the questions from the group reporters.

Challenge: Have students look at the Food Guide Pyramid in their books for one minute. Draw an empty pyramid on the board with the six compartments but no other information. Have volunteers come to the board one at a time, and give them each the name of a food pictured in the Pyramid. They write the food in the correct compartment. Ask the rest of the class to make sure the categorizations are correct.

Challenge: Tell students that the United States Department of Agriculture had trouble designing a graphic that conveyed the information about nutrition in the most effective way. Ask pairs of students to design another graphic to inform people about different kinds of foods and persuade them to eat nutritious food.

C. Write all the foods you ate yesterday.

➤ Write on the board *Breakfast / Quantity* and tell students that they are going to list what they ate for breakfast yesterday. Write *toast—2 slices* and any other food that you ate. Ask volunteers for the foods they ate. Make sure students include the amounts.

➤ Have students look at the chart on page 108. Tell them to complete the chart with everything they ate yesterday and the amount.

Option: On a separate sheet of paper, students copy the chart. They interview a partner and complete the chart with the partner's information. Partners look at the two charts and discuss similarities and differences.

D. Discussion . . .

➤ Ask students to look at their charts and write a letter next to each entry to indicate what group it belongs to: G—grains, V—vegetables, and so on.

➤ Write the names of the groups of foods on the board. As you read each group, ask students to raise their hands if that is the group that most of their foods came from yesterday. Put tally marks next to the groups.

E. Read about the Food Guide Pyramid.

➤ After students read the information from the United States Department of Agriculture (USDA) Web site, check comprehension by asking questions such as *What is the Pyramid designed to help you do?* (eat better every day) *What group should you eat the least from?* (fats, oils, and sweets) *How many servings from the meat group should you have each day?* (two to three) *What is one serving of bread?* (one slice) *What is one serving of peanut butter?* (two tablespoons) *What is one serving of milk?* (one cup)

Option: Have students create five comprehension questions based on the reading. Then have students exchange papers with a partner and answer their partner's questions.

Option: Have students create a food pyramid based on the diet of their home country or culture. For example, instead of bread, students from northern Africa might list couscous in the grains group at the bottom of the pyramid.

Option: Have students log on to the following Web site and look up a pyramid for their culture or a culture similar to theirs:
www.semda.org.info/pyramid.
If students have created their own cultural food pyramid, they can compare them to the ones on the Web site.

Option: Students can get more information about each food group by visiting the following Web site and clicking on the group:
www.nal.usda.gov:8001/py/pmap/htm.

➤ Do it yourself!

(For general suggestions, see *Introduction*, page Txiii.)

Procedure:

A–B.

➤ Remind students to use the Food Guide Pyramid in planning their food choices. Have them refer to the USDA information on serving sizes.

➤ Tell students that their plans should be realistic and include foods and portions they will probably really eat tomorrow. For example, they shouldn't write down 3 ounces of fish if they know they won't have time to buy any.

➤ In pairs or small groups, students talk about their completed meal plans. Put these questions on the board to guide discussion: *Have I included enough food from each group? Have I included too few servings from any group or groups? Where do I need to improve my choices? Have I included too many fattening, fatty, or salty foods?*

C. Culture talk . . .

➤ If students created food pyramids based on the diet of their home country or culture, ask them to get them out.

➤ Put students in small groups by country or culture, if possible. Have students list typical foods eaten in their countries and the usual amounts of those foods. Ask students to indicate which of those foods are healthful.

➤ Restructure the groups so that the new groups consist of members from different countries or cultures. Have them compare diets.

➤ Lead a class discussion, asking questions such as *What do your diets have in common? What are some significant differences? How do the diets in your home countries compare to the diet of this country?*

Option: Put students in small groups to discuss how their eating habits have changed since their arrival in this country.

E. Read about the Food Guide Pyramid.

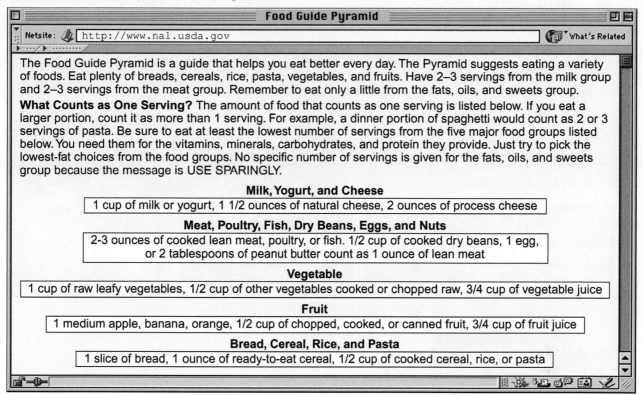

Food Guide Pyramid

Netsite: http://www.nal.usda.gov   What's Related

The Food Guide Pyramid is a guide that helps you eat better every day. The Pyramid suggests eating a variety of foods. Eat plenty of breads, cereals, rice, pasta, vegetables, and fruits. Have 2–3 servings from the milk group and 2–3 servings from the meat group. Remember to eat only a little from the fats, oils, and sweets group.

What Counts as One Serving? The amount of food that counts as one serving is listed below. If you eat a larger portion, count it as more than 1 serving. For example, a dinner portion of spaghetti would count as 2 or 3 servings of pasta. Be sure to eat at least the lowest number of servings from the five major food groups listed below. You need them for the vitamins, minerals, carbohydrates, and protein they provide. Just try to pick the lowest-fat choices from the food groups. No specific number of servings is given for the fats, oils, and sweets group because the message is USE SPARINGLY.

Milk, Yogurt, and Cheese
1 cup of milk or yogurt, 1 1/2 ounces of natural cheese, 2 ounces of process cheese

Meat, Poultry, Fish, Dry Beans, Eggs, and Nuts
2-3 ounces of cooked lean meat, poultry, or fish. 1/2 cup of cooked dry beans, 1 egg, or 2 tablespoons of peanut butter count as 1 ounce of lean meat

Vegetable
1 cup of raw leafy vegetables, 1/2 cup of other vegetables cooked or chopped raw, 3/4 cup of vegetable juice

Fruit
1 medium apple, banana, orange, 1/2 cup of chopped, cooked, or canned fruit, 3/4 cup of fruit juice

Bread, Cereal, Rice, and Pasta
1 slice of bread, 1 ounce of ready-to-eat cereal, 1/2 cup of cooked cereal, rice, or pasta

➤ Do it yourself!

A. Write a meal plan for yourself for tomorrow. Use the Pyramid.

Breakfast / Quantity	Lunch / Quantity	Dinner / Quantity	Snacks / Quantity

B. Discussion. Does your meal plan follow the guidelines of the Pyramid?

C. Culture talk. In the country you come from, what do people consider a healthful diet? Compare cultures with your classmates.

> **Review**

A. Pair work or group work.

- Who are the people?
- What are the problems?

Ask and answer questions.

Create conversations.

Tell a story.

Say as much as you can.

Review

(For general suggestions, see *Introduction*, page Txii.)

Procedure:

A. Pair work or group work.

Ask and answer questions.

➤ Ask questions about the picture, such as *Where are the man and woman in the first scene?* (a restaurant) *What is the man looking at in the second scene?* (an ad for Fat-B-Gone) *What is he doing in the last scene?* (cooking a healthy meal)

➤ Partners take turns pointing to different things in the picture and asking and answering questions.

Option: Let pairs of students study the picture for one minute. Then have Student A close his or her book while Student B asks questions about the three scenes.

Option: Let partners study the picture for one minute. Then have both students close their books and list as many objects in the scenes as they can remember. Have partners compare lists.

Create conversations.

➤ Focus students' attention on the first scene. Tell them to imagine that the man is sorry that he's eaten so much dessert. Have pairs complete this sentence for the man: *I shouldn't have . . .* Tell them to continue the conversation between the couple.

Challenge: Talkathon. Ask pairs of students to come to the front of the room and role-play a conversation between the couple. Time each pair. The pair that can sustain a logical conversation for the longest period of time wins.

Tell a story.

➤ Tell students that although the same man is shown in all three scenes, many details are needed to connect the scenes so the picture as a whole tells a coherent story. Ask students to describe the events in each picture and to add as much information as they can to make the scenes connect more smoothly. Before students begin, you may want to brainstorm possible questions to answer, such as *How much time has gone by between each scene? What was the man's experience with Fat-B-Gone? Why did he decide to use the Food Guide Pyramid for help in meal planning? Does he have any regrets now?*

Option: Ask *Who do you think the woman is?* Have students tell her story. They should include information about how long she has known the man, how she feels about her weight, whether she has any health problems, any regrets she has about her recent behavior.

Option: Divide the class in half. Have half the students imagine they are the man in the picture and that he has lost a lot of weight. Now he makes inspirational speeches to groups and describes his experience successfully losing weight. Tell students to create a talk for the man to give to the class. Have the other half of the class think up questions to ask the speaker, such as *What do you think of Fat-B-Gone? Do you have any healthful recipes to share? Do you ever eat dessert now?*

🎧 B–C.

➤ Tell students that they are going to listen to a radio call-in show on nutrition.

➤ Brainstorm questions that callers might have for a nutritionist. Write examples on the board.

➤ After students have listened the first time, ask *What did the caller want to know?* (how to use the Food Guide Pyramid)

➤ Have students read the advice in column A of Exercise C. Then have students listen to the call-in show again and match the advice in column A with its purpose in column B.

➤ Note that reasons in column B are written as infinitives of purpose. Remind students that they saw this structure in Unit 3.

➤ When students have completed the matching activity, check answers by asking *why* questions such as *Why should you eat a variety of foods?* Students should answer with an infinitive of purpose: *to get necessary nutrients.*

Option: In pairs, have students ask and answer *why* questions about the advice in the listening.

D–E.

➤ Students work individually to complete the review exercises. Tell students that Exercise E continues on page 112 and that they should complete the entire exercise.

➤ Circulate to offer help as needed.

➤ Have students check answers with a partner. Review answers as a class.

➤ Identify any areas of difficulty that may require additional instruction and practice.

Tapescript

Edwin: This is Edwin Crane. Welcome to "Ask the Nutritionist." Today's questions relate to the Food Guide Pyramid. Our first caller is Meredith. Meredith, you're on the air.

Meredith: Hello, Edwin. Thank you for taking my call. I don't understand how to use this Pyramid thing that everybody's talking about. Can you help me?

Edwin: Sure, Meredith. What specifically do you want to know about the Pyramid?

Meredith: Well, first, do I have to eat all these things at every meal? If I do that, I'll be fat as a house!

Edwin: No, of course not. The Pyramid tells you how much you need in a day, not in a meal.

Meredith: Oh, that makes sense. Another question: You know the milk, yogurt, and cheese group?

Edwin: Yes.

Meredith: Well, I absolutely hate yogurt!

Edwin: You don't have to eat yogurt just because it's in the Pyramid. That group also contains milk and cheese. You can have two to three servings of any of those.

Meredith: You mean I can have three servings of cheese? I love cheese.

Edwin: Of course. The Pyramid doesn't tell you *what* to eat, it just gives you guidelines to follow.

Meredith: The Pyramid is still too complicated for me. Can't you just give me some general advice?

Edwin: Sure. Here's some advice. It's not complete, but I hope it helps:

Eat a variety of foods to get all the nutrients you need.

Balance the foods you eat with exercise, to maintain or improve your weight.

Choose a diet with lots of grains, fruits, and vegetables to help you avoid eating too much fat.

Choose a diet low in fat and cholesterol to reduce your risk of heart disease.

Choose a diet moderate in sugars to help avoid tooth decay.

Choose a diet moderate in salt and sodium to help reduce your risk of high blood pressure.

If you drink alcoholic beverages, do so in moderation to avoid accidents, addiction, and health problems.

Meredith: That's easy as pie! Thanks, Edwin!

🎧 **B.** Listening comprehension. Listen to the radio call-in show.

🎧 **C.** Listen again and match the dietary advice in column A with its purpose in column B, according to the radio program.

A	B
__d__ 1. Eat a variety of foods.	a. to avoid accidents and health problems
__f__ 2. Eat a lot of grains, fruits, and vegetables.	b. to avoid heart disease
__c__ 3. Exercise.	c. to maintain your weight
__b__ 4. Don't eat a lot of fat and cholesterol.	d. to get necessary nutrients
__g__ 5. Don't eat a lot of sugar.	e. to avoid high blood pressure
__e__ 6. Don't eat a lot of salt.	f. to avoid eating a lot of fatty foods
__a__ 7. Don't drink a lot of alcohol.	g. to avoid tooth decay

D. Read each sentence or question. Underline your response.

1. "Don't eat all that salt."

   YOU <u>You're right. I have high blood pressure.</u>   **YOU** You're right. I need some exercise.

2. "Why don't you buy some Fat-B-Gone?"

   YOU <u>I'm not gullible!</u>   **YOU** It's too fattening. I'm on a diet.

3. "If it's natural, it's safe!"

   YOU <u>I think that's a myth.</u>   **YOU** But it's so hard to pass up!

4. "You look terrific. How did you get in such great shape?"

   YOU <u>I cut down on calories and started exercising.</u>   **YOU** I sent away for it.

E. Complete each sentence with a regret. Use *should have* or *shouldn't have* and a past participle.

1. He ___shouldn't have eaten___ four servings of ice cream. You're supposed to eat ice
   (not eat)
   cream sparingly!

2. They ___should have taken___ my word when I told them that Fat-B-Gone is a fraud.
   (take)

3. You ___shouldn't have believed___ that silly ad about the muscle-building machine. No
   (not believe)
   pain, no gain.

4. I __shouldn't have wasted__ my money on that cabbage-soup pill. Nothing burns fat.
   <small>not waste</small>

5. When I saw my doctor last week, I __should have asked__ her about those
   <small>ask</small>

   injections for my migraines.

F. **Write two regrets that you have about your life. Use *should have* and *shouldn't have*.**

1. (Answers will vary.) _____

2. _____

G. **Complete each conversation with a negative question.**

1. **A:** __Doesn't celery burn fat_____?
   <small>celery / burn fat</small>

   B: No. Take my word. It doesn't.

2. **A:** __Isn't the Pyramid terrific_____?
   <small>Pyramid / be terrific</small>

   B: Yes, it is. But it's a little complicated.

3. **A:** __Didn't you buy that muscle machine_____?
   <small>you / buy that muscle machine</small>

   B: Are you kidding? Of course I didn't.

H. **Composition. On a separate sheet of paper, write about the picture on page 110. Say as much as you can.**

Now I can
❑ express regret.
❑ suggest a remedy.
❑ avoid quackery.
❑ separate weight-loss facts from myths.
❑ make daily food choices based on the Food Guide Pyramid.

F–G.

➤ Students work individually to complete the review exercises.

➤ Circulate to offer help as needed.

➤ Have students check answers with a partner. Review answers as a class.

➤ Identify any areas of difficulty that may require additional instruction and practice.

Option: Students practice reading Exercise G in pairs.

H. Composition . . .

➤ Provide students with concrete approaches to writing about the picture on page 110. Use one of the options that follow, give students a choice of options, or assign options based on students' levels of proficiency. Model what is expected of students for each option.

➤ Advise students to look back through the unit for help and ideas as they write.

➤ Circulate to offer help as needed.

Option: Tell students to imagine what the man is thinking in scenes 2 and 3. Have them write his thoughts; for example, *Wow! That's a terrific offer! I could lose 50 pounds in a week!* Ask volunteers to read their thought balloons aloud.

Option: Have students write a conversation between the man and woman in the first scene. They can look at the model conversation on page 100 for an example of the format to follow.

Option: Have students write a letter of complaint to the maker of Fat-B-Gone or Muscle Man Cream in which they complain that the claims were not true. The letter should include when the product was purchased, how long it was used, and what the results were.

Challenge: Have students write a public service announcement to encourage people to follow the Food Guide Pyramid in making their daily food choices.

Now I can

➤ Read the first item in the box out loud: *Now I can express regret.* Elicit from the class an example of how to do express regret, such as *I shouldn't have eaten that pizza.*

➤ Put students in pairs, tell students to take turns reading each item in the box and giving an example of what they have learned. When students can provide an example, they should check that objective. If there are items students aren't able to check, have them look back through the unit for ideas.

➤ When students are finished reviewing with their partners, read each item out loud and elicit an example from the class.

Oral test (optional)

You may want to use the *Now I can* box as an informal evaluation. While students are working on the *Composition* activity, you can call them up individually and check their ability with two or three objectives.

Your money

Note: For the plan-ahead project on page 123, ask students to bring in car ads and ads for credit and for work-at-home opportunities. Suggest that students look in magazines and newspapers.

 Preview

(For general suggestions, see *Introduction*, page Tviii.)

Warm up. Is this a good opportunity? Would you call 1-800-BIG-SIGN? Why or why not?

Procedure:

➤ Put students in small groups to look at the picture and answer these questions: *Would you want to go into business with this man? Why or why not?* Elicit reasons why working with this man might not be a good idea and write them on the board; for example, *There are many indications that he is running an unprofitable business, such as peeling paint, hand-lettered signs, a bare light bulb. He is unprofessionally dressed in a T-shirt.*

➤ Tell students that the slogan *Get rich quick* is often a clue that a business may be using unethical schemes. Point out the unorthodox spelling: *Earn x-tra $$$* instead of *Earn extra money.*

➤ Now read the *Warm up* questions and elicit responses: *Is this a good opportunity?* (probably not) *Would you call 1-800-BIG-SIGN? Why or why not?* (maybe, you don't know until you call, it doesn't look like a good business opportunity to get involved with)

Option: Have students write a one-paragraph description of the office. Remind them to indent the first line and use appropriate punctuation and capitalization. They can comment on the list on the board of reasons why working with this man might not be a good idea.

Option: Students from some cultures may be shocked by the man's disrespectful posture, especially the placement of his feet. Explain that the man is supposed to look sleazy and unreliable and that he is probably a scam operator, running a business that may not be quite legal. You may want to use this picture as a point of departure for a brief discussion on behavior that different cultures find rude or offensive. Remind students to express their opinions respectfully.

Unit 9 objectives

Procedure:

➤ Tell students that sometimes objectives relate to knowledge gained and sometimes to skills acquired. Ask students to read the objectives and write an *S* next to the skills and a *K* next to the knowledge-based objectives.

➤ Have each student identify the objective that he or she thinks will be hardest to meet. Write 1 through 8 on the board to indicate the objectives. Read the objectives aloud and have students raise their hands for the one that seems most difficult. Tally the results next to each objective.

➤ Some of these objectives may be treated differently in other cultures. Allow students to discuss how their home cultures view the borrowing and lending of money.

➤ Refer students to objective 6. Tell them that the picture shows a work-at-home scheme. Note that the word *scheme* often has a negative connotation, implying something manipulative or dishonest.

Your money

 Preview

Warm up. Is this a good opportunity? Would you call 1-800-BIG-SIGN? Why or why not?

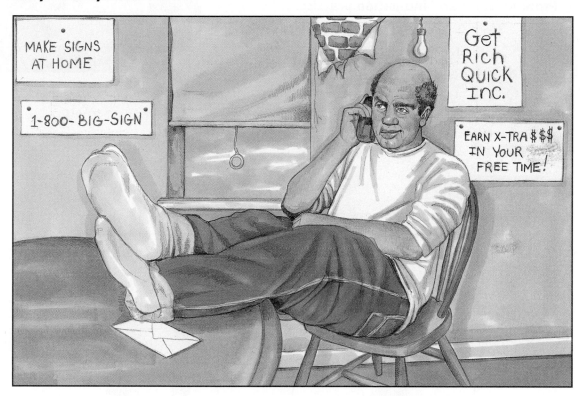

Unit 9 objectives

- Borrow money from a friend or co-worker.
- Agree to repay the loan.
- Remind a person to pay back a loan.
- Share wishes and dreams.
- Offer advice on financial aid.
- Understand work-at-home schemes.
- Understand credit unions.
- Understand the problems with payday loans.

Model 1   Borrow money from a friend. Give a reason. Commit to repay.

A. Listen and read.

A: I left my wallet home. Do you think I could borrow $10?

B: Let me check what I have. Here you go.

A: Thanks so much. I'll pay you back tomorrow.

B: No problem.

B. Pronunciation and intonation practice.

Ways to agree and decline

Agree: Here you go.

Decline: Actually, I'm short of cash myself. I'm sorry.

Vocabulary

Reasons to borrow money from a friend

I left my wallet at home.

I'm out of cash.

They won't accept my check.

I have to go to the cash machine.

They only take Master Charge or Quick Buy.

C. Pair work. Ask a friend for money.

A: _____. Do you think I could borrow $_____?

B: Let me check what I have. _____.

A: _____.

B: _____.

Practical conversations

(For general suggestions, see *Introduction*, page Tviii.)

Model 1

Content: borrowing money from a friend, giving a reason, committing to repay, ways to agree or decline

Procedure:

🎧A–B.

➤ Before students listen and read, ask *What would you do if you got to work and discovered you had left your money at home?* Elicit attitudes about borrowing and lending money at work. Discuss possible solutions to the problem.

➤ To set the scene for the conversation, ask questions about the photo, such as *Where are these people?* (in an office, at work) *What do you think their relationship is?* (co-workers) *What is happening?* (The man is giving the woman money.) *Why do you think he is giving her money?* (maybe he is returning a loan, maybe she is borrowing money)

➤ After students listen to the conversation, check comprehension by asking questions such as *What does the woman want?* (to borrow $10) *Why?* (She left her wallet at home.) *Does the man lend her the money?* (yes)

➤ Before students repeat the lines, tell them that although native speakers often say groups of words quickly, pauses at the end of sentences are also important. Ask them to focus on the number of sentences in each line of the conversation (2, 2, 2, 1). Then have students repeat, making sure to pause appropriately at the periods.

Option: Put students in pairs or small groups to discuss attitudes toward borrowing money. Ask them to list different people they would feel comfortable borrowing money from, such as a relative or a good friend. Then have students discuss how much money they would be willing to borrow from these people. Lead a class discussion to compare students' attitudes.

🎧Ways to agree and decline

➤ Have students listen to and repeat the statements.

➤ Brainstorm other polite ways to agree and decline and write them on the board. Suggestions may include *Sure, You're in luck* and *Sorry, I don't have that much.*

➤ Tell students *A co-worker just asked me for $10, but I only have $8.* Point out that sometimes a middle option is appropriate: *I'm sorry, I don't have $10, but would $5 help?*

🎧Vocabulary

➤ Have students listen to and repeat the reasons to borrow money from a friend.

➤ Brainstorm other reasons to borrow money. Prompt with *Why might you need money and not have it?* Elicit examples such as *I have to buy a book, I forgot my lunch, I lost my wallet.* Write students' ideas on the board.

C. Pair work . . .

➤ Note that Student B can either agree or decline to lend the money. If Student B declines, Student A does not say *Thanks so much. I'll pay you back tomorrow.* Brainstorm other responses Student A might make, such as *That's okay, Thanks anyway.* Discuss possibilities for Student B's last line, such as *I'm really sorry* or *Maybe Student C has cash today.*

➤ Model the conversation with a more advanced student. Play the role of Student A, demonstrating how to give a reason to borrow money, request a dollar amount, and respond appropriately to Student B's agreement or refusal.

➤ Have pairs practice the conversation, using reasons from the *Vocabulary* and the ways to agree or decline.

Option: Ask students what expressions they have heard for not having money. On the board write ideas such as *I'm broke, I'm tapped out, I'm strapped for cash, I'm low on funds.* In pairs, students can use these expressions in the conversation. They can also use them to practice declining invitations, as in this conversation:

A: Can you go to the movies tonight?

B: Sorry, I'm broke.

Model 2

Content: sharing your wishes and dreams, offering advice on financial aid, wishes and dreams, ways to fund dreams that are hard to afford, *but* to connect ideas

Procedure:

🎧 A–B.

➤ After students listen to the conversation, check comprehension by asking questions such as *What does the woman on the left want to do?* (go to college) *What is the problem?* (It's so expensive.) *What does the woman on the right suggest?* (Her friend should apply for a scholarship.)

➤ Preview the grammar topic by saying *The woman on the left would love to go to college.* Then ask *What information contradicts her wish to go to college?* (It's so expensive.) *What key word tells you that the second part of the sentence contradicts the first?* (but)

➤ Remind students that *Why don't you* begins a negative question, but it is used to make a suggestion. Elicit examples of other ways to make a suggestion, such as *You could . . .* or *You might. . . .* An imperative can also be used to make a suggestion: *Just do it!*

➤ Tell students that the letter *o* can be pronounced in several different ways. In this conversation, the following words contain different vowel sounds: *love, college, don't,* and *do.* Have students repeat these words after you.

➤ Tell students to concentrate on saying the correct vowel sounds as they repeat the conversation.

🎧 Wishes and dreams

➤ Ask *What are wishes and dreams?* Elicit that both words express something that is wanted or hoped for.

➤ After students repeat the phrases in the book, elicit examples of their own wishes and dreams and write them on the board.

🎧 Vocabulary

➤ Make sure students understand the meaning of *scholarship, college loan, tuition assistance, credit union, finance,* and any other difficult terms.

Option: Have students work in small groups and tell a true story about using one of the ways to fund dreams.

C. Pair work . . .

➤ Model the conversation with a more advanced student. Play the role of Student B to demonstrate choosing a way to fund dreams from the *Vocabulary.*

➤ In pairs, students practice the conversation.

➤ Circulate to offer help as needed.

➤ Do it yourself!

(For general suggestions, see *Introduction*, page Txiii.)

Procedure:

A. Complete the chart . . .

➤ On the board, copy the chart from the book. Ask students if getting married is really free. Elicit or point out that although weddings can cost a lot of money, a simple civil ceremony can be had for the price of a marriage license, so it is practically free.

➤ Ask students to think about their wishes and dreams that require money and those that don't. Since it may be easier to think of wishes and dreams that cost money, brainstorm examples that are free, such as *I'd like to get in shape, spend more time with my family, get in touch with my old friends.*

➤ Working individually, students complete the chart in their books. Students can refer to the examples of wishes and dreams on the board or think of their own.

B. Discussion . . .

➤ On one side of the board, write *The best things in life are free.* Ask students to explain this saying (really important things don't cost money) and offer examples, such as health, a positive outlook, good family relationships.

➤ On the other side of the board, write *You get what you pay for.* Ask students to explain this saying (things that have value also cost something) and offer examples, such as buying an appliance on sale that you can't get parts for. Elicit or point out that the two sayings are almost opposite in meaning.

➤ Put students in small groups to brainstorm other sayings on the same topic from their home cultures or from this one. Elicit examples and write them under one of sayings on the board; for example, *There's no such thing as a free lunch* and *Money is the root of all evil.*

➤ In small groups, students discuss which idea they agree with most and why.

A. Listen and read.

A: I'd love to go to college, but it's so expensive!

B: Why don't you apply for a scholarship?

A: Do you think that would be possible?

B: You'll never know if you don't give it a try.

B. Pronunciation and intonation practice.

Wishes and dreams

go to college
get some more training
go to graduate or technical school

renovate my house
build a new garage
buy a new car

Vocabulary

Ways to fund dreams that are hard to afford

apply for a scholarship	get a bank loan
apply for a college loan	finance the car
get tuition assistance at work	borrow money from your relatives
borrow from the credit union at work	

C. Pair work. **Share your wishes and dreams. Offer advice.**

A: I'd love to _____, but it's so expensive!

B: Why don't you _____?

A: Do you think that would be possible?

B: You'll never know if you don't give it a try.

➤ Do it yourself!

A. Complete the chart with wishes and dreams.

Wishes and dreams that cost money	Wishes and dreams that are free
I'd like central air conditioning.	I'd like to get married.

B. Discussion. **There's a saying that "the best things in life are free." Is that true?**

Practical grammar

Common misspellings

Review the following spelling reminders. Don't make errors with these words.

they're, their, there

> they're: **They're** writing a resume right now. (*they + are*)
>
> their: It's **their** car. (possessive)
>
> there: Look. It's right over **there**. (a place)

it's, its

> it's: **It's** 5:15. Time to go home! (*it + is*)
>
> its: The thing I like about this office is **its** location. (possessive)

then, than

> then: First I called, and **then** I sent an e-mail. (a time)
>
> than: This resume is newer **than** that one. (a comparison)

your, you're

> your: This is **your** new office. (possessive)
>
> you're: I hope **you're** happy here. (*you + are*)

two, too, to

> two: I applied for **two** loans to help with tuition. (a number)
>
> too: I wrote and I called **too**. (adds information)
>
> to: It's too early **to** know if she got the job. (part of infinitive construction)

See page 144 for a more complete list of commonly misspelled words.

A. Choose the correct word to complete each sentence.

1. It's _____their_____ loan, not my loan.

they're / their / there

2. _____It's_____ OK. I can borrow from the credit union at work.

It's / Its

3. A low-interest loan is better _____than_____ a high-interest one.

then / than

4. _____You're_____ late. The deadline for loan applications was yesterday.

Your / You're

5. Those _____two_____ offers are _____too_____ good _____to_____ refuse!

to / two / too   to / two / too   to / two / too

Practical grammar

(For general suggestions, see *Introduction*, page Tix.)

Common misspellings

Procedure:

➤ Write on the board the three example sentences using *two, too,* and *to.* Read the sentences aloud and circle the words *two, too,* and *to.* Ask *What's the meaning of each of these words?* Elicit that *two* is a number, *too* refers to added information, and *to* plus a base form is an infinitive.

➤ Tell students that *two, too,* and *to* are examples of homonyms, or words with the same sound but different meanings and usually different spellings. Because even native speakers can make mistakes with these words, students are going to study the spelling of some of the more common homonyms.

➤ Write on the board the three example sentences with *they're, it's,* and *you're,* but do not use the contracted forms: *They are writing a resume right now, It is 5:15, I hope you are happy here.* Tell students that if they can rewrite a sentence with a pronoun and a form of *be* then the term is a contraction and is spelled with an apostrophe. Model this pattern with by reading the sentences on the board with contractions (*They're, It's,* and *You're*).

➤ Write on the board *The book's cover is red* and *The books have red covers.* Elicit or point out the difference between *'s* (to show possession) and *s* (to make a noun plural). Remind students not to use an apostrophe to make a noun plural.

➤ Have volunteers read aloud each of the example sentences in the box. Make sure students understand the differences in meaning among the homonyms.

Option: Bring to class and hand out paragraphs from newspapers or magazines. Have students work in pairs to find examples of the homonyms they've studied here. Read the material beforehand to insure that the paragraphs contain enough examples.

A. Choose the correct word...

➤ Write the first example on the board, including the word choices below the line. Elicit the correct choice and write it in the blank. If necessary, focus students' attention on *they're* and ask them to try reading the sentence with the uncontracted form, *they are.*

➤ Working individually, students complete the sentences. Tell them to refer to the examples in the box if necessary.

➤ Review answers as a class.

Option: Spell check game. Divide the class into teams with three or four members each. Have each team create 12 different flashcards on which students write one of the homonyms. Read a sentence from the box or Exercise A that contains one of the homonyms: *They're writing a resume right now.* Student 1 from Team 1 holds up the correct flashcard when he or she hears the homonym: *they're.* Holding up the correct card earns 1 point. Student 1 from Team 2 responds to the next sentence, and so on, until everyone has had a turn. In a variation of this game, teams compete at the same time.

Challenge: Dictation. Each student dictates a sentence for the rest of the class to write. Have students use sentences from the box or Exercise A.

Challenge: Have students brainstorm other homonyms that cause confusion. Write them on the board and elicit or explain meanings. Students can add these words to the list in their books and include them in the *Option* and *Challenge* activities above.

Connecting ideas with *but* and *so*

Procedure:

➤ Write on the board the following pairs of sentences: *I asked for money. They lent it to me* and *I asked for money. They didn't lend it to me.* Also write the three connecting words *and, but,* and *so.* Read the first pair aloud. Then ask students what word they would use to connect the sentences. Elicit *and* to join two sentences when the second sentence gives additional information. Rewrite the sentences as two connected clauses and include a comma: *I asked for money, and they lent it to me.*

➤ Repeat the procedure with the second pair of sentences. Elicit the connecting word *but* to connect two sentences when the second sentence gives contradictory information. Rewrite with a comma.

➤ Write this sentence from Model 2, page 115: *I'd love to go to college, but it's so expensive.* Point out the comma and the connecting word *but.* Ask *Why do we connect these two sentences with "but"?* Elicit the fact that the second sentence gives contradictory information. Remind students of the earlier discussion.

➤ Write on the board a third pair of example sentences: *They didn't give me the loan. I borrowed the money from my family.* Repeat the procedure. Elicit the connecting word *so* to connect two sentences when the second sentence gives a result. Rewrite with a comma.

➤ Ask *What is a sentence?* Elicit that a sentence has a subject and a verb and expresses a complete thought. Ask *What is a clause?* Remind students that a clause is like a sentence in that it has a subject and a verb, but that it is part of a larger sentence. You may want to review the discussion of clauses and sentences in Unit 5. Have the students read the information in the box.

➤ Point out the comma before *and, but,* and *so.* Note that even educated writers sometimes omit the comma. The use of the comma also varies depending on the style of writing; for example, it is often dropped in newspaper articles. Tell students that they will practice connecting sentences with *and, but,* and *so* and a comma.

B. Complete each sentence ...

➤ Write the first sentence on the board with the blank rule. Read it aloud and ask *Does the second clause introduce a result, or does it provide contradictory information?* Elicit that it is a result. Ask *Should we complete the sentence with "but" or "so"?* Elicit the answer *so* and write it on the line.

T117

➤ Tell students to read each remaining sentence and decide if the second clause introduces a result or provides contradictory information. Then they can decide whether to use *but* or *so.*

➤ Working individually, students write the appropriate conjunction on the line.

➤ In pairs, students compare answers.

C. Complete each clause ...

➤ Write the first item on the board and read it aloud. Elicit possible completions such as *I'm going to take out a loan, I decided to buy a bicycle.*

➤ If necessary, remind students what a clause is (it is like a sentence in that it has a subject and a verb, but that it is part of a larger sentence). Make sure students know when to use *but* and *so* (to introduce a contradiction; to introduce a result).

➤ Students complete the sentences by writing original clauses that tell a result or provide contradictory information.

➤ In pairs, students read their sentences.

➤ Do it yourself!

(For general suggestions, see *Introduction,* page Txiii.)

Procedure:

A–B.

➤ Write on the board the two following sentences: *I'd like central air conditioning, I'd like to get married,* and the conjunctions *but* and *so.* Ask volunteers to add a clause beginning with *but* or *so* to one of the sentences. Students may offer *I'd like central air conditioning, but I can't afford it* or *I'd like to get married, so I'm dating a lot of new people.*

➤ Tell students to look at the chart on page 115 that they completed with their own wishes and dreams. Have them write each wish or dream on a separate line. Then have them add to each one a clause beginning with *so* that expresses a result or a clause beginning with *but* that expresses contradictory information.

➤ In pairs, students read their sentences.

Challenge: An extended conversation. After Student A reads a sentence, Student B responds appropriately, as if in a conversation. For example, if Student A says *I want to renovate my house, but it's very expensive,* Student B might respond *Why don't you take out a loan?* Have students continue the conversation with as many exchanges as possible.

You can connect two complete sentences with *and*. The second sentence presents additional information. Use a comma between the clauses.

I asked for money. They lent it to me → I asked for money, **and they lent it to me**.

Two other connecting words are *but* and *so*. Use *but* to introduce a clause with contradictory information. Use *so* to introduce a result clause.

contradictory information

I asked for money, **but they didn't lend it to me.**

a result

They didn't give me the loan, **so I borrowed the money from my family.**

B. **Complete each sentence with *but* or *so*.**

1. I wanted to finish my degree, ____so____ I applied for tuition assistance at work.

2. I work at Starlight Electric, ____but____ unfortunately they don't have a tuition assistance program.

3. Her lifelong dream was to have a pool, ____but____ she could never afford it.

4. She couldn't get a house with a pool, ____so____ she joined a health club.

5. He asked for $4,000 to build a garage, ____but____ it wasn't enough.

C. **Complete each clause with contradictory information or a result.**

1. I don't have enough money to get a new car, so _____(Answers will vary.)_____.

2. I don't have enough money to get a new car, but _____.

3. The company they work for has terrible benefits, so _____.

4. The company they work for has terrible benefits, but _____.

➤ Do it yourself!

A. **Revisit the wishes and dreams you wrote on page 115. Write a statement about each one with *but* or *so*.**

I want to renovate my house, but it's very expensive.

I want to renovate my house, so I'm not taking a vacation this year.

_____

_____

B. **Pair work. Compare statements with a partner.**

Work-at-home schemes

A. Read the picture story again. Answer the questions.

1. What kind of job are the people talking about? _____They are talking about sign-making._____

2. What does the woman have to do before she begins making signs? _____

   The woman has to pay a start-up fee of $2500 and sign a contract before she begins.

B. Vocabulary. Choose the word or phrase closer in meaning to the underlined word or phrase.

1. Earn extra cash <u>in your free time</u>!

   ⓐ when you don't have to pay   ⓑ when you're not working

2. Well, this is <u>right up your alley</u>.

   ⓐ on your street   ⓑ just right for you

➤ Authentic practice

(For general suggestions, see *Introduction*, page Tx.)

Work-at-home schemes

Procedure:

➤ Before students open their books, ask if they have ever heard of jobs where employees can work at home. Elicit examples of jobs such as telemarketing and stuffing envelopes. Point out that sometimes a reputable company allows employees to work from home on the computer. This arrangement differs from a typical work-at-home scheme because it is a flexible benefit rather than a condition of employment.

➤ Have students open their books and read the bar. Point out that *schemes* here has a negative meaning.

➤ Have students read along silently as they listen to the conversation. Then check comprehension by asking questions such as *What's the name of the man's company?* (Get Rich Quick Inc.) *Does the company seem profitable and well run?* (no) *Why not?* (It's in a room and not an office, the wall is peeling, there are paint cans on the floor, the man is dressed sloppily) *Does the woman take the job immediately?* (no) *Why not?* (She wants to think about paying $2500 to get started.)

➤ Discuss the meanings of any unfamiliar terms such as *make your own hours, beats, right up my alley, got it, zap, start-up fee, put you down, on second thought, never mind, suit yourself.*

A. Read the picture story again . . .

➤ Have students write complete sentences in response to the questions. Ask volunteers to read their answers aloud.

Option: Have two or more students write their answers on the board. Check content as a class. Review capitalization and punctuation as well.

B. Vocabulary . . .

➤ Model the exercise. Read the first item aloud. Ask *What phrase do I have to define?* (in your free time). Have students read the two responses. Ask *Which response means in your free time?* (when you're not working) Remind students to indicate their answers by filling in the ovals.

➤ Working individually, students complete the remaining seven items, including those on page 119.

➤ Have students compare answers with a partner.

Option: Have students work in pairs to create original conversations that begin with the first line in each item. Students add an appropriate rejoinder, as in the following example:

A: Earn extra cash in your free time!

B: Well, what do I have to do?

As a variation, students can create extended conversations that include the first line.

If your students are ready . . .

Language note: The phrase *work-at-home* is hyphenated because it is a phrasal modifier, meaning that the whole phrase together conveys one idea that modifies the noun *scheme*. It requires hyphens between each word in the phrase. A phrasal modifier is different from a string of adjectives, each of which modifies a noun: *an interesting, productive computer job*. In this example, the job is interesting and productive and in the field of computers. The three modifiers give three different pieces of information. On the other hand, the modifier *work-at-home* conveys only one idea about the job—the employee works at home. You can ask students to find these other phrasal modifiers in the story: *sign-making (job, machine), start-up (fee).*

C. Critical thinking...

➤ Have students read the questions and then look at the picture story again.

➤ Working individually, students answer the questions.

➤ In small groups, students discuss the pros and cons of the job offer. Have them create a table to list advantages and disadvantages. See the example below for possible entries.

Advantages	Disadvantages
Work at home Set your own hours Could make $12.50 to $15/hour	Start-up cost of $2500 May not make a good wage because you don't work fast enough Equipment might be messy and need a lot of space No benefits Pushy manager

➤ When students have finished their charts, write their ideas in a similar chart on the board. Ask *Do you think the woman should take the job?*

Challenge: In this two-part activity, students first write a letter to *Ask Joan* asking for advice on this job opportunity. Remind students to include the information from the picture story. When finished, students exchange letters with a partner. In response, partners write a letter of advice from Joan. Partners should refer to some of the disadvantages listed in their charts.

➤ Do it yourself!

(For general suggestions, see *Introduction*, page Txiii.)

Procedure:

A. Write your own response...

➤ Have students look at the pictures of the man on the phone. Point out that since the same person appears in all three pictures, this is meant to be one consecutive conversation.

➤ Read the first speech balloon. Ask *Who do you think this person is?* (a scam operator, a sleazy business person) *What do you think of the start-up fee?* (It's not "low," The amount makes me suspicious.)

➤ Working individually, students write responses to each of the speech balloons. Have them compare responses with a partner.

➤ In pairs, students read their conversations out loud.

B. Discussion...

➤ Read the first question in the directions. Remind students that *scheme* has a negative connotation and suggests a business that is not altogether legal.

➤ Elicit examples of work-at-home schemes such as telemarketing and stuffing envelopes. Point out that usually such jobs are based on piecework, that is, workers get paid for how many pieces of work are finished, not how long they work. Ask students if they think this is a good way to pay people.

➤ Ask students if they have ever had such a job or if they know someone who has. Put students in small groups to discuss the terms of any work-at-home schemes they know about and whether or not they decided to get involved. Have students give reasons for their decision.

Option: Have students look for work-at-home notices in local magazines and newspapers as well as in flyers and brochures. Ask them to bring in the notices or copy the information. They can also report on phone solicitations they have received for work-at-home possibilities. Have students note the type of work, what costs must be paid up front, and other terms of the offers.

3. <u>Beats</u> an office job!

   ⓐ It's better than   ⓑ It costs less than

4. I'm calling to <u>find out</u> more.

   ⓐ learn   ⓑ look for

5. <u>Got it</u>.

   ⓐ I heard you.   ⓑ I know you.

6. Can I <u>put you down</u> for that?

   ⓐ insult you   ⓑ write your name on the list

7. On second thought, <u>never mind</u> the contract.

   ⓐ I want   ⓑ I don't want

8. <u>Suit yourself</u>.

   ⓐ You need to be well dressed.   ⓑ It's your choice.

C. Critical thinking. Answer the questions. Then explain your opinions.

1. What's good about the offer? _____ (Answers will vary.) _____

2. What's bad about the offer? _____

3. Should the woman take the offer? Why? Why not? _____

   _____

➤ Do it yourself!

A. Write your own response. Then read the conversation out loud with a partner.

There's a low start-up fee of $5000. Can I put you down for that?

YOU _____

Do you have fax or e-mail?

YOU _____

You'd better act fast. After today, the fee is going up.

YOU _____

B. Discussion. Have you ever heard of a work-at-home scheme? What were the terms? Did you get involved? Why or why not?

Authentic practice

Loans

🎧 **A. Listening comprehension. Listen to the conversations about money.**

> January 15
> I promise to repay George Klagsbrun
> $450 by February 28.
> Melvin Clark

GET CASH UNTIL PAYDAY!
$100 or MORE ... FAST.

Metro Credit Union ——————————————— **MCU**
Consumer Loan Rates

New Car Loans	Used Car Loans
36 Months	60 Months
5.5%	5.75%*

Effective as of 7/1/04. Rates are based on term of loan. Additional discount may be available for automatic payment plan.

*Used Car Loan rates depend on the model year of the vehicle.

🎧 **B. Read the statements. Then listen to the conversations again and check *True*, *False*, or *?* (No information) for each statement.**

	True	False	?
Conversation 1			
1. They're talking about a bank loan.	☐	☑	☐
2. An IOU is a personal note in which someone promises to repay a loan.	☑	☐	☐
3. The man wants to buy a boat.	☐	☐	☑
Conversation 2			
1. They're talking about rates.	☑	☐	☐
2. A credit union is a car dealer.	☐	☑	☐
3. They want to buy a used car.	☐	☐	☑
Conversation 3			
1. They're talking about a paycheck.	☐	☑	☐
2. The woman wants to repaint her house.	☐	☐	☑
3. The woman needs cash.	☑	☐	☐

💻 **FYI. For a good glossary of credit and borrowing terms, log on to this Web site:**

http://www.cardreport.com/glossary.html

Authentic practice

(For general suggestions, see *Introduction*, page Tx.)

Loans

Procedure:

A–B.

➤ Point to the handwritten note and ask *What is this?* Elicit that it is an IOU, which stands for I owe you. It is a note that says the writer promises to repay money. *Who would you write an IOU to?* (a friend, a co-worker, a relative) Make sure students understand that writing an IOU is a way we commit to repaying a personal loan. It is more formal than a verbal promise.

➤ Ask questions about the other two documents, such as *What information is given on the Metro Credit Union document?* (consumer loan rates, car loan rates) *What does the other document promise?* (cash until payday)

➤ Make sure students know that a credit union is an organization that people can join, often at a workplace. One of the benefits a credit union offers to its members is loans at low interest rates. Tell students they will learn more about credit unions on the next page.

➤ Tell students that they are going to listen to three short conversations about money.

➤ After students have listened the first time, have them read the statements in Exercise B. As they listen the second time, have them check the appropriate boxes for each conversation. If necessary, have students read the statements for only one conversation at a time, and then have them listen to just that conversation.

Option: Have pairs of students rewrite the false statements to make them true.

Challenge: Have students take notes during the listening. As a way of supporting their answers, they should write down as much of the conversation as they can that relates to each statement. For example, next to item 1 under Conversation 1, students might write *I really appreciate your lending me this cash on such short notice, George.* After students have listened to the three conversations, elicit examples of the notes, and ask how the information pertains to the statement. Students might say, for example, that George lent the money, not a bank, and that using the first name implies a personal relationship.

FYI . . .

Option: If students have access to the Internet, assign each pair of students two to three terms from the glossary. Have them make notes on the glossary definitions, put them into their own words, and share the information with the class.

Tapescript

Conversation 1

Man 1: I really appreciate your lending me this cash on such short notice, George. It came right in the nick of time. I can pay you back by the end of February. Is that all right?

Man 2: Sure, no problem. But I'd feel more comfortable if you'd sign an IOU. Amelia would never forgive me if I didn't ask you for one.

Man 1: Absolutely. I understand. *My* wife would feel the same way. How should we do this?

Man 2: I could draft a note. Look it over and see if you agree to the terms. OK?

Man 1: Good plan.

Conversation 2

Woman: What kind of loan rates can we get at the Credit Union?

Man: The Credit Union—good idea! I'll check. Credit unions are usually fairer than dealers. What's the Web address?

Woman: Metro.cu.org/rates.

Man: OK. Here it is. Not bad. Have a look.

Woman: That *is* pretty good. Much better than the rates in this car ad.

Conversation 3

Man: You need some fast cash?

Woman: You bet. And my credit's not great. What should I do?

Man: You can always get a payday loan. There's this place that advertises, on the corner of First and Elm. Easy, fast. Why don't you pass by and see about a loan?

Woman: Are you sure? There must be some catch. Something that looks too good to be true usually is.

C. Read the information...

➤ Scanning for specific information is an important academic skill. Before students read about credit unions and payday loans, write several questions on the board. You can use the ones listed below or create your own. Remind students that when they scan, they are looking for key words that will help them locate specific pieces of information. Often phrases in the question itself are repeated in the sentence where the information can be found.

1. What is a credit union?
2. How many people are served by credit unions?
3. How can you join a credit union?
4. What is a payday loan?
5. Is this kind of credit cheap?
6. What are some other names for payday loans?

➤ Organizing information from readings in charts and tables is another important academic skill. After students read about the two topics, have them summarize the information with bulleted items. To review as a class, put a similar table on the board and elicit students' ideas. See the following table for an example.

CREDIT UNIONS	PAYDAY LOANS
Nonprofit financial institutions Owned and run by members Safe, reasonable Serve a specific community	Small, short-term, high-rate loans Very expensive rates Also called cash advance loans, check post-dated check loans, deferred deposit check loans

➤ To encourage critical thinking, ask *If you needed a loan, where would you rather go, to a credit union or a place that offered payday loans? Why?*

Option: In pairs, students underline all the adjectives used to describe the two different services. Elicit examples and write them on the board. Your lists should resemble the following: Credit union: nonprofit, cooperative, financial, safe, reasonable. Payday loans: small, short-term, high-rate, expensive.

D. True story...

➤ Tell students that there are many types of loans—some informal, some formal contracts. Put students in pairs to talk about any experience they have had borrowing money. They can use these questions as prompts: *Did you borrow from a financial institution or a person? How long did you have to pay the money back? What kind of fee or interest did you have to pay on the loan? Was it a good experience? What kind of advice would you give about borrowing money?* If students are comfortable sharing this information, they can also say how much money they borrowed.

➤ Lead a class discussion about borrowing money, drawing on students' experience. Ask questions such as *Who borrowed money from friends or relatives? Who took out a bank loan? What advice would you give someone who needed to borrow money?*

➤ Do it yourself!

(For general suggestions, see *Introduction*, page Txiii.)

Procedure:

A–B.

➤ Put students in pairs or small groups to answer the two questions. Tell them to support their opinions with reasons and examples. Encourage students to jot down their ideas on a separate sheet of paper.

➤ Then put students in small groups that include people from different countries. Have them compare and contrast borrowing and lending customs in their home countries and in this one.

Option: Have each small group make a list of situations when it is not a good idea to borrow money. Then have groups share their ideas with the whole class.

Challenge: Have students present the findings from their discussion in a chart or Venn diagram. In a chart, they should list the countries across the top and the various features down the left column. If they decide to use a Venn diagram, they should compare only two or three countries at a time.

C. Read the information about credit unions and payday loans taken from government Web sites.

About Credit Unions

Address: @ http://www.ncua.gov

What Is a Credit Union?

A credit union is a nonprofit, cooperative financial institution owned and run by its members. Credit unions are a safe place to save and borrow at reasonable rates. Members pool their funds to make loans to one another. Today, over 10,000 credit unions with over $480 billion in assets serve more than 79 million people. Credit unions have been rated No. 1 in customer satisfaction at financial institutions for 10 years, according to the *American Banker Newspaper's* customer satisfaction survey.

To join a credit union, you must be eligible for membership. Each institution decides who it will serve. Most credit unions are organized to serve people in a particular community, group or groups of employees, or members of an organization or association.

If you want to know about credit unions in your state or city, log on to http://www.ncua.gov/indexabout.html

Web zone

Payday Loans

Netsite: http://www.ftc.gov   What's Related

Payday Loans

Payday* loans are small, short-term, high-rate loans. Usually, a borrower writes a personal check payable to the lender for the amount he or she wishes to borrow plus a fee. This kind of credit is very expensive.

Let's say you write a personal check for $115 to borrow $100 for up to 14 days. The check casher or payday lender agrees to hold the check until your next payday. At that time, depending on the particular plan, you pay the lender $115 in cash and he or she discards the check. If you are unable to pay the lender the $115, you may extend, or "roll over," the loan for another two weeks until your next payday for another $15. In this example, the cost of the initial loan is a $15 finance charge and a 391% APR (annual percentage rate). If you roll over the loan three times, the finance charge would climb to a total of $60 to borrow $100.

Payday loans are also called cash advance loans, check advance loans, post-dated check loans, or deferred deposit check loans.

D. True story. Have you ever borrowed money from a credit union or a friend? Have you ever taken out a payday loan, a personal loan, or a bank loan? Tell your story.

➤ Do it yourself!

A. Discussion. Discuss borrowing and lending.

1. Is it sometimes necessary to borrow money?
2. When is it not a good idea to borrow money?

B. Culture talk. Compare and contrast customs of borrowing and lending money in your home countries and here.

"Neither a borrower nor a lender be."

A. Read and listen to the letters.

Ask Joan

Culture tips for newcomers

Dear Joan:

In my office there are a lot of people of different nationalities, and we have a tradition that's a lot of fun. Once a month, we go out to lunch to a different kind of restaurant—Chinese, Italian, Korean, Greek, Polish, Mexican, Cuban. You get the idea, Joan.

When the check comes, one co-worker (I'll call her Jenna) is always short a dollar or two, so she asks me to lend her the money. Jenna always forgets to pay me back. It's very hard to ask her to repay the money because it makes me feel stingy and unfriendly since it's only a dollar or two at a time. But I'm beginning to feel angry inside, and now I don't enjoy the lunches. Any advice?

Shelly, tired of shelling out

Dear Shelly:

It's awkward to ask friends or co-workers to pay back money you lent them, especially when it's only a small sum. But it's inconsiderate of Jenna to continue borrowing without paying you back. I think you simply have to take the bull by the horns and say as politely as you can: "Jenna, it's really hard to ask you this, but do you think you could repay me the money I've been lending you when we go out? Even though it's only a dollar or two each time, it's starting to add up. I'd estimate that I've given you about $___ (fill in what you estimate the total is) by now, and I would feel a lot better if you could pay me back." Unless Jenna is a really terrible person, she'll apologize and pay. And you'll feel better that you spoke up!

Joan

Dear Joan:

I have not-so-great credit, and I made the mistake of borrowing money from a check-cashing place that gives payday loans. But the cost is exorbitant, and when you figure the yearly interest, it's more than 300%. Is that legal? What should I do?

Gullible Gus

Dear Gullible:

I haven't heard from you in a while. As you have learned the hard way, payday loans are <u>not</u> a good way to borrow money. Read this information from the Federal Trade Commission regarding alternatives to payday loans:

> When you need credit, shop carefully. Compare offers. Look for the credit offer with the lowest APR (annual percentage rate). Consider
> - a small loan from your credit union or small loan company
> - an advance on pay from your employer
> - a loan from family or friends
>
> A cash advance on a credit card may also be a possibility, but it may have a higher interest rate than your other sources of funds. Find out the terms before you decide.
>
> Also, a local community-based organization may make small business loans to individuals.
>
> If you decide you must use a payday loan, borrow only as much as you can afford to pay with your next paycheck and still have enough to make it to the following payday.

Remember, Gus, to plan a budget so that you don't have to borrow money on a week-to-week basis.

Joan

B. Role play. Role-play a conversation in which you borrow money from a friend or co-worker and agree to repay. Then role-play a conversation in which the friend doesn't repay. Review the practical conversation on page 114 to enrich your role plays.

C. Discussion. Talk about different ways to get money. What are the pros and cons of each way?

Authentic practice

(For general suggestions, see *Introduction*, page Tx.)

"Neither a borrower nor a lender be."

Procedure:

🎧 A. Read and listen to the letters.

➤ Have students read the bar. Ask them to rephrase the quotation in their own words; for example, *Don't borrow or lend money.* Ask *Do you agree or disagree with the advice?* Have students give reasons to support their opinions. Ask *What do the quotation marks tell us?* Elicit that this is quoted speech, somebody's actual words. Tell students that it is a quotation from *Hamlet,* a play by Shakespeare.

➤ After students read and listen to the letters, check comprehension by asking questions such as *What is Shelly's problem?* (A co-worker keeps borrowing money and doesn't pay it back.) *What does Joan advise her to do?* (Tell the co-worker how much she owes and ask for the money.) *What is Gus's problem?* (He took out a payday loan.) *What are some loan options that the FTC suggests?* (a credit union loan, a pay advance, a loan from family or friends, a cash advance on a credit card, a business loan from a local community-based organization)

➤ Explain any unfamiliar terms such as *be short a dollar or two, take the bull by the horns, exorbitant, cash advance.* Pronounce the word *stingy* and explain if necessary. Make sure students know what a *budget* is (a plan for spending money).

Challenge: In developing academic reading skills, students need to answer interpretive or critical thinking questions as well as literal questions. A literal question asks for information that is directly stated in the reading, such as *Are the people in Shelly's office all of the same nationality?* (No. There are a lot of people of different nationalities.) Interpretive questions ask for information that is implied in the reading, such as *Do you think Shelly has trouble refusing to loan Jenna money?* (Yes. Shelly continues to lend Jenna money even though Shelly feels angry inside and doesn't enjoy the lunches anymore.) Ask students to write one literal question and one critical thinking question about the letters. Have students exchange questions with a partner and discuss the answers.

B. Role play . . .

➤ Put students in pairs. Let them decide who will play the borrower and the lender. Have them create two conversations, one in which the borrower agrees to repay the loan and another in which the borrower doesn't repay. Refer students to the conversation on page 114 for suggestions.

➤ Circulate to help students with their conversations.

➤ Have volunteers perform their role play for the class.

C. Discussion . . .

➤ As a class, brainstorm different ways of getting money. Refer students to the documents on page 120 and to the boxed information in the *Ask Joan* column.

➤ In small groups, students discuss the advantages and disadvantages of different ways of getting money.

Option: Put students in groups of four and assign each group one way of getting money, such as a bank loan, a credit-union loan, a credit card advance, tuition assistance, or a car loan. Tell students that group members must each have a role: facilitator, recorder, reporter on advantages, and reporter on disadvantages. When students have completed their discussions, have groups present the pros and cons of the methods they discussed.

➤ Do it yourself!

(For general suggestions, see *Introduction,* page Txiii.)

Procedure:

A. Read the ads.

➤ After students have looked at the ads, ask questions such as *Which work-at-home opportunity pays a better rate?* ($5 for every envelope) *Is the interest rate higher on a 15-year loan or a 30-year loan?* (the 30-year loan) *How much is the Honda Accord?* ($15,495 or $17,060 with all its equipment)

➤ Elicit or tell students that a *SASE* is a self-addressed stamped envelope. Ask *Why should you send a self-addressed stamped envelope?* (to receive more information) Explain any terms or abbreviations that are difficult or unfamiliar.

B–C.

➤ Ask students to take out the car ads and ads for credit and for work-at-home opportunities they found in magazines and newspapers. Contribute some of your own as well.

➤ Assign students to groups depending on the type of ad they brought in: all the car ads in one group, the ads for credit in another, and the ads for work-at-home opportunities in a third. If necessary, subdivide groups so that there are only five members in each group.

➤ Have groups create two lists, one for elements of the ads that are similar and one for elements that are different.

➤ Create new groups of three students consisting of a member from each of the original groups (one car ad, one credit ad, one work-at-home opportunity). Have group members tell about typical features of the ads they studied.

Option: Based on their ad research, have pairs or small groups create a car ad, an ad for credit, or an ad for a work-at-home opportunity. Have them first discuss the elements that make each type of ad attractive, eye-catching, or interesting.

➤ Do it yourself!   A plan-ahead project

A. Read the ads.

1000 Envelopes Equals $2000!!
Independent Home Workers wanted to process bulk mail w/ our sales material. SASE to:
J.R. Quick
1999 Hillside
Bogota, NJ 07603

$2,000+/WK
$5 for every envelope you stuff. For info. send $5 & a SASE to
C. Rose
125 Ridge St.

15 YEAR FIXED	5.375%	5.495% APR
30 YEAR FIXED	5.875%	5.990% APR

Also Available
- 1st Time Buyers Program
- Debt Consolidation
- Free Pre-Approval
- 100% Financing
- No-Income Check Loans
- Credit Problem Programs
- Cash Out Refinance Loans
- Home Equity Loans

4.9% APR AVAIL. AT THESE PRICES

INCLUDES DESTINATION & PREP FEES.

BUY FOR $15,495

BRAND NEW 2004 HONDA ACCORD 4DR
Automatic, P/W, Tilt, AM/FM/CD, Dual Airbags, Telescopic Steering, Floor Mats & More!
Model# CM5613PLW $17,060

$135 PER MO. FOR 42 MOS.

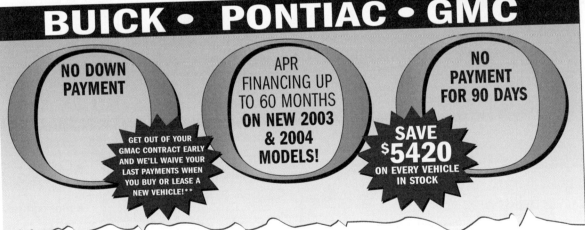

BUICK • PONTIAC • GMC

NO DOWN PAYMENT

GET OUT OF YOUR GMAC CONTRACT EARLY AND WE'LL WAIVE YOUR LAST PAYMENTS WHEN YOU BUY OR LEASE A NEW VEHICLE!**

APR FINANCING UP TO 60 MONTHS ON NEW 2003 & 2004 MODELS!

SAVE $5420 ON EVERY VEHICLE IN STOCK

NO PAYMENT FOR 90 DAYS

B. Find and bring in one or more items similar to the ones above:
- car ads from the newspaper to compare the terms of the loans
- ads for credit
- ads for work-at-home opportunities

C. Discussion. Compare what you found with your classmates.

Review

(For general suggestions, see *Introduction*, page Txii.)

Procedure:

A. Pair work or group work.

Ask and answer questions.

➤ Ask the class general questions about the pictures, such as *What do you think the women in the restaurant are talking about?* (the bill, a loan) *What kind of ad is on the bus stop wall?* (an ad for a work-at-home scheme) *What do you think the woman at the bottom left is doing?* (getting a payday loan) *What is the man at the bottom right filling out?* (a credit union membership application)

➤ For each picture, have partners take turns answering these questions: *What is happening? What are the people doing?*

Challenge: Divide the class into two teams. Tell the teams that they must create questions about the pictures using the following question words: *why, where, who, what,* and *when.* They should write three questions for each question word. Elicit one or two examples and write them on the board, such as *Why is the woman on the right in the top picture holding some money? Where is the man filling out an application?* Collect all the questions. In random order, ask the questions, alternating between the two teams. Each correct answer gets 1 point.

Create conversations.

➤ Have pairs number the speech balloons and, on a separate sheet of paper, write one line of conversation for each person in the pictures. Then have students read their lines aloud for the rest of the class to guess who is speaking.

Option: In pairs, students create conversations for each of the four interactions pictured. Have volunteers read one of the conversations aloud.

Option: Have pairs choose one of the pictures and create an extended conversation for the characters.

Challenge: Assign half the class the role of the borrower in the top picture and half the role of the lender. Allow students a few minutes to look back through the unit for ideas. Then have students stand up and form two concentric circles, with the students on the inside playing the role of the lender and the students on the outside playing the role of the borrower. Students face each other, pair up, and have a conversation. After a minute, the "borrowers" walk to their right, pairing up with the new "lender," who is one student down from the previous partner. These two students then have a conversation. Repeat until all students have had an opportunity to practice the conversation with several partners. After students have practiced with two partners, you can change the scenario and have the lender ask for the money back.

Tell a story.

Option: One-minute speech. Assign each student one of the pictures. Give students several minutes to look at the picture and review ideas from the unit. Each student must then describe what is going on in the picture, talking for one minute if possible.

Option: Create a character. Have students choose one person in the pictures and tell what he or she is doing and thinking at the moment. Have students imagine a reason why the character might need extra money.

Option: Fortuneteller. Ask students to choose one of the four situations and predict what will happen in the future.

⌒B. Listening comprehension...

➤ Tell students that they are going to hear two speakers talk about financial matters.

➤ After listening, students work individually to write advice to each of the speakers.

➤ In pairs, they compare answers.

Challenge: Have students create their own statements about a money problem, and then read their statements to a partner. The partners offer advice orally or in writing.

C–D.

➤ Students work individually to complete the review exercises.

➤ Circulate to offer help as needed.

➤ Have students check answers with a partner. Review answers as a class.

➤ Identify any areas of difficulty that may require additional instruction and practice.

Tapescript

1. Male: Look at this ad for making flags! "Work your own hours, in the comfort of your own home!" How hard could *that* be?

2. Female: I saw this great deal on a used computer, and I can buy it for only four hundred dollars! The original cost was eleven hundred and ninety-nine dollars! The problem is I don't have that kind of money. I think I'll get a payday loan.

---

1. My advice: _____ (Answers will vary.) _____

   _____

2. My advice: _____

   _____

C. **Read each sentence. Underline your response.**

1. "Here's a good opportunity for you. Telemarketing from home would be right up your alley."

   YOU But I have no e-mail.   **YOU** <u>Really? How do I get started?</u>

2. "My phone number is 325-0091."

   YOU <u>Got it.</u>   **YOU** I'm not that gullible.

3. "Never mind the offer. It doesn't sound good."

   YOU <u>Suit yourself.</u>   **YOU** There's a low start-up fee.

4. "I'd like to go to architecture school, but it's too expensive."

   YOU <u>Have you applied for a scholarship?</u>   **YOU** I'll have to give this some thought.

D. **Choose one of the words or phrases to complete each sentence.**

1. When you ask another person for money and he or she gives it to you, you are

   _____ borrowing _____ money.
      borrowing / lending

2. When you give someone money and he or she agrees to pay you back, you are

   _____ lending _____ money.
      borrowing / lending

3. Money that you receive from a bank, a friend, or a relative and that you agree to

   repay is a _____ loan _____.
                  loan / rate

4. A note in which one person agrees to repay another is _____ an IOU _____.
                                                      a payday loan / an IOU

5. _____ Interest _____ is money you owe to a lender in addition to the money
      A loan / Interest
   you borrowed.

E. Complete each sentence with *but* or *so*.

1. Joan advised Gus not to borrow money from a check-cashing business, ___so___ he went to the credit union instead.

2. The credit union offered much better terms, ___so___ Gus borrowed from them.

3. The check-cashing place and the credit union are both in the same neighborhood, ___but___ the credit union gives better terms on credit.

4. Mr. Santoro asked his sister-in-law for a loan, ___but___ she was short of cash and couldn't give him the money.

F. Complete each sentence with a comma and a logical statement beginning with *but* or *so*.

1. I needed money ___(Answers will vary.)___ .

2. The bank advertised low rates _____ .

3. The scholarship committee offered her a scholarship _____

_____ .

4. Gus saw an ad for a great work-at-home opportunity _____

_____ .

5. We didn't know the terms _____ .

G. Answer the questions.

1. Why should you be careful of work-at-home offers? ___(Answers will vary.)___

_____

2. Why should you be careful about payday loans? _____

_____

3. What's the difference between getting a payday loan and borrowing money from a credit union or a bank? _____

_____

H. Composition. On a separate sheet of paper, write about the picture on page 124.

Now I can
- ❑ borrow money from a friend or co-worker.
- ❑ agree to repay the loan.
- ❑ remind a person to pay back a loan.
- ❑ share wishes and dreams.
- ❑ offer advice on financial aid.
- ❑ understand work-at-home schemes.
- ❑ understand credit unions.
- ❑ understand the problems with payday loans.

E–G.

➤ Students work individually to complete the review exercises.

➤ Circulate to offer help as needed.

➤ Have students check answers with a partner. Review answers as a class.

➤ Identify any areas of difficulty that may require additional instruction and practice.

Challenge: For Exercise E, have students write a new ending for the sentences. They should use the other conjunction and an original clause. For example, students might rewrite item 1 as *Joan advised Gus not to borrow money from a check-cashing business, but he did it anyway.*

H. Composition...

➤ Provide students with concrete approaches to writing about the picture on page 124. Use one of the options that follow, give students a choice of options, or assign options based on students' levels of proficiency. Model what is expected of students for each option.

➤ Advise students to look back through the unit for help and ideas as they write.

➤ Circulate to offer help as needed.

Option: Students write a description, in paragraph form, of what happened in one of the pictures. The paragraph should have at least five sentences. One of the sentences should use *but* and one should use *so*. Remind students to indent the first sentence and to use correct punctuation and capitalization.

Option: Students write an IOU for the woman borrowing money in the first picture. They can follow the model on page 120 and make up names for the two women.

Option: Students write an extended conversation between any two speakers in the pictures. Refer them to the conversation on page 114 for format and ideas.

Challenge: Students write down the information they think would be asked for on a loan application.

Now I can

➤ Read the first item in the box out loud: *Now I can borrow money from a friend or co-worker.* Elicit from the class an example, such as *I'm out of cash. Do you think you could lend me $5?*

➤ Put students in pairs. Tell students to take turns reading each item in the box and giving an example of what they have learned. When students can provide an example, they should check that objective. If there are items students aren't able to check, have them look back through the unit for ideas.

➤ When students are finished reviewing with their partners, read each item out loud and elicit an example from the class.

Oral test (optional)

You may want to use the *Now I can* box as an informal evaluation. While students are working on the *Composition* activity, you can call them up individually and check their ability with two or three objectives.

Your career

 Preview

(For general suggestions, see *Introduction*, page Tviii.)

Warm up. Look at the resume. What's the purpose of a resume?

Procedure:

➤ Before students open their books, brainstorm initial contacts with a potential employer. If necessary, prompt with questions such as *When does a potential employer have the first contact with you? What are some ways an employer can form an impression of you?* Elicit responses, including *a phone inquiry, an application form, a resume, an interview*. List students' ideas on the board.

➤ Brainstorm ways to create a good impression through each of the contacts listed on the board. You may end up with a list like this one.

A phone inquiry: Be polite; get all the necessary information

An application form: Be neat, thorough, and truthful; spell words correctly

A resume: Be neat and clear; use good grammar and spelling; tailor the resume to the job

An interview: Be punctual, well-groomed, prepared, and polite; ask good questions; answer questions completely

➤ Have students open their books. Read the *Warm up* question and elicit responses. Make sure students know that *a resume* is a summary of a person's work and educational experience. Writing a resume is generally part of a job application process.

➤ Ask students what Carlos Sinkoff has included on his resume. They should respond with the resume headings *objective, summary of qualifications, strengths, work experience, education,* and *references.*

➤ Note that the word *resume* is spelled like the verb *resume,* but it is pronounced *rayzumay,* because it was originally a French word. Students may also see the word spelled with accent marks: *résumé.*

Challenge: Working individually, students create questions about the information covered on the resume. They should phrase the questions as if they were addressing Carlos Sinkoff; for example, *What kind of education do you have?* Or *Can you tell me about your educational background?* Review questions briefly and then put students in pairs to take turns asking and answering the questions.

Challenge: Have students research various methods of getting a job. Students with Internet access can check resume-posting Web sites such as monster.com. Other class members can investigate the free resources at the public library, such as resume and interviewing workshops, the classified section of the local paper, and computers with word-processing and resume-writing programs. Have students share their findings with the class.

Unit 10 objectives

Procedure:

➤ Have students read the objectives.

➤ Have students count off by 6 (the number of objectives). Direct all the 1s to one area of the room, 2s to another, and so on, until six groups have formed. Ask groups to list steps they would follow in meeting that objective. For example, the 1s might include *Look into other job opportunities by checking the classified ads.* Ask groups to put their lists on transparencies or big sheets of paper. Then have the groups present their ideas. Save the transparencies or sheets to refer to at the end of the unit.

Your career

 Preview

Warm up. Look at the resume. What's the purpose of a resume?

Carlos Sinkoff
uribres@mytimes.com

45 McCabe Avenue, Hadley Beach, NJ 07865   (201) 555-6743

OBJECTIVE
   Position as an architectural draftsperson or commercial artist

SUMMARY OF QUALIFICATIONS
   8 years of experience in the magazine publishing industry as an illustrator
   4 years of experience in a civil engineering concern as a draftsperson

STRENGTHS
   Visual creativity
   Careful execution of projects on a timely basis

WORK EXPERIENCE
   Elegant Interiors, Little Rumson, NJ
      Colorist and painter: 1998 to present

   TAXI-FAST, Miramar, NJ
      Taxi driver: 1996-1998

   Chilean Life Magazine, Osorno, Chile
      Illustrator and layout person: Full-time for two years, then part-time
      while full-time at Klimpft Associates: 1987-1995

   Klimpft Associates, Temuco, Chile
      Chief draftsman in office of more than 200 architects and civil engineers:
      1991-1995

EDUCATION
   University of the West, Vina del Mar, Chile
      Bachelor of Arts, major in architectural drafting, minor in fine arts: 1987

REFERENCES
   Available upon request

Unit 10 objectives

- Apply for a better job.
- Tell your employer about a job offer.
- Get a counteroffer.
- Give notice.
- Write a job history.
- Write a resume.

Practical conversations

A. Listen and read.

A: How long have you been in your current job?

B: Two years.

A: And why do you want to change jobs?

B: Well, I've completed my degree, and I'm ready for a bigger challenge.

A: That's great. Let's see what we have for you.

B. Pronunciation and intonation practice.

> ### Ideas
>
> **Some reasons to apply for a better job**
>
> I've completed my degree, and I'm ready for a bigger challenge.
>
> My husband / wife has been transferred here, and I need to find a new job.
>
> My English has improved, and I'm ready for a professional job.
>
> There's not much room to advance where I work now.
>
> I'd like to make a career change, and that's impossible in my company.
>
> Your own reason: _____

C. Pair work. Explain why you'd like to change jobs. Use the resumes or your own resume.

SCOTT FURILLO
2000 to present: Assistant front-desk manager, Kinkade Hotel, 3499 North Main, Medford, NJ 07080.

Marina Oxcraft
2002 to present: Bookkeeper, Accurate Accountancy, 12 Bank Street, White Plains, NY 10605.

Alan Petak
1996 to present: Service manager, German Motor Works, 3617 White Rock Turnpike, Fairfield, CT 06432.

Anne Chang
1995 to present: Teacher's aide, Seattle Public Schools, 814 Fifth Avenue South, Seattle, WA 98109.

A: How long have you been in your current job?

B: _____.

A: And why do you want to change jobs?

B: Well, _____.

A: _____.

Practical conversations

(For general suggestions, see *Introduction*, page Tviii.)

Model 1

Content: applying for a better job, reasons to apply for a better job, resume excerpts

Procedure:

A-B.

➤ To set the scene for the conversation, ask students questions about the photo, such as *Where are the two speakers?* (in an office) *Whose office is it?* (the woman's) *How do you know?* (The phone is facing her, She is writing.) *Why do you think the man is in her office?* (Maybe he's a co-worker or a job applicant.)

➤ After students read and listen to the conversation, check comprehension by asking questions such as *What questions does the interviewer ask?* (How long have you been in your current job? Why do you want to change jobs?) *Why does the job applicant want a new job?* (He's completed his degree, and he's ready for a bigger challenge.)

➤ Tell students that we often alternate strongly stressed syllables with more weakly stressed ones. The longer sentences in this conversation have a distinctive rhythm that students should try to attune their ears to.

➤ Ask students to listen to the conversation again and put a dot above each syllable. They should use a small dot for a weakly stressed syllable and a large dot for a strongly stressed syllable.

➤ Write the sentences in the conversation on the board. Read each sentence and elicit information about the stress of each syllable. Place an appropriately sized dot above each syllable. Finally, have students repeat the sentences after you.

Ideas

➤ After students listen and repeat, brainstorm other reasons to apply for a better job, such as a *better schedule* or *the opportunity to learn new skills*. Write the ideas on the board.

Option: Have students rewrite the ideas using clauses introduced by *but* (item 5) or *so* (items 1, 2, 3). They will have to rewrite item 4 to use a clause with *but*.

C. Pair work ...

➤ Have students read the four resume excerpts.

➤ Ask students to assume the role of one of the four job applicants. Give them time to think of answers to the following questions: *How long have you been in your current job? Why do you want to change jobs? What are your career goals?*

➤ Model the conversation with a more advanced student. Play the role of Student B, the job applicant, to demonstrate giving a reason to apply for a better job.

➤ In pairs, students practice the conversation, first giving reasons for one of the job applicants and then for themselves.

Challenge: Working in pairs, students extend the conversation to include more of the job interview. As a class, first brainstorm questions the interviewer might ask. Then, alternating the roles of the interviewer and the applicant, students role-play a job interview. They can answer for themselves or assume the role of one of the four applicants.

Model 2

Content: telling your employer about a job offer; getting a counteroffer; telling someone about a hard choice; perks, benefits, and other features of good jobs

Procedure:

🎧A–B.

➤ To set the scene for the conversation, ask questions about the photo, such as *Where are the two speakers?* (in an office) *Whose office do you think it is?* (the man's) *Why do you think so?* (The woman is entering, He's behind the desk.)

➤ Discuss appropriate ways to enter a co-worker's or supervisor's office. Elicit ideas such as *Knock, say "Excuse me," and ask if you can interrupt.*

➤ After students read and listen to the conversation, check comprehension by asking questions such as *What does Oliva want to talk about?* (a job offer) *Does John want her to leave?* (No. He asks if there is some way they can get her to stay.) *What is better about the other position?* (The salary is much higher.)

➤ Before listening to the conversation again and repeating, tell students to listen for the stressed words and syllables. Then have them mark the text with a large dot for a strongly stressed syllable and a smaller dot for a weakly stressed syllable, as they did for Model 1.

🎧Telling someone about a hard choice

➤ Students listen to and repeat ways to tell someone about a hard choice.

➤ Read the conversation with the class playing the role of Student B. Play the role of Student A and substitute one of the ways to tell someone about a hard choice.

🎧Vocabulary

➤ Tell students that *a perk* is a benefit or advantage. It is a short form of the word *perquisite*.

➤ Have students listen and repeat.

➤ Brainstorm other features of good jobs and write them on the board, such as *more flexibility* or *a better schedule.*

Option: Have students rank the perks, benefits, and other features of good jobs from 1 to 6. Let 1 be the most important feature to them. Put students in small groups to discuss the reasons for their rankings.

C. Pair work ...

➤ Model the conversation with a more advanced student. Play the role of Student A. Demonstrate telling someone about a hard choice and describing a perk or benefit. Choose a feature from the *Vocabulary* box or from the list on the board.

➤ Have pairs practice the conversation, alternating the roles of Students A and B. Make sure they first choose names for the characters.

➤ Do it yourself!

(For general suggestions, see *Introduction*, page Txiii.)

Procedure:

➤ Have students refer to page 128 to see how the job seekers in Exercise C set up their resumes.

➤ Explain that a *draft* is a first attempt at writing something. A draft for a resume needs to be rewritten in order to include all relevant details under the appropriate headings; to polish the wording; and to check spelling, capitalization, and punctuation.

➤ Copy the form from the book on the board and fill it out for yourself. Read the information aloud and answer any questions about format.

➤ Tell students to begin their own resumes by writing their names on the top line. In the first slot on the second line, they should write the month and year or just the year that they began their current job.

➤ Note that *to present* on a resume indicates that the job applicant is still employed in that same capacity at that same company. If students are no longer working, they should adapt the form as follows: 2000 (the year they began) *to* 2003 (the year they stopped working).

➤ In the remaining space, students write their position, the company, and the company address.

Option: In pairs, students ask and answer questions about their resumes, such as *How long have you worked there? What is your present position?*

A. Listen and read.

A: John, do you have a moment to talk?

B: Sure, Oliva. What's on your mind?

A: Well, I've been offered another position. And I'm trying to decide what to do.

B: Really? Is there some way we can get you to stay?

A: Well, I don't know. They're offering a much higher salary.

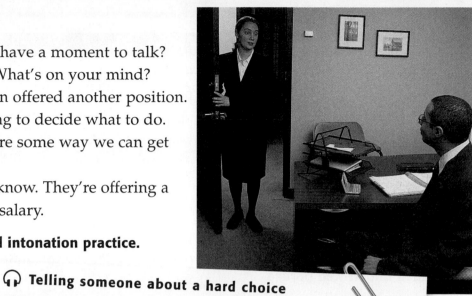

B. Pronunciation and intonation practice.

Telling someone about a hard choice

I'm trying to decide what to do.
I've decided to take it.

I can't make up my mind.
The offer is just too good to refuse.

Vocabulary

Perks, benefits, and other features of good jobs

a higher salary	tuition assistance
more responsibility	better working conditions
more opportunity for growth	better benefits

C. Pair work. Talk about a job offer.

A: _____, do you have a moment to talk?

B: Sure, _____. What's on your mind?

A: Well, I've been offered another position. And _____.

B: Really? Is there some way we can get you to stay?

A: Well, I don't know. They're offering _____.

➤ Do it yourself!

Draft the beginning of your own resume. Begin with your name. Then add your last job and the date you began. Look at the resumes on page 128 as models.

_____
(Name)

_____ to present: _____

_____

The past unreal conditional

Explain consequences of unreal conditions in the past with the past unreal conditional.
Use *had* and a past participle in the *if* clause.
Use *would have* or *could have* + a past participle in the result clause.

> If Paul **had seen** that ad, he **would have applied** for the job. (But he didn't see the ad: unreal)
>
> I **wouldn't have studied** law if my mother **hadn't been** a lawyer. (But I did study law: unreal)

Don't use *would* or *could* in the *if* clause.

> ~~If Paul would have seen that ad~~…

A. **Distinguish between real and unreal conditions. Choose the statement closer in meaning to each underlined phrase.**

1. Al would have left <u>if they hadn't offered him an opportunity to advance</u>.

   ⓐ They offered him an opportunity. ⓑ They didn't offer him an opportunity.

2. <u>If she had known about the job in quality control</u>, she would have taken it.

   ⓐ She knew about the job. **ⓑ** She didn't know about the job.

3. <u>If they had told him about the promotion</u>, he would have accepted it.

   ⓐ They told him about the promotion. **ⓑ** They didn't tell him about the promotion.

4. <u>If he had been there</u>, he could have told them about the opening.

   ⓐ He was there. **ⓑ** He wasn't there.

5. The resume would have been better <u>if someone had helped her write it</u>.

   ⓐ Someone helped her write it. **ⓑ** No one helped her write it.

B. **Choose the correct forms to complete each past unreal conditional sentence.**

1. What would you have done if they _____had offered_____ you a promotion?
   would have offered / had offered

2. If the opportunities to advance _____had been_____ better, would you have stayed?
   would be / had been

Practical grammar

(For general suggestions, see *Introduction*, page Tix.)

The past unreal conditional

Procedure:

➤ Review with students the information on unreal conditional sentences from Unit 5. Put on the board a series of unreal conditions; for example, *If I wanted to save money, If I paid my bills on time.* Brainstorm result clauses and write students' ideas on the board, making sure to use *would*; for example, *I would buy a used car, I wouldn't have to pay a late fee.* Ask *Are these real situations?* (no) Tell students that unreal conditional sentences express hypothetical or imaginary situations.

➤ Tell students that we can explain the consequences of unreal conditions in the past using the past unreal conditional. Write on the board *If I had wanted to save money, I would have bought a used car; If I had paid my bills on time, I wouldn't have had to pay a late fee.* Underline *had* and the past participle in the *if* clause and *would have* and the past participle in the result clause.

➤ Focus students' attention by asking questions such as *What verb form do we use in the "if" clause?* (*had* + past participle) *What verb form do we use in the result clause?* (*would have* + past participle).

➤ Reread the sentences on the board, giving the result clause first. Remind students that the order of the clauses does not change the meaning. However, when the *if* clause comes first, it is separated from the result clause by a comma.

➤ Have students read the information in the box. Create other examples of past unreal conditions and write them on the board. Use these clauses or your own: *If I had applied for the job, If the company had gotten your resume, If she had completed her degree.* Have students suggest clauses to complete the sentences, making sure to use *would have* or *could have* plus a past participle in the result clause.

A. Distinguish ...

➤ Have students read item 1. Ask *Did Al leave?* (no) *Did they offer him an opportunity to advance?* (yes) Tell students to fill in the first oval because that statement is closer in meaning to the underlined *if* clause.

➤ Tell students that in this exercise the underlined *if* clauses express something that didn't happen. Tell them to select the statement that tells what did happen.

➤ Working individually, students complete the exercise. Have pairs compare answers, and then review as a class.

Option: A story about the past. To help students practice formation of the past unreal conditional, explain that you are going to tell a story about the past. After each sentence you say, students are to ask a question beginning with *What if.* Begin by saying *I went to college.* Elicit the question *What if you hadn't gone to college?* Give an answer such as *If I hadn't gone to college, I couldn't have become a teacher.* Continue this activity until students can ask *What if* questions quickly and accurately.

Challenge: Have students work in pairs to rewrite the sentences in Exercise A. In each item, the *if* clause should match the meaning they didn't choose. In item 1, for example, the sentence would read *Al wouldn't have left if they had offered him an opportunity to advance.*

B. Choose the correct forms ...

➤ Review with students the verb forms in past unconditional sentences: *had* + past participle in the *if* clause, *would / could have* + past participle in the result clause. For practice, have students identify the verb forms in Exercise A.

➤ Have students work individually to complete the exercise. Remind them that the exercise continues on page 131.

➤ After students have compared answers with a partner, review as a class. Ask students to support their verb form choices; for example, *In item 1, the situation described is unreal. It takes place in the past. I can't use "would have" in the "if" clause. Therefore the correct form is "had offered."*

C. Complete each of the following...

➤ Complete item 1 with the class. Have students underline the *if* clause. Ask *What verb form is used?* (*had* + past participle). Ask *What verb form is used in the result clause?* (*would / could have* + past participle)

➤ Have students look through the remaining sentences and underline the *if* clauses. Remind them that *if* clauses in past conditional sentences use *had* + past participle and result clauses use *would / could have* + past participle.

➤ Working individually, students complete the sentences. Review as a class. Check that students completed the sentences with the past unreal forms since the sentences also make sense as present unreal conditionals.

➤ The last sentence is very challenging, and students may need help. Be sure students see the passive construction in the result clause. Compare the differences in items 5 and 6. Item 6 can serve as a model if students want to produce the passive in the *Do it yourself!* activity.

Option: You might wish to contrast the meaning of the following:

1. If she applied for that job, she would get it.
2. If she had applied for that job, she would have gotten it.

Elicit from students that the first implies a future consequence of a present condition. The second implies a past consequence of a past condition.

Option: Have students make the sentences negative: *If she hadn't applied for that job, she wouldn't have gotten it.*

If your students are ready...

Language note: Unreal past conditionals can also be formed using inversion rather than an *if* clause. It's not important for students to be able to manipulate this grammatical form, but they may hear it and should understand what it means. For example, item 1 in Exercise A on page 130 would appear as *Had they not offered him an opportunity to advance, Al would have left.* Item 2 could be rewritten *Had she known about the job in quality control, she would have taken it.* The meaning is the same, but the clause that states the condition is formed by inverting the auxiliary verb *had* and the subject. This is not a question formation but a different type of inverted form. The past unreal conditional expressed with inversion occurs in the last frame of the picture story on page 132.

➤ Do it yourself!

(For general suggestions, see *Introduction*, page Txiii.)

Procedure:

A–B.

➤ Tell students that when we speculate we think about unreal situations—what might happen or might have happened.

➤ Model Exercise A with a sentence about yourself, such as *If my first language had not been English, I could have learned it in school.*

➤ Working individually, students complete the sentences. Students exchange sentences with a partner to check for the correct verb forms in the clauses.

➤ When students have finished, write the two *if* clauses as headings on the board.

➤ Students write their result clauses under the appropriate *if* clauses.

➤ Have the students read the sentences aloud.

Option: Put students in small groups to compare and contrast their result clauses. Elicit from each group the ways in which their speculations were similar or different.

Option: Brainstorm other life-changing or life-defining situations. Elicit ideas by asking *What events or conditions have determined the way your life has turned out?* Write these ideas on the board as *if* clauses; for example, *If I hadn't gotten married, If I hadn't gone to college, If I had been an only child.* Have students create endings for several of the sentences.

3. If the company had offered a retirement plan, fewer employees __would have left__ .

 would leave / would have left

4. If Ace Paints __had posted__ a list of openings, they __wouldn't have had__

 would post / had posted

 hadn't had / wouldn't have had

such a hard time hiring from within the company.

C. Complete each of the following past unreal conditional sentences.

1. If she ___*had applied*___ for that job, she *would have gotten* it.

 apply

 get

2. If they ___had offered___ a better salary, more people ___would have been___

 offer

 be

available.

3. I ___would have interviewed___ you if there ___had been___ an opening in my

 interview

 be

department.

4. If they ___had paid___ me a better salary, they ___could have convinced___

 pay

 convince

me to stay.

5. If you ___had shown___ them your resume, they ___would have hired___

 show

 hire

you on the spot.

6. If you ___had shown___ them your resume, you ___would have been hired___

 show

 be hired

on the spot.

➤ Do it yourself!

A. Speculate on what would have happened in your life if things had been different. Complete the sentences with true information about yourself.

1. If I had stayed in my home country, _____

_____ .

2. If my first language had been English, _____

_____ .

B. Collaborative activity. With your classmates, write your result clauses from Exercise A on the board.

Consider a counteroffer.

① Mike: Fred? Excuse the interruption. Have you got a minute?

Fred: For you? Anytime. Come in and have a seat, Mike. What's on your mind?

Mike: Sorry to spring this on you, but I've been offered a position at Fischbach, and I guess I'm going to have to give you notice.

② Fred: Well, I must say I'm not surprised. If it's not too late, would you consider a counteroffer? It would be a shame to lose you.

Mike: Thanks, Fred. I appreciate the kind words.

③ Mike: But I'm not sure. The position at Fischbach is at a much higher level.

And—forgive me for saying this—but in the two years I've been here, it never occurred to me that there was much room for growth. I know it's not your fault....

④ Fred: Had we known you were interested in more responsibility, we certainly would have paid attention. You can take my word for that.

Let me see what I can do. Would you be willing to hang in there till the end of the day? I could get back to you by three.

Mike: Well, OK. No harm in trying!

A. Check *True, False,* or *? (No information)* for each statement.

	True	False	?
1. Mike is a programmer.	☐	☐	☑
2. Mike's work is very good.	☑	☐	☐
3. Fred wants Mike to take the offer.	☐	☑	☐
4. Mike is going to take the Fischbach offer.	☐	☐	☑
5. Fred gets another job for Mike.	☐	☐	☑

B. Listen. Read each response out loud from the text.

C. Check the subjects Fred and Mike talk about.

☑ 1. a job offer from another company

☐ 2. a mistake Mike has made on the job

➤ Authentic practice

(For general suggestions, see *Introduction*, page Tx.)

Consider a counteroffer.

Procedure:

➤ Help students focus their attention before they listen to the picture story. Write on the board questions such as *Why is Mike talking to Fred? What is Fred's reaction to Mike's news?* Tell students to listen for answers to these questions.

➤ With books still closed, have students listen to the picture story. If necessary, let them listen again.

➤ Elicit responses to the two questions on the board: *Mike wants to tell Fred he got another offer and is giving notice; Fred wants Mike to stay, so he makes a counteroffer.*

A. Check...

➤ Have students read the statements. Then have students read the picture story while they listen again.

➤ Some expressions may be unfamiliar to students. Have students find and circle *spring this on you, give you notice, it would be a shame, take my word, hang in there, no harm in trying.* Ask them to think of a different word or phrase for each of these. For example, instead of *Sorry to spring this on you,* you could say *Sorry to give you this unexpected news.*

➤ Ask students to locate the past unreal conditional in this story (frame 4: *Had we known . . .*). Remind them that inverting *had* and the subject has the same meaning as an *if* clause in a past unreal conditional. If necessary, refer students to the *Language note* on page T131.

➤ Working individually, students check the appropriate boxes. Have students compare answers with a partner.

Option: Making inferences is an important academic skill. Have students identify the statements that require the reader to look beyond the literal information given in the story. For example, no one says that Mike's work is very good, but Fred says he's not surprised that Mike got another offer and that it would be a shame to lose him. From these statements, we can infer that Mike's work is good. For each statement that requires making inferences, ask students to cite the information in the story that led to their answers.

B. Listen...

➤ Play the cassette or read the tapescript.

➤ Students respond to the three items.

Option: Dictation. Have the students write each of the three items. Let them listen as many times as necessary to complete the activity.

C. Check the subjects...

➤ Make sure students complete the exercise on page 133.

➤ Students work individually to check the subjects discussed.

➤ For each topic discussed, students underline the supporting information in the story.

➤ In pairs, students check their answers.

Tapescript

1. Fred? Excuse the interruption. Have you got a minute?

2. It would be a shame to lose you.

3. Would you be willing to hang in there till the end of the day? I could get back to you by three.

D–E.

➤ Put students in pairs. Student A opens the book to page 133 while Student B listens with closed book.

➤ Student A reads each item. Student B responds appropriately.

➤ Student B opens to page 133, and pairs choose the appropriate responses together.

➤ In pairs, students take turns reading the items and the appropriate responses.

Option: Have students create original sentences or questions that could lead to the other responses. In item 1, for example, the question *Why do you want to leave?* could lead to the response *Forgive me for saying this, but...*

Option: Give students time to review the responses, and then have them close their books. Read the items in random order and have students answer chorally with the appropriate response.

F. Critical thinking...

➤ Working individually, students answer the question.

➤ Put students in small groups to compare answers. Ask students to discuss what contributes to job satisfaction. Have them create a list of these factors and reach a consensus on which two or three factors are most important.

➤ Lead a class discussion about what the groups decided were the most important factors in job satisfaction. Write their ideas on the board.

Challenge: Tally the results for each factor listed on the board that contributes to job satisfaction. Have students present these findings as a pie chart. See the sample below.

Friendly work environment   6

Good pay / benefits   11

Challenge   5

Opportunity for advancement   8

➤ Do it yourself!

(For general suggestions, see *Introduction*, page Txiii.)

Procedure:

A. Write your own response...

➤ Have students read the speech balloons. Ask *Who is talking?* (a boss, a supervisor) Point out that since the same person appears in all three pictures that this activity is meant as a single conversation.

➤ Have a more advanced student read the first speech balloon out loud. Model an appropriate response such as *Maybe, but the other position pays a much higher salary.*

➤ Have students write responses individually and then compare responses with a partner.

➤ In pairs, students practice their conversations.

B. Culture talk...

➤ Put students in groups with others from the same or a similar culture. Have them discuss what people do when they get an offer for another job.

➤ Have the students create a role play about the situation. Ask volunteers to perform their role plays for the class.

➤ Lead a discussion about the different responses that were presented in the role plays.

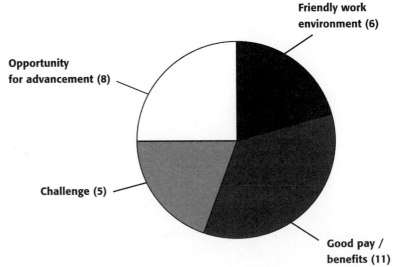

Friendly work environment (6)

Opportunity for advancement (8)

Challenge (5)

Good pay / benefits (11)

❏ 3. problems at Fischbach

☑ 4. a lack of opportunity for growth

☑ 5. a possible counteroffer

D. **Read each sentence or question. Underline your response.**

1. "If I made a counteroffer, could I get you to reconsider?"

   YOU Forgive me for saying this.   **YOU** <u>Possibly. There's no harm in trying.</u>

2. "I'm going to have to give you notice."

   YOU I didn't see it.   **YOU** <u>That's a shame.</u>

3. "I'm sorry to spring this on you, but I've taken another job."

   YOU I appreciate the kind words.   **YOU** <u>I'm not surprised.</u>

4. "Thanks for the kind words."

   YOU You can take my word for that.   **YOU** <u>For you? Anytime.</u>

E. **Pair work. Take turns reading the items and responses in Exercise D.**

F. **Critical thinking. Answer the question. Then discuss your opinion with a partner or a group.**

What do you think Mike really wants? _____ (Answers will vary.) _____

➤ Do it yourself!

A. **Write your own response. Then read the conversation out loud with a partner.**

Would you be willing to consider a counteroffer?

YOU _____

It would be a shame to lose you.

YOU _____

If we'd known you wanted to move up, we would have offered you something sooner. Let me see what I can do.

YOU _____

B. **Culture talk. In the country where you come from, what do people do when they get an offer for another job? Role-play a conversation.**

Authentic practice

How to get a better job

A. Listening comprehension. Listen to the conversations. Then answer the questions.

1. Why is Sara unhappy at her job? <u>She wants to move up, have a more managerial position.</u>

2. Why has Sara been underemployed in this country? <u>Her English was weak.</u>

B. Read the statements. Then listen to the conversations again to complete each statement. Fill in the ovals.

1. Sara is tired of _____.

   ⓐ Evan   **ⓑ** the assembly line

2. She has worked at her present job _____.

   ⓐ for two and a half years   ⓑ for two and a half months

3. Sara is afraid to tell Evan she wants a better job because _____.

   ⓐ he wouldn't have anyone to do her work   ⓑ her English isn't very good

4. When Sara speaks up, Evan _____.

   ⓐ says he will try to help   ⓑ is angry with her

5. In Venezuela, Sara was _____.

   ⓐ a manager   ⓑ an assembly-line worker

6. Sara's English is _____ now.

   ⓐ weaker   **ⓑ** better

C. Role play. Role-play a conversation between two employees. One wants to move up but doesn't know how to make it happen.

I'm ready to get a job with more responsibility. What should I do?

Authentic practice

(For general suggestions, see *Introduction*, page Tx.)

How to get a better job

Procedure:

⌒A. Listening comprehension . . .

➤ To set the scene for the listening activity, have students look at the picture. Ask questions such as *Where are the speakers?* (in a cafeteria) *What kind of relationship do you think they have?* (friends or co-workers)

➤ Have students read the questions. Ask students why immigrants are often underemployed in their new country. Elicit reasons such as the following: *Immigrants don't know the language, The educational requirements for some jobs are different.*

➤ Play the cassette or read the tapescript. Have students write answers to the questions.

➤ Put students in pairs to compare answers.

⌒B. Read the statements . . .

➤ Students read the statements and possible completions.

➤ Have students listen to the conversations again and then select a completion for each statement.

➤ Review as a class.

C. Role play . . .

➤ Have a volunteer read the man's speech balloon. Ask *What advice could you give this man?* Write students' suggestions on the board.

➤ Tell students that they are going to create a role play between two co-workers. One wants to move up, and the other gives advice.

➤ Put students in pairs to brainstorm ideas. Refer students to the list on the board.

Tapescript

Conversation 1

Mary Lou: Hey, Sara, why the long face?

Sara: Mary Lou, I just can't stand it any more. I've been in this same assembly job now for two and a half years, and there's no way to move up. What should I do?

Mary Lou: Have you told Evan?

Sara: No. I'm afraid he'd get mad. After all, who would do all this work?

Mary Lou: Believe me, if you got another job, they'd find someone to do the work. Speak up.

Sara: What do you mean?

Mary Lou: Well, you've got nothing to lose. If you'd spoken up two years ago, you'd be earning a whole lot more by now.

Sara: Do you think? What do I tell Evan?

Mary Lou: Just tell him that in Venezuela you were a plant manager. Now that your English is better, you'd like to find work at a higher level—like you used to do. Ask him if there are any possibilities for you to move up.

Sara: Hey, look. There's Evan, and he's alone. . . . I'll go talk to him now. Wish me luck.

Conversation 2

Sara: Evan? Excuse the interruption, but I really need to talk to you.

Evan: Sure, Sara. Something wrong?

Sara: Well, not wrong, but . . . I just need to know if there's any possibility you might consider promoting me to a more . . . managerial spot. I've been on the assembly line for a couple of years now. But compared to what I did in Venezuela, I feel a little underemployed.

Evan: What kind of work did you do in Venezuela?

Sara: I was plant manager in a manufacturing business. I had 35 people reporting to me. I have a college degree.

Evan: No kidding. If you'd told me that a while back, I would have kept an eye open for a higher-level position.

Sara: It's not your fault. When I first got here, my English was pretty weak. But I've been studying at night, and now with my American husband and my in-laws and everything, my English has really improved. I'm sort of bored in this job. I think it's time to move on. That's why I wanted to talk to you.

Evan: Well, I'm glad you spoke up. I'll be on the lookout. I think I heard there's something in the Center Street branch. Just hang in there. I'll give the chief a call today and get back to you soon.

Sara: Thanks, Evan. I appreciate it.

D. Culture talk...

➤ On the board, write two headings: *My job now* and *My last job in my home country.* Ask students what factors they might consider as they compare the jobs they have now with the jobs they had in their home countries. Students may suggest salary, medical insurance, paid vacations, and other ideas. If necessary, remind students of the discussion generated during the critical thinking exercise on page 133 of factors that contribute to job satisfaction.

➤ Working individually, students jot down notes about the jobs they had in their home countries and the jobs they have now. Students who don't work now or who didn't work before can jot down notes about how their lives in general are the same or different. Have them list several factors to consider, such as household chores, child care, and contact with friends.

➤ Have students display the similarities and differences in a Venn diagram.

➤ In pairs or small groups, have students explain their diagrams.

➤ Lead a group discussion on any patterns that students noticed when comparing past and present jobs or lives. If necessary, prompt with questions such as *Are most students employed now? Is their standard of living better or worse? Have their goals changed? How?*

➤ Do it yourself!

(For general suggestions, see *Introduction*, page Txiii.)

Procedure:

➤ Tell students that they are going to fill out the employment history section of a job application. Students who do not have an employment history can use that of a friend or relative, or work with partner.

➤ Have students read the directions under *Employment History.* Make sure students understand the terms and abbreviations on the application by asking questions such as *What does "mo" stand for?* (month) *What does "yr" mean?* (year) *What does "wk" mean?* (week) *What is a base salary?* (the salary before any tips or overtime is added on) *What is a starting position title?* (the name of the position you had when you began work at the company)

➤ Remind students to begin with the position they have now. If they are not working, they should discuss the last job they had.

➤ Note that salaries can be figured by the week or by the year. Students should circle *wk* or *yr,* depending on which one applies to them.

➤ Tell students to look at the *Ideas* box on page 128 and the *Vocabulary* box on page 129 for examples of reasons for leaving a job. Students should phrase this reason as a positive step; for example, they might cite *no opportunities for advancement* rather than *boring job.*

➤ Tell students that when they are listing duties and responsibilities they should follow parallel structure. For example, they might want to list everything as a gerund: *filing, answering the phone, keeping a correspondence log, operating and maintaining the fax machine.*

Option: Have students exchange forms and practice peer review on the job applications. Provide these and similar questions as guidelines: *Are all names, addresses, and phone numbers complete? Can you read the handwriting? Are dates and dollar amounts clear? Are the duties and responsibilities listed in parallel structure?*

Option: Have students list on a card or slip of paper their duties and responsibilities without any further description. Collect the cards and read the duties and responsibilities aloud. Have other students guess the job position.

Challenge: Have students work in pairs to role-play an interviewer and a job applicant. The questions and answers should be based on the information in the employment history. Make sure the job applicant describes the duties and responsibilities in complete sentences rather than just a list; for example, *I was responsible for all the filing and answering the phone. I also kept the correspondence log and was responsible for operating and maintaining the fax machine.*

D. Culture talk. Compare the job you have now with the last job you had in your home country. If you are not working now, compare your life today with your life in your home country. Talk about how they are the same and how they are different.

➤ Do it yourself!

Look at the employment history section of a job application from a major company. Fill out the section for yourself. (*Note*: You may omit the section on salary for confidentiality.)

Employment History

List all employment since high school, including summer, cooperative education, and U.S. military service (you need to provide dates and relevant duties only). Start with your most recent position. Periods of unemployment should also be noted. Leave no gaps in time sequence. If you need more space, please use an additional sheet of paper.

Company Name				Type of Business		Company Address	Phone Number
Starting Date		Leaving Date		Starting Base Salary	Final Base Salary	Starting Position Title	Last Position Title
Mo	Yr	Mo.	Yr				
				$ ___ wk yr	$ ___ wk yr		

Name of immediate supervisor _____

Supervisor's position title _____

Reason for leaving _____

Please describe your duties and responsibilities _____
_____
_____
_____

May we contact that employer now? ☐ Yes ☐ No If no, when? _____ Employer's Phone Number _____

Company Name				Type of Business		Company Address	Phone Number
Starting Date		Leaving Date		Starting Base Salary	Final Base Salary	Starting Position Title	Last Position Title
Mo	Yr	Mo.	Yr				
				$ ___ wk yr	$ ___ wk yr		

Name of immediate supervisor _____

Supervisor's position title _____

Reason for leaving _____

Please describe your duties and responsibilities _____
_____
_____
_____

May we contact that employer now? ☐ Yes ☐ No If no, when? _____ Employer's Phone Number _____

Writing a resume

 A. Read and listen to the letters.

Ask Joan
Culture tips for newcomers

Dear Joan:

In my country I was a commercial artist and draftsman. Eight years ago my employer went out of business, and I was having trouble finding work. But I was very lucky. I married a wonderful American woman and came to this country. My English was very bad when I got here, and I couldn't get work in my field. For the first two years I worked as a taxi driver. And since then, I've been working as a painter for a large company. The work is good, Joan, and I feel very lucky to be in such a wonderful country where there is so much opportunity, so I don't want you to feel sorry for me. But I speak good English now and I would like to go back to my profession. Do you have any advice for me?

Carlos Sinkoff

Dear Carlos:

Thank you for the kind words about this country! My advice to you, since you are seeking professional employment, is to write a resume. A resume is a brief presentation of your background, skills, and employment history. It is the traditional way to introduce yourself to a potential employer.

A reader sent me an article on resume tips from *Modern Professional* Magazine, and I've included it below. I hope it's helpful. I look forward to seeing your art in an advertisement or a magazine soon!

Joan

Modern Professional

■ Tips for a winning resume

Before setting off on that job hunt, polish up your resume to showcase your strengths and make yourself irresistible to an employer. The two most popular formats for resumes are chronological and functional.

Chronological: Lists work experience and education in chronological order, with the most recent dates first. It is common to subdivide the information into categories such as "work experience," "education," "professional affiliations," "languages," and "awards."

Functional: Organizes the information by skill and accomplishment areas. These do not have to be arranged chronologically. The functional resume is most effective for persons wishing to change careers or for persons who have not been in the job market for a number of years.

Resume red flags

Don't put the following on your resume:

- salary information
- reasons for leaving jobs
- personal statistics (weight, height, health, marital status, children)
- names of supervisors
- names and addresses of references

Above all: **BE ACCURATE, TRUTHFUL, AND DON'T MISSPELL ANYTHING!**

B. Critical thinking. Read the "Resume red flags." Why do you think it's not a good idea to put each one of those items on a resume? Discuss with your classmates.

C. Discussion. In your opinion, which kind of resume should Carlos Sinkoff write? Why?

Authentic practice

(For general suggestions, see *Introduction*, page Tx.)

Writing a resume

Procedure:

A. Read and listen to the letters.

➤ Have students read along silently as they listen to the letters. Check comprehension by asking questions such as *What was Carlos's job in his country?* (He was a commercial artist and draftsman.) *What has he done in this country?* (He's driven a taxi and worked as a painter.) *What is his problem?* (He wants to go back to his profession, work as a commercial artist and draftsman.) *What does Joan advise Carlos to do?* (write a resume)

➤ Have students read the *Tips for a winning resume.* Check comprehension by asking questions such as *What are two types of resumes?* (chronological and functional) *How are they different?* (A chronological format organizes information by date, with the most recent date first. A functional format presents information according to skills and accomplishments.) *Who should use a functional resume?* (people changing careers or people who have been out of the job market for a number of years) *What are some things you should not put on a resume?* (salary information, reasons for leaving jobs, personal statistics, names of supervisors, names and addresses of references)

➤ Some terms may be unfamiliar to students. Make sure they know the meaning of *setting off, showcase,* and *red flags.*

Option: In small groups or pairs, have students speculate about Carlos and what his life might have been like if it had taken a different turn. Put on the board past unreal conditional *if* clauses such as *If Carlos had not left his country, If Carlos hadn't married an American, If Carlos hadn't learned English.* Elicit speculations such as *If Carlos had not left his country, he might have found another job as a commercial artist, If Carlos hadn't gotten married, he might not have come to this country.*

Option: Creating a timeline can be a helpful way to organize information. Ask students to create a timeline for Carlos, including everything they know about him. Have students underline information in his letter that they will use, such as *eight years ago, two years—taxi driver, painter.* Put an empty timeline on the board and elicit information that corresponds

to specific dates; for example, *1995—lost my job as a commercial artist and draftsman.*

Challenge: When students have finished creating a timeline for Carlos, have them create an employment and education timeline for themselves. Tell them to include all education and training as well as employment experience. Have students share their completed timelines in pairs.

Challenge: Put students in pairs or small groups to compare Carlos's employment experience to that of Sara. Have them create a graphic organizer such as a Venn diagram to present the similarities and differences. Students can then use their ideas about Carlos and Sara to write a paragraph that compares their work histories.

B. Critical thinking . . .

➤ Direct students' attention to the *Resume red flags.*

➤ Ask *Why shouldn't you put this information on a resume?* Working individually, students jot down their ideas.

➤ In pairs or small groups, students compare ideas.

➤ Then lead a class discussion about reasons not to put this information on a resume. Elicit students' ideas and write them on the board. Ideas might include the following: *Salary information is best discussed in a private conversation, Giving salary information might limit the amount a potential employer would be willing to offer, Giving reasons for leaving a job might appear too negative, Listing names of supervisors adds unnecessary length to a resume.* Tell students that personal statistics are irrelevant to most jobs and, in fact, it is illegal for a perspective employer to ask about some of them.

C. Discussion . . .

➤ Review with students the features of the two types of resumes.

➤ Put students in small groups to discuss which format Carlos should use for his resume. Have them give reasons for their choices.

➤ Ask students which type of resume they think they should write for themselves. Have volunteers explain their reasoning.

➤ Do it yourself!

(For general suggestions, see *Introduction,* page Txiii.)

Procedure:

A. Look at Carlos Sinkoff's resume.

➤ Have students read Carlos's resume. Check comprehension by asking questions such as *What kind of resume did Carlos write—functional or chronological?* (functional) *What are his strengths?* (visual creativity and careful execution of projects on a timely basis) *What commercial art experience has Carlos had?* (He was an illustrator and layout person for eight years in Chile.) *Where did he go to school?* (University of the West, Vina del Mar, Chile) *What kind of job does Carlos want now?* (a position as an architectural draftsperson or commercial artist)

Option: Using the resume as a reference point, students work in pairs to develop a role play between Carlos and an interviewer. The interviewer should ask Carlos questions about his education, job experience, and goals. Have students switch roles to practice both parts.

Option: If your students have access to the Internet, have them research resume formats. If possible, they should print out a variety of resume formats and bring them to class. In small groups, students compare the various formats and select one for their own use.

B. Write your own resume . . .

➤ Have students decide on the format and general categories that they want to use in their resume. Tell students to review the resume tips on page 136 and Carlos's resume on this page. They may want to change the categories Carlos used or add others.

➤ Have students draft a resume on a separate sheet of paper.

Option: Ask how students feel about sharing the information in their resumes. If appropriate, have students exchange resumes and practice peer review. They should check spelling, punctuation, use of parallel structure, and consistent formatting.

A. Look at Carlos Sinkoff's resume.

Carlos Sinkoff

uribres@mytimes.com

45 McCabe Avenue, Hadley Beach, NJ 07865

(201) 555-6743

OBJECTIVE

Position as an architectural draftsperson or commercial artist

SUMMARY OF QUALIFICATIONS

8 years of experience in the magazine publishing industry as an illustrator
4 years of experience in a civil engineering concern as a draftsperson

STRENGTHS

Visual creativity
Careful execution of projects on a timely basis

WORK EXPERIENCE

Elegant Interiors, Little Rumson, NJ
Colorist and painter: 1998 to present

TAXI-FAST, Miramar, NJ
Taxi driver: 1996-1998

Chilean Life Magazine, Osorno, Chile
Illustrator and layout person: Full-time for two years, then part-time
while full-time at Klimpft Associates: 1987-1995

Klimpft Associates, Temuco, Chile
Chief draftsman in office of more than 200 architects and civil engineers:
1991-1995

EDUCATION

University of the West, Vina del Mar, Chile
Bachelor of Arts, major in architectural drafting, minor in fine arts: 1987

REFERENCES

Available upon request

B. Write your own resume on a separate sheet of paper. You can use Carlos Sinkoff's resume as a model, or refer to the resume tips on page 136.

Review

(For general suggestions, see *Introduction,* page Txii.)

Procedure:

A. Pair work or group work.

Ask and answer questions.

➤ Ask the class general questions about the picture, such as *Where is the woman in the first picture?* (in her home country, in a drugstore) *What do you think her job was there?* (pharmacist) *When did she come to this country?* (in 2000) *What kind of job did she have when she first came here?* (She worked in a restaurant.)

➤ Partners take turns pointing to different things in the picture and asking questions. For each picture, students should ask *What is happening? What are the people doing?* in addition to their own questions.

Option: On a separate sheet of paper, have groups write as many questions as they can about each picture. Students should put questions for each picture under the appropriate date. Have groups exchange questions. Students take turns reading the questions, and the group discusses the answers.

Create conversations.

➤ Have pairs of students create a conversation between the woman and the pharmacist at Health Note or the woman and the restaurant manager. Or students may choose to create a conversation for one of the earlier dated pictures, even though no speech balloons are used.

➤ If students need help or ideas, they can look back over the unit.

➤ Ask volunteers to role-play their conversation for the class. Have pairs present their conversations in chronological order so that the conversations create a continuous story.

Tell a story.

Option: Scenes. Assign students one of the six pictures. Give them a few minutes to look at the picture and review ideas from the unit. Each student must explain what is going on in the picture, including the date and place and who the characters are. Ask students to talk for one minute if they can.

Option: The woman's story. Have students tell the woman's story, alternating the simple past tense with past unreal conditional sentences. For example, a student might begin *Tina used to be a pharmacist in her country. If she had stayed there, she might have owned her own pharmacy.* In a variation, you could have one student begin in the simple past tense, have the second speculate in the past unreal conditional, the third advance the real story in the simple past tense, and so on.

Option: Sequencing. Dictate the following sentences. Have students write down the sentences and then put them in the correct order (3, 4, 6, 2, 5, 7, 1).

She went to talk to the restaurant manager.

She took English classes so she could speak the language better.

She used to work as a pharmacist.

She arrived in her new country.

One day she decided to try returning to her profession.

She got a job in a restaurant.

She had an interview with a pharmacist at Health Note.

⌂B–C.

➤ Tell students they are going to listen to two conversations between the same people. One takes place over the phone, and the other is in person.

➤ After students listen to the conversations the first time, have volunteers read the statements in Exercise C out loud.

➤ After students listen a second time, they check the appropriate boxes.

➤ Have students work in pairs to check answers.

D–E.

➤ Tell students to complete Exercise E on page 140.

➤ Students work individually to complete the review exercises.

➤ Circulate to offer help as needed.

➤ Have students check answers with a partner. Review answers as a class.

➤ Identify any areas of difficulty that may require additional instruction and practice.

Tapescript

Mr. Lerner: Lerner's Drugs. How may I help you?

Ms. Schacter: This is Sofia Schacter. I'm responding to the ad for an assistant pharmacist in today's paper?

Mr. Lerner: Yes. Are you a pharmacist?

Ms. Schacter: Yes, I am.

Mr. Lerner: Are you currently employed?

Ms. Schacter: No, not at the moment. I was a pharmacist in Peru, but I haven't worked as a pharmacist in this country. I just passed the licensing exam.

Mr. Lerner: Peru. So you speak Spanish?

Ms. Schacter: Yes, I do.

Mr. Lerner: That's great, since a lot of our clients speak Spanish. Would you like to come in for an interview?

Ms. Schacter: Yes, I would. When would be good?

At the interview

Mr. Lerner: Ms. Schacter? Art Lerner. Nice to meet you. Please have a seat.

Ms. Schacter: Thanks. Nice to meet you too.

Mr. Lerner: Do you have a resume?

Ms. Schacter: Yes. Right here.

Mr. Lerner: Hmm. Very nice.

Ms. Schacter: Can you tell me something about the job?

Mr. Lerner: Sure. There are two senior pharmacists and one opening for an assistant pharmacist. One of the senior pharmacists just gave notice, to go to dental school. We promoted the assistant pharmacist to a senior.

Ms. Schacter: That's great. So there's opportunity to grow into a senior position here.

Mr. Lerner: Absolutely. Would you like to hear more about the job?

Ms. Schacter: Yes, thanks.

🎧 **C.** Read the statements. Then listen to the conversations again and check *True*, *False*, or *?* *(No information)* for each statement.

		True	False	?
1.	Ms. Schacter saw an ad in the paper.	☑	☐	☐
2.	She is currently working as a pharmacist.	☐	☑	☐
3.	She is from Peru.	☑	☐	☐
4.	She is married.	☐	☐	☑
5.	She doesn't have a resume.	☐	☑	☐
6.	She is going to study dentistry.	☐	☑	☐
7.	She takes the job.	☐	☐	☑

D. Read each sentence or question. Underline your response.

1. "I can't believe you're taking another job!"

   YOU Yeah. Sorry to spring that on you.   **YOU** Forgive me for saying this.

2. "What kind of job are they offering?"

   YOU A resume.   **YOU** A high-level position.

3. "Why do you want to change jobs?"

   YOU I can't make up my mind.   **YOU** My husband was transferred.

4. "Would you be willing to consider a counteroffer?"

   YOU It would be a shame.   **YOU** No, the offer is just too good to refuse.

E. Distinguish between real and unreal conditions. Choose the statement closer in meaning to each underlined phrase.

1. He would have accepted the position <u>if he had known about it.</u>

   ⓐ He knew about it.   ⓑ He didn't know about it.

2. <u>If she had written a chronological resume,</u> they would have hired her.

   ⓐ She wrote a chronological resume.   ⓑ She didn't write a chronological resume.

3. <u>If you had included your supervisors</u>, your resume would have been too long.

    (a) You included your supervisors.   **(b)** You didn't include your supervisors.

4. You would never have gotten that job <u>if you hadn't written such a good resume</u>.

    (a) You wrote a good resume.   (b) You didn't write a good resume.

F. **Choose the correct forms to complete each past unreal conditional sentence.**

1. If she _____hadn't sent_____ in her resume, they _____wouldn't have given_____ her the job.
             wouldn't send / hadn't sent   didn't give / wouldn't have given

2. If the company _____had known_____ earlier, they _____would have made_____ a
             had known / would know   had made / would have made
counteroffer.

G. **Composition. On a separate sheet of paper, write about the picture on page 138. Say as much as you can.**

> **Now I can**
> ❑ apply for a better job.
> ❑ tell my employer about a job offer.
> ❑ get a counteroffer.
> ❑ give notice.
> ❑ write a job history.
> ❑ write a resume.

F. Choose the correct forms ...

➤ Students work individually to complete the review exercise.

➤ Circulate to offer help as needed.

➤ Have students check answers with a partner. Review answers as a class.

➤ Identify any areas of difficulty that may require additional instruction and practice.

G. Composition ...

➤ Provide students with concrete approaches to writing about the picture on page 138. Use one of the options that follow, give students a choice of options, or assign options based on students' levels of proficiency. Model what is expected of students for each option.

➤ Advise students to look back through the unit for help and ideas as they write.

➤ Circulate to offer help as needed.

Option: Have students write a chronological story in the simple past tense, making sure to write at least one sentence about each picture.

Option: Have students create part of a resume for the woman. Using Carlos Sinkoff's resume on page 137 as a guide, they can include the woman's objective and her work experience as a pharmacist and as a restaurant worker. If students want to write a more complete resume, they can fill in any gaps with information they make up.

Option: Have students write a conversation between the woman and the pharmacist at the interview or between the woman and the restaurant manager. Refer students to pages 128 and 129 for the format to follow and for ideas for their conversation.

Challenge: Have students speculate on the woman's life now if she had not left her home country. Remind them to use past unreal conditional sentences where appropriate.

Now I can

➤ Read the first item in the box out loud: Now *I can apply for a better job.* Elicit from the class an example of how to apply for a better job, such as *Write a resume* or *Give a reason to change jobs.*

➤ Put students in pairs. Tell students to take turns reading each item in the box and giving an example of what they have learned. When students can provide an example, they should check that objective. If there are items students aren't able to check, have them look back through the unit for ideas.

➤ When students have finished reviewing with their partners, read each item out loud and elicit an example from the class.

Oral test (optional)

You may want to use the *Now I can* box as an informal evaluation. While students are working on the *Composition* activity, you can call them up individually and check their ability with two or three objectives.

Review notes

Areas for further review and practice

This is an alphabetical list of all active vocabulary in *Workplace Plus 4*. The numbers refer to the page on which the word first appears.

A

accept   114
accident   31
act   24
advance   128
advice   58
against   86
aggressive driving   36
agree   2
air conditioning   16
another   17
any   46
apartment   16
apartment hunter   22
apologize   59
apology   45
apply   115
appointment   59
appropriately   30
approval   20
army   87
arrest   92
ask for   16
at fault   20
audiovisual
   equipment   45
auto club
   membership   42
auto repair   72
available   48
avoid   8

B

bait trap   22
bake   2
bake sale   2
bank loan   115
beat   118
bellman   48
benefit from   73
benefits   129
beverage   44
bid   78
bill   45
blanket   42
borrow   114
borrower   122
broken   16
burst   16
but   117

C

cable   17
capital punishment   86
car service   59
career change   128
cash   114
cause   2
cash machine   114
cell phone   42
censorship   86
challenge   128
charity   7
check   114
cholesterol   100
circuit breaker   22
circumstances   86
claim   76
class   58
college   115
college loan   115
commit   114
commitment   62
competitive   78
complain   45
complaint   24
con   86
consequences   58
consider   132
construction   72
contribute   2
controversial   86
couch potato   104
counteroffer   129
cover   76
credit union   115
cure   101
current   128
cut another driver
   off   36

D

dairy foods   107
damage   20
data port   51
dead-bolt lock   22
deadline   58
deal   76
decline   3
degree   128
dental work   72

dentist   59
describe   31
description   73
diet   106
disability   24
disagree   86
discrimination   24
discuss   17
dismay   58
distribute   2
doctor   59
donation   2
double   48
double room   51
dream   115
drink   87
driver's license   58
dwelling   24

E

efficient   73
election   58
electrical work   72
element   94
emergency repair   16
employer   129
equal opportunity   24
estimate   72
expensive   115
express   58

F

fair   20
fair housing   24
fast   72
fats   107
fatty foods   100
favor   86
fender bender   31
finance   115
financial aid   115
find out   118
fine   58
flash   36
flashlight   42
flyer   2
Food Guide
   Pyramid   108
food pantry   2
for   19
fraud   8

front desk   44
fruits   107

G

gas   17
gesture   36
get   72
glass   44
Golden Rule   38
good cause   2
government
   censorship   86
graduate school   115
grains   107
growth   129
gullible   104
gun   87

H

hairdresser   59
hand-held cell
   phone   30
hanger   44
health   106
heat   16
helmet   87
high blood
   pressure   100
high cholesterol   100
hit   31
honest   73
honk   36
hot water
hotel check-in   48
hotel room   50
hotel services   45
household   16

I

idea   86
impossible   128
imprint   48
improve   128
in writing   72
included   20
insurance   76
insurance claim   76
insure   76
interest   59
ironing board   44

This is a unit-by-unit list of all the social language from the practical conversations in *Workplace Plus 4*.

Unit 1

I'm collecting for _____.
Would you be willing to _____?
What did you say it was for?
I'd be happy to.
Thanks so much.
Hello?
Good evening.
Is this (a sales call)?
I'm sorry. (to refuse)
Thank you very much.

Unit 2

What's the problem?
I'm sorry. (to disagree)
OK. I'll see what I can do.
Hi, _____.
How's it going?
Not great.
(Our cable's) out.
I hope not.
I'll check and let you know.
Thanks.

Unit 3

I'm going to have to _____.
You're right.
I'm sorry. (to apologize)
Here you go.
I'll be back in (a few minutes).
Oh, no.
No, thank goodness.
Well, take it easy.

Unit 4

May I help you?
Hello. This is _____.
Would it be possible to _____?
Absolutely.

Right away.
Is there anything else?
Actually, . . .
Sure, no problem.
Is there some way we can make
   that up to you?
Of course.
Please accept my apology.

Unit 5

I don't believe it!
What?
I was supposed to _____.
Can I give you some advice?
You're right!
I missed it.
Would you like to _____?

Unit 6

Can you give me an estimate?
It'll be about ($500).
How long will it take?
Will you put that in writing?
Do you know (a good painter)?
As a matter of fact, I do.
Would you like me to _____?
That sounds like a good
   reference.

Unit 7

Are you in favor of _____?
What about you?
I'm against it.
I think it's wrong to _____.
We'll have to agree to disagree.
You want to know what I think?
I think it's ridiculous that _____.
You have a point.

Unit 8

I shouldn't have (eaten _____)!
Why not?
Didn't you like (them)?
Are you kidding?
Of course I did.
Oh, really?
That's too bad.
Don't you have (migraines)?
Yes, I do.
They say _____.
Really?
Right here.
It couldn't hurt to give it a try.

Unit 9

Do you think I could borrow
   ($10)?
Let me check what I have
I'll pay you back tomorrow.
I'd love to _____.
Why don't you _____?
Do you think that would be
   possible?
You'll never know if you don't
   give it a try.

Unit 10

How long have you been in your
   current job?
That's great.
Let's see what we have for you.
Do you have a moment to talk?
What's on your mind?
Is there some way we can get
   you to stay?

The following words are often misspelled, especially by people whose first language is not English. Pay particular attention to the words with an asterisk (*).

across	hundred	really	then
address	information*	receive	there
advice*	instead	recommend	therefore
afraid	its	referring	these
against	it's	responsibility	they
airplane	knowledge*	restaurant	this
all right	known	rhythm	thought
anything*	learn	right	thousand
behavior*	marriage	running	through
believe	maybe	Saturday	tomorrow
brought	medicine	scenery*	too
bury	men	science	traffic*
can't	minute	seat	traveling
choose	money*	sense	tried
chose	Mr.	separate	two
chosen	necessary	should	typical
clothes	neighbor	soccer	unforgettable
committee	occurred	somebody*	unfortunately
convenient	of course	something*	until
criticize	off	sometimes	used to
decide	opposite	special	usually
decision	paid	speech	very
describe	passed	spend	wait
destroy	people	spent	watch
didn't	physical	standard	wear
doesn't	plan	stopped	weather
don't	plane	story	were
effect	pleasant	strength	where
embarrass	possibility	studied	whether
etc.	possible	studying	which
everybody*	prefer	succeed	whole
everyone*	preferred	success	with
everything*	pretty	suddenly	without
exaggerate	privilege	summer	woman
excellent	profession	Sunday	women
exercise	professor	sugar	would
foreign	program	sure	writing
forty	pronunciation	surprise	written
fourth	proof	swimming	young
friend	psychology	taught	
grammar	quiet	than	
hear	quite	theater	
heard	read	their	* This word is always
heart	realize	themselves	singular. Never add –s.

Irregular verbs

The following verbs have irregular past-tense forms.

Base form	Past-tense form	Past participle		Base form	Past-tense form	Past participle
be	was / were	been		leave	left	left
begin	began	begun		let	let	let
break	broke	broken		lose	lost	lost
bring	brought	brought		make	made	made
buy	bought	bought		mean	meant	meant
can	could	been able to		meet	met	met
choose	chose	chosen		pay	paid	paid
come	came	come		put	put	put
do	did	done		read	read	read
drink	drank	drunk		ring	rang	rung
drive	drove	driven		run	ran	run
eat	ate	eaten		say	said	said
fall	fell	fallen		see	saw	seen
fight	fought	fought		sell	sold	sold
find	found	found		send	sent	sent
forget	forgot	forgotten		speak	spoke	spoken
get	got	gotten		take	took	taken
give	gave	given		tell	told	told
go	went	gone		think	thought	thought
have	had	had		understand	understood	understood
hear	heard	heard		wear	wore	worn
hurt	hurt	hurt		withdraw	withdrew	withdrawn
know	knew	known		write	wrote	written

Non-action verbs

Emotions	Mental states		The Senses		Appearances
adore	agree	know	feel	see	appear
appreciate	assume	mean	hear	sound	be
care	believe	mind	notice	smell	cost
detest	consider	realize	observe	taste	look
dislike	disagree	recognize	perceive		seem
doubt	estimate	remember			
fear	expect	see (understand)	**Preferences**		**Possession**
hate	feel (believe)	suppose	desire		belong
hope	find	suspect	need		contain
like	guess	think (believe)	prefer		have
love	hope	understand	want		own
regret	imagine	wonder	wish		
respect					

Verbs followed by gerunds

admit	discontinue	imagine	prohibit
appreciate	discuss	keep (continue)	quit
avoid	dislike	mention	recommend
can't help	enjoy	mind (object to)	report
can't stand	explain	miss	resist
consider	feel like	postpone	risk
delay	finish	practice	suggest
deny	give up (stop)	prevent	understand
detest			

Verbs followed by infinitives

afford	choose	learn	promise
agree	decide	manage	refuse
appear	deserve	need	seem
ask	expect	offer	struggle
arrange	fail	pay	volunteer
attempt	help	plan	want
can't afford	hope	prepare	wish
can't wait	hurry	pretend	would like

Verbs followed by gerunds or infinitives

begin	hate	love	start
can't stand	intend	prefer	stop
continue	like	remember	try
forget			

Verbs followed by objects and infinitives

advise	encourage	need*	require
allow	expect*	order	teach
ask*	force	pay*	tell
cause	help*	permit	want*
choose*	hire	promise*	warn
convince	invite	remind	would like*

* Words with an asterisk can also be followed by an infinitive without an object.

How to spell the gerund and the present participle

Add *-ing* to the simple (or "base") form of the verb.

      speak   →   speaking

If the simple form ends in *-e*, drop the *-e* and add *-ing*.

      have   →   having

In verbs of one syllable, if the last three letters are a consonant-vowel-consonant (C-V-C) series, double the last consonant and then add *- ing*.

      C V C
      ↓ ↓ ↓
      s i t   →   sitting

Exception: Don't double the last consonant in words that end in *-w*, *-x*, or *-y*.

      fix   →   fixing

In verbs of more than one syllable that end in a consonant-vowel-consonant series, double the last consonant *only* if the stress is on the last syllable.

      permít → permitting
      contról → controlling
but not   órder   ordering

Internet sources for civics and consumer information

The following Internet sources are taken from the pages of *Workplace Plus 4*. For fuller information, see the text and exercises on the indicated pages.

page 9: **www.ftc.gov** (telemarketing complaint form from the Federal Trade Commission)

page 11: **www.hud.gov** (information on volunteerism from the U.S. Department of Housing and Urban Development)

page 23: **www.apartments.about.com/ library/tools/bl_huntingchecklist.htm** (information on finding an apartment)

page 24: **www.hud.gov/offices/fheo/ FHLaws/index.cfm** (the Fair Housing Act from the U.S. Department of Housing and Urban Development)

page 53: **www.ftc.gov** (information on travel fraud from the Federal Trade Commission)

page 80: **www.bbb.org/bureaus** (consumer information on insurance from the Better Business Bureau)

page 80: **www.insurancefraud.org** (consumer information on insurance from the Coalition Against Insurance Fraud)

page 80: **www.iii.org** (consumer information on insurance from the Insurance Information Institute)

page 80: **www.ftc.gov** (consumer information on insurance from the Federal Trade Commission)

page 94: **www.access.gpo.gov/congress/ senate/constitution/toc.html** (the complete U.S. Constitution and amendments)

page 95: **www.usdoj.gov/usao/eousa/ kidspage/glossary.html** (glossary of terms relating to the U.S. justice system)

page 106: **www.niddk.nih.gov/health/ nutrit/pubs/statobes.htm** (information on overweight from the National Institute of Health)

page 108: **www.nal.usda.gov** (the Food Guide Pyramid from the U.S. Department of Agriculture)

page 120: **www.cardreport.com/glossary/ html** (glossary of credit and borrowing terms)

page 121: **www.ncua.gov** (information on credit unions from the National Credit Union Association)

page 121: **www.ftc.gov** (information on payday loans from the Federal Trade Commission)

The first 10 amendments to the Constitution were ratified on December 15, 1791 and form what is known as the Bill of Rights. The capitalization and punctuation in this version are from the original Bill of Rights, which is on permanent display in the Rotunda of the National Archives Building in Washington, DC. (See the National Archives and Records Administration Web site at **www.nara.gov**.)

Amendment I

Congress shall make no law respecting an establishment of religion, or prohibiting the free exercise thereof; or abridging the freedom of speech, or of the press; or the right of the people peaceably to assemble, and to petition the Government for a redress of grievances.

Amendment II

A well regulated Militia, being necessary to the security of a free State, the right of the people to keep and bear Arms, shall not be infringed.

Amendment III

No Soldier shall, in time of peace be quartered in any house, without the consent of the Owner, nor in time of war, but in a manner to be prescribed by law.

Amendment IV

The right of the people to be secure in their persons, houses, papers, and effects, against unreasonable searches and seizures, shall not be violated, and no Warrants shall issue, but upon probable cause, supported by Oath or affirmation, and particularly describing the place to be searched, and the persons or things to be seized.

Amendment V

No person shall be held to answer for a capital, or otherwise infamous crime, unless on a presentment or indictment of a Grand Jury, except in cases arising in the land or naval forces, or in the Militia, when in actual service in time of War or public danger; nor shall any person be subject for the same offence to be twice put in jeopardy of life or limb; nor shall be compelled in any criminal case to be a witness against himself, nor be deprived of life, liberty, or property, without due process of law; nor shall private property be taken for public use, without just compensation.

Amendment VI

In all criminal prosecutions, the accused shall enjoy the right to a speedy and public trial, by an impartial jury of the State and district wherein the crime shall have been committed, which district shall have been previously ascertained by law, and to be informed of the nature and cause of the accusation; to be confronted with the witnesses against him; to have compulsory process for obtaining witnesses in his favor, and to have the Assistance of Counsel for his defence.

Amendment VII

In suits at common law, where the value in controversy shall exceed twenty dollars, the right of trial by jury shall be preserved, and no fact tried by a jury, shall be otherwise reexamined in any Court of the United States, than according to the rules of the common law.

Amendment VIII

Excessive bail shall not be required, nor excessive fines imposed, nor cruel and unusual punishments inflicted.

Amendment IX

The enumeration in the Constitution, of certain rights, shall not be construed to deny or disparage others retained by the people.

Amendment X

The powers not delegated to the United States by the Constitution, nor prohibited by it to the States, are reserved to the States respectively, or to the people.

Workbook Answer Key

Note: In communicative exercises where several answers are possible, this answer key contains some examples of correct answers, not all possible answers. Any valid answer in this type of exercise should be accepted.

UNIT 1

Exercise 1

1. c   2. e   3. b   4. d   5. a

Exercise 2

Answers will vary.

Exercise 3

1. speak   2. calling   3. loans   4. busy
5. send   6. flyers   7. interested 8. time

Exercise 4

Conversations will vary. Following is one example of what students may write.

1. A: I'd like to get involved in some volunteer work. Tell me, _Aggie_, do you volunteer?

   B: Yes, I do. I _volunteer at the animal shelter_ on Saturdays.

   A: _That's a good cause._ Do they need any more help?

   B: Yes, they do. Would you be willing to _distribute some flyers_?

   A: _I'd be happy to._

2. A: Good afternoon. May I speak to _Mrs. Osmond_?

   B: Who's calling, please?

   A: This is _Melissa_. I'm calling from _the Children's Fund_ about _our magazine_.

   B: Is this a sales call?

   A: Yes, it is.

   B: I'm sorry. _We don't take offers over the phone._

   A: _Thank you for your time._

Exercise 5

1. volunteer
2. are collecting
3. try
4. use
5. is having
6. are taking

Exercise 6

2. helps
3. call
4. takes
5. is
6. come
7. are waiting

Exercise 7

2. am taking
3. donate
4. am trying
5. want
6. need
7. have

Exercise 8

2. are you doing (right now)?
3. do you want to go tonight?
4. is running the car wash on Saturday?
5. do you say to (or tell) telemarketers (when they call)?

Exercise 9

Answers will vary.

Exercise 10

1. b   2. a   3. a   4. b   5. a

Exercise 11

1. d   2. e   3. a   4. c   5. b

Exercise 12

1. Unsolicited
2. cut down
3. updates
4. write
5. registered

Exercise 13

1. The Direct Marketing Association (DMA).
2. For five years.
3. Four times a year.
4. No.
5. Two to three months.

Exercise 14

Answers will vary.

Exercise 15

1. F   2. T   3. T   4. F   5. F   6. T

Exercise 16

1. Sunday, April 23, 2004.
2. T-shirts, gloves, and jeans.
3. You can make a cash contribution.
4. County Park Clean-Up.

UNIT 2

Exercise 1

2. The window is broken.
3. A pipe burst.
4. There's no hot water.
5. There's no air conditioning.
6. The lock is broken.

Exercise 2

1. e   2. d   3. a   4. b   5. c

Exercise 3

1. burst
2. water
3. call
4. working
5. pipes
6. give

Exercise 4

Answers will vary.

Exercise 5

Conversations will vary. Following is one example of what students may write.

A: Manager's office. How may I help you?

B: Hi. This is *Enrique* in apartment *3F*. I've got a problem.

A: What's wrong?

B: *The window is broken*.

A: Well, I'm busy right now. Is it urgent?

B: *I'm sorry, but yes*.

A: OK. I'll *see what I can do*.

Exercise 6

1. signed
2. haven't fixed
3. asked
4. hasn't seen
5. Has, called

Exercise 7

1. for
2. since
3. for
4. since

Exercise 8

Answers will vary.

Exercise 9

1. has lived / has been living, one month
2. started
3. stopped working
4. has been calling / has called
5. visited

Exercise 10

Answers will vary.

Exercise 11

1. b   2. b   3. b   4. a   5. a

Exercise 12

Tenant	phone, cable TV
Rental agent	gas, electricity
Building supervisor	emergencies (a pipe burst, no heat)

Exercise 13

1. security
2. dead-bolt
3. electrical
4. circuit breakers
5. switches
6. burners
7. leaks
8. burst pipe

Exercise 14

Answers will vary.

Exercise 15

1. a   2. b   3. b

Exercise 16

1. a   2. d   3. c   4. b   5. e

Exercise 17

Students should check items 2, 4, and 6.

Exercise 18

1. b   2. a   3. b   4. a   5. a

UNIT 3

Exercise 1

1. not stopping
2. totaled
3. sideswiped
4. rear-ended
5. tailgate
6. signal

Exercise 2

1. signal
2. stop
3. cell phone
4. registration

Exercise 3

1. I had to take the bus today. My car is at the auto repair shop.

2. Why? Did you have an accident?

3. Yes. I was turning right out of a parking lot, and another car hit me.

4. Oh, no! Were you hurt?

5. No, thank goodness. It was just a fender bender.

6. That's good. Did you get a ticket?

7. No, but the other driver did. He didn't stop at the stop sign.

Exercise 4

Conversations will vary. Following is one example of what students may write.

A: You look upset. Is there anything wrong?

B: Oh, I got a ticket today.

A: Really? What for?

B: For *not stopping at a red light*.

A: This has been a bad week for driving. My husband had an accident yesterday.

B: Oh, no! What happened?

A: *Someone rear-ended him and he totaled his car*.

B: Was anyone hurt?

A: *The other driver broke his ankle*.

B: And will the insurance cover the damage?

A: *Yes, thank goodness*.

Exercise 5

2. asking
3. observing
4. driving
5. stopping
6. seeing
7. using
8. breaking

Exercise 6

1. to get an oil change
2. to buy cans of juice for Tim's party
3. to make a doctor's appointment for Paulo
4. to pay her speeding ticket
5. to mail her registration renewal

Exercise 7

1. to yield
2. to get
3. Being
4. for totaling
5. to signal, changing
6. to driving
7. to park

Exercise 8

2. did you call the insurance company
3. did she stop
4. is having a car important

Exercise 9

Answers will vary.

Exercise 10

1. b   2. a   3. b   4. a   5. b

Exercise 11

1. c   2. e   3. d   4. b   5. a

Exercise 12

1. T   2. ?   3. F   4. F   5. T   6. F

Exercise 13

2. good driver
3. aggressive driver
4. aggressive driver
5. good driver
6. good driver
7. aggressive driver
8. aggressive driver

Exercise 14

Answers will vary.

Exercise 15

1. Not OK
2. OK
3. OK
4. Not OK
5. OK

Exercise 16

1. b   2. a   3. c   4. a   5. c

Exercise 17

1. flashlight
2. jumper cables
3. flares
4. jack, spare tire
5. map
6. cell phone

UNIT 4

Exercise 1

1. b   2. c   3. d   4. e   5. f   6. a

Exercise 2

1. Front desk
2. pillows
3. never
4. brought
5. right
6. use
7. newspaper
8. apology

Exercise 3

1. Right away.
2. I'm so sorry.
3. I'm so sorry.
4. Right away.
5. I'm so sorry.
6. Right away.

Exercise 4

Conversations will vary. Following is one example of what students may write.

A: Housekeeping.

B: Hi. This is _Margarite_ at the front desk. Would it be possible to take _some towels_ to Room _307_ right away?

A: Of course. Is there anything else?

B: Yes. They'd also like _some glasses_.

A: Sure, no problem.

Exercise 5

Answers will vary.

Exercise 6

1. any   2. some   3. some   4. any   5. some
6. some   7. any   8. some   9. some

Exercise 7

Answers will vary.

Exercise 8

2. Did you see any / some
3. Are there any / some
4. Did you make any / some
5. Could you use some

Exercise 9

Answers will vary.

Exercise 10

1. b   2. a   3. a   4. b   5. a

Exercise 11

1. hotel guest   2. hotel clerk   3. hotel clerk   4. hotel guest   5. hotel clerk   6. hotel guest   7. hotel clerk   8. hotel guest

Exercise 12

1. Edward Morgan   2. Skyview Suites
3. February 1   4. February 8   5. two   6. double
7. two queen-size   8. USExpress   9. Hai
10. T290

Exercise 13

2. 235   3. 127   4. 518   5. 301

Exercise 14

1. c   2. a   3. b   4. a   5. c

Exercise 15

1. The Federal Trade Commission.

2. Get the total cost in writing and know what it includes.

3. It gives you more protection than cash or check. / If you don't get what you pay for, you may be able to dispute the charges with your credit card company.

4. Blocks of dates usually around holidays or peak season when no discount travel is available.

Exercise 16

Answers will vary.

UNIT 5

Exercise 1

1. c   2. d   3. a   4. e   5. b

Exercise 2

1. deadline
2. register
3. yesterday
4. believe
5. supposed
6. forgot
7. term
8. advice
9. way
10. wait

Exercise 3

Answers will vary. Following is an example of what students may write.

Things you renew	Things you return	Things you register for
driver's license	library books	to vote
library books	videos	art class

Exercise 4

1. c   2. g   3. d   4. f   5. e   6. b   7. a

Exercise 5

Conversations will vary. Following is one example of what students may write.

A: I don't believe it.

B: What's wrong?

A: Oh, I was supposed to *return this video* by *Saturday*, but I forgot.

B: That's too bad. Now you'll have to *pay a late fee* Maybe you should *use a calendar*. That way you won't forget again.

A: That's good advice. Thanks!

Exercise 6

1. real condition
2. unreal condition
3. real condition
4. real condition
5. unreal condition
6. unreal condition
7. real condition
8. real condition

Exercise 7

2. Ivan would help me with my homework if he had time.

3. We wouldn't pay late fees if we paid our bills on time.

4. If Sheila's computer skills improved, she would get a better job.

5. I would ask my friends for help if I had too much on my plate.

Exercise 8

2. if she doesn't practice driving
3. if she doesn't renew her permit today
4. she would be ready to take the driving test
5. she wouldn't have to ask friends to help her practice driving
6. she wouldn't be worried

Exercise 9

Answers will vary.

Exercise 10

1. a 2. a 3. b 4. a 5. b

Exercise 11

1. T 2. F 3. T 4. ? 5. F

Exercise 12

2. perfectionism
3. prioritization
4. perfectionism
5. prioritization

Exercise 13

Answers may vary. Following is an example of what students may write.

1. pick up the kids, drop off registration forms before 5:00

2. make a haircut appointment, call Karen, pick up the dry cleaning, mail medical insurance forms, and bake cookies

3. pick up the dry cleaning, mail medical insurance forms, and pick up the kids

Exercise 14

1. March 6, 2004
2. Wednesday
3. Thursday
4. Friday
5. 10:00
6. 2:00
7. $15.00
8. $12.00
9. the due date (*or* March 6, 2004)

Exercise 15

2. coming late to someone's house for a party

3. bringing a book back to the library a couple of days late

4. paying rent a day or two late

Exercise 16

1. starts
2. expires
4. calendar
5. return
6. deadlines
7. miss
8. list
9. plate

Exercise 17

Answers will vary.

UNIT 6

Exercise 1

1. yes 2. yes 3. no 4. no 5. yes 6. no

Exercise 2

1. yes 2. yes 3. no 4. no 5. no 6. yes

Exercise 3

1. d 2. b 3. a 4. c

Exercise 4

1. reasonable
2. honest
3. fast
4. recommend
5. estimate
6. efficient

Exercise 5

Conversations will vary. Following is one example of what students may write.

A: I'm looking for a good *babysitter*. Can you recommend anyone?

B: Well actually, I can. *Her* name is *Aimee Herring*.

A: Is *she reliable*?

B: Yes. And *she* is very *reasonable*.

A: *Sounds great*. I'll give *her* a call.

Exercise 6

2. (They) wasted a lot of time.

3. (The work) took longer than we thought.

4. (Those mechanics) were reasonable but not very fast.

5. (I) volunteered to help.

6. (Pete's plumbing) does a really good job.

7. (New construction) is too expensive.

Exercise 7

2. The job will take seven or eight hours. / Will the job take seven or eight hours?

3. Ms. Lopez needs a good electrician.

4. We think the insurance will cover the repairs.

5. Would you like me to give you some references?

6. How long will the auto repair take?

Exercise 8

1. My daughter Edith is eight years old. She's in the third grade. Her school is on Martin Luther King Drive. Her teacher's name is Miss Tam.

2. We've lived in St. Louis for three years. Our doctor's name is Dr. Cherala. Her office is in Greenville. She's the best doctor in Missouri.

Exercise 9

Answers will vary.

Exercise 10

1. b   2. b   3. a   4. a   5. b

Exercise 11

1. broke down
2. towed
3. locked
4. coverage
5. add
6. auto
7. cover
8. flat tire
9. battery
10. policy

Exercise 12

1. Konstantanides Building Service.
2. Velela Household Painting.
3. Konstantanides Building Service.
4. (It would be) $530.
5. Answers will vary.

Exercise 13

2. assets   3. short-term expenses   4. injury
5. generally

Exercise 14

1. c   2. a   3. c   4. d

Exercise 15

Answers will vary.

Exercise 16

1. good rates, excellent service
2. a higher deductible
3. worth less than $1,000
4. low-profile
5. discount

UNIT 7

Exercise 1

1. con   2. con   3. pro   4. con
5. pro   6. con   7. pro   8. con

Exercise 2

1. think
2. against
3. wrong
4. opinion
5. favor
6. guess
7. circumstances
8. matter

Exercise 3

Answers will vary.

Exercise 4

Conversations will vary. Following is one example of what students may write.

1. A: There are just too many rules these days!

   B: What do you mean?

   A: Well, did you know that _you can't smoke indoors in a public place_.

   B: Yes, I did. I'm in favor of it, because _cigarette smoke is very unhealthy_.

   A: I guess you have a point.

2. A: What's your opinion about _organized prayer in schools_?

   B: Well, I'_m against it_. What do you think?

   A: Actually, I'm _for_ it. I believe _if children prayed more, they would behave better_.

   B: _I think it's wrong no matter what._

Exercise 5

1. Asha asked, "Does this restaurant have a non-smoking section?"

2. The waitress answered, "Yes. It's in the back."

3. Danielle said, "I thought all restaurants were entirely nonsmoking now."

4. The waitress said, "Maybe in some states, but not here."

5. Asha asked, "Would you rather eat somewhere else?"

6. Danielle replied, "No, this is fine."

Exercise 6

2. Marcela said, "I thought that law was only for children."

3. Luis responded, "No, it's for everyone."

4. Marcela asked, "Where can I get a helmet?"

5. Luis answered, "They're on sale at the bike store in Old Town."

6. Marcela said, "Thanks. I'll get one tomorrow."

Exercise 7

2. Lia says (that) it's ridiculous that we can't smoke in the building.

3. Mr. Tan says (that) he's against prayer in schools.

4. Yuri says (that) he believes that censorship is necessary.

5. Sophia says (that) there are way too many rules.

6. Arturo says (that) he disagrees with that law.

7. Maria says (that) it's wrong to take more than you can eat at a buffet.

8. Ava says (that) she heard about that on the news.

Exercise 8

Answers will vary.

Exercise 9

1. a   2. b   3. a   4. b   5. b

Exercise 10

1. I think the Internet is a dangerous thing.

2. Dangerous? Why?

3. There are a lot of things on it that children shouldn't see.

4. True. But that's why there is parental control software.

5. Parental control software? What's that?

6. It's software that allows parents to restrict what children can see on the Web.

7. That's a great idea. But I still think there should be limits to the Internet.

8. But that would be censorship. Are you in favor of that?

9. Hmmm . . . I'll have to think about that.

Exercise 11

1. b   2. e   3. d   4. a   5. c

Exercise 12

1. argument
2. calm
3. against
4. touch
5. innocent
6. complain
7. lawyer
8. badge
9. witnesses

Exercise 13

1. Amendment I
2. Amendment IV
3. Amendment I
4. Amendment VI
5. Amendment VI
6. Amendment VII

Exercise 14

2. jury box
3. flag
4. judge
5. witness
6. witness stand
7. state's attorney
8. defense attorney
9. defendant

Exercise 15

Answers will vary.

UNIT 8

Exercise 1

1. report
2. overweight
3. cholesterol
4. too
5. fatty
6. weight
7. milkshake
8. limit

Exercise 2

Answers will vary.

Exercise 3

1. migraine
2. cure
3. remedy
4. prescription
5. limit
6. cholesterol

Exercise 4

Conversations will vary. Following is one example of what students may write.

1. A: What do you take when you have *a cold*?

   B: I usually take *vitamin C*.

   A: Does it help?

   B: *Sometimes*.

2. A: Do you know of anything that cures *arthritis*?

   B: They say *Rackinusha* can help.

   A: Where did you hear that?

   B: *I read about it in a magazine*.

   A: OK. I guess it couldn't hurt to give it a try.

Exercise 5

2. Luisa should have asked her doctor to call her prescription in to the pharmacy.

3. The Olsons shouldn't have tried to move a heavy bookcase themselves.

4. Hanna shouldn't have given her sister some of her prescription medicine.

5. Alain should have asked his doctor to check his cholesterol.

6. I should have started this exercise plan a long time ago.

Exercise 6

Answers will vary.

Exercise 7

1. Don't you need
2. Isn't smoking
3. Didn't Mehmet lose
4. Aren't health clubs
5. Didn't you buy

Exercise 8

2. Didn't Maya have a check-up last week?
3. Doesn't Linda look wonderful?
4. Aren't you taking medicine for your cholesterol?
5. Didn't you try the same diet last year?
6. Isn't Eric a volunteer paramedic?
7. Didn't Leon stop smoking?

Exercise 9

1. b   2. a   3. b   4. b   5. a

Exercise 10

1 c   2. b   3. d   4. e   5. a

Exercise 11

1. remedy
2. suggests
3. limiting
4. gullible
5. safe
6. headaches

Exercise 12

1. a   2. a   3. c   4. b   5. b

Exercise 13

1. meats
2. fats and oils
3. seafood
4. dairy foods
5. grains
6. fruits
7. sweets
8. vegetables

Exercise 14

1. six (6)
2. one (1)
3. one (1)
4. three (3)
5. four (4)
6. five (5)

Exercise 15

Answers will vary.

UNIT 9

Exercise 1

1. wallet
2. credit cards
3. out of cash
4. cash machine
5. personal checks

Exercise 2

1. I'm collecting for a birthday cake for Patsy. Do you want to contribute?

2. Yes, but I'm a little short of cash right now. I left my wallet at home this morning.

3. That's too bad. Would you like me to put in $5 for you?

4. That would be really great. I'll pay you back tomorrow.

5. No problem.

6. Thanks. I really appreciate it.

Exercise 3

1. graduate
2. scholarship
3. credit union
4. money
5. assistance
6. dreams

Exercise 4

Answers will vary.

Exercise 5

Conversations will vary. Following is one example of what students may write.

A: I've always wanted to _go to technical school,_ but it's so expensive.

B: Maybe you could _apply for a scholarship._

A: I guess that's possible. Or I could _borrow money from my parents._

B: That's right. It couldn't hurt to give it a try!

Exercise 6

1. to
2. their
3. its, than
4. You're, your
5. then
6. it's, too
7. They're
8. There, two

Exercise 7

1. c   2. e   3. a   4. d   5. b

Exercise 8

1. Reina applied for a car loan, and she got it.

2. I get paid Friday, so I can pay you back then.

3. The house is wonderful, but it needs a lot of renovation.

4. I've always wanted to learn to swim, so I'm taking lessons.

5. The car is in good condition, and it's reasonably priced.

6. Victor would love to go to technical school, but it's very expensive.

Exercise 9

1. Because he didn't need a loan then.
2. Because he wants to buy a new car.
3. Because their rates are (pretty) good.

Exercise 10

Answers will vary.

Exercise 11

1. a   2. b   3. b   4. a   5. b

Exercise 12

1. car

2. credit union

3. the credit union

4. their terms are better than the bank's, and the office is in his building

5. join the credit union

Exercise 13

1. b   2. c   3. a   4. a   5. c

Exercise 14

Answers will vary.

Exercise 15

1. expires
2. pass
3. paycheck
4. personal check
5. fee
6. before
7. after
8. finance

Exercise 16

1. b   2. a   3. b   4. c   5. b   6. a

Exercise 17

Answers will vary.

UNIT 10

Exercise 1

1. challenge
2. improved
3. complete
4. transferred
5. career
6. room, advance
7. degree

Exercise 2

1. d   2. e   3. b   4. a   5. f   6. c

Exercise 3

1. tuition assistance
2. benefits
3. responsibility
4. salary
5. counteroffer
6. perks
7. refuse
8. opportunities for growth

Exercise 4

Conversations will vary. Following is one example of what students may write.

A: Hey _Al_, what's _wrong_?

B: Well, you know I've been looking for another job because _I'd like to make a career change_.

A: Yes, I know. Have you had any luck?

B: Actually, I've been offered a job.

A: Really? Where?

B: At _the Iki Mart_.

A: That's great. Is it a good job?

B: Well, they're offering _a good salary_ and _room to advance_.

A: Sounds good. Have you made your choice?

B: _I can't make up my mind_.

Exercise 5

2. had known, would've called
3. would've made, had had
4. had typed, would've looked
5. had worked, would've been
6. would've written, had asked

Exercise 6

2. If I hadn't taken that job, I wouldn't have learned about working with customers.
3. If Cindy hadn't spoken Spanish, she wouldn't have gotten the job.
4. If Pedro hadn't known how to do data entry, he wouldn't have gotten the promotion.
5. If I hadn't been ready for a challenge, I wouldn't have applied for this transfer.
6. If I had known there was an opening, I would've brought my resume.

Exercise 7

Answers will vary.

Exercise 8

Answers will vary.

Exercise 9

1. a   2. b   3. b   4. a   5. a

Exercise 10

1. b   2. a   3. a   4. b   5. a

Exercise 11

Answers will vary.

Exercise 12

Answers will vary.

Exercise 13

1. laundry worker I, May, 1998

2. $200

3. no opportunity for advancement, salary

4. September, 2000, Parkland Properties, maintenance worker

5. supervising a crew of 6, performing maintenance and landscaping, assigning tasks, evaluating work, and keeping records

6. Mr. Larry Tiet

Exercise 14

1. F   2. T   3. F   4. T   5. F   6. T   7. T

Exercise 15

Answers will vary.

Skills for test taking

UNIT 1

1. A   2. B   3. B   4. D   5. C

UNIT 2

1. C   2. A   3. B   4. D   5. C

UNIT 3

1. C   2. D   3. B   4. C   5. A

UNIT 4

1. D   2. C   3. B   4. A   5. D

UNIT 5

1. D   2. A   3. A   4. B   5. C

UNIT 6

1. A   2. D   3. D   4. C   5. B

UNIT 7

1. D   2. B   3. D   4. C   5. A

UNIT 8

1. B   2. D   3. A   4. B   5. B

UNIT 9

1. C   2. B   3. B   4. D   5. C

UNIT 10

1. B   2. A   3. C   4. A   5. B